I0114358

THE WORKS OF SRI CHINMOY

POETRY

VOLUME I

THE WORKS OF SRI CHINMOY

POETRY

VOLUME I

★

THE DANCE OF LIFE

THE WINGS OF LIGHT

THE GOLDEN BOAT

LYON · OXFORD

GANAPATI PRESS

LXXXVI

© 2016 THE SRI CHINMOY CENTRE

ISBN 978-0-9933080-6-2

See appendix for notice regarding this edition.

FIRST EDITION WENT TO PRESS ON 13 APRIL 2016

POETRY

VOLUME I

PART I

THE DANCE OF LIFE

1. I BUTCHERED YOUR IGNORANCE

When I thought I was the doer
Of all my deeds,
I turned to mist.
I died.
I became the emperor of giant
failures.
My soul came to the fore,
Consoled my visionless ignorance.
God made His Appearance
supreme.
"You fool, be not wedded to
impossibility's lifeless beauty.
I waste not a leaf.
I butchered your ignorance wild
for you
To equal My Transcendental
Throne."

2. SHE WAS THE SUPREME AUTHORITY

She was a woman of exquisite
beauty.
Her career she started
As the Queen of the universe.
She was the supreme Authority
On human failure
And
Perfection divine.

3. WHEN I SAY

When I say,
"God is powerful,"
The world is ready to endorse my
view.

When I say,
"God is considerate,"
The world hesitates to endorse my
view.

When I say,
"God is impartial,"
The world endeavours to negate
my view.

When I say,
"God is merciful,"
The world devours my view.

4. WHEN I INSULTED

I insulted God.
In return
He infused wisdom-light
Into my eyeless mind.

I insulted the world.
In return
The world landed death-blows on
me.

I insulted my inner strength.
In return
It compelled my fall:
A clean-cut forest tree.

5. THE RESULT OF WORLD-ACCEPTANCE

He was a stalwart spiritual figure.
Above blemish he always was.
He loved the world deeply and
unconditionally.
No response.
He dispatched his frustrated
Failure to the other world.
He fought and fought
Against his own solid realisation
Until he passed
Behind
The curtain of eternity.
The realisation read:
"In your world-acceptance
You fostered in your life-breath
A venom-snake."

6. IN THE GRAND OLD DAYS

In the grand old days
My thought was my life's sole
pole-star.
My mouth and my heart,
In forms they were two
But
In spirit they were one.
I saw God, my All.
He embraced me.
He needed my love.
I demanded His Love.
His Love nullified all my
Vainglorious power in a
twinkling.
My love developed into
A hushed silence.
In that silence grew a seething
Amazement:
My death in God's Immortality
And
God's Immortality in my death
Bloomed in excellence supreme.

7. PRETENCE NO MORE

I live in a zone of silence
To decipher my hostile past.
No, my life is not
A speck of dust
Flawed and doomed to
nothingness.
Useless words I pronounced.
Therefore suicide I committed
Time and again.
In my life from now on
Only
The essential is permissible.
No more shall I pretend to be
What I am not:
IGNORANCE.

8. DESIRE-SUN, ASPIRATION-MOON

Desire-Sun makes me tremble.
Aspiration-Moon makes me
dream.
O Desire-Sun, in you
I have my silent death.
O Aspiration-Moon, with you
I have my endless Life.

9. AT LAST I SHALL LISTEN

My past is heavy with
The lifeless
Meaning.
A frightened thought
My fast-approaching future
Is.
I have the body and soul
Of hope completely in my
Thoughts.
I shout at the top of my lungs.
My soul embodies the weight of
Despair.
At last I am now learning the art
of listening
To God's
Voice.
"Son, in your soulful silence is
My fruitful message,
My All."

10. I CRY AND SMILE

I grant my seconds
No respite.
Always in tornado-motion,
Always.
My heart's Cry, my soul's
Smile
Are my birthless teachings
Endless.
They shall cover the world,
They shall.
I foresaw the thirst and hunger of
the
World.
And here I bring the remedy:
Nectar-flood.
I cry with man
And
Smile with God.

11. IN THE CORE OF SILENCE

Yes, I was deported
To a distant
Land uncharted
By the eyeless hunger of
ignorance-sea.
A wait-and-see attitude
Failed
To breathe within my
Reality's throes.
Burning with impatience-noon
My dauntless vital horse
Freed me from the sea
Of ignorance unplumbed.
And now, here I remain,
Here
In the snow-capped core of
Silence,
Alone, all alone, unchallenged,
Triumphant,
Eternity's pride, Lord eternal
Supreme.

12. A SYMBOL OF PROMISE

Every life is a rich
Storehouse
Of experience.
I dare declare:
We live not,
NOT
In an epoch of
Chaotic decay.
I plumb the depths
Of light
At each hush-gap.

Every life
Is a symbol of
Promise,
Streaming forth from a realm
Where
No one is a stranger, unwanted
None,
Where Love blossoms for the One
And Truth for the many.

13. THE TRUTH-EMPEROR OF LOVE

Soon
My earth-pilgrimage shall
End.
Today, today I shall
Arouse
With my clarion call
All
The slumbering universal
Eyes.
I saw the light of
Day
With a world-message:
"Each
Man is the Truth-Emperor of
Love."

14. CHILDREN OF THE HIMALAYAN CAVES

The Master said in public:
"My hope and my faith
Are centred in my young
disciples."
The old disciples groaned:
"Master, good-bye.
We are leaving you for good."
The Master then said:
"My real disciples are those
Who have denied themselves."
The young disciples roared:
"Master, we are leaving you,
immediately.
We have done so much for you.
Your shameless ungratefulness
Deserves us not."
Who remained?
Only children, Children of the
Himalayan caves
For the Transcendental Palace.

15. I AM HAPPY

I am happy
Because
My mind has forgotten how to
Calculate.
I am happy
Because
My heart has forgotten how to
Hesitate.
I am happy
Because
My life always knows how to
Tolerate.

16. HOW I DEAL WITH GOD

I steeled my nerves to brave God.
I strengthened my will to capture
God.
I stilled my mind to welcome God.
I emptied my heart to treasure
God.

17. HIDE-AND-SEEK

Every minute inspires me
To attempt.
Every hour perfects me
To ascend.
Every day illumines me
To reach.
In my attempt,
I have come to learn what I can be.
In my ascension,
I have come to learn who I
eternally Am.
On my arrival,
God and I shall stop playing our
age-long
Game,
Hide-and-Seek.

18. THE STORY OF MY COMMON SENSE

When my common sense
Was fast asleep,
I lived in the animal kingdom.
I felt and filled my hungry abyss.
When I surrendered
My common sense to my Inner
  Pilot,
Peace-sea, sun-world, love-Heaven
At long last
Discovered their permanence
In my God-hunger supreme.

19. MAGNIFICENT DISASTER

All my youthful hopes of blazing
  noon
Are smashed by calamity's giant
  strokes.
No ray of life to sustain my inner
  faith.
Grim necessity dare not command
  me
To sustain my outer belief.
I loved the throes of the human
  world.
Indeed, a fatal love!
My reward is a magnificent
  disaster
Of a universal tornado-character.

20. IN MY HEART-DAWN AND SOUL-SUN

I loved my life's morning walks.
Hope-beauty led my eyes and
  guided my steps.
I love my life's midday runs.
Reality's naked life
Has sent uncertainty into
  destruction-exile.
I shall love my life's evening
  stumblings.
Life divine shall embrace the abyss
  of science.
Evening does not mark the end.
Evening is the precursor of a purer
Dawn and a brighter sun.
In my Heart-Dawn, my
  preparation shall begin.
In my Soul-Sun, my perfection
  shall bloom.

21. EACH THOUGHT

A vivacious infant,
Each thought
In the vital world.

A helpless orphan,
Each thought
In the physical world.

A doubting youth,
Each thought
In the mental world.

A growing God,
Each thought
In the psychic world.

22. VISIONS OF THE EMERALD BEYOND

No more am I the foolish
customer
Of a dry, sterile, intellectual
breeze.
I shall buy only
The weaving visions of the
emerald Beyond.
My heart-tapestry
Shall capture the Himalayan
Smiles
Of my Pilot Supreme.
In the burial of my sunken mind
Is the revival of my climbing
heart.
In the burial of my deceased mind
Is the festival of my all-embracing
life.

23. WHERE IS IT?

Heaven cries out: "Where is it?"
Earth cries out: "Where is it?"
God cries out: "Where is it?"
Man smiles and asks: "What is it?"
God, earth and Heaven cry:
"Gratitude, your gratitude."
Man says: "O earth, your choice
deserves it not.
O Heaven, Your voice retains it
not.
O God, Your Forgiveness needs it
not.
Never."

24. FRUSTRATION-NIGHT DETHRONED

Man's untiring groans of
Sharp accusation
Pierce the compassion-canopy
Of Heaven's life.
Heaven says:
"Man, what can I do?
Yours are the talents that jump
  and run
Below the lowest standard of
  recommendation
At every place, always.
Break asunder your eternity's
  lifeless isolation.
Lose your existence in the many
  and become One.
Your tenebrous frustration-night
Shall be dethroned by the
  ocean-deep delight
Of Victory's Crown."

25. IN MY HERMIT HEART

In my hermit heart
I dread noise and love silence.
I have wrestled with heavy doubts
And now I wear victory's crown.
The length of my aspiring life
Is increasing fast, very fast.
The length of my desiring life
Is becoming slender, very slender.
Soon it will perish in the abyss
Of lifeless nothingness.
In my hermit heart
God's Compassion is invoked by
  me to sing,
God's Love is invited by me to play.
My heart of gratitude,
My life of surrender
Will watch them sing and play.

26. VISION-SKIES

The body
Loves to be swayed by the wind of
  emotion.
The vital
Loves the prickings of desire.
The mind
Loves the confines of the finite.
The heart
Loves to be in the galaxy of saints.
The soul
Loves the life of unhorizoned
  vision-skies.

27. DESTRUCTION-TREE

I insulted
Danger, disaster and destruction
Bitterly.
They answered
Me with a shower of arrows
Immediately.
I saw
Into the hollowness of their wild
Schemes.
I shall
Uproot
danger-disaster-destruction
Trees
With the easy
Ease of removing seedlings.

28. THE KINGDOM OF SELF-DELUSION

It took me a long time
To settle up all my accounts
With hope.
Hope-flames gave birth
To the body of immortal
Frustration-chaos in me.
O hope!
Before you were born,
I ruled the Kingdom of dust and
stone.
And now with you,
I rule the Kingdom of
self-delusion.
I am the King, the present saviour,
Without
The presence of certainty's smile.

29. I LONG TO BE ONE

I long to be one
With the Dust of Your Feet.
I long to be one
With the Smile of Your Eyes.
I long to be one
With the Love of Your Heart.
I long to be one
With the Oars of Your Boat.
I long to be one
With the Glow of Your Promise.
I long to be one
With the Flow of Your Life.
I long to be one
With the Victory of Your Banner.

30. MY GOD-BECOMING

His Compassion is
The cure of my body.
His Vision is
The cure of my soul.
My life owes
To His creative Will within me.
My earthly role owes
To His ceaseless sun-vast Smiles.
My Heavenly goal will owe
To Him for my permanent
God-becoming.

31. WHEN THE GODS CAME TO ME

When the infernal gods came to
 me,
They brought with them their
 fatal love.
When the oriental gods came to
 me,
They brought with them their
 soaring love.
When the occidental gods came to
 me,
They brought with them their
 glowing love.
When the supernal gods came to
 me,
They brought with them my
 long-lost forgotten self.

32. O FAILURE'S BROKEN WINGS

O resplendent Sun,
Your core, my only haven.
O unceasing sigh,
My breath, your only haven.
O Victory's golden wings,
Do carry me into the skies of
 nectar-love.
O failure's broken wings,
In me you have your perfect
 solace.

33. BUBBLES OF HUMAN PHILOSOPHY

My mother's ageless grace
Waves in my heart's starry skies.
My father's ageless face
Smiles inside the bubbles
Of my human philosophy.

34. I LOVE

I love the music of silence.
I love the breath of rottenness.
I love the bliss of angels.
I love the body of chaos.

O silence, you are my all.
O rottenness, you need
My constant attention.
O angels, my soaring
Hope shakes hands with
Your glowing smiles.
O chaos, you prove to the
World at large
The boundless power
Of my endless patience.

35. WHEN I LOVE

When I love the steps of my
thoughts,
My life becomes a series of
calamities.
When I love the flights of my will,
My life becomes a series of daring
visions.
When I love the boat of my life,
My life becomes the divine
compeer
Of perfection's heights.

36. HOPE-BOAT AND LIFE-BOAT

My hope-boat is plying
Between uncertainty and
frustration.
My thought-boat is plying
Between disaster and destruction.
My will-boat is plying
Between silence and sound.
My life-boat is plying
Between beauty's Shore and duty's
Goal.

37. MY DISAPPOINTMENT AND MY GOD-APPOINTMENT

No more shall I speak
In self-defence.
My disappointment in the world
Is hastening my
God-appointment.
Broken are my teeming earthly
bonds.
Illumined is my climbing
Heavenly heart.

38. GREAT IS HE, GREAT IS SHE, GREAT IS GOD

He is great.
He negates his train of passion
By voluntarily enjoying it.

She is great.
She negates her stream of
insecurity
By voluntarily cherishing it.

God is great.
His Compassion forgives man and
woman.
God is great.
His Love hides them soulfully.
God is great.
His Light liberates them
unconditionally.

39. THE COLLECTOR

Man's mind is an eager searcher of
space.
Man's heart is a torch-bearer of
God's Grace.
Man's soul is the transformer of
human contempt into divine
praise.
Man's God-life is the collector of
the broken ones, the forsaken
and forlorn.

40. MY MIND'S SUNSET AND MY HEART'S SUNRISE

O my mind's sunset,
Behold, my heart's sunrise.

O my heart's sunrise,
You are travelling towards Light.
Light shall unveil
Your Beloved, The Beloved.

O my mind's sunset,
Your vision has totally failed.
Wonder and wander no more,
Homeless
And
Godless
And
Lifeless.

41. I NEED

The human in me
Needs Crucifixion-night.

The Divine in me
Needs Ascension-day.

The Immortal in me
Needs Perfection-noon.

And whom do I need?

I need God.
I need Ishwara.
I need Adonai.
I need Lord.
I need Ahurmazda.
I need Allah.
I need Amitabha.

Many more, all, all
Inside the boundless Net
of the Absolute Supreme.

42. I DO THE IMPOSSIBLE, HOW?

I have decided what I want.
I shall listen to the voice within.
I believe
It is all-loving, all-fulfilling.
I know
It is all-loving, all-fulfilling.
And it is exactly so.
My belief is my power.
My knowledge is my power.
I do the impossible because
My life of constant surrender
To the Will of the Supreme
Has taught me how.

43. MY RELATIONSHIP WITH BOOKS

I don't read a book.
I study it!
I don't study a book.
I love it!
I don't love a book.
I just become it!
I know there is only one book:
God's Reality.
I know there is only one reader:
God's Vision.
I know there is only one enjoyer:
God the eternal Child.

44. ANOTHER BEGGAR

There is something.
What is it?
Realisation?
I had it.

There is something.
What is it?
Revelation?
I am achieving it.

There is something.
What is it?
Manifestation?
I don't have it.
I need it.

Like me,
Another beggar needs it.
Who is He?

He, the Father of the Big Heart.
He, the Son of the Big Eye.

45. TWO SMILES

O height of understanding,
I want you not.
O height of becoming,
I want you.
O height of oneness,
I am you.
In me you see the smile of
Here.
In you I see the smile of
Now.
Here eventually becomes.
Now eternally is.

46. TO SEE THE FACE OF JOY

To see the face of joy
He went along with the world.
No joy.

To see the face of joy
He adapted himself to wishes of
others.
No joy.

To see the face of joy
He allowed others to out-talk him.
No joy.

To see the face of joy
He fasted for two long weeks.
No joy.

To see the face of joy
He denied himself even an iota of
human love.
No joy.

To see the face of joy
He entered into the zone of
silence.
No joy.

Finally a little bird whispered:
"Joy on earth no longer is.
Prepare yourself for the world
Beyond
Where joy is married to Eternity's
Life."

47. THE MIRACLE MAKER

His is the life of a miracle-maker.
He started with himself.
Himself he loved.
Himself he caught.
Himself he taught.

He has started teaching.
Nobody passes through him
 unchanged.
His life is a constant movement
 upward and inward.
Doctrine he has none.

His Heavenly beauty and God
Live under the same roof.
His earthly duty and God
Live in the same room.

48. IN HIS SHADOW

I wish to live in His shadow.
Why?
Because His heart of deeds
Gets priority
Over His mind of thoughts.

I wish to live in His shadow.
Why?
Because His one single smile
Is fraught with more meaning
Than
All the sermons of the world
 collected together.

I wish to live in His shadow.
Why?
Because His Silence is the Source
Of my countless freedom-deeds.

49. SHE

To think of Her
Is to become a chosen instrument
 of God.

To meditate on Her
Is to reach the heights of Paradise
 unchallenged.

To see Her
Is to sit on Infinity's
 Transcendental Throne.

To feel Her
Is to become Immortality's Bliss.

50. THE DATE OF HIS BIRTH IS CONTROVERSIAL

The date of his birth is
controversial.
The soul of the earth says:
"He was born on August 27, 1931."

The heart of the earth says:
"He was born on August 30, 1931."

The vital of the earth says:
"He was born on August 27, 1936."

The mind of the earth says:
"He was born on August 27, 1938."

The body of the earth says:
"He was born on August 27, 1950."

God says:
"He was born twice:
Once before the beginning of Life
in the Heart of Silence,
Once after the end of Death
in the Head of Sound."

51. I AM LEARNING

I am learning the art of listening.
I wish to be an eternal student.

I am learning the art of believing.
I wish to be an eternal believer.

I am learning the art of serving.
I wish to be an eternal servant.

I am learning the art of becoming.
I wish to be
The father of my silver dreams.
I wish to be
The son of my golden realities.

52. WHAT IT HAS

His concentration has given him
What it has: Power.
With Power he has changed
The lives of multitudes.

His meditation has given him
What it has: Love.
With Love he has changed
The face of humanity.

His contemplation has given him
What it has: Oneness.
With his Oneness he becomes man
the lover divine;
With his Oneness he becomes God
the Beloved Supreme.

53. MY MIND

No more Eternity's madness
Can hound my mind.
My heart has discovered the Key
For its junior partner.
My heart has unlocked the Door
For its junior partner.

From now on
My mind never shall sleep.
It will watch my inner Treasures:
The sun of Light, the sea of Peace
And the sky of Love.

54. REAL HOPES

The Heaven of real hopes
Arches over me.
Surrender, the master in me,
Knowledge, the servant in me,
Are together playing.
The Heaven of real realities
Starts my unfailing engine: Truth.
The Heaven of real realities
Generates my illumining
  electricity: Love.
My sure will moves the world
  within;
My pure thought moves the world
  without.

55. THREE IMMORTAL PRESENTS

I have received three immortal
  presents
On life's Christmas tree:
Detachment-bud
Concern-flower
Love-fruit.

With the bud I shall begin
My self-enquiry.
With the flower I shall achieve
My self-discovery.
With the fruit I shall enjoy
My self-mastery.

56. I CHALLENGED THE INVISIBLE

I drove the chariot of the sun
Athwart the arch of blue-gold
  Heaven,
Dissolving the negative intruders,
Fear and doubt,
Embracing the positive
  prompters,
Faith and Love.
Thousands of years ago
I challenged the invisible.
At long last, today
My challenge has been accepted.
Enlightenment fondly braves
The untiring searcher.

57. IN QUEST OF THE SATISFACTION-QUEEN

His life was an infinitude of quest.
Satisfaction denied him her presence.
Helpless he was.
Miserable he became.
At last a blue bird
From deep within lovingly announced:
"Argue not with your brooding self.
Satisfaction-queen will be yours.
Your meditation shall shake hands
with God-manifestation.
God-manifestation shall shake hands
with your perfection."

58. HIS FACE AND FEET

O unbridled demands and commands
Of doubt, jealousy and insecurity,
Stop! Stop your lurid game.
Thrust not upon me
All man-made discoveries.
I need only my God-made achievements:
My God's smiling Face,
My God's dancing Feet.

59. WHISPERINGS

The whisper of temptation
Took him to hell.
There he saw his animal face.

The whisper of aspiration
Took him to Heaven.
There he saw his God-Face.

The whisper of realisation
Took him to the World of Silence.
There he became the Endless Race.

60. HE FOUND, HE FINDS

At the rim of sorrow
He found his heartless mind.
On the brink of despair
He found his soulless heart.

In the sea of destruction
He found his goalless soul.
Centuries dropped dead.

Now
On the shore of Time
He finds his searching mind
He finds his crying heart
He finds his illumining soul.

61. THE GOSPEL OF FAITH

O magnificent aspiration,
You have shown me the life of
reality.
O magnificent realisation,
You have given me the soul of
acceptance.
O magnificent God,
You have given me the gospel of
faith:
My faith in Your descending
Smiles
Your faith in my ascending cries.

62. A YAWNING GULF

A yawning gulf between
My vision-tree and my
reality-plant.
A yawning gulf between
The place I love to live and the
place I live.
I love to live under the vault of
Heaven.
Alas, my existence lives
In the valley of the shadow of
death.
Peace has escaped my
remembrance;
Delight, too.
But I know a swing of the
pendulum
Will change my face and fate.
My surrender supreme
Shall marry my dream-boat
With my reality-shore.

63. THE WEAVER

The world weaves
A garland of curses
For me
When I forget to admire her
beauty.

The world weaves
A garland of curses
For me
When I underestimate the value
of her gifts.

The world weaves
A garland of curses
For me
When I adore the Light and
Delight of Heaven.

The world weaves
A garland of curses
For me
When I love the Silence-King
inside my heart.

64. A SIN, A CRIME

A sin against man
I commit
When I love myself alone.

A crime against God
I commit
When I love only mankind.

A sin and a crime
Against myself I commit
When
I forget what I was, Truth,
And what I am, Love.

65. MY NEW TASK

When I saw my life
In the silent room of death
I was thrilled.
I smiled because
I was given a new job
By my Lord Supreme:
To discover an oasis
In the spanless desert of death.
Jobless, aimless, helpless and
hopeless
No more am I.
No more my heartbeats
A standing jest, derision.
I shall perform my God-ordained
task
And become infinity's Dream and
Eternity's Reality.

66. I BECOME

No daring is fatal.
No loving is mortal.
No serving is fruitless.

In my daring I become
The Truth Transcendental.
In my loving I become
The soul supreme.
In my serving I become
The Oneness absolute.

67. THE STORY OF HIS DESTINATION

Before he reached
His destination, Heaven,
On his way
He hurled his mind hellward
With all its finite nonsense.
On reaching
His destination
He offered God
His surrendered heart
And
His fulfilled soul.

68. HE HAS

He has the mind
That never sleeps.
It always fights
Against its own existence.

He has the heart
That ever plays
On the Elysian lap of his soul.

He has the body,
He knows not what it does.

He has the vital,
He knows not what to do with it.

69. IT STEALS INTO MY HEART

There was a time when I loved
The fantastic fabrics of the mind.
There was a time
When I lived my life
Based on culled fictions.
There was a time
When I was satisfied
With a fragment of reality,
Splintered, broken and smashed.
But now a lucid illumination
Steals into my heart.
The eternal Presence
Of Infinity's Light
Feeds my Vision's Dawn.

70. LOVE AND BECOME

I looked for the mainland
Of Reality,
And I found it.
It whispered:
"Love or suffer,
Love or die,
Love and grow,
Love and become.
The world of hesitation has
frightened your heart.
The world of calculation has
puzzled your mind.
The world of temptation has
captured your vital.
The world of depression has
devoured your body."

71. THE DANCE OF TRANSCENDENCE-BLISS

O mind, argue not with yourself,
And suffer no remorse.
O heart, O my senior partner,
How long will you remain
An unuttered part of my life?
O soul, O our general manager,
Do use me, my many selves.
Allow me not to stumble any more
In the world of tragedy and tears.
Today you give me the power
To conquer my puny "I"
And be the song of
Transformation-Light.
Tomorrow you will give me the
power
To conquer my giant "I"
And be the dance of
Transcendence-Bliss.

72. EGO-PUBLICITY AND FRUSTRATION-FUTILITY

Each of his spiritual children
Was convinced that he saw
No one but him,
No one but her;
Loved no one but him,
No one but her;
Blessed no one but her,
No one but him;
Admired no one but her,
No one but him.
He lost his existence
Between their blind ego-publicity,
And his giant frustration-futility.

73. TO SEE HER

Each of her spiritual children
Thought of her differently,
Spoke of her differently,
Saw her differently,
Loved her differently,
Judged her differently.
To each she represented
Something else.
But one sweet fact they all
affirmed:
"To see her is to own her."

74. I AM PREPARED

You have come to me
To share your teeming worries.
I am prepared.

You have come to me
To throw your serpent-doubt at
me.
I am prepared.

You have come to me
To challenge my compassion-net.
I am prepared.

My child, I am the sole
intermediary
Between
The animal in you and the
Supreme for you.

75. YOU WANT TO BE FREE

You want to be free
From the drag of the flesh.
You want to be free
From the pull of desire.
You want to be free
From the push of frustration.
You want to be free
From the confines of your finite self.
You want to be free
From the prison-house of your own creation.
Then submit your fear to God's tears.
This is the only way
To regain and safeguard your proudest pride.

76. GOD HAS GIVEN ME

God has given me
Nothing but love and concern.
I have given God
Nothing but ignorance and self-defence.

God has given me
Nothing but Grace and praise.
I have given God
Nothing but frustration and accusation.

God has given me
Unconditionally
What He eternally has: Forgiveness.
I have given God
Unreservedly
What I eternally am: Ingratitude.

77. WHEN I WAS BORN

When I was born
In the heart of my sun
I was my Duty's role.

When I was born
In the heart of my moon
I was my Beauty's Soul.

When I was born
In the heart of my surrender-will
I was my Perfection-Goal.

78. HE KNEW

He knew
The impotence of human doubt.
He knows
The importance of Faith divine.
He knew
The impotence of human love.
He knows
The importance of Love divine.
He knew
The impotence of human
sovereignty.
He knows
The importance of Surrender
divine.
He knew
The impotence of human success.
He knows
The importance of Failure divine.
He knew
The impotence of human goal.
He knows
The importance of Role divine.

79. I DESIRE

I desire
To live remote from the stupid
babble of
Multitudes.
I desire
To snap the bonds and twists of
every snare of
Multitudes.
I desire
To see my hidden soul in the
hidden Goal of
Multitudes.
I desire,
I desire,
I desire
To walk the humble ways of life of
Multitudes.

80. HE FOUND HIS PLACE

Sloth and vagary
Found no place in him.
Fear and doubt
Found no place in him.
Worry and despair
Found no place in him.
God's Love and Pride
Found place in him.
He found his place,
His Eternal Place
On the Lap of Singing God,
In the Heart of Dancing God.

81. WITHIN THE SPAN OF A SINGLE HUMAN LIFE

Within the span of a single human life
I shall see the Eye of God's Vision-Boat.

Within the span of a single human life
I shall feel the Hand of God's Reality-Sun.

Within the span of a single human life
I shall become the Heart of God's Perfection-Goal.

Within the span of a single human life
I shall hide Eternity's ignorance.

Within the span of a single human life
I shall embody Immortality's Shore.

Within the span of a single human life
I shall reveal Infinity's Bliss.

82. YOU MUST TEACH

Only one body,
You must teach it.

Only one vital,
You must guide it.

Only one mind,
You must perfect it.

Only one heart,
You must use it.

Only one soul,
You must treasure it.

Only one Goal,
You must become it.

83. IS HE YOUR MASTER?

Is he your Master?
He then must be
An instructor of hard toils.

Is he your Master?
He then must be
A trainer of undying Patience.

Is he your Master?
He then must be
A transmitter of perfecting Light.

Is he your Master?
He then must be
Your only unconditional Lover.

84. I HEARD

In the abyss of doubt and despair
I heard my Master's call.

In the depth of love and joy
I heard my Master's footfall.

In the smile of silence
I heard my Master's
Salvation-Message.

In the life of surrender
I heard my Master's
immortality-Joy.

85. TRANSFORMATION, TRANSCENDENCE AND BEYOND

His body,
A picture of austerity.
His vital,
A picture of humility.
His mind,
A picture of serenity.
His heart,
A picture of purity.
His soul,
A picture of nobility.
His Goal,
A picture of Reality.
And he himself is the picture
Of yesterday's transformation,
Today's transcendence
And tomorrow's
Perfection-Beyond.

86. INCONSCIENCE AND FORGIVENESS

His are the lips that do the best
preaching.
His is the life that does the worst
deceiving.
His is the body that does the
longest sleeping.
His is the vital that does the
wildest ridiculing.
His is the mind that does the
meanest snobbing.
His is the heart that does the
filthiest defiling.
His is the realisation that
sempiternally shines
Between
Man's hopeless inconscience
And
God's endless Forgiveness.

87. THE VOYAGER OF SELF-DISCOVERY, THE EMPEROR OF LIFE-MASTERY

I yearn and ache for Thee.
Every day I become
Love-seed,
Devotion-plant,
Surrender-tree.
O Lord, forget me not
In my outer goalless wandering
Far and wide.
O Lord, make my pilgrim-heart
The voyager of self-discovery,
The emperor of life-mastery.

88. BEHOLD, YOUR BELOVED IS COME

O shining heart of expectation,
O searching mind of expectation,
O struggling vital of expectation,
O dying body of expectation,
Behold, your Beloved is come
With His Silence-Light,
Promise-Height,
Victory-Kite.

89. I AM A

I am a searcher of expanding
space.
I am a lover of running race.
I am an adorer of glowing beauty.
I am a performer of fulfilling duty.
I am a sower of God's crying
necessity.
I am a grower of man's mounting
divinity.

90. YOU WILL TRANSFORM AND TRANSCEND

O humility's soul,
Your life-garden is eternally
In bloom.
You were born in the
Silence-Palace
Of the moon.
You sport with the Heart of
The Eternity-Sun.
Your surrender-existence is your
sole friend.
In your eternal pilgrimage
To the Supreme,
Soon, very soon
You will transform today's face
And transcend tomorrow's smile.

91. HE IS GREAT

He is great,
Not because of his cosmopolitan
education.
He is great,
Not because of his international
name and fame.
He is great,
Because he touched the Feet
Of his Beloved in the temple.
He is great,
Because he kissed the Feet
Of his Beloved in the mosque.
He is great,
Because he breathed the Life
Of his Beloved's Feet in the
synagogue.
He is great,
Because he has become
His Beloved's Feet in the church.

92. THE SOUL-BIRD

O world-ignorance,
Although
You have shackled my feet,
I am free.
Although
You have chained my hands,
I am free.
Although
You have enslaved my body,
I am free.
I am free because I am not of the
body.
I am free because I am not the
body,
I am free because I am the
soul-bird
That flies in Infinity-Sky.
I am the soul-child that dreams
On the Lap of the immortal King
Supreme.

93. THEREFORE I LOVE YOU

Lord, You are a stranger to
tiredness;
Therefore I love You.
Lord, You are a stranger to sleep;
Therefore I love You.
Lord, You are a stranger to dream;
Therefore I love You.
Lord, my darkness hates Your
Light;
Therefore I am puzzled.
Lord, my bondage hates Your
Freedom;
Therefore I am bewildered.
Lord, my ignorance hates Your
Compassion;
Therefore, I am lost, totally lost.

94. TWO KILLERS

Lord, when You kill me
With Your Love supreme
I kill you with my undying
ingratitude.

Lord, when You kill me
With Your Power supreme
I kill you with my hopeless
helplessness.

Lord, when You kill me
With Your Indifference supreme
I kill you with my bleeding
insecurity.

95. HE ACTS

He acts.
His actions are stung
By the serpent of ambition.

He acts.
His actions unmistakably
Organise ego-publicity.

He acts.
His actions ruthlessly
Disturb the role of his soul.

He acts.
His actions are always
For the luxury of self-indulgence.

96. THE LOCK AND THE KEY

Doubt is the lock,
Faith is the key.
Hate is the lock,
Love is the key.
Body is the lock,
Soul is the key.
Ignorance is the lock,
Light is the key.
God's Heart has no lock,
Man's mind has no key.

97. HE HAS HEARD HIS MASTER'S FOOTFALLS

His life is full of din,
His life is full of rush,
His life is full of hurry.
He is a picture of insincerity,
He is a picture of ingratitude,
He is a picture of failure.
He fails to silence the storm of his
flesh,
He fails to come out of the abyss of
his doubt,
He fails to bury the coffin of his
fear.
Yet
He shall be saved,
He shall be liberated,
He shall be fulfilled.
For
He has heard his Master's
footfalls.

98. MARCH ON! MARCH ON!

March on, don't beat retreat!
Sunder not your life from Reality.
March on, respond to the call
Of the Universal Life.
Liberation-flood is yours.
Perfection-sky is yours.
March on, don't beat retreat!
Don't argue with yourself.
You are destined to reap the full
harvest.
March on, don't beat retreat!

99. SURRENDER THEN SURRENDER NOW

When I surrendered
To the yoke of public opinion,
My life-forest
Teemed with fear, doubt and
despair.
An endless series
Of misfortunes and serpentine
windings
Imprisoned my soul.
I have now surrendered
To the Love-Will of my Inner Pilot.
Under the Vault of Heaven
My earthly existence now
breathes.
I live to proclaim
My Beauty's descent and Duty's
ascent.

100. NOW I AM HAPPY

I was not happy,
Although my fame reached
Unprecedented heights.

I was not happy,
Although the world kissed
The dust of my feet.

I was not happy,
Although God offered me
His Transcendental Pride.

But now I am happy,
Because
The Blossoms of my service-tree
Have all been devoured
By man's ignorance-night and
God's Blessing-Light.

101. TICKET

Realisation is the one-way ticket
From the man-station
To the God-junction.

Manifestation is the round-trip
ticket.

Aspiration is the money-power
That buys the ticket.

Surrender divine needs no ticket,
No money-power.
It has what it needs:
The Compassion-Feet
Of the Lord Supreme.

102. WHY ARE YOU SENSITIVE?

You are sensitive to noise
Because
You have not invented
The Atom Bomb
And
The Hydrogen Bomb.

You are sensitive to noise
Because
The outer world's vast
achievement is determined
Not
To touch your feet.

You are sensitive to noise
Because
God the Player divine,
God the Singer eternal,
God the Dancer immortal,
Has not claimed you in Heaven
As His partner on earth.

103. ABOVE AND BEYOND

Above the ignorance of birth and
death he is.
Above destruction-night he is.
Beyond the world of suspicion his
life of integrity is.
Beyond question his miracle-faith
is.
Above all earth-awards he is.
Above all Heaven-rewards he is.
Beyond the universal insecurity
he is.
He embodies Eternity's Cry.
He reveals Infinity's Smile.
He manifests Immortality's Life.
Earth loves his heart of
dedication.
Heaven adores his feet of
protection.

104. DEPENDENT AND INDEPENDENT

My outer poverty follows
In the train of luxury.
My inner poverty follows
In the train of desire.

I know two things:
My helpless hope is dependent on
all.
My ageless faith is independent of
all.

105. COMPLETE TRANSFORMATION-CHANGE

There is only one serious danger,
And that danger is doubt.
My Inner Pilot warned me of that
danger.

There is only one serious
temptation,
And that temptation is supremacy.
My Inner Pilot warned me against
this temptation.

There is only one dark death,
And that death is fear.
There is only one true life,
And that life is love:
Love of the soul for the body's
Complete transformation-change.

106. THE ACHIEVEMENT OF NON-POSSESSION

When he was a man of
non-possession,
He became the marvellous blend
Of love and action.
His religion was not noisy,
His philosophy was not showy.
He advanced and achieved,
He achieved and advanced.
He knew that he was a descendent
of God.
He knew that he was on a footing
of equality with God.
Heaven gave him Heaven's
possession:
Delight.
Earth gave him earth's possession:
Perfection.

107. OUR MANY SELVES

We see
Only what we are.
We are
Our skin-deep selves.
We are
Our dissatisfied million selves.
We are
Our eyeless emotion-selves.
We are
Our helpless frustration-selves.
We are
Reaping the full harvest of our
forgotten selves.

108. I DEPEND

When I am in the mind,
I depend on doubt and fear.
When I am in the vital,
I depend on aggression and
regression.
When I am in the body,
I depend on hopelessness and
helplessness.
When I am in the heart,
I depend on insecurity and
uncertainty.
When I am in the soul,
I depend on love and joy.
When I am in God,
I depend on His Forgiveness and
Assurance.

109. HE IS A DESCENDANT OF GOD

He is a descendant of Satan,
Therefore he is ignorant of
love-light.
He is a descendant of Man,
Therefore he is ignorant of
gratitude-might.
He is a descendant of God,
Therefore he is ignorant of
ignorance-night.

110. MY INNER PILOT DISCOURAGES ME

In the morning
My Inner Pilot
Discourages me from bitter
complaining.

In the afternoon
My Inner Pilot
Discourages me from constant
competing.

In the evening
My Inner Pilot
Discourages me from useless
brooding.

At night
My Inner Pilot
Discourages me from fruitless
dreaming.

111. MY LIFE ALTERNATES WITH GOD

My day alternates with night
My fear alternates with strength
My doubt alternates with
certainty
My love alternates with hatred
My defeat alternates with victory
I alternate with God
My soul alternates with God the
Dream
My heart alternates with God the
Lover
My life alternates with God the
Player.

112. I HAVE DONE

O Lord, You are requesting me
To offer You an iota of love.
Hard is it to accede to Your
request,
But I shall try.

O Lord, You want me to give You
My pleasure-life and take from
You
Your Joy-Life in return.
Hard is it to consent to Your
terms,
But I shall try.

O Lord, You propose that I
represent
You on earth.
Easy, mighty easy, to consent to
Your liberal proposal.
And I am doing it.
Lo, I have done it!

113. O SWEET ONES

O Sweet Lord,
Forget me not
In my wanderings far and wide.

O sweet Heaven,
Ignore not
The outpouring of my heart.

O sweet earth,
Underestimate not
The eternal voyager in me.

Lord, we two are one.
Heaven, we are of each other's
Dream-boat.
Earth, we are for each other's
Reality-shore.

114. CLARION CALL

My eternal children sweet,
Hearken to my clarion call:
No fall there is, no fall,
Just quit, ignorance, quit.

115. I LOOK

I look within and see
My Lord's Nectar-Delight.
I look without and see
The face of destruction-night.
I look forward and see
The golden dance of life.
I look backward and see
The smile of a naked knife.

116. SLOWLY

Slowly my heart ascends
To kindle the flame of love divine.
Slowly my heart descends
To plumb the life of beauty's
mine.

Slowly my heart transforms
The ceaseless pride of
ignorance-night.
Slowly my heart fulfils
The Golden Hour of God-Delight.

117. NOT NOW

My light shall flood the world.
Not now, not now, not now!
My will shall feed the world.
Not now, not now, not now!

My smile shall lift the world.
Not now, not now, not now!
My boat shall sail the world.
Not now, not now, not now!

My light, my will, my smile,
My boat, shall change the face
Of earth and inspire the world
To win the Godward Race.

118. I KNOW AND I KNOW NOT

I love the world;
I know not why and how.
The world loves me;
I know not why and how.

I love my Lord;
Oh, I know why and how.
My Lord loves me;
Oh, I know why and how.

Two strangers, the world and I.
O world, where are we, where?
Two friends, my Lord and I.
Here we are, eternally here.

119. I SEE

In the beams of the moon
I see my beauty's face.
In the rays of the sun
I see my duty's race.
In the flames of the sky
I see my oneness divine,
I feel my oneness immortal
With my Pilot's Nectar-Embrace.

120. MY LIFE IS TRANSCENDING

From the blue of the sky
My soul began its descending
flight.
In the black of my body
My life is sleeping and sleeping.
In the green of my vital
My life is struggling and
struggling.
In the red of my mind
My life is searching and searching.
In the white of my heart
My life is becoming and
becoming.
In the gold of my soul
My life is transcending and
transcending.

121. THE BANNER

In the core of the hoary past
There lived a Master
Of loftiest magnitude.

He believed in his disciples'
Constant and striking promises.
Therefore he was entitled
To hoist the Banner of
Transcendental Pride.

Alas, there the story ended not.
Sorrowfully and helplessly
He watched his disciples'
Hopeless achievements.
Therefore he was doomed
To hold the flag of permanent
failure.

122. SHE SPEAKS

Softly she speaks;
Therefore she is kind.
Slowly she speaks;
Therefore she is confident.
Soulfully she speaks;
Therefore she is divine.
Compassionately she speaks;
Therefore she is immortal.
Unconditionally she speaks;
Therefore she alone is
indispensable.

123. WHEN I MEDITATE

When I meditate on God,
My world becomes the sunshine
Of Immortality's Birth.
When I meditate on mankind,
My world becomes the thick
clouds
Of uncertainty's life.
When I meditate on my puny "I",
My world becomes the destined
dance
Of blind destruction-flood.

124. GOD FEELS

God feels good
When you embody
The life of sincerity.

God feels great
When you embody
The breath of purity.

God feels proud
When you embody
The soul of humility.

God feels victorious
When you embody
The role of His Duty.

125. I FLY

I fly on the wings of morning
To see in Heaven God's Beauty.
I fly on the wings of noon
To see on earth God's Power.
I fly on the wings of evening
To feel in my heart God's Silence.
I fly on the wings of night
To feel in my soul God's Bliss.

126. WHEN I BLOW THE TRUMPET

When I blow the trumpet of the
  sky,
God smiles at me.
When I blow the trumpet of the
  earth,
God shakes hands with me.
When I blow the trumpet of
  ego-life,
God devours my pride.
When I blow the trumpet of God's
  Silence,
God embraces my height.

127. YOUR GIFTS FOR THE WORLD

Your tongue filled with
  venom-praise
For the world.
Your heart filled with deathless
  hatred
For the world.
Your mind filled with lifeless love
For the world.
Your vital filled with
  elephant-madness
For the world.
Your body filled with
  ignorance-dream
For the world.
Your life filled with
  uncertainty-sea
For the world.
Your soul filled with
  indifference-sky
For the world.

128. I BECOME

Slowly and steadily
With silver tears
I see the Head of God.

Lovingly and silently
With gold tears
I breathe the Heart of God.

Constantly and unconditionally
With diamond tears
I become the Feet of God.

129. HIS LIFE

His life of aspiration
Buys and buys
Expensive will-flames divine.

His life of desire
Sells and sells
Explosive vital human thoughts.

In his life of ascent
He is
An unchallenged capacity.

In his life of descent
He is
Poorer than the poorest stability.

130. WHAT I AM

Ability is my soul
Stability is my heart
Reality is my Goal
Necessity is my Lord
Infinity is my smile
Eternity is my cry
Divinity is my face
Immortality is my race.

131. HE WANTS HE NEEDS

Freedom of religion,
He wants.
Freedom of church,
He needs.

Freedom of bondage,
He wants.
Freedom of ignorance,
He needs.

Freedom of life,
He wants.
Freedom of silence,
He needs.

132. YET YOU ARE FOND OF ME

God, I am absent-minded;
Yet You are fond of me.

God, I am negligent;
Yet You are fond of me.

God, I am insecure;
Yet You are fond of me.

God, I am impure;
Yet You are fond of me.

God, why are You so fond of me?
"My child, I am fond of you,
Because
You try,
Because
You cry."

133. HE THINKS, HE FEELS, HE KNOWS

His vital thinks
To live with God the
disciplinarian
Is ridiculous.

His mind thinks
To live with God the simpleton
Is ridiculous.

His body thinks
To live with God the inconsiderate
Is ridiculous.

His heart feels
To live without God the Beloved
Is ridiculous.

His soul knows
To live without God the Lover
Is ridiculous.

134. NONE

None will try for me
When I try.
None will cry with me
When I fail.
None will sigh over me
When I am doomed.
None will think of me
When I am gone.

135. THE STORIES OF HIS LIVES

He started his pilgrim-life
With implicit faith in man.
He ends his pilgrim-life
With a frustration-mountain.

He started his vagabond-life
With no faith in God.
He ends his vagabond-life
With God's Face in his heart
And God's Heart in his eyes.

136. WHEN I DO

When I do
One thing at a time,
I am successful.

When I do
Two things at a time,
I am doubtful.

When I do
Three things at a time,
I am fearful.

When I do
Four things at a time,
God smiles at me.

When I do
Five things at a time,
God cries with me.

When I do
Six things at a time,
God dies with me.

When I do
Seven things at a time,
God does them all for me.

137. THE STRANGERS

His deeds
Are strangers to deception.
His words
Are strangers to truth.
His life
Is a stranger to success.
His death
Is a stranger to hope.

138. SECRETLY AND OPENLY

Secretly he borrows from God
His Illumination-flood.
Openly he lends an iota to
  mankind
With an exorbitant interest.

Secretly he learns free from God
His infinite Songs of Oneness
  supreme.
Openly he teaches only one to
  mankind
For an unsurpassable fee.

139. HE SPOKE

He spoke to his past.
Alas, he is clothed
In soulless tears
And lifeless sighs.

He spoke to his present.
Alas, he is clothed
In brooding fears
And teeming doubts.

He spoke to his future.
Alas, he is clothed
In a visionless soul
And a missionless goal.

140. THE LIBERAL

Liberal was he then
In constant advice.
Liberal is he now
In continuous promise.
Liberal will he be
In ceaseless self-giving.
His advice: Be divine.
His promise: You I shall make
  divine.
His self-giving: Lo, you are divine!

141. ALL ARE UNSELFISH

Doubt shares its capacity
With the mind.
Therefore, unselfish is doubt.

Arrogance shares its capacity
With the vital.
Therefore, unselfish is arrogance.

Lethargy shares its capacity
With the body.
Therefore, unselfish is lethargy.

Insecurity shares its capacity
With the heart.
Therefore, unselfish is insecurity.

Uncertainty shares its capacity
With the soul.
Therefore, unselfish is
uncertainty.

Man shares his ignorance-capacity
With God.
Therefore, unselfish is man.

142. TWO BIRTHDAYS

I count my age
From two different years.

To celebrate my human life,
I count my age
Right from 1931.

To celebrate my life divine,
I count my age
Only from 1944.

143. A SEEKER'S THREE BIRTHDAYS

Each seeker can count his age
From three different dates:
The day he saw the light of day,
The day he sat at his Master's feet,
The day he became the Heart
Of the Pilot Supreme.

144. BE THOU

Be Thou my body
That I may wake.
Be Thou my vital
That I may run.
Be Thou my mind
That I may fly.
Be Thou my heart
That I may dive.
Be Thou my soul
That I may reveal.
Be Thou my goal
That I may fulfil.
Be Thou my all
That I may only be Yours.

145. I ENTERED

I entered
Into the sombre care of human
thought.
Nothing there was.

I entered
Into the illumined Palace of
Thought divine.
Something there was.

I entered
Into the conditionally
surrendered
Soul of human life.
There I saw God smiling.

I entered
Into the unconditionally
surrendered
Soul of Life divine.
There I saw God becoming.

146. WHAT DO THE TEACHERS TEACH?

Death's lifeless night I was.
Life's endless day I am.
God's ceaseless Bliss I shall be.

Night taught me how to sigh.
Day teaches me how to try.
Bliss shall teach me how to cry.

I taught night how to surrender.
I teach day how to endeavour.
I shall teach Bliss how to devour.

147. O MY POOR LONELINESS

O my poor loneliness,
You live in thought's wilderness.
O my poor loneliness,
Your wings are clipped.

O my poor loneliness,
How long must you cherish
The cave of tenebrous night?

O my poor loneliness,
Why do you stay
With the lifeless body of
destruction-night?

O my poor loneliness,
The tallest pavilion of Heaven,
The Golden Radiance of Eternity,
Are cancelling the fate of your
death
And immortalising the
transformed face of your life.

148. MY THREE POSSESSIONS

When I pray,
My inspiration owns
The fount of eternal Peace.

When I meditate,
My aspiration owns
The fount of immortal Light.

When I dedicate,
My realisation owns
The fount of supreme Bliss.

149. MUTUAL LOVE

I adore God
For what He has:
Yesterday's Promise,
Today's Assurance,
Tomorrow's Gift.

God loves me
For what I am:
Curiosity-Prince,
Stupidity-King,
Futility-Emperor.

150. HE DIED IN HIS LIFE-CAR

He died
In his life-car
When his mind was in high,
His body in neutral.

He died
In his life-car
When his vision-race was in high,
His reality-face in neutral.

He died
In his life-car
When his elephant-confidence
was in high,
His rabbit-capacity in neutral.

151. JOY-GIFTS

My heart gives me infant joy.
My soul gives me instant joy.
My Goal gives me constant joy.
My Supreme gives me
Birthless and measureless
Deathless and ceaseless
Joy.

152. IF I LISTEN

My Lord asks me
Whom to listen to?

"If I listen to the demands of your body,
You will grow into a blind beggar.

"If I listen to the demands of your vital,
You will grow into a wild elephant.

"If I listen to the demands of your mind,
You will grow into unparalleled insanity.

"If I listen to the demands of your heart,
You will grow into the ignorance-king."

153. YOU ARE INSECURE

You are insecure
Because
Your belief is not sustained
By the inner faith.

You are insecure
Because
Your faith is not sustained
By the unconditional surrender.

You are insecure
Because
Your surrender has not
Breathed the life of oneness supreme.

154. IN LONELINESS

When
He is in the well of loneliness,
He thinks of doubt.

When
He is in the pool of loneliness,
He thinks of despair.

When
He is in the lake of loneliness,
He thinks of consolation.

When
He is in the river of loneliness,
He thinks of hope.

When
He is in the sea of loneliness,
He thinks of God.

155. I SAW IN HIS EYES

He slept in silence.
I saw in his closed eyes
The Peace of God.

He woke up in silence.
I saw in his blossomed eyes
The Joy of God.

He walked in silence.
I saw in his glowing eyes
The Light of God.

He ran in silence.
I saw in his ambrosial eyes
The Life of God.

156. WHEN PANGS FLASHED

When pangs flashed
Across your heart,
You criticised God.

When pangs flashed
Across your mind,
You blamed God.

When pangs flashed
Across your vital,
You cursed God.

When pangs flashed
Across your body,
You deserted God.

157. PLEASE

O generous earth!
Pray for me, please.

O generous sky!
Think of me, please.

O generous Heaven!
Meditate on me, please.

O generous God!
Love me, Love me, Love me,
please.

158. DO YOU KNOW?

Do you know
Your lowest and strongest
temptation?
It is your evening doubt.
It is your evening doubt.

Do you know
Your lower and stronger
temptation?
It is your afternoon jealousy.
It is your afternoon jealousy.

Do you know
Your low and strong temptation?
It is your morning insecurity.
It is your morning insecurity.

159. HIS LOYALTY

He was helpless.
Therefore
He declared his loyalty to fear.

He was hopeless.
Therefore
He offered his loyalty to
unhappiness.

He was useless.
Therefore
He surrendered his loyalty to
doubt.

160. BEFORE HE SAW

Before he saw
The face of the world,
He was the smile of an
angel-child.

Before he saw
The Face of God,
He was the tempest of despair.

Before he saw
The face of God-manifestation,
He was the life of uncertainty.

161. TO BE THE VOICE

To become the voice of humanity,
He touched the Feet of God.

To become the voice of divinity,
He breathed the Heart of God.

To become the Voice of God,
He dined with the Soul of God.

162. IN HIM I SEE A RASCAL

When he gives
His birthless and deathless
sermon,
In him I see a superlative rascal.

When he offers
The message of Love divine,
In him I see an unparalleled rascal.

When he distributes
The Life of the Absolute Supreme,
In him I see the transcendental
rascal.

163. THE BEGGAR

His smiles
Are lovelier than the moon.
His cries
Are quieter than death.
His thoughts
Are faster than the bullet.
His heart
Is feebler than the tiniest ant.
His hopes
Are richer than the Emperor
supreme.
His life
Is poorer than Eternity's beggar.

164. A DROP OF TEARS

A drop of my tears
Is enough to make my Lord
Embrace my ageless
Inner poverty.

A drop of my Lord's tears
Is enough to transform my life of
ignorance-dream
Into Reality's
Divinity-Love.

165. HE SEES

In his doubting mind,
He sees Eternity's Cloud.

In his sleepless heart,
He sees Infinity's Rainbow.

In his warrior-soul,
He sees Immortality's Life.

166. THE COSMIC RIVER

His body flows
With the river of cosmic sadness.

His vital flows
With the river of cosmic madness.

His mind flows
With the river of cosmic blindness.

His heart flows
With the river of cosmic kindness.

His soul flows
With the river of cosmic gladness.

His goal flows
With the river of cosmic oneness.

167. HE BECOMES

When he is angry,
He becomes a mountain.

When he is peaceful,
He becomes an ocean.

When he is happy,
He becomes the vision of the skies.

When he is sad,
He becomes the slave of death.

168. MY LIFE

My desire-life
Lighted the candle of God.

My aspiration-life
Kindled the lamp of God.

My realisation-life
Glorified the sun of God.

My manifestation-life
Fulfilled the LIGHT of God.

169. NO DIFFERENCE

No difference
Between
The sleeping spirit and
destruction-power.

No difference
Between
The stainless Pride and
transcendental Height.

No difference
Between
Humanity's gratitude and
divinity's plenitude.

170. MUSIC

O music of love,
From you I learn
The secret of closeness.

O music of will,
From you I learn
The secret of future-creation.

O music of silence,
From you I learn
The secret of universal oneness.

O music of surrender,
From you I learn
The secret of cosmic perfection.

171. I AM NOT READY

Earth is waiting for me;
I am not ready.
I want to rest more.

Heaven is waiting for me;
I am not ready.
I want to sleep more.

God is waiting for me;
I am not ready.
I want to dream more.

I shall rest with Eternity's Body.
I shall sleep with Infinity's Heart.
I shall dream with Immortality's
Soul.

172. MY LONGINGS

A sad longing
I have for Peace.

A sweet longing
I have for Light.

A conscious longing
I have for self-transcendence.

A surrendered longing
I have for God-realisation.

A sleepless longing
I have for my perfect Perfection.

173. I CRY

I cry
When my heart-sea
Is black with desires.

I cry
When my mind-sky
Is grey with desires.

I cry
When my vital-forest
Is green with desires.

I cry
When my body-desert
Is red with desires.

174. MY PROMISES AND MY FAILURES

My morning promise:
I shall be divine.
I fail.

My afternoon promise:
All my actions shall be divine.
I fail.

My evening promise:
In everything I shall see the
divine.
I fail.

My night promise:
I shall think of the divine alone.
I fail.

175. THE WAVES OF TEMPTATION, FRUSTRATION AND DESTRUCTION

Temptation-waves
Are the armies of the day.
In vain my vital fights with them,
In vain.

Frustration-waves
Are the armies of the night.
In vain my heart fights with them,
In vain.

Destruction-waves
Are the armies of tomorrow.
In vain my soul fights with them,
In vain.

176. I AM NOT ALONE

I am not alone.
The burial ground of hope
Is within my heart.

I am not alone.
The burial ground of hope
Is before my eyes.

I am not alone.
The burial ground of hope
Is around my life.

I am not alone.
The burial ground of hope
Is above my soul.

177. YESTERDAY AND TODAY

Yesterday
She was the bride of enthusiasm.
Today
She is the widow of hope.

Yesterday
She was the bride of humility.
Today
She is the widow of humiliation.

Yesterday
She was the bride of confidence.
Today
She is the widow of doubt.

178. MY NECESSITIES

A fatal necessity:
The whisper of my temptation.

A promising necessity:
The whisper of my prayers.

A fruitful necessity:
The whisper of my surrender.

A fulfilled necessity:
The whisper of my oneness.

179. HE WAS MISUNDERSTOOD

He preached the gospel of purest love.
He was misunderstood.

He preached the gospel of sweetest devotion.
He was misunderstood.

He preached the gospel of quickest surrender.
He was misunderstood.

He preached the gospel of slowest repentance.
He was misunderstood.
YES,
This time
He was misunderstood
Far beyond the power of his receptivity.
He became the worst victim
Of the world's wild derision.

180. SIN AND CRIME

It is a sin against the human
In my mind
When I think of fear.

It is a crime against the God
In my heart
When I think of doubt.

It is a sin against my
God-becoming
In my life-river
When I deliberately feed despair.

It is a crime against my
God-manifestation
In my body-field
When I unconditionally surrender
to shameless death.

181. FOUR IMMORTAL GIFTS

His life is a gift
Of God's Silent Compassion.

His heart is a gift
Of God's Silent Attention.

His soul is a gift
Of God's Silent Illumination.

His Goal is a gift
Of God's Silent Perfection.

182. DISCUSSIONS

The mind and the heart
Do not discuss.

The mind and the vital discuss,
But never conclude.

The vital and the body discuss,
Include and exclude.

The soul and the heart
Never discuss,
Just include and conclude.

183. HOPELESS, USELESS AND HELPLESS

He is hopeless.
His darkness
Has corrupted the beauty of his
mind.

He is useless.
His insincerity
Has corrupted the lustre of his
heart.

He is helpless.
His ingratitude
Has corrupted the effulgence of
his soul.

184. THERE IS NO OTHER

After the first Soul
There is no other.

After the first Race
There is no other.

After the first Goal
There is no other.

After the first God
There is no other.

185. AGAINST

Against the shore of death,
The waves of science beat in vain.

Against the peak of life,
The arrows of science strike in
vain.

Against the vision of the soul,
The soldiers of science fight in
vain.

186. WHO CAN STAND?

Against man's impurity,
Who can stand?
No, not even a saint.

Against man's insincerity,
Who can stand?
No, not even a sage.

Against man's obscurity,
Who can stand?
No, not even a seer.

Against man's insecurity,
Who can stand?
No, not even a yogi.

Against man's stupidity,
Who can stand?
No, not even an Avatar.

Against man's futility,
Who can stand?
No, not even God.

187. ANSWER ME

Answer me in one word:
Who is God?
Answer me in two words:
Where is God?
Answer me in three words:
How to realise God?
Answer me in four words:
How to become God?

Who is God?
Truth.
Where is God?
With Light.
How to realise God?
Through constant offering.
How to become God?
Through
surrender-devotion-love.

The seeker's surrender
Embodies God's Soul.
The seeker's devotion
Embodies God's Heart.
The seeker's love
Embodies God's Life.

188. AT EVERY WORD

At every word my real necessity
dies.
At every word my strong capacity
dies.
At every word my illumining
beauty dies.
At every word my liberating duty
dies.
At every word my fulfilling
promise dies.
At every word my Himalayan Goal
dies.

189. ASK ME NO QUESTIONS

Ask me no questions,
I shall not possess you.

Ask me no questions,
I shall not desert you.

Ask me no questions,
I shall not disappoint you.

Ask me no questions,
I shall not dislike you.

Ask me no questions,
I shall bring God to you.

Ask me no questions,
I shall make God feed you.

Ask me no questions,
I shall place you on God's
blue-gold Throne.

190. BEAUTY

Beauty that must die
Is the human face.

Beauty that must live
Is the human heart.

Beauty that must increase
Is the human soul.

Beauty that must enlighten
The life of the world
Is the flame-wave of love.

191. BE NOT

Body, be not impure.
Vital, be not restless.
Mind, be not obscure.
Heart, be not insecure.
Life, be not hopeless.
Death, be not so sure.

192. DO AS I SAY, NOT AS I DO

Do as I say, not as I do.
I ask you to tell the truth;
Hence, you must.
I am far beyond the snares of lies;
Hence, I need not stick to truth.

Do as I say, not as I do.
I ask you to realise God;
Hence, you must.
I am far beyond the domain of
  ignorance;
Hence, I need no God-realisation.

193. I DO MY DUTY

I do my duty
And
Let God's Compassion do the rest.

I do my duty
And
Let God's Blessing do the rest.

I do my duty
And
Let God's Assurance do the rest.

I do my duty
And
Let God's Will do the rest.

I do my duty
And
Let God's Pride do the rest.

I do my duty
And
Let God's Oneness do the rest.

194. THERE WAS A TIME

There was a time
When I
Was a dreamer of dreams.
But now I am a lover of realities.

There was a time
When I
Killed God with my
venom-doubts.
But now I kill God
With my love-fire.

There was a time
When I
Was ignorant of the life of
nectar-sea.
But now I have become
Within and without
Infinity's Nectar-Sea.

195. WHEN THE TIME CAME

He loved the things he wanted.
He killed the things he wanted.

When the time came,
He loved doubt dearly.
When the time came,
He killed doubt ruthlessly.

When the time came,
He loved autocracy shamelessly.
When the time came,
He killed autocracy ruthlessly.

When the time came,
He loved ignorance supremely.
When the time came,
He killed ignorance ruthlessly.

196. ARE YOU A FAVOURITE SON OF GOD?

Are you a favourite son of God?
Then expect no friend from the world.

Are you a favourite son of God?
Then expect jealousy from the world
Far beyond the power of your receptivity.

Are you a favourite son of God?
Then expect contempt from the world
Far beyond the end of your imagination's flight.

Are you a favourite son of God?
Then rest assured the length and breadth of the world
Will misunderstand you:
Your love-light, your devotion-height, your surrender-delight.

For you the Supreme is Compassion.
In you the Supreme is Illumination.
With you the Supreme is Perfection.

197. ARE YOU A FAVOURITE DAUGHTER OF GOD?

Are you a favourite daughter of
God?
Then you need nothing,
absolutely nothing,
Either from Heaven or from earth.

Are you a favourite daughter of
God?
Then feel that your Lord
Is not only within your soul-boat
But also of your life-river.

Are you a favourite daughter of
God?
If you think that your Father does
everything for you,
Then you are mistaken.

If you feel that your Father will do
everything for you,
Then you are mistaken.
If you feel that He has already
done everything for you,
Then you are right, absolutely
right.

Indeed, He had done everything
for you
Long before your soul came into
the field of manifestation.
You just become in the life of your
heart
What you eternally are in His
Soul:
His, only His.

198. HE IS FOR GOD ONLY

There was a time
When he was for God on earth
only.

There was a time
When he was for God in Heaven
only.

There was a time
When he was for God in his heart
only.

But now he is for God only,
For God only.

199. HELL

Hell is a thing like doubt.
Hell is a thing like jealousy.

Hell is an animal like a panther.
Hell is an animal like a tiger.

Hell is a man like the poorest
beggar.
Hell is a man like the fiercest
brute.

Hell is a road paved with good
intentions.
Hell is a road that compels us to
think of perfection.

200. HE BARKS BUT HE BITES NOT

He barks and barks;
That is what he knows.

He bites not, he bites not.
How can he bite?
Since he knows not,
Since he knows not.

He barks and barks;
That is his self-styled role.

He bites not and bites not,
That is his God-ordained Goal.

201. THE STORY OF PERHAPS

When he lives in the mind
He speaks to the fruitless perhaps.

When he lives in the heart
He sings for the hopeless perhaps.

When he lives in the vital
He plays with the worthless
perhaps.

When he lives in the body
He dances with the lifeless
perhaps.

202. MY SOUL IS THE PLAYER

My thought is the doubt,
My mind the doubter.

My feeling is the love,
My heart the lover.

My desire is the destruction,
My vital the destroyer.

My ignorance is the sleep,
My body the sleeper.

My will is the play,
My soul the player.

203. REALITY'S IMMORTALITY

Thousands of years ago
He cried for the Throne.
Hundreds of years ago
He saw the Throne.
Two hundred years ago
He touched the Throne.
One hundred years ago
He sat on the Throne.
He was captured by Divinity's
Beauty.

Now he has become the Throne.
He is claimed by
Reality's Immortality.

204. SAVE AND EXCEPT

He can resist everything
Save and except temptation.

He can resist everything
Save and except his yesterday's
failure.

He can resist everything
Save and except his today's
frustration.

He can resist everything
Save and except his tomorrow's
perhaps.

He can resist everything
Save and except his Master's
Compassion.

205. HE DIED

He died for the Goddess of Beauty.
She saw him not.

He died for the Goddess of
Wealth.
She blessed him not.

He died for the Goddess of Love.
She granted not an iota of love to
him.

He died for the Goddess of Duty.
She descended.
She came.
She blessed.
She perfected.
She fulfilled.
She immortalised
His life of desire without,
His life of aspiration within.

206. DON'T WORRY!

O Body, don't worry!
I have not yet
Begun to rest.

O Vital, don't worry!
I have not yet
Begun to fight.

O Mind, don't worry!
I have not yet
Begun to think.

O Heart, don't worry!
I have not yet
Begun to love.

O Soul, don't worry!
I have not yet
Begun to manifest.

My dear friends,
When the hour strikes
I shall play my roles
In your inspiration-flowers,
With your aspiration-flames,
And for your realisation-Sun.

207. I WASTED TIME

Foolishly I wasted time.
Time now wastes me cheerfully.

Unconditionally I wasted time.
Time now wastes me sovereignly.

I wasted time
Because
Time was heavily
Hanging on me,
My impotent shoulders.

Time wastes me
Because
Time knows that I am
An unimportant member,
A beggar in the universal family of
beggars.

208. COMMAND AND OBEY

Faith to command,
Doubt to obey.

Purity to command,
Impurity to obey.

Light to command,
Darkness to obey.

But
Soul-Love to command,
Soul-Love to obey.

God-Will to command,
God-Will to obey.

209. MY GOD, MY GOD!

My God, my God,
Why have You forsaken me?
Have I told a lie?
"No, never!"
Have I betrayed You?
"No, never!"
Have I condemned Your world?
"No, never!"
Have I tried to dethrone You?
"No, never!"

My Lord, my Lord,
Why have You then
Forsaken me?
Why?
"Dive deep within,
And discover the answer."

210. NECESSARY AND UNNECESSARY EVILS

Desire,
A necessary evil.
Money-power,
A necessary evil.
Compromise-net,
A necessary evil.

BUT

Doubt,
An unnecessary evil.
Jealousy,
An unnecessary evil.
Insecurity,
An unnecessary evil.

211. NEVER AND EVER

Never the two shall meet:
Doubt and faith.
Never the two shall meet.

Never the two shall meet:
Love and hatred.
Never the two shall meet.

Never the two shall meet:
Aspiration-flame and
desire-cloud.
Never the two shall meet.

Ever the two shall meet:
God and man,
Life and death,
Ignorance-sea and Reality-Shore.
Ever the two shall meet.

212. WHO SAYS NO?

Who says
No man can serve two masters?
I say one can.
One can serve his master, Doubt.
One can serve his master, Faith.

Who says
No one can serve two masters?
I say one can.
One can serve his master,
Frustration-Life.
One can serve his master,
God-Compassion.

213. ALAS!

No man thinks
He is weak.
No woman thinks
She is ugly.
No thought thinks
It is poor.
No doubt feels
It can be vanquished.
No old man feels
He is empty of advice.
No young man suspects
He shall ever die.

214. NOT THAT I LOVE YOU LESS

O Earth, not that I love you less,
But I love Heaven more.

O Dream, not that I love you less,
But I love Reality more.

O Man, not that I love you less,
But I love God more.

O God-realisation, not that I love
you less,
But I love God-fulfilment more.

215. LISTEN TO ME

Sleep, my body, sleep,
It is a gentle thing.

March, my vital, march.
It is a brave thing.

Think, my mind, think.
It is an important thing.

Feel, my heart, feel.
It is a noble thing.

Sacrifice, my soul, sacrifice.
It is the perfect thing.

216. NOTHING CAN IMPROVE

Nothing can improve his
thoughts,
But purity-flame.
Nothing can improve his feelings,
But love-moon.
Nothing can improve his actions,
But service-tree.
Nothing can improve his life,
But death-rest.

217. OPEN

Open my body.
You will see engraved
"Service-Life."

Open my vital.
You will see engraved
"Compassion-Life."

Open my mind.
You will see engraved
"Will-Life."

Open my heart.
You will see engraved
"Love-Life."

Open my life.
You will see engraved
"Promise-Life.
Failure-Life.
Surrender-Life.
Perfection-Life."

218. TEARS

Tears, idle tears,
Stop!
Tears, soulful tears,
Start!
Tears, helpless tears,
Continue!
Tears, determined tears,
Reach!

219. TALK ABOUT YOURSELF

Why don't you talk
About yourself, Mr. Ghose?

"Sir God, there is no difference
Between
My spiritual children and my own
life."

Then Mr. Ghose, say something
Nice about them.

"Sir God, my children
In the hoary past
Dared to love You.
And now they dare think of You.
In the near or distant future
They will dare
To live without You."

Mr. Ghose, your shameless
prophecy
Equals your futile realisation.

220. FAITH AND DOUBT

Faith is unfolded from within,
Doubt is imposed from without.

Knowledge is unfolded from within,
Ignorance is imposed from without.

A life of faith
Is a life of God-simplicity
And
God-immensity.

A life of doubt
Is a life of Frustration-Desert
And
Destruction-Volcano.

A life of knowledge
Is a life of Promise-Tree
And
Progress-Fruits.

A life of ignorance
Is a life of Bondage-Crown
And
Death-Frown.

221. AT THE PINNACLE

At the pinnacle
Of the Rama-enlightenment,
I became Sacrifice divine.

At the pinnacle
Of the Krishna-enlightenment,
I became Love divine.

At the pinnacle
Of the Buddha-enlightenment,
I became Compassion divine.

At the pinnacle
Of the Christ-enlightenment,
I became Concern divine.

At the pinnacle
Of the Ramakrishna-enlightenment,
I became Cry divine.

At the pinnacle
Of the Chinmoy-enlightenment,
I became Surrender divine.

222. LORD AND SON

Lord,
My service is at Your disposal.
Tell me what I can do for You.
Son,
Empty your mind.

Lord,
My service is at Your disposal.
Tell me what I should do for You.
Son,
Fill up your heart.

Lord,
My service is at Your disposal.
Tell me what I must do for You.
Son,
Smile! Smile in the heart of the
body,
Smile in the life of the soul.

223. MY MAIDEN EXPERIENCE

With doubt I had
My maiden conflict.

With faith I had
My maiden triumph.

With fear I had
My maiden disgust.

With courage I had
My maiden ecstasy.

With man I had
My maiden failure.

With God I had
My maiden Silence.

224. ONLY REMEDY

Only remedy
For the delinquent world:
austerity.
Only remedy
For the fallen world: concern.
Only remedy
For the helpless world: Love.
Only remedy
For the dying world: Oneness.

225. LIGHT, BLISS AND CONSCIOUSNESS

Light, you have nullified
My yesterday's fear.
I am grateful.

Bliss, you have nullified
My today's doubt.
I am grateful.

Consciousness, you have nullified
My tomorrow's pride.
I am grateful.

226. HIS HEART

His heart of love
Became Krishna's Kadamba-tree.

His heart of wisdom
Became Buddha's Bodhi-tree.

His heart of cries
Became Ramakrishna's
Panchavati-trees.

His heart of service
Became Chinmoy's Rupantar-tree.

227. NAREN AND THAKUR

My Naren,
You have struggled and struggled,
You have fought and fought
To manifest me.

Our Thakur,
You have cried and cried,
You have served and served
To illumine me.

My Naren,
Your heart of love,
Your mind of light
Are my giant shoulders.

Our Thakur,
Your Feet of Compassion,
Your Eyes of Perfection
Are my Dream-Boat
And
Reality-Shore.

228. QUESTION AND ANSWER

Maharshi Ramana's question:
"Who am I?"
You are the cry of your ascending
heart,
You are the smile of your
descending soul.

Ramakrishna Paramahansa's
answer:
"Mother Kali."
Where is She?
In the battlefield of life.
Who is She?
Chaser of volcano-passion,
Bringer of Compassion-flood.

Swami Vivekananda's answer:
"The Olympian Will-power."
What is it?
The only Reality.
Whose is it?
Yours, only yours, absolutely
yours.

229. A FELLOW-PILGRIM

A man-made umbrella,
A God-made hand
Protected the chosen Son of God
From Indra's passion-shower.

Indra desired to extinguish the
faith-flames
Of the disciple in his Master.

God increased the disciple's
faith-flames, love-beams,
Making him realise
His Master, too,
Was a human being,
A fellow-pilgrim.

230. HOW WE LIVE

Without God
An atheist lives.
With God
A theist lives.
Around God
A devotee lives.
For God
A seeker lives.
In God
A lover lives.

231. I CAME TO HIM

I came to him doubtful.
He smiled and said:
"Stay with me for three minutes."

I came to him uncertain.
He caressed the sleeping Eye
between my eyebrows and said:
"Stay with me for three years."

I came to him with a student's
eagerness.
He blessed my devoted head and
said:
"Stay with me for thirty years."

I came to him with the heart of a
child.
He embraced my surrendered life
and said:
"Stay with me for eternity."

232. GIANTS OF THE SPIRIT

Naren, When are you planning
To come down to the earth?
"I have no such plans."

Gadadhar, When are you thinking
Of coming down to the earth?
"I don't cherish that kind of
thought any more."

Jesus, When will you illumine the
world
To celebrate your second
resurrection?
"I am more than satisfied
With my advent and with my first
and last resurrection on earth."

Siddhartha, Have you ever
thought of moving
From your Nihil house to Earth
house?
"Oh no! I shall forever
Remain in my Nihil house
Of Immortal Peace
And
Immortal Bliss."

Kanu, You declared that you enter
into the world-arena
Whenever righteousness declines
And
Unrighteousness prevails,
To destroy the dark hands
And save, elevate and illumine the
snow-white hearts.
Since then, how many times
Have you appeared and
disappeared
From the earth-scene?
"I am not accountable to the
world for my lofty promise.
In top secret I tell you:
The absolute Supreme is not
going to fire me
Even if I hopelessly fail to stick to
my well-intentioned promise."

233. THE MANIFOLD GOD

God the Power
Was the Idol of my thought.

God the Bliss
Is the Idol of my thought.

God the Peace
Shall be the Idol of my thought.

God the Creator
Was the Idol of my Will.

God the Player
Is the Idol of my Will.

God the Lover
Shall be the Idol of my Will.

234. WARMTH AND ILLUMINATION

Desire-oven warms his vital.
Aspiration-flames illumine his heart.

Doubt-heat warms his mind-cave.
Faith-fire illumines his life-palace.

Temptation-furnace warms his body.
Perfection-sun illumines his soul.

235. O MY FAMILY

O my mind,
In you I see a lampless world.

O my heart,
In you I see a faithless world.

O my vital,
In you I see a soulless world.

O my body,
In you I see a lifeless world.

O my soul,
In you I see a helpless world.

236. MAN, GOD AND ANGEL

I am man;
I need forgiveness.
God has it for me.

I am God;
I need indifference.
Man has it for me.

I am man;
I need beauty.
An angel has it for me.

I am an angel;
I need duty.
Man has it for me.

237. NOTHING HAPPENED

Nothing really exciting happened
When I fell down from Heaven.
I just fell down.

Nothing really exciting happened
When I climbed up to the skies.
I just climbed up.

Nothing really exciting happened
When I starved with darkness.
I just starved.

Nothing really exciting happened
When I dined with Light.
I just dined.

238. I BELONG

I belong to a universal family.
Thinking is a family thing.
Feeling is a family thing.
Loving is a family thing.
Becoming is a family thing.

We all think of God's Mind.
We all feel God's Heart.
We all love God's Body.
We all become what God eternally
is:
Immortality's Soul, Reality's Goal.

239. HOW TO HANDLE

How to handle the crowds?
Just shout at the top of your voice.

How to handle evil thoughts?
Just frown at them.

How to handle venom-doubts?
Just don't eat them.

How to handle the painful past?
Just think of your silver present
And
Imagine your golden future.

240. NEWS

Man, give me some news, please.
"My news will surprise you:
At last I want to think of God."

God, give me some news, please.
"My news will confuse you.
At last I have decided to retire."

241. THE ADJECTIVE

"Helpless" is the adjective
To describe his heart.

"Hopeless" is the adjective
To describe his mind.

"Senseless" is the adjective
To describe his vital.

"Useless" is the adjective
To describe his body.

"Fruitless" is the adjective
To describe his soul.

242. I LEARNT

Working with God
I learnt how to bless
Efficiently.

Working with man
I learnt how to cry
Sufficiently.

Working with children
I learnt how to dream
Endlessly.

Working with angels
I learnt how to smile
Divinely.

243. HE IS AND HE IS NOT

He is confident,
But
He is not calm.

He is calm,
But
He is not confident.

He is pure,
But
He is not sure.

He is sure,
But
He is not pure.

He can be confident and calm,
He can be pure and sure,
The day
Surrender-might from the realm
Of the Beyond
Embraces his snow-white heart.

244. HE IS NOT THE SAME MAN

He is not the same man
I accepted as my divine Guru.
The changes in his personality,
Appearances and interests
Have badly disappointed me.
Alas!

He is not the same man
I accepted as my true disciple.
His sleeping heart,
His doubting mind,
His roaring vital life,
His physical impurity
Have sadly disappointed me.
Alas!

245. MASTER MAN AND MASTER GOD

Master man,
I am unemployed.
Please give me a job.
"Massage my feet.
This will be your regular job.
I assure you,
You will draw an exorbitant salary."

Master God,
I am unemployed.
Please give me a job.
"Massage My Head.
By the way, you can do this at your sweet will
Every day or any day.
BUT
I shall pay you regularly,
I shall pay you unreservedly
With My eternal Gratitude-Plenitude."

246. IN PRAISE

In praise of women
I must say
They love and they want to be
  loved.

In praise of men
I must say
They want to be loved only.

In praise of God
I must say
He is trying to live
Without human love.

247. AGAINST

Against his doctor's warnings,
He slept very little.

Against his disciples' beggings,
He ate too much.

Against humanity's heavy
  snorings,
He has little to say.

Against divinity's measured
  blessing,
He has much to say.

248. IN THE ASSEMBLY

In the assembly of animals
He knew where he stood:
A roaring lion.

In the assembly of men
He knows where he stands:
A barking dog.

In the assembly of the gods
He knows where he will stand:
A bleating lamb.

249. THE MASTERS ARE FOND OF HIM

He has a child's heart.
Therefore
Ramakrishna is fond of him.

He is always dancing and
roaming.
Therefore
Chaitanya is fond of him.

He is always humble and meek.
Therefore
Christ is fond of him.

He is always kind and benevolent.
Therefore
Buddha is fond of him.

He is always loving and playing.
Therefore
Krishna is fond of him.

He is always crying and smiling.
Therefore
God is fond of him.

250. I SEARCHED AND SEARCHED

I searched and searched
For my soul.
At last I found my soul in the
Flute of Krishna.

I searched and searched
For my heart.
At last I found my heart in the
Cross of Christ.

I searched and searched
For my mind.
At last I found my mind in the
Meditation of Buddha.

I searched and searched
For my vital.
At last I found my vital in the Life
of Vivekananda.

I searched and searched
For my body.
At last I found my body on the Lap
of the Supreme.

251. CURRENT EVENTS

God has at last found
A home on earth.
Man's gratitude
Has agreed to grant God
A temporary shelter.

Man is tired of his frustration.

Human doubt is doubting
Its proud judgement
And sure assurance.

Man's pleasure-life
Has realised its folly
And it now wants the joy-life
To replace its long-standing
career.

252. MY RIGHTS

I stood up for my rights.
My rights demanded
The life of universal acceptance
And the life of universal
recognition.

I stand up for my rights.
My rights demand
My heart's cry and my life's smile.

I shall stand up for my rights.
My rights shall demand
The surrender-moon
From the world of aspiration-sun.

253. ADVENTURE AND PROGRESS

Truth-adventure
Is
Life-progress.

Life-adventure
Is
Soul-progress.

Soul-adventure
Is
God-progress.

God-adventure
Is
Mineral-progress
Plant-progress
Man-progress
Creation-progress
Creator-progress.

254. WHERE IS THE SECRET PLACE OF SAFETY?

Where is the secret place of safety?
In the mind-pond? No!
Where is the secret place of safety?
In the heart-lake? No!
Where is the secret place of safety?
In the soul-river? No!
Where is the secret place of safety?
In the self-sea? No!
Where is the secret place of safety?
In the life of Love divine? Yes!

255. MY DIARY

In the early hours of dawn,
In the late hours of night
I write my diary.
My diary houses only one word:
Gratitude.
Gratitude to God's Compassion,
Gratitude to man's service,
Gratitude to the thought of my
 self-transcendence,
Gratitude to my self-enquiry,
Gratitude to my God-discovery.

256. HUMAN AND DIVINE

A human communist
Is he
Who takes from some
And gives to others.

A divine communist
Is he
Who takes from himself
And offers to others.

A human socialist
Is he
Whom the vital of society loves.

A divine socialist
Is he
Who loves the heart of society.

A human god
Is he
Who lives in ignorance-sea.

A divine God
Is He
Who lives for ignorance-sea.

257. ONENESS-LIGHT

One mouth spoke,
One hand wrote,
One hand drove.
Destination offered its pride
sublime
To their perfection-height.
Perfection offered its pride
sublime
To their aspiration-might.
Aspiration offered its pride
sublime
To their oneness-light.

258. THE DANCE

The dance of desires
Never ends.
Although the dancers
Become tired and breathless,
The dance of desires
Never ends.

The dance of fulfilment
Never begins.
Although man
Cries and sighs,
The dance of fulfilment
Never begins.

259. YOUR RICHEST GAIN

Your richest gain
Was not in silver.

Your richest gain
Is not in gold.

Your richest gain
Shall not be in diamonds.

Your richest gain
Was in Realisation-seed.

Your richest gain
Is in Revelation-plant.

Your richest gain
Shall be in Manifestation-tree.

260. ETERNALLY YOU CAN BE HAPPY

You are unhappy.
Therefore you walk
From the mental pillar to the vital post
And
From the vital post to the mental pillar.

You are happy.
Therefore you run
From your surrendering heart to your illumining soul
And
From your illumining soul to your surrendering heart.

You will be eternally happy
If you fly
From man's dream-land to God's Reality-sky
And
From God's Reality-sky to man's dream-land.

261. MAN FORGETS

Man forgets
That his vital is swayed by desires.

Man forgets
That his mind constantly wanders.

Man forgets
That his days on earth are short.

Man forgets
That his real needs are very few.

Man forgets
That he has only God to call his own,
His very own.

262. FOURTEEN HAPPY DAYS

Tolstoy had fourteen happy days
During his entire earth-pilgrimage.

I still have not counted
My happy days on earth.
But I am so proud
To tell the world
That man, angel and God
Have kindly done the job for me.

Man's conclusion: fourteen seconds.
Angel's assumption: fourteen years.
God's revelation: fourteen aeons.

263. I AM OF GOD AND I AM FOR GOD

Helpless is Time
When I sleep.

Useless is Time
When I doubt.

Hopeless is Time
When I despair.

Godless is Time
When I halt.

Measureless is Time
When I move.

Birthless is Time
When I am of God.

Deathless is Time
When I am for God.

264. EVERYBODY HAS HIS ALLOTTED JOB

I don't speak ill of myself.
Why?
I don't want to take away
The job of my enemies.

I don't speak well of myself.
Why?
I am afraid it won't look nice
If I do the job of God.

265. MY PROBLEMS SOLVED

Ignorance was my problem
Bondage was my problem
Weakness was my problem.

Fear is my problem
Doubt is my problem
Jealousy is my problem.

Love will be my problem
Light will be my problem
God will be my problem.

I have survived my past
I brave my present
I shall transform my future.

266. YOU ARE SOMEONE

You are someone worth knowing
Because
In you I see the knowledge of
Socrates.

You are someone worth fighting
Because
In you I see the will of Napoleon.

You are someone worth loving
Because
In you I feel the heart of Christ.

You are someone worth pleasing
Because
In you I become divinely
complete.

267. MY NEEDS

Yesterday my need was
world-conquest.
I failed.

Today my need is my own
survival.
I am failing.

Tomorrow my need will be a
surrendered life.
I shall fail.

268. THE SCIENCE

The science of the Old Man said:
Look upward, see the Eye of God.

The science of the New Man says:
Look forward, see the Mind of
God.

The science of the God-Man will
say:
Look inward, become
The Heart of the Absolute.

269. WHO MAKES MY DECISIONS?

Who makes my decisions?

In the morning
God makes my decisions.
Therefore I sing and dance.

In the afternoon
I make my decisions.
Therefore I try and cry.

In the evening
Satan makes my decisions.
Therefore I sigh and die.

270. AT THE ENTRANCE

He entered into the vital world
To feel its hunger wild.
At the entrance Alexander, Caesar,
  Napoleon,
Hitler and Stalin greeted
Him with solemnity.

He entered into the mental world
To feel its hunger great.
At the entrance Socrates, Plato,
  Aristotle,
Shankara and Madhava greeted
Him with a series of smiles.

He entered into the psychic world
To feed his hunger deep.
At the entrance Rama, Krishna,
  Christ,
Chaitanya and Ramakrishna
  greeted
Him with the warmest embrace.

271. WHERE DO YOU SLEEP?

O Electricity,
Where do you sleep?
"I sleep in the clouds."

O Beauty,
Where do you sleep?
"I sleep in God's descending
  Grace."

O God,
Where do You sleep?
"I sleep between
Earth's ingratitude
And
Heaven's indifference."

272. THE ETERNAL PARTNER

St. Teresa discovered
Her life's eternal Partner in Christ.

Mira discovered
Her soul's eternal Partner in
Krishna.

You can discover
Your heart's eternal Partner
In God the Beloved Supreme.

St. Teresa offered to Christ
What she had: Love-world.

Mira offered to Krishna
What she had: Devotion-world.

You can offer to the Supreme
What you have: Surrender-world.

273. RAMAKRISHNA

He was born in a tiny
Obscure Bengali village in India.
He lived in a tiny corner
Of a big temple.
A Kali-worshipper he was.
A man-lover he became.
A world-teacher he is
And
Forever shall remain.

274. WITHOUT

Love without wisdom
Is today's lover.
Wisdom without love
Is today's saviour.

Beauty without duty
Is today's choice.
Duty without beauty
Is today's noise.

275. HIS PERSONALITY AND HIS INDIVIDUALITY

No length, no breadth
His personality has.
No height, no depth
His individuality has.
Total and perfect isolation
His real name is.
He is a body
With no voice of the soul.
He is a soul
With no life of the body.

276. A SWEET LONGING

A sweet longing have I
For the mainland of Reality.
No more shall I live
A life founded upon
Culled fictions.
Splintered, broken and smashed
Realities of life
No more can torture my intrepid
heart.
From now in my mind
Only God-Reality will grow.
In my heart
Only God-Love will grow.
In my life
Only God-Embrace will grow.

277. HIS REVELATION

His eyes reveal
The mountain of false smiles.
His heart reveals
The river of cheap smiles.
His soul reveals
The sea of ugly smiles.
His Goal reveals
The beauty of empty smiles.

278. I TOUCHED

I touched
The tail of jealousy.
It threw at me
A garland of curses.

I touched
The eyes of doubt.
They gave me
A glass of venom-water.

I touched
The heart of fear.
It presented me
With incapacity-sea.

I touched
The soul of faith.
It offered me
God's Garland of Roses.

279. O ARMIES

O Armies of Night,
You were the strength
Of my eyeless yesterdays.

O Armies of Light,
You are the strength
Of my soulful todays.

O Armies of Bliss,
You shall be the strength
Of my immortal tomorrows.

280. HIS LIFE

His thought is a dream
Beyond repair.

His hope is a dream
Pregnant with despair.

His life is a dream
Past correction.

His soul is a dream
Ignorant of imperfection.

281. HIS INHERITANCE

From God,
Promise-Land he inherited.

From man,
Hope-moon he inherited.

From life,
Failure-mountain he inherited.

From death,
Nothingness-night he inherited.

282. FORGOTTEN, FORGIVEN AND UNSEEN

O forgotten yesterdays,
Take back, take back
Your sorrow-treasure.

O forgiven todays,
Go back, go back
To your home of night.

O unseen tomorrows,
Come soon, come soon
To awaken my ignorance-dream.

283. THE BRIDE AND THE WIDOW

You were the bride of a
dream-boat.
You are the widow of a
reality-shore.

You were the bride of a
hope-dawn.
You are the widow of a
despair-eve.

You were the bride of an
illumination-sun.
You are the widow of
destruction-fun.

284. IN DIFFERENT KINGDOMS

In the animal kingdom
I was a holocaust of
donkey-laughter.

In the human kingdom
I am a holocaust of
frustration-advice.

In the divine kingdom
I shall be a holocaust of
angel-illumination.

285. NECESSITY

God begged me
To start my life
With a fateful necessity.

God asked me
To continue my life
With a hopeful necessity.

God commanded me
To end my life
With a meaningful necessity.

286. RESURRECTIONS

My past is resurrected:
I was God the Vision-power.

God's past is resurrected:
He was man the Will-power.

In the past
I lived under the Throne of
God-Light.

In the past
God lived above the Throne of my
Surrender-might.

287. A SIN AND A CRIME

Endless whispers of temptation
Alas, he shamelessly was.
Unbridled demands of passion
Alas, he supremely was.
Now
His forward look:
A sin against man.
Now
His backward look:
A crime against God.

288. O YOGI

O Yogi, when shall I love and seek
God?
"You can love and seek God
Only after He has loved
And
Sought you as His own,
His very own."

O Yogi, when will it be?
"The day you feel
Your soul-seed is of God
And
Your life-fruit is for God."

289. BLESSED

Blessed are the ugly;
They care for God's Beauty.

Blessed are the poor;
They care for God's Treasure.

Blessed are the weak;
They care for God's Power.

Blessed are the pure;
They care for God's Heart.

Thrice blessed are the
surrendered;
They care only for God's
Existence-Light.

290. WE ALL LAUGH

My immediate world
Laughs at my fragile silence.
The entire world
Laughs at my fragile promise.
In the morning
I laugh and laugh
At the fragile discoveries of my
mind.
In the evening
I laugh and laugh
At the fragile dreams of my heart.
At night
I laugh and laugh
At the fragile realities of my life.

291. ONLY TWICE HE LOVED HIMSELF

His rich life
Is a variety of absurdities.
He became God before he was
born.
He married Heaven, his mother,
When he was a minute old.
He married earth, his daughter,
When he was a trillion years old.
He loved himself only twice:
Once when he denied his
supremacy,
Once when he affirmed his total
surrender.

292. I SURRENDER

I surrender to joy
Because
Joy is power.
I surrender to love
Because
Love is a power sublime.
I surrender to oneness
Because
Oneness is the measureless power.
I surrender to God
Because
God is the absolute Power
supreme.

293. GOD, DO YOU THINK OF ME?

God, do You ever think of me?
"I do."
When do You think of me?
"My son, I think of you
When you do not think of Me."
God, why? Why do You do that?
"My son, when you think of Me
I feel you are safe
And well-protected.
But when you forget to think of
Me
I feel I am under obligation
To think of you,
To care for you
So that you do not go astray."

294. ALAS, IT IS TOO LATE

Why did I not take
Fighting lessons from Sri Rama?
Alas, it is too late.

Why did I not take
Playing lessons from Sri Krishna?
Alas, it is too late.

Why did I not take
Suffering lessons from the
Buddha?
Alas, it is too late.

Why did I not take
Forgiving lessons from the Christ?
Alas, it is too late.

Why did I not take
Dancing lessons from Sri
Chaitanya?
Alas, it is too late.

Why did I not take
Long-distance walking lessons
from Sri Shankara?
Alas, it is too late.

Why did I not take
Crying lessons from Sri
Ramakrishna?
Alas, it is too late.

Why did I not take
Struggling lessons from Swamiji?
Alas, it is too late.

Why did I not take
Surrendering lessons from Sri
Chinmoy?
Alas, it is too late.

295. WASTE OF YEARS

In his animal life
He was in love
With a wild waste of years.

In his human life
He was in love
With a sad waste of years.

In his divine life
He is in love
With the proud gain of years.

296. THE MEMORIES OF TIME

I was unrealised;
Therefore
I faded from the merciless
 memory of Time.

I was unrevealed;
Therefore
I faded from the unsympathetic
 memory of Time.

I was unmanifested;
Therefore
I faded from the indifferent
 memory of Time.

BUT NOW

Time shakes hands with me,
Time dines with me,
Time dances with me.

297. THE DESIRE OF POWER

The desire of love-power
Raised him high, very high.

The desire of indifference-power
Dragged him down
Beyond his imagination.

The desire of thought-power
Killed his inner silence.

The desire of money-power
Fooled him, his life, his all.

298. COUNSEL

Smiling counsel
Cuts off one foe.
Friendly counsel
Cuts off ten foes.
Loving counsel
Cuts off ninety foes.
Sacrificing counsel
Cuts off three hundred foes.
Oneness counsel
Cuts off all foes.

299. TAX-EXEMPT

Humility
Is exempt from fear-tax.
Nobility
Is exempt from jealousy-tax.
Generosity
Is exempt from doubt-tax.
Divinity
Is exempt from ignorance-tax.

300. KILL THEM

Shakespeare said:
"The first thing we do, let's kill all
the lawyers."

My ascetic-fanatic friend says:
The first thing I do,
Let me kill all the singers.
They have no right
To destroy my Lord's Ears.

The second thing I do,
Let me kill all the dancers.
They have no right
To destroy my Lord's Eyes.

The third thing I do,
Let me kill all the loud
God-worshippers.
They have no right
To destroy my Lord's
Silence-Peace.

301. HIS KNOWLEDGE AND HIS UNDERSTANDING

He knows everything.
He knows everything
And understands nothing.

He understands everything.
He understands everything
And knows nothing.

To be in the world of the soul
Is to know everything.
To be in the world of the mind
Is to understand nothing.

To be in the world of the vital
Is to understand everything.
To be in the world of the body
Is to know nothing.

302. NOBODY'S BUSINESS

Nobody's business
Is everybody's necessity.

Nobody's business
Is everybody's duty.

Nobody's business
Is everybody's depth of
realisation.

Nobody's business
Is everybody's sense of universal
perfection.

303. TWO DIFFERENT THINGS

Love is one thing,
Possession is another.

Possession is one thing,
Happiness is another.

Happiness is one thing,
Accomplishment is another.

Accomplishment is one thing,
Perfection is another.

304. I CAN'T FOLLOW

I can't follow God
Because
He wants, instead, to follow me
most faithfully.

I follow man
Because
He wants to lead me constantly.

Staying behind,
God inspires me
To reach my sun-world.

Staying ahead,
Man instigates me
To ignore my aspiration-world.

305. WHEN I LIVE

When I live in the vital world
I find it easier to break than to
build.

When I live in the physical world
I find it easier to sleep than to
work.

When I live in the mental world
I find it easier to doubt and
suspect
Than to love and embrace.

When I live in the psychic world
I find it easier to build than to
break,
I find it easier to work than to
sleep,
I find it easier to love and embrace
Than to doubt and suspect.

Unlike in other worlds,
In my psychic world
I want what I need,
I get what I want.

306. WHEN

When I smile,
I make everything out of nothing.
When I love,
I make everything out of nothing.
When I offer,
I make everything out of nothing.
But
When I hesitate to smile,
I make nothing out of everything.
When I delay in loving,
I make nothing out of everything.
When I calculate in my offering,
I make nothing out of everything.

307. GOD DEPENDS ON YOU

God's arrival-appearance
Entirely
Depends upon your divine
audacity
And
Divine tenacity.
Claim Him as your unconditional
slave;
He will be exceedingly pleased.
Stick to your realisation and
assertion;
He will offer His Heart-Crown to
you.

308. SHE AND HE COUNT DIFFERENTLY

She counts God's Blessings.
Therefore
She is happy.

He counts his failings.
Therefore
He is unhappy.

She counts devotedly God's divine
approvals.
Therefore
She is happy.

He counts greedily his
achievements only.
Therefore
He is unhappy.

309. HE IS GREAT

He is hopelessly great.
In the vital world
He pushes the door marked *Pull*,
In the mental world
He pulls the door marked *Push*.
In the psychic world
He neither pulls nor pushes
But waits for the hour to strike.
He knows that at the choice hour
God Himself will open
The door for him
Quietly,
Proudly,
Unconditionally.

310. DEATH AND GOD

Only two persons
On earth and in Heaven
Do not contradict.

These are Death and God.

Death-hush knows not
How to contradict.
God-Wisdom feels
It is not worthwhile to contradict.

311. SHE AND HE

She is very rich
Because
She always gives,
She always gives.

He is very poor
Because
He always needs,
He always needs.

She is always beautiful.
She is always beautiful
Because
Her surrender divine
Drinks the Beauty of God.

He is always ugly.
He is always ugly
Because
His undivine autocracy devours
the freedom of man.

312. DO YOU NEED?

Do you need peace of mind?
Then think that the world does
not need you.

Do you need peace of mind?
Then feel that the world
Is not nearly as useless as you
think.

Do you need peace of mind?
Then see that you do not make
The same mistakes
That the world quite often makes.

313. WHEN HE IS

When he is in the soul
He speaks nothing.
He quietly listens,
He cheerfully agrees.

When he is in the heart
He speaks very little.
He tries to listen,
He tries to agree.

When he is in the mind
He speaks constantly.
He never listens,
He totally disagrees.

314. WHEN I

When I imitate God
To please Him,
He feels quite uneasy.

When I love God
To please Him,
He feels quite uneasy.

When I serve God
To please Him,
He feels quite uneasy.

When I become another God
To please Him,
He feels divinely happy;
He feels supremely fulfilled.

315. MY HUMAN CONFIDENCE AND MY CONFIDENCE DIVINE

My
Human confidence
Is
The proud feeling
Of knowing everything,
Of understanding everything.

My
Divine confidence
Is
To identify myself with the heart of everything,
See God and the world
With the soul of everything,
And
Become one with God the Aspiration-Light
And God the Realisation-Delight of everything.

316. TWO CONDUCTORS

Man the conductor
Sees the players
And
Sees not the audience.
His hunger for growing
appreciation
Is
Half fed.

God the conductor
Hears the aspiration-music of the
cosmic gods
And
Becomes the
appreciation-applause of the
divine audience.
His hunger for the
joy-distribution
Is
Sumptuously fed.

317. HIS DOUBT AND HIS FAITH

His doubt dares to solve
All his problems
Save and except
The unemployment problem
For faith, which it so maliciously
creates.

His faith faithfully solves
All his problems
Created by his morning
doubt-clouds
And
Nourished by his evening
doubt-storms.

318. MACHINE AND MAN

When a machine
Wants to think like a man,
God feels proud of His
Dream-Boat.
He starts singing and dancing.

When a man
Wants to think like a machine,
God feels sorry for man's
unevolving life.
He buries His Mind and Vital
In the soil of despair-night
And
He drowns His Heart and Soul
In the giant bosom of failure-sea.

319. FEAR AND DOUBT

Fear of truth grows on his hope
tree
To weaken him.

Doubt in God grows on his hope
tree
To poison him.

His self-doubt grows on his hope
tree
To destroy him.

320. BEFORE COLUMBUS DISCOVERS YOU

Don't sleep,
Get up at least.
Don't stand still,
Walk a little at least.

Before Columbus
Dares to discover you,
Fly your wings
Into the unknowable Beyond
Where
Your doubt-Columbus,
Your fear-Columbus
Shall have no access.

There you can reign
Unseen,
Unchallenged,
Unfathomed,
Sovereign,
Absolute,
Supreme.

321. TRANSFORMATION

"Everyone thinks of
Changing the world, but no one
thinks of
Changing himself."
–*Tolstoy*

I tried to change myself;
I badly failed.

I tried to change the world;
To my wide surprise,
The world had achieved
Its perfection-light long before
I made my surrendered attempt.

I failed to change my life
Because
I mixed too much
With my Master, Ego,
With my Disciple, Doubt.

322. HOW DO WE USE ENGLISH?

Stephen Leacock said:
"Canadians use English for literature,
Scotch for sermons,
American for conversation."

I use English to betray my roaring stupidity.
I use English to ignore my doubtful capacity.
I use English to reveal my soulful divinity.
I use English to manifest God's glowing Authenticity.

323. EXPECTATION AND ATTAINMENT

Love is what we expect;
Hatred is what we get.

Concern is what we expect;
Indifference is what we get.

Union is what we expect;
Division is what we get.

Triumph is what we expect;
Defeat is what we get.

Transformation is what we expect;
Frustration is what we get.

324. COMMUNICATION-PROBLEMS

O Telephone,
You have solved
My communication-problems;
Between
North and South,
East and West.
Therefore
To you I bow and bow.
But
Alas, who will solve
The age-long communication-problems
Between
My doubting mind
And
My crying heart,
Between
My restless vital
And
My joyless body?

325. MY FAMILY IN ACTION

My heart practises
The Truth,
My mind preaches
The Truth.

My heart achieves
The Truth,
My vital distributes
The Truth.

My heart treasures
The Truth,
My body discards
The Truth.

My heart becomes
The Truth,
My soul is
The Truth.

326. BEING AMERICAN MEANS

Mr. Heinrich Boll, West
Germany's
1972 Nobel Laureate in literature,
declared:
"Being American means the
chance to be what you want."

I asked my God two small
questions:
What is the meaning of chance?
What do Americans want to be?
"My son, you are a God-lover.
For a God-lover there is no such
thing as chance.
My dictionary does not house that
particular word.
What you and I call Grace, others
call chance.

"My son, here is My answer
To your second question:
Americans want to be perfect
slaves to their freedom."
Father, what do You mean?
I don't understand Your answer.
Please be a little more explicit.

"What I mean is this:
Americans are not profitably,
Consciously and unreservedly
Using their freedom-soul
To reach the acme of their
Freedom-Goal."

327. BACK TO MY DESK

Mr. Boll said:
"I am travelling too much and I want to go
Back to my desk."

Since I have the same problem,
Although in an infinitesimal measure,
I sought my God's advice.
God said: "My son, to Me your bed is your perfect desk.
To Me, your car is your perfect desk.
To Me, a jet plane is your perfect desk.

"Inspiration
Is in your heart.
Aspiration
Is in your soul.
Revelation
Is in your eyes.
Manifestation
Is in your hands."

328. I CAME, I SAW, I CONQUERED

Caesar thundered:
"I came,
I saw,
I conquered."

Satan thundered:
"I came,
I conquered,
I saw not."

I thundered:
"I came not,
I saw not,
I conquered not."

God thundered:
"I came,
I was seen,
I was conquered."

329. WHEN I DRIVE

When I drive
I never feel
I own the car
Or
I own the road.

I feel
God's Protection
Owns the car
And
Man's sympathy owns the road.

330. I STUDIED

I studied in three schools
That do not believe in failure:
My first school was the school of
Aspiration,
My second school was the school
of
Transformation,
My third school was the school of
Satisfaction.

331. COMEDY AND TRAGEDY

In life's comedy
False fear dies.

In life's tragedy
False hope dies.

Through life's comedy
God reveals His Grace.

Through life's tragedy
God perfects His Face.

332. GOD AND I SMILE

God gave me a smile,
I gave Him a smile.
His smile made me feel
That I am not yet
Past correction.
My smile made Him feel
That I am still a lover of
Perfection.

333. WHEN I AM

When I am
In the hands of a doctor,
Fear and Death
Quietly think of me.

When I am
In the hands of a lawyer,
Anxiety and deception
Bravely think of me.

When I am
In the hands of a Spiritual Master,
Confidence and joy
Constantly think of me.

334. ONE SOWS AND ANOTHER REAPS

The cook laboriously cooks;
The waitress gets the immediate
appreciation.

Nature and Fate cure;
The doctor demands the fee.

God's Grace illumines and fulfils
mankind;
Man feels it is all due to his own
personal effort.

335. PEACE

God's Grace
Wants to offer man the soul's
eternal Peace.
Man's cry
Wants to acquire the heart's
immediate Peace.
The United Nations
Wants to offer the mind's
universal Peace.
Divorcing couples
Want to give birth to the vital's
demanding peace.

336. I AM LUCKY AND FORTUNATE

I am lucky
In my outer life:
Success ascends
Before labour.

I am fortunate
In my inner life:
Grace descends
Before success.

337. HE IS LUCKY

He is lucky,
He did not get what he deserved.
He is lucky,
He did not say what he intended.
He is lucky,
He does not find anything wrong
with the world.
He is lucky,
He does not know when death
will knock at his door.

338. I WAS A FOOL

I was a fool,
I depended on my personal
efforts.
I was a fool,
I depended on man's assistance.
I was a fool,
I depended on God's Grace.

But
Now I have become a wise man
Since I revised the order.
I now depend on God's
unconditional Grace first,
Ninety-eight and a half per cent.
And then I depend on my puny
personal efforts,
One per cent.
Finally I depend on man's
conditional assistance,
One-half of one per cent.

339. THREE EXAMINATIONS

I have
Three examinations to pass:
Death, Life and God.
I must say,
These are all most difficult
examinations.

I have
Two examinations to pass:
Life and God.
I feel I shall fare well.

I have
One examination to pass:
God.
It seems I have already passed it.

340. THEY SAY

They say, "After middle age
The days go two at a time."
I wholeheartedly
See eye to eye with them.
I just want to add
A few things:
After middle age
The mind-deer wants to run
faster,
The vital-horse wants to run
slower,
The body-bull wants to enjoy rest.

341. TWO TEACHERS

As a dance-teacher,
God teaches me
How to dance soulfully
Before the cosmic gods.

As an ignorance-teacher,
I teach God
How to cry pitifully
Before the human multitudes.

342. IN MY PAST, PRESENT AND FUTURE

There was a time
When I lived to eat.
I ate and ate and ate.

Now
I eat to live.
I regularly eat,
I devotedly eat.

There shall come a time
When I shall eat
At God's Will,
At God's Hour;
From God's Kitchen,
With God's Smile.

343. BECAUSE

Because
I am unsuccessful,
My desire suffers.

Because
I am unsuccessful,
My aspiration suffers.

Because
I am unsuccessful,
My life suffers.

Because
I am unsuccessful,
My goal suffers.

Alas, there is someone
Who constantly suffers for me.
He is my God,
He is my Lord,
He is my All.
He suffers for me
Not because I am unsuccessful,
But because
I have deliberately kept myself
Out of employment.

344. FORTUNE OR MISFORTUNE

Lord, a woman's beauty:
Is it her fortune or misfortune?
Son, it is her fortune.
I gave her the beauty,
I am that beauty.

Lord, a man's duty:
Is it his fortune or misfortune?
Son, it is his fortune.
I gave him the duty,
I am that duty.

Lord, a Yogi's heart:
Is it his fortune or misfortune?
Son, it is his fortune.
I gave him the heart,
I am that heart.

345. I DON'T PRAY

I don't pray.
Why?
Because God does not need my prayer.

I don't pray.
Why?
Because man does not understand my prayer.

I don't pray.
Why?
Because my enemies don't believe in my prayer.

Finally I have come to the conclusion that
I don't have to pray.
Why?
Because my friends believe that I always pray.

346. THE STORY OF MY FAILURE

When I failed
In man's examination,
God came to my immediate rescue.
He explained
Emphatically
Why I had failed:
Because the examination was very difficult.

When I failed
In God's examination,
Man deeply enjoyed my failure
And whisperingly said:
You rightly deserved it
Because
Your rich ignorance beggars description.

347. THREE SEEKERS

A beginner seeker
Is he who has started
The art of believing.

An advanced seeker
Is he who has started
The art of believing, loving,
serving.

A realised seeker
Is he who has started
The art of surrendering:
Surrendering cheerfully to God's
Will,
Surrendering helplessly to man's
ignorance.

348. EXPERIENCE, REALISATION AND MANIFESTATION

Experience
Gives me no vacation.

Realisation
Gives me no frustration.

Revelation
Gives me no uncertainty.

Manifestation
Gives me no futility.

349. TWO ADVISERS

God's advice to Man:
"Don't lie!"

Man's advice to God:
"Don't sigh!"

God's advice to Man:
"Don't hide!
Are you a thief?"

Man's advice to God:
"Don't chide!
Am I a thief?"

350. UNDERESTIMATION AND OVERESTIMATION

When I underestimated
My Power,
God placed me on His throne of Bliss.

When I underestimated
My Light,
God offered me His Garland of Victory.

When I overestimated
My Power,
Satan demanded and confiscated my passport.

When I overestimated
My Light,
Death mocked my height
And
Deported me into the Land of Destruction-Night.

351. NEVER SHALL I FAIL

Failure
Is not falling down.
Failure
Is desiring to live
Where I have fallen.

I cry for Heaven.
Therefore
Never
Shall I fail.

I try for earth.
Therefore
Never
Shall I fail.

352. I AM HAPPY

I believe everybody;
Therefore
I am happy.

I love everybody;
Therefore
I am happy.

I think of God every day,
  everywhere;
Therefore
I am happy.

I am happy, I am always happy
Because
Heaven lives for the cries of my
  heart
And
Earth lives for the smiles of my
  soul.

353. BEFORE TIME KILLS ME

I shall think of Time
Before
Time kills me.

I shall love Time
Before
Time kills me.

I shall use Time
Before
Time kills me.

I shall reveal God
Before
Time kills me.

I shall fulfil God
Before
Time kills me.

354. MOTHER'S DAY AND FATHER'S DAY

Mother's Day is great
Because
At least once a year
Children allow their minds
To think of their mother's heart
And
Allow their hearts to house
And treasure their mother.

Father's Day is great
Because
At least once a year
Each father tells his children
That he really wants to equal the
Heavenly Father in Compassion
and Concern.

355. ONLY FAULT

His body's only fault is that
It sleeps too much.
His vital's only fault is that
It runs too much.
His mind's only fault is that
It doubts too much.
His heart's only fault is that
It believes too much.
His soul's only fault is that
It has none, really none.

356. MY GOD IS ANGRY WITH ME

My God is angry with me
Because
I forget.
My God is angry with me
Because
I forgive.

What do I forget?
I forget the world's
Dedicated service to me.
What do I forgive?
I forgive
My ignorance,
My flowing ignorance,
My increasing ignorance,
My undying ignorance.

357. GOD WILL BE PLEASED

Serve in the physical world;
God will be pleased.
Fight in the vital world;
God will be pleased.
Watch in the mental world;
God will be pleased.
Love in the psychic world;
God will be pleased.
Surrender in the world of Light;
God will be pleased.
Become in the world of Perfection;
God will be pleased.

358. NOBODY LOVES

Nobody loves
A great flatterer.
Nobody loves
A gross lover.
Nobody loves
A wicked man.
Nobody loves
An immodest woman.
Nobody loves
An indifferent Heaven.
Nobody loves
An unprogressive earth.

359. FOOD IS GOD AND GOD IS FOOD

India's great Mahatma Gandhi
revealed:
"To a man with an empty
stomach, food is God."
India's great Nobody, Sri
Chinmoy, reveals:
"My full stomach feels that God is
food."

Food is God
When I think of Gandhi's
Countless hungry and starving
children.
God is food
When I think of God's
Countless dreaming, revealing
and illumining children.

360. YOUR HUMAN LIFE AND YOUR LIFE DIVINE

In your human life
You notice that the world
Is full of fools.
You are right, absolutely right.
But let me add just a little to your
great discovery:
There is just one more fool than
you think
And that is you,
And that is you.

In your life divine
You feel that the world
Is full of fools.
You are right, absolutely right.
But let me add just a little to your
great discovery:
There is just one less fool than you
feel
And that is you,
And that is you.

361. I UNDERSTAND

I perfectly understand God
Even without knowing His
language.
I never understand man
Although I know man's language
thoroughly.
I always misunderstand
The language of love
Although it sounds
Sweet,
Soulful
And
Meaningful.

362. A USUAL THING

To err is a usual thing;
To forgive is an unusual thing.
To love is to forget all troubles;
To repent is to revive all troubles.
To own Light is to govern night;
To fear Truth is to disown God.

363. FORTUNE-TELLER AND FORTUNE-BESTOWER

When man the fortune-teller
Promises me a bright future
My heart of gratitude
Makes his present immediately
brighter.

But when God the
fortune-bestower
Promises me the brightest future
My impatient heart of ingratitude
Questions God's sincerity
And
Questions His motive.

364. WHEN I THINK

When I think once,
I say what I intended to say.
When I think twice,
I hesitate to open my mouth.
When I think thrice,
I never fail to keep my proud
mouth shut.

365. I THANK YOU, FATHER

My Father tells me
What to do.
I ask Him,
How can I do it?
My Father shows me
How to do it.
I ask Him,
Why does He not do it for me?
My Father does it for me,
He does everything for me.

Then
What do I tell Him?
I tell Him,
Father, I am sorry,
I could have done it far better;
I could have done everything
infinitely better.
Anyway, I thank You, Father,
Since Your intention was good.

366. THE FIRST AND THE LAST

The first woman
Tempted
The first man
To eat.

The last woman
Shall inspire
The last man
To be divine,
To be perfect,
To be supreme.

367. TWICE TO MY RESCUE

My Lord
Came to my rescue twice:
Once when my admiring friends
Turned me into an ego-balloon,
Once when my enemies
Doubted my realisation,
The God-ordained boon.

368. THINKING AND THANKING

I stopped thinking;
Therefore
I don't have to thank any more.

I stopped thanking;
Therefore
I don't have to love any more.

I stopped loving;
Therefore
I don't have to repent any more.

I stopped repenting;
Therefore
I don't have to sleep any more.
I must act,
I must become.
I must act to become,
I must become to act.

369. WE ARE ALL GREEDY

You are greedy.
I definitely know it.
He is greedy.
I unmistakably feel it.
I am greedy.
I modestly exaggerate it.
Your greed tempts me.
His greed instigates me.
My greed destroys me.

370. O NECTAR-SON

You are your parents'
Earthly pride.
You are your spiritual parents'
Heavenly pride.
You are the Supreme's
Immortal Pride,
Infinite Joy,
Eternal Life,
O Nectar-Son of humanity in the
  Heart of God,
O Nectar-Son of God for the soul
  of humanity!

371. THE STORY OF GUILT

The body is guilty
For the things it has delayed,
For the things it has forgotten.

The vital is guilty
For the things it has accepted,
For the things it has rejected.

The mind is guilty
For the things it has suspected,
For the things it has believed.

The heart is guilty
For the things it has discovered,
For the things it has avoided.

The soul is guilty
For the things it has promised,
For the things it has omitted.

372. IMPARTIAL, NEUTRAL AND PARTIAL

He is impartial
And
Not neutral.
Therefore, He is God.

He is partial
And
Not neutral.
Therefore, he is man.

God's impartiality
Only a brave soul enjoys.
Man's partiality
Only a sick soul enjoys.

373. THE MAN OF ETERNITY

My aspiration-candle
Is the man of the hour.

My realisation-lamp
Is the man of the day.

My revelation-moon
Is the man of the year.

My manifestation-sun
Is the man of Eternity.

374. NO HOLIDAYS

Her jealousy has no holidays,
His doubt has no holidays.

Her insecurity has no holidays,
His impurity has no holidays.

But
Her desire has a few holidays
And
His aspiration has nothing
But holidays.

375. YOU HAVE NO SENSE

Son, you have no sense.
Father, that is why I think of You,
Ceaselessly.
Father, You have no sense.
Son, that is why I am within you,
I am for you, unconditionally.

Son, let us not quarrel any more.
Bring the candle.
Father, let us not quarrel any
more.
Light the candle.
Son, you look so beautiful!
Father, You are truly merciful,
You are truly thoughtful,
You are truly fruitful.

376. WHERE ARE YOU, MOTHER?

Inspiration,
I want you, friend.
Aspiration,
I need you, son.
Realisation,
I had you, Father.
Revelation,
Where have you been, daughter?
Manifestation,
Where are you, Mother?

377. THE DIVINE SEPARATION

Desire
Is your divine separation
From the mineral life.

Aspiration
Is your divine separation
From the animal life.

But
Realisation
Is your divine union
With the mindless mineral life,
With the heartless animal life,
With the soulless human life.

378. ON GOD'S BEHALF

I am sick.
But
My God is not sick.
Why is He not sick?
He just can't afford to be sick.
If He too falls sick
Then who will look after me?

God does not sleep.
But
I sleep. I sleep ceaselessly.
Why?
I feel that God needs some rest.
He deserves some rest
Since He works so hard
Day in, day out.
I have a sympathetic heart;
Therefore
I feel that it is my bounden duty
To sleep and rest on God's behalf.

379. ADDITION AND SUBTRACTION

I wanted to be really rich;
Therefore
Constantly I wanted to add
To my possessions.

God wanted me to be supremely rich;
Therefore
He most carefully subtracted
My possessions
From
My desire-life,
And
Most carefully added
My renunciation
To my aspiration-soul
And
Realisation-Goal.

380. NOBODY KNOWS WHERE IT IS

My soul spreads happiness
When it enters into my heart.
My vital spreads happiness
When it leaves my heart.

Happiness:
Everybody knows what it is,
But
Nobody knows where it is.
Ah, I see the Face of happiness
In my sleepless heart,
In my deathless soul,
In my horizonless Goal.

381. MAN, BE CAREFUL OF WOMAN

Sri Ramakrishna said,
Man, be careful of woman.

Mother Kali said,
Son, your advice needs some explanation.

Mother, what I meant was this:
Man, be careful of the human in woman.

Son, still it is not quite clear to me.

Mother, let me simplify it for you.
What I meant was this:
Man, do not use your human eyes to see and corrupt
The divine in woman.

Son, now I understand your philosophy.
It is simply fascinating,
It is divinely illumining,
It is supremely fulfilling.

382. I HAVE INHERITED

My sister Lily's love and
determination
I have inherited.

My sister Arpita's concern and
service
I have inherited.

My brother Chitta's poetry and
sacrifice
I have inherited.

My brother Hriday's philosophy
and wisdom
I have inherited.

My brother Mantu's patience and
detachment
I have inherited.

My sister Ahana's music and
immensity
I have inherited.

My mother Yogamaya's psychic
tears and surrender
I have inherited.

My father Shashi Kumar's inner
confidence and outer triumph
I have inherited.

383. NEVER

Never
He thinks out of fear;
Never
He fears to think.
Never
He loves out of fear;
Never
He fears to love.
Never
He becomes one out of fear;
Never
He fears to become one.
He thinks only of his life divine,
He fears only his ignorance,
He loves only his soul,
He becomes only his goal.

384. THE STORIES OF FOUR FRIENDS

Inspiration is a runner
That starts its journey from you.

Aspiration is a kite
That comes out of you
And flies above you.

Intuition is a magnet
That pulls the world towards you.

Realisation is a sun
That shines always within you.

385. IN MY CASE

In my case,
My forgiveness is kind to me.
In my case,
My ignorance is kind to me.
In my case,
My Lord is kind to me.

My forgiveness lovingly says:
"I will give you infinite chances
To perfect your life."

My ignorance cheerfully says:
"Don't be in a hurry.
I have spoken to the Mother,
   Eternal Time, about you.
She will wait for you indefinitely;
So, you can take your own time."

My Lord compassionately says:
"Son, you are a sick man,
You are a weak soldier,
You are a poor seeker.
Therefore
It is my duty supreme
To do everything within you,
Everything for you."

386. HIDDEN TREASURES

Love is hidden
Even from those who express it.

Joy is hidden
Even from those who feel it.

Truth is hidden
Even from those who know it.

But
God is not hidden
Even from those
Who want Him not,
Who need Him not.

387. FOUR STORIES

The story of his vital
Is unreadable.

The story of his mind
Is yet unread.

The story of his heart
Will take time to read.

The story of his soul
Will never be read.

388. WHEN

When doubt ceases,
Faith begins.
When fear ceases,
Courage begins.
When hatred ceases,
Love begins.
When jealousy ceases,
Oneness begins.

When faith ceases,
I am lost.
When courage ceases,
I am caught.
When love ceases,
I am useless.
When oneness ceases,
Everything ceases.

389. A REFORMED CHARACTER

Woodrow Wilson said:
"I used to be a lawyer,
But now I am a reformed
character."

I say:
I used to be a doubter,
But now I am a reformed
character.
I am now a staunch believer.

I used to be a man-hater,
But now I am a reformed
character.
I am now a universal lover.

I used to be a truth-examiner,
But now I am a reformed
character.
I am now a constant truth-learner.

390. O MY DEAR FRIENDS

"All Americans lecture. I suppose
It is something in their climate."
–*Oscar Wilde*

All Indians procrastinate too long.
I suppose it is something
In our climate.

All Englishmen think too much.
I suppose it is something
In their climate.

All Canadians follow too far.
I suppose it is something
In their climate.

O American friend of mine,
I wish to hear your lecture.
O Indian friend of mine,
Let us not sleep any more.
O English friend of mine,
I am sure you know
There is something far
Beyond thinking.
O Canadian friend of mine,
Your own goal
Is infinitely more beautiful
Than the goal of others.

391. MY CORRESPONDENCE-GURU

Dear Robert Frost,
To you I immensely owe.
You are my only
correspondence-Guru,
And you shall remain so
Forever and forever.
You have freed me and
enlightened me
From the correspondence-world.
I humbly repeat your message
sublime:
"For God's sake, don't give up
Writing to me simply because I
don't write to you."

392. WHEN I WRITE LETTERS

When I write letters to God,
I tell Him how happy I am.

When I write letters to man,
I tell him how unhappy I am.

When I write to God,
I tell Him how fresh I am.

When I write to man,
I tell him how tired I am.

God's replies are as follows:
"Dear son, since you are happy
and fresh,
Then work hard and more for Me
on earth."

Man's replies are as follows:
"Dear friend, since you are
unhappy
And tired, we want to fire you.
We are looking for another
instrument
To serve us,
To please us,
To fulfil us."

393. A GREAT LESSON

I always get a great lesson
From my musical capacity.
It takes all my pride out of me.

I always get a great lesson
From my ceaseless barking.
It takes all my pride out of me.

But
My ever-compassionate Lord,
Out of His infinite Bounty,
Consoles me:
"My son, in your past incarnation
You were a musician of the
highest magnitude.
Your soul does not want to eat the
same fruit again.
My son, this is not your last
incarnation.
I assure you, in your
Next incarnation, without fail,
You will turn over a new leaf."

394. THEY TALK

Joy talks, but it does not
Always
Tell the truth.

Love talks, but it does not
Always
Tell the truth.

Oneness talks, and it
Always
Tells the truth.
What is truth?
God's first invention
And
Man's last discovery.

395. HIS INVITATIONS

To cheer his divine birth
He invited the cosmic gods.
The gods simply flew down
To the earth to cheer him, love
him, embrace him.

To mourn his human death
He invited his earthly comrades,
earthly devotees, earthly
adorers.
Some came late,
Some came not at all,
Some just sneered
At his audacious invitation.

396. THE DIFFERENCE

O Lord Buddha,
Please tell me the difference
Between
Sujata's sweetmeat
And
Chunda's venom-meat.

"Brother, the difference?
Practically none!
Sujata's sweetmeat
Helped me openly in unlearning
The lessons of Ignorance.
Chunda's venom-meat
Helped me secretly in learning
The message of Nirvana."

397. WHAT DID YOU MEAN?

O Saviour-Christ,
Please tell me,
What did you mean
By your strongest affirmation:
'I and my Father are one'?
Tell me in what sense you and
your Father are one.

"O dear brother,
Of all people, how is it that You,
my wise brother,
Do not understand my simple
message?
On earth I am my Father's Face,
In Heaven I am my Father's Eye.
In that sense we are one,
inseparable.
This is what I meant when I said:
'I and my Father are one.'"

398. DEAR NAREN

Dear Naren,
Did America love you?
"That I don't know, Chinmoy,
But I loved America and forever
shall love America."

Dear Naren,
Did America satisfy you?
"That I don't know, Chinmoy,
But I satisfied America beyond her
imagination."

Dear Naren,
What will be the fate of America?
"Chinmoy, I love you and bless
you
For asking me such a divine
question.
You know, brother,
America's fate is exactly the way
You and your Supreme see it.
America's fate is exactly the way
You and your Supreme feel it.
America's fate is exactly the way
You and your Supreme shape it."

399. URGENT BUSINESS

Mother Mary, Please tell me,
where is your son?
I have been searching and
searching for him
In the ecstasy-sun of Heaven.
I have something most important
To discuss with him.

"Son,
Are you here?
For the last ten years
My Jesus has been searching and
searching for you
In the ignorance-sea and hell-fire
of earth.
He has left me a note saying
He has a piece of urgent business
With you on earth."

400. MY LORD, WHAT WILL HAPPEN?

My Lord, what will happen if I
deceive You?
"Son, I shall simply die."
My Lord, what will happen if You
deceive me?
"Son, nothing will happen to you.
Your ignorance-friends
Will console you, strengthen you,
To pay Me back in My own coin.
But in My case, if you, My all,
Ever deceive Me, I shall simply
die,
Since I have no other friend and
none to call My own."

401. A JOINT BANK ACCOUNT

God and I
Have a joint bank account.
He earns and deposits;
I neither earn nor deposit.
"Son," He says, "why don't you
Withdraw and buy your desires
So that at the end of the year
We shall be paying
Less income tax to Satan?
And also for another reason
I would like you to withdraw
Our wealth from the bank:
If you issue cheques to others,
The world will see that
You and I are good partners,
Loving partners, eternal
partners."

402. I AM NOT GOING TO TALK BACK

I am not going to talk back
To anyone any more.
No, not even to God.
Let Him scold me,
Let Him insult me.
I shall prove to Him
That I have not one,
But three striking qualities:
I know how to hear,
I know how to bear,
I know how to transfigure.
Of course,
It is for our mutual good.

If I become perfect,
God will definitely be proud of
me.
If I become perfect,
I won't have to fight
Constantly against Him.

403. MY MIRROR

In the morning
When I look in my mirror
I see the face of pure aspiration.

At noon
When I look in my mirror
I see the face of sad dissatisfaction.

In the evening
When I look in my mirror
I see that I am totally lost.

At night
When I look in my mirror
I see my broken heart
Replaced by God's Heart of
Determination,
And my sunken face
Replaced by God's
Perfection-Grace.

404. THE SONG OF EVOLUTION

A monkey climbed down a tree;
Lo, he became a man.

A man looked up;
Lo, he became a god.

A god looked within;
Lo, he became
The energy of a monkey,
The patience of a tree,
The forgiveness of a man,
The dedication of the Supreme.

405. A BETTER GURU AND A BETTER DISCIPLE

I hoped to get a better Guru;
Alas, there was none.

I hoped to get a better disciple;
Alas, there was none.

I hoped to get a better God;
I saw so many,
I saw them so willing,
I immediately felt
That
They were worth loving
And
Worth becoming.

406. ANOTHER GOD NEEDED

Rabelais said:
"A mother-in-law dies
Only when another devil
Is needed in hell."

I say:
"A seeker is born
Only when another God
Is needed on earth."

407. TOP SECRETS

The biggest secret
Came out of my little mouth:
God is still alive.

The sweetest secret
Came out of my little mouth:
God loves me.

The purest secret
Came out of my little mouth:
God is for all,
Including me:
My uselessness,
My unwillingness.

408. RELIGIOUS DISEASE AND RELIGIOUS CURE

Conversion is not a religion,
But a religious disease.
Yoga is not a religion,
But a religious cure.

Fear of God is not a religion,
But a fatal disease.
Love of God is not a religion,
But a normal life,
A perfecting soul,
A fulfilling Goal.

409. NAPOLEONS

The vital Napoleon
Braves and wins.
The mental Napoleon
Unlearns and becomes the
knowledge-sun.
The psychic Napoleon
Surrenders and becomes the
God-Love.

410. I BORROW

I borrow
Everything from God
Save and except His Perfection.

I borrow
Everything from God
Save and except His Realisation.

I borrow
Everything from God
Save and except His Aspiration.

God never borrows.
He just grabs my ignorance
And claims it as His, His alone.

411. CELEBRATIONS

My hope celebrates
The arrival of the New Year.

My doubt celebrates
The survival of the old year.

My soul celebrates
The arrival of my realisation-year.

My God celebrates
The survival of my
aspiration-year.

412. GOD, TELL ME THE REASON, PLEASE

In six days, God,
You created and completed
Heaven and earth.
How is it that my love-room
Still remains unfinished,
My devotion-room untouched,
My surrender-room unbuilt?
God, tell me the reason, please.

"My son, to complete your
love-room,
I need more satisfaction-power.
Unfortunately
I have run short of it.

"My son, in order to start working
On your devotion-room,
I need more
determination-power.
Unfortunately
Right now I don't have it.

"My son, you want Me to build
Your surrender-room.
Believe Me,
I am desperately searching
For My patience-power."

413. FATHER, HOW IS IT?

Father, how is it that
You do not love me
As You did before?
Have I done anything wrong?

"My son, ask your doubt-friend."

Father, how is it that
You do not care for me any more?
Have I done anything serious?

"My son, ask your
insecurity-friend."

414. FATHER, HAVE I DONE SOMETHING SPECIAL FOR YOU?

Father, how is it that
You love me nowadays
Much more than You ever did before?
Have I done something inwardly special for You?

"My son, ask My Compassion."

Father, how is it that
You care for me nowadays
At every second of my life,
And You are making me feel
My real closeness to You,
My divine oneness with You,
My supreme fulfilment in You?
Have I done something special for You
In the inner world?

"My son, ask My unconditional Compassion."

415. WHEN I LOOK

When I look at myself
I forget to learn.
When I look at the world
I learn to listen.
When I look at God
I listen to learn.

416. WITHOUT

Without air
Man cannot live.
Without the sun
Earth cannot live.
Without love
Life cannot live.
Without man's smile
God cannot live.

417. EXCEPT THREE THINGS

I remember everything
Except three things:
God Himself sent me
Into the world;
God Himself gave me
His Message of love to offer
To the world;
God Himself asked me
To be one with the world
For God-manifestation,
For God-perfection
On earth.

418. HE IS BLIND AND HE IS NOT BLIND

God's Compassion is blind,
But
His Wisdom is not.

God's Love is blind,
But
His Concern is not.

God's Promise is blind,
But
His Fulfilment is not.

God is blind;
Therefore He is available.

God is not blind;
Therefore He is unapproachable.

419. NO AND YES

No is not
A rejection
From a woman's heart.

Yes is not
An acceptance
Of a man's heart.

Cosmic Law is not
A rejection
From God's heart.

Forced Smile is not
The fulfilment
Of God's Promise.

420. I HAVE DONE AND I HAVE NOT DONE

The most difficult thing on earth
I have done:
I have squared the circle.

The easiest thing on earth
I have not done
And I cannot do.
I cannot make my disciples
Fearlessly and soulfully
SMILE!

421. ASK

How to know
If you have done the right thing?
Ask your soul.

How to know
If you are doing the right thing?
Ask your heart.

How to know
If you will be doing the right thing?
Ask your Will.

Your soul can unlock the door of the past.
Your heart can unlock the door of the present.
Your Will can unlock the door of the future.

422. THREE WORLDS

No vital world means
What it says.

No mental world says
What it means.

No psychic world says
If it does not mean.

423. HE BELIEVES

He believes
In divine miracles.
Therefore
He believes
That the earthly
marriage-oneness can last and fulfil.

He believes
In human miracles.
Therefore
He believes
That God-realisation can be achieved
With no aspiration and with no dedication.

424. FOLLOW MY WAY

He is a puritan friend of mine.
He wants me to live
My life in his way.
Why should I?

I am a seeker.
I want to live my life
In my own way.
Why should I not?

To the puritan friend of mine,
God says:
"Don't be a beggar,
You will fail."

To me, God says:
"Don't be a chooser,
You will fail.
Follow My Way:
My Way is the only filler
Of your empty life.
My Way is the only fulfiller
Of your soul's ancient promise."

425. THEY KNOCKED

Opportunity knocked
At my door only once.

Opportunists knocked
At my door thousands of times.

God knocked
At my door twice:
Once after I dined with ignorance,
Once before I went to sleep with
inconscience.

426. HOW THEY ACT

The soul proposes,
The vital opposes.

The mind hesitates,
The heart dedicates.

The body fears,
God cheers.

427. I AM AN ORPHAN

Adam and Eve
Had no human parents;
Yet
They were not orphans,
For God the divine Father became
their Father
And
God the divine Mother became
their Mother.

I
Have two visible and tangible
parents;
Yet
I am an orphan,
For my father
Does not know how to feed me
with wisdom-light,
And
My mother
Does not know how to feed me
with concern-might.

428. IS THERE ANYTHING PERMANENT?

My Lord,
How is it that there is nothing
Permanent on earth?

"Who told you so?
Is jealousy not permanent on
earth?
Is doubt not permanent on earth?
Is insecurity not permanent on
earth?"

My Lord,
True, they are.
But when are You
Going to make them
impermanent?

"Son, the moment the world
wants Me to."

My Lord,
Why do You blame the poor
innocent world?
After all, who created the world?

"Son, by creating the world
I feel I have played My role.
Now I feel the world should play
its role
By embracing love,
Faith and oneness.
And you know, son,
I am more than ready,
I am more than eager
To assist the world
In its noble adventure."

429. HERE IS THE PLACE

Is your goal to love?
Then here is the place.

Is your goal to love God in His
own Way?
Then here is the place.

Is your goal to become another
God?
Then here is the place.

Is your goal to transcend the
previous God?
Then here is the place.

Is your goal to transcend the
present God?
Then here is the place.

Is your goal, your only goal, to
become the future God?
Then here is the place.
Here is the place:
Earth, Mother Earth.

430. DISEASE, DEATH AND GOD

Disease is the revenge
Of a neglected thought.

Death is the result
Of a forgotten will.

God is the prize
Of a remembered love.

431. SINCE

Since
I escaped from Dream,
I have grown blind.

Since
I escaped from Reality,
I have become lame.

Since
I escaped from God,
I have become helpless.

Since
I escaped from myself,
I have become worthless.

432. THE STORY OF GOD

Where is God?
"I don't know."

How is God?
"I don't know."

Who is God?
"I don't know."

Who is the future God?
"Ah, I know, I know.
Not one but three future Gods:
My Transformation-Feet,
My Illumination-Mind,
My Oneness-Heart."

433. WHERE DO I LOOK FOR GUIDANCE?

Where do I look for guidance?
I look for guidance
In the body of grey fears.

Where do I look for guidance?
I look for guidance
In the vital of red jealousies.

Where do I look for guidance?
I look for guidance
In the mind of black doubts.

Where do I look for guidance?
I look for guidance
In the heart of white insecurities.

My Lord says:
"If you need further guidance,
Then
Think of Me,
Count on Me,
I am at your disposal.
My Light is at your disposal,
My Delight is at your disposal,
My Perfection is at your disposal."

434. DON'T JUST EXIST

Don't just exist. Live!
Don't just live. See!
Don't just see. Feel!
Don't just feel. Become!
And what happens
When you become?
When you become,
You really exist
Both on earth
And in Heaven.
You proudly live
In God's Heart.
You use God's Eye to see.
You use God's Heart to feel.
When you see,
You see your own omnipotence.
When you feel,
You feel your own omnipresence.

435. FAITH AND PERSONAL EFFORT

Lord, can faith be increased
By personal effort?
"Yes, faith can be increased
By personal effort
Provided
One knows the real meaning
Of personal effort."
What is personal effort?
"Personal effort is nothing but
Unseen and unrecognised Grace."
What is the other Grace,
I mean normal Grace?
"That Grace is called
Universal shower."

436. HE NEEDED ONLY THREE PERSONS

He needed
Only three persons
In this vast world:
A constant praiser,
A grateful learner,
An unconditional lover.
Alas, he found not even one.
Since
All mortals with no exception failed him,
He appointed God.

God touched his feet
And emphatically praised his ignorance.

God touched his feet
And unmistakably learnt from him
How to drink ignorance.

God touched his feet
And unconditionally became
His eternal Lover.

437. WHEN I LIVE

When I
Live in the mind,
I know less but say more.

When I
Live in the heart,
I know more but say less.

When I
Live in the soul,
I know most but say least.

When I
Live in God,
I know most and say most.

438. MIRACLE

What? Do I have to see any
miracle?
Am I not the world's greatest
miracle?

Who can equal me in performing
miracles?
One miracle I have already shown:
I was the God supreme,
And now I am a feeble man.

My second miracle will take place
In the distant future:
I shall become
Once more the Lord of the
Universe.

439. APPRECIATION, ADMIRATION AND LOVE

I appreciate myself not;
Therefore
I deserve more appreciation.

I admire myself not;
Therefore
I deserve more admiration.

I love myself not;
Therefore
I deserve more love.

But, since
I love not God,
I deserve no love, no admiration,
No appreciation, nothing,
Absolutely nothing.

440. A SELF-MADE MAN

He says
He is a self-made man.
I pity him.
I feel sorry for him.
I accept his apology,
Immediately.

He says
He is a self-made man.
I hate him.
I hate his haughtiness.
I trust not his insincere claim.
I discard his meaningless life
With its useless achievements,
Immediately.

441. GOD AND I LOVE

God loves me
For one particular reason:
I take my service
More selflessly than I take my life.

I love God
For two particular reasons:
He has forgotten how to think,
And
He is never busy.

442. WHEN I PREACH, WHEN I MEDITATE

When I preach,
My preaching finishes
Long before it actually stops.

When I meditate,
My meditation continues
Long after it has definitely
stopped.

443. THEIR OPINIONS DIFFER

The mind says:
Love is sex.

The vital says:
Sex is love.

The heart says:
Love is love.

The body says:
There is no such thing as love.

The soul says:
There is nothing but love.

444. WHY DO I LOVE GOD?

I love God
For two special reasons:
He is not afraid
Of my ignorance-sea
And
I am not afraid
Of His Omnipotence-Reality.

445. THREE FRIENDS

My Lord, I have thousands of
friends;
Of course, that includes You.

Now tell me, please,
How many friends do You have?

"Son, I have only three regular
friends:
World-love is My one-half friend,
World-devotion is My one full
friend,
World-surrender is My
one-and-a-half friend.

"If I have not miscalculated,
Then I have three friends.
Son, this is, of course, excluding
you."

446. I BECOME PERFECT

Lord, I am sufficient
Only when I have You
On my side.

"Son, I am sufficient
Only when I take
Your side.

"When I add Peace
To your achievements,
I become complete.

"When I add Light
To your achievements,
I become perfect."

447. I AM A GENIUS

I am a dependent genius.
I depend on the world's
appreciation.
I am happy.

I am a dependable genius.
The world depends on me.
I am really miserable.
I have no holidays.

I am an independent genius.
I am really happy
Because
I don't depend on the world's
appreciation
And
The world does not depend on my
genius.
The world is free to bark.
I am free to bray.

448. ANOTHER GOD

If I could only love myself
Divinely,
I would become
Another God.

If I could only reveal myself
Selflessly,
I would become
Another God.

If I could only manifest myself
Unconditionally,
I would become
Another God.

If I could only forget and forgive
myself,
I would become
The only God.

449. SHE CRIES

She cries every second
To please the Lord.

She cries every second
To love the Lord.

She cries every second
To serve the Lord.

The Lord cries every second
To make each of them feel that
She is indispensable,
She is indispensable,
She is indispensable,
And also
He grants them the boon
That they will have three hundred
incarnations less
To realise His Transcendental
Height
And become His Universal Life.

450. SHE JUMPED, SHE RAN, SHE DIVED

She jumped and jumped
Before the Lord.
She ran and ran
Before the Lord.
She dived and dived
Before the Lord.

Finally the Lord
Jumped with His jumper-seeker
Only to break His knees,
Ran with His runner-seeker
Only to damage His heart,
Dived with His diver-seeker
Only to break His head.

Lo,
The jumper reached
The Height of the Supreme.
The runner reached
The Length of the Supreme.
The diver reached
The Depth of the Supreme.

451. HE AND HIS

He and his ego worship each
other,
He and his doubt love each other,
He and his fear torture each other,
He and his failure hate each other,
He and his perfection reject each
other,
He and his death live in each
other.

452. YOUR INGRATITUDE IS AN EXCEPTION

Your pride confuses my mind.
Your pride amuses my heart.
Your life receives nothing but
A ceaseless tribute from the
foolish world.
I know not how
Your swollen head
And
Your sunken mind
Live together.
You know not how to implore,
You know not how to explore,
You know only how to explode.
Here on earth,
There in Heaven
Nothing grows without
nourishment.
But
Your ingratitude is an exception,
Indeed, an unbelievable
exception.

453. GOD IN HIM IS STILL ALIVE

In the morning
He shakes hands with I-dolatry.
In the evening
He embraces his self-infatuation.
At night
He suffers from I-strain.
Yet
His is not a hopeless case;
God in him is still alive,
Vividly alive.

454. THE SAME PALACE

Truth and dignity
Share the same palace.
Love and joy
Share the same palace.
Father and son
Share the same palace.
Faith and doubt
Share not the same palace.
Fear and courage
Share not the same palace.
Alas, ingratitude has no palace,
none at all.

455. HIS ABSENCE

His physical absence
Diminishes my little hopes
And increases my great hopes.

His spiritual absence destroys
All my hopes, little and great.

In his physical absence
I see my Goal,
Although quite far.
In his spiritual absence
I see only a goalless shore.

456. IN THE GOAL OF THE SOUL

Pleasure is the absence
Of temporary physical pain.

Joy is the presence
Of eternal gain
In the heart of life.

Doubt is the absence
Of temporary mental relief.

Faith is the presence
Of eternal release
In the Goal of the soul.

457. ACCEPTANCE

Acceptance human
Is the acknowledgement
Of painful obligation.

Acceptance divine
Is the acknowledgement
Of soulful perfection.

God accepted man
To make him happy.
Man accepted God
To make himself great.

458. OCCURRENCE AND EXPERIENCE

The body thinks
Accident is an inevitable
occurrence.
The mind discovers
Accident is an undeniable
occurrence.
The heart feels
Accident is an avoidable
occurrence.
The soul knows
Accident leads
To profitable experience.

459. STRIVE

Strive blindly,
And achieve nothing.

Strive carefully,
And achieve something.

Strive soulfully,
And achieve everything.

Strive unconditionally,
And, lo, you have won
Everything,
Including God.

460. DEATH

Death, how often do you speak to
God?

"I speak to God constantly."

Can you tell me
What both of you talk about?

"We talk about our achievements
And
Our disappointments.
I tell Him about my achievements
On earth
And my disappointments in
Heaven.
God tells me about His
achievements
In Heaven
And His disappointments on
earth."

I see.
Thank you, Death.

461. HIS KINGDOMS

His desire-kingdom
Is bounded on the north by fear,
On the south by doubt,
On the west by jealousy,
On the east by insecurity.

His aspiration-kingdom
Is bounded on the east by faith,
On the west by love,
On the north by devotion,
On the south by surrender.

His realisation-kingdom
Is bounded on the east by God's
Compassion,
On the west by God's
Illumination,
On the north by God's Realisation,
On the south by God's Perfection.

462. A ZERO AND A HERO

I am a zero.
Therefore
I pray to God.

I am a hero.
Therefore
I take care of man.

When I am in the body,
I represent the nothingness
Of a zero.

When I am in the soul,
I represent the Treasure
Of Eternity.

463. WHEN

When he concentrates,
Everything matters.

When he meditates,
Nothing matters.

When he contemplates,
Only God matters.

464. THEY RISE

When the vital retires,
The mind rises.

When the mind retires,
The heart rises.

When the heart aspires,
The soul rises.

When the body aspires,
God rises.

465. SHE NURSES

She nurses love,
He nurses indifference.
She nurses devotion,
He nurses indifference.
She nurses surrender,
He nurses indifference.
She nurses grievances,
He nurses indifference.
She nurses despair,
He nurses indifference.

She nurses indifference.
He touches her feet,
He kisses her shoes,
He becomes her slave.

466. ALL OBEY ME

My doubt obeys me
When I tell him
To do as he wishes.

My jealousy obeys me
When I tell her
To do as she wishes.

My pride obeys me
When I tell him
To do as he wishes.

My fear obeys me
When I tell her
To do as she wishes.

My God obeys me
When He sees me
Smiling and dancing.

The world obeys me
When she sees me
Crying and sighing.

467. BETTER AND BITTER

Obstacles appear
To make us better, not bitter.

Failure appears
To make us better, not bitter.

Obstacles disappear;
We wait and look around.

Failure disappears;
We wonder and wander around.

468. I TELL YOU

I tell you,
Even when worst comes to worst,
It will not be so bad.

I tell you,
Even when best comes to best,
It will not be so good.

Unwillingness to see
The Face of Light
Is by far the worst thing on earth.

Surrender to God's Will
Is by far the best thing on earth.

To defeat the worst in life,
We must unlearn in the heart
The lessons given us by the mind.

To win the best in life,
We must learn in the mind
The lessons given us by the heart.

469. WHO IS HE?

Even his own shadow
Is afraid of him.
Even his own eyes
Are afraid of him.
Even his own Goal
Is afraid of him.

Who is he?
Impurity, the only son
of our venom doubts.

470. HIS SOVEREIGN DREAM

His sovereign dream
Of God-manifestation on earth
Is collapsing fast, very fast,
Into its own self:
An explosion with no life in it,
A realisation with no light in it,
A perfection with no love in it.

471. SHE

In the morning
She is the passion of
aspiration-light.

In the afternoon
She is the passion of
transformation-might.

In the evening
She is the passion of
realisation-height.

At night
She is the passion of
immortality-right.

472. PASSION

Passion is possession.
Live in the vital,
You will know it.

Passion is frustration.
Live in the mind,
You will feel it.

Passion is perdition.
Live in the heart,
You will discover it.

Yet
Passion is not rejection
By God's Compassion.
Passion is illumination
When it shakes hands with
aspiration.

473. WHEN HE LEFT HEAVEN

When he left Heaven,
The owner of Heaven
Soulfully cried with gratitude,
Hoping that he would soon
return.

When he touched earth,
The owner of earth
Vehemently protested his arrival.
Furious, Mother Earth said to
Father Heaven:
"Stop dropping your garbage on
me."

Trembling, Father Heaven
replied:
"O my better half, forgive me,
This will be absolutely
My last torture,
My greatest relief."

474. HE IS A PECULIAR MAN

He is a peculiar man
Privately and publicly.

Privately he steals from God,
Publicly he gives to mankind.

Privately he shakes hands with
God,
Publicly he touches God's feet.

Privately he advises God,
Publicly he obeys God.

Privately he feeds on God's
Compassion,
Publicly he finds fault with God's
creation.

475. HIS REALISATION AND HIS MANIFESTATION

He never remembers his
realisation,
Once he has decided
To tell the world
What it looked like.

He never forgets his
manifestation,
Once he has decided
To tell the world
What it looks like.

476. ONLY

Only Heaven can
Deserve his pride.

Only earth can
Preserve his sacrifice.

Only he can
Observe his birthright.

Only God can
Serve his aspiration-delight.

477. HE IS VERY LOYAL

He is very loyal to God;
Therefore
He reached God's Head.

He is very loyal to man;
Therefore
He kissed man's feet.

He is very loyal to God;
Therefore
He touched God's Heart.

He is very loyal to man;
Therefore
He breathed in man's mind.

478. FRIENDLESS AM I

No friend have I
In Heaven.
They all have descended
To work for the world.

No friend have I
On earth.
They all have ascended
To rest in Heaven.

Friendless in Heaven,
I cry for earth-entrance.
Friendless on earth,
I cry for Heaven-exit.

479. HIS FRIENDS SPEAK

His mind says to him:
"You are useless.
You cannot entertain
Even one charming doubt."

His heart says to him:
"You are useless.
You cannot maintain
Even one particle of faith."

His soul says to him:
"You are useless.
You cannot contain
Even one secret of God."

480. HE AND GOD ILLUMINE

He illumines Heaven
When he leaves it.
He illumines man
When he leaves earth.

God illumines him
When he teaches.
God illumines him
When he reaches.
All illumine him
When he ceases.

481. HIS ONLY SHORTCOMING

On earth
His long staying
Is his only shortcoming.

In Heaven
His short staying
Is his only shortcoming.

In man
His very staying
Is his only shortcoming.

482. BEFORE HIM

Before Him
My Imagination dies,
My Aspiration runs.

Before Him
My Aspiration dies,
My Realisation flies.

Before Him
My Realisation dies,
My Perfection spreads.

Before Him
My Perfection dies,
My Oneness prevails.

483. THE SUPERLATIVE FAILURE

He has not only the last word,
But the last ten thousand words.

He sings not only the last song,
But the worst possible song
Composed by any man on earth.

He reveals not only the last
experience,
But the saddest experience
Experienced by the superlative
failure.

484. HE THINKS, HE FEELS, HE KNOWS

He thinks the world loves him.
Truth is thinking
Through his searching mind.

He feels the world loves him.
Truth is feeling
Through his serving heart.

He knows the world loves him.
Truth is singing
Through his glowing life.

485. GOD, FOR GOD'S SAKE!

God, for God's sake,
Don't be so cruel,
Don't make me Your equal!

God, for God's sake,
Don't be so stupid,
Don't make me Your equal!

God, for God's sake,
Don't be so absurd,
Don't make me Your equal!

If I equal You, God,
I shall lose my purest love-life,
I shall lose my sweetest
devotion-world,
I shall lose my brightest
surrender-sky.

486. DESIRE-WORLD AND ASPIRATION-WORLD

In the morning
Aspiration-world
Brushes her teeth,
Desire-world
Sharpens her tongue.

In the evening
Aspiration-world
Illumines her Ignorance-tree,
Desire-world
Destroys her life.

487. WHAT HAPPENS IS THIS

When I am in Heaven,
I pull my ant weight.

When I am on earth,
I throw my elephant weight
around.

When I am with God,
I have no weight.
He just empties my weight.

488. LORD, IF IT IS YOUR WILL

Lord, if it is Your Will,
I shall love my enemies.

Lord, if it is Your Will,
I shall illumine my friends.

Lord, if it is Your Will,
I shall forgive my earthly
existence.

Lord, if it is Your Will,
I shall live without You.

But
If it is Your Will
That I should equal You
And become another God,
Then
I shall cry around You,
I shall sigh within You,
I shall die before You.

Lord, give me only one boon:
First and last,
That You will remain my eternal
Lord.

489. THE GREATEST FAULT

The greatest fault
He discovered in Heaven
Was ecstasy.

The greatest fault
He discovered on earth
Was complacency.

The greatest fault
He discovered in himself
Was love.

The greatest fault
He discovered in God
Was
FORGIVENESS.

490. HE

He is so indecisive.
He has been meditating
For thirty-three long years;
But still he has not given himself
A spiritual name.

He is so possessive.
He wants to know the names of his
Spiritual great-grandchildren
Who are still sleeping in Heaven.

He is so obsessive.
He wants world-perfection
This very moment.
He feels his own perfection
Can delay;
No harm,
His big heart can wait
And sleep in Eternity's Life.

He is so progressive.
He asks God
To beg him to create
A new world, a world infinitely
 better
Than God's own world.

491. HE CHALLENGED GOD

During his entire life
He challenged God
Not once, but thrice.

In the morning of his life
He challenged God's Power,
Only to be liberated.

In the afternoon of his life
He challenged God's Forgiveness,
Only to be forgiven.

In the evening of his life
He challenged God's Immortality,
Only to be embraced.

492. I BELIEVE, I LIKE AND I LOVE

I believe everything.
It saves me from thinking,
It saves me from criticising,
It saves me from doubting.

I like everything.
It saves me from being ignored,
It saves me from being
 misunderstood,
It saves me from being obstructed.

I love everything.
It saves me from sovereignty,
It saves me from curiosity,
It saves me from futility.

493. HIS TWO ADMIRERS

He has two staunch admirers:
God and Satan.

God admires his presence of mind
In the inner world.

Satan admires his absence from
mind
In the outer world.

God asks him to remember
Everything that God says and
does.
This will help God.

Satan asks him to forget
Everything that Satan says and
does.
This will help Satan.

494. WHEN I SPEAK

I never speak ill of man,
Except in self-defence.

I never speak well of God,
Except in self-glorification.

I neither speak ill nor well of
Truth.
Why?
Because Truth needs
No comment from me,
From my judgement-seat.

495. REINCARNATION

He is the clear proof
Of reincarnation.

In his previous incarnation
He spoke excessively
Ill of God.

In this incarnation
He is trying to compensate.

He is appreciating God
Beyond his sincerity.

He is admiring God
Beyond his capacity.

He is loving God
Beyond his necessity.

496. HE TAKES AND LEAVES

When he deals with men,
First he takes them
And then he leaves them.

When he deals with angels,
First he ignores them
And then he invokes them.

When he deals with God,
First he loves God with his love,
And then he kills Him with his
surrender.

497. LOOK AND OVERLOOK

After we look doubt over,
We overlook doubt.

After we overlook faith,
We look faith over.

After we look Satan over
When he smiles,
We overlook him
When he cries.

After we overlook God
When He cries,
We look Him over
When He smiles.

498. IN VAIN

In vain
His superlative adorers
Fight against
His sleepless gravediggers.

In vain
His proud creation
Fights against
His earth's oblivion.

499. FIRST AND LAST

Love is Heaven's first sacrifice,
Love is earth's last achievement.

Dream is Heaven's first invention,
Dream is earth's last discovery.

God is Heaven's first Voice,
God is earth's last Choice.

500. WHAT IS WRONG WITH ME?

Even
A turtle makes progress.
What is wrong with me?

Even
A fool makes progress.
What is wrong with me?

Even
A sunken hope makes progress.
What is wrong with me?

Even
A broken heart makes progress.
What is wrong with me?

Even
A deceased life makes progress.
What is wrong with me?

501. NOTHING TO DO WITH IT

Insecurity is for women only;
Men have nothing to do with it.

Impurity is for men only;
Women have nothing to do with it.

Love is for God only;
Human beings have nothing to do with it.

Ingratitude is for human beings only;
God has nothing to do with it.

502. DESTINATION GUARANTEED

Human thought has degenerated,
Human hope has degenerated,
Human love has degenerated,
Human soul has degenerated,
Human goal has degenerated.

But God's Thought for man is still the same,
God's Hope for man is still the same,
God's Love for man is still the same,
God's Soul for man is still the same,
God's Goal for man is still the same.
Therefore,
Man's higher destination
Is guaranteed.

503. WHO HAS ALL THE ANSWERS?

Have you all the answers?
No!

Has he all the answers?
No!

Have I all the answers?
No!

Who has all the answers?
Faith, man's faith,
His faith in himself,
His faith in God.

504. GRATITUDE

A desiring man
Never gets tired of offering his
  gratitude
To his own efforts.

An aspiring man
Never gets tired of offering his
  gratitude
To his own faith.

A surrendered seeker
Never gets tired of offering his
  gratitude
To his Lord divine.

The Lord Supreme
Never gets tired of offering His
  Gratitude
To His Infinite Compassion.

505. SUCCESS

Desire waits for the future
To make it successful.

Aspiration actually makes the
  future
Successful.

Realisation itself is the glorious
  success.
Realisation is
The seed of the past,
The flower of the present,
The fruit of the future.

506. EVILS

O fear, O doubt,
You two are unnecessary evils.

O money, O power,
You two are necessary evils.

O impurity, O insecurity,
You two are Satan's necessities.

507. MY PROGRESS

There was a time
When I tried hard to avoid desires.
Now desires avoid me, my
  aspiration.

There was a time
When I tried hard to avoid doubts.
Now doubts avoid me, my faith.

There was a time
When I tried hard to avoid fear.
Now fear avoids me, my courage.

There was a time
When I tried hard to avoid
  temptation.
Now temptation avoids me, my
  liberation.

508. HE IS BRAVE

He who hears is brave.
He who sees is brave.
He who feels is brave.
He who thinks is brave.
He who desires is brave.
He who aspires is brave.
He who surrenders is brave.
But he who braves is God.

509. I LEAVE AND I TAKE

I leave my fears inside my room,
I take my courage when I go out.

I leave my pride inside my room,
I take my humility when I go out.

I leave my despair inside my room,
I take my hope when I go out.

I leave my darkness inside my room,
I take my illumination when I go out.

510. THEY HATE HIM

Fear hates him
Because
He speaks ill of fear
To his friend, courage.

Doubt hates him
Because
He speaks ill of doubt
To his friend, faith.

Impurity hates him
Because
He speaks ill of impurity
To his friend, purity.

Bondage hates him
Because
He speaks ill of bondage
To his friend, liberation.

511. TODAY AND TOMORROW

Today courage endures;
Tomorrow courage shall prevail.

Today love endures;
Tomorrow love shall prevail.

Today truth endures;
Tomorrow truth shall prevail.

Likewise,
O Lord, today in me You endure;
Tomorrow, I assure You, in me You shall prevail.

512. WISDOM

Faith is the wisdom
That has said its prayers.

Surrender is the wisdom
That has fulfilled its life.

Love is the wisdom
That has done its duty.

God is the Wisdom
Who has opened His Heart.

513. I SEE, I HAVE AND I AM

Doubt I see,
Faith I have,
Courage I am.

Ignorance I see,
Wisdom I have,
Bliss I am.

Separation I see,
Union I have,
God I am.

514. HE IS

He is a sufferer.
Therefore
He lives five minutes longer.

He is a hero.
Therefore
He lives ten minutes longer.

He is a sacrificer.
Therefore
He lives fifteen minutes longer.

He is a believer.
Therefore
He lives twenty minutes longer.

He is a lover.
Therefore
He lives forever.

515. HE WHO MISSES

He who misses
God's Eye
Misses much.

He who misses
God's Smile
Misses more.

He who misses
God's Heart
Misses most.

He who misses
God's Love
Misses everything.

516. IT IS ALWAYS EASY

It is always easy
To brave ignorance
From a safe distance.

It is always easy
To adore man
From a safe distance.

It is always easy
To deny Truth
From a safe distance.

It is always easy
To doubt God
From a safe distance.

517. WE ALL NEED HOPE

Courage needs hope
For its aspiration.

Faith needs hope
For its realisation.

Love needs hope
For its revelation.

I need hope
For my manifestation.

518. TOGETHER THEY GO

Courage and Love
Together go.

Courage and Peace
Together go.

Courage and Bliss
Together go.

Courage and God
Together go.

519. EVERYONE ASKS ME FOR A FAVOUR

Doubt asks me
To cherish him
And boast of him.

Fear asks me
To nourish her
And boast of her.

Courage asks me
To feed him
And look after him.

Faith asks me
To strengthen her
And immortalise her.

520. MY NEEDS

I need a sleepless body
To see God.

I need a tireless vital
To play with God.

I need a fearless mind
To travel with God.

I need a selfless heart
To converse with God.

I need a deathless life
To dance with God.

521. SINCE EVERYTHING IS IN THE HANDS OF GOD

I have insulted the world;
I deserve a severe punishment.
But I must not
Be frightened to death,
Since
Everything is in the Hands of God.

I have criticised God;
I deserve a severe punishment.
But I must not
Be frightened to death,
Since
Everything is in the Hands of God.

I have doubted myself;
I deserve ceaseless punishment.
And the law of Karma
Shall dog me and dog me and dog
me.

522. ABOVE ALL

Man above all:
This is the height
Of my animal realisation.

Love above all:
This is the height
Of my human realisation.

Oneness above all:
This is the height
Of my divine realisation.

God-manifestation above all:
This is the height
Of my absolute Perfection.

523. BEFORE AND AFTER

Before God-realisation
My renunciation
Was my supreme sacrifice.

After God-realisation
My unconditional oneness
With the ignorance-world
Is my supreme sacrifice.

524. HOW CAN I ATTAIN GOD?

Not by rituals
Can I attain God.

Not by austerity
Can I attain God.

Not by self-denial
Can I attain God.

I can attain God
With a love-heart,
With soul-bliss.

525. MY IMMORTALITY

My beauty
Is immortal in Heaven.

My duty
Is immortal on earth.

My aspiration
Is immortal in life.

My surrender
Is immortal in God.

526. IN ME THEY NEED

The animal
In me needs
Freedom from aggression.

The human
In me needs
Freedom from fear.

The divine
In me needs
Freedom from ignorance.

The Supreme
In me needs
Freedom from Compassion.

527. GOD-DISCOVERY AND MAN-PERFECTION

His philosophy,
Explained and expanded,
Becomes God-Discovery.

God-Discovery,
Condensed and made practical,
Becomes Man-Perfection.

528. NOT GOING TO LAST

Lord, my life
Always bristles with problems
Of varying magnitude.

Son, this realisation of yours
Is not going to last.

Lord, when will You prove
The authenticity
Of Your prophecy?

Son, just smile
And see
If I am right.

529. WHAT IS IT?

An incarnation: what is it?
A manifestation of God.

An animal incarnation: what is it?
A general manifestation of God.

A human incarnation: what is it?
A special manifestation of God.

A divine incarnation: what is it?
The supreme manifestation of
God.

530. LOVE

Human love
Originates in the whispers
Of uncertainty.

Divine love
Originates in the whiteness
Of purity.

God's Love
Originates in the oneness
Of beauty.

531. HIS BIRTHRIGHT

He has only one friend:
Love.
Three times a day
His friend helps him.

In the morning,
Love energises him.

In the afternoon,
Love enfolds the best in him.

In the evening,
Love tells him
That God-Discovery is his
birthright.

532. NO PEACE HERE OR HEREAFTER

A weakling
Has no peace,
Here or hereafter.

An unthinking man
Has no peace,
Here or hereafter.

An unloving heart
Has no peace,
Here or hereafter.

An unfulfilled life
Has no peace,
Here or hereafter.

533. HE WILL WAKE UP

He talks.
He is a man of empty talk.

He lives.
He lives a purposeless life.

He yields.
He constantly yields to cowardice.

He is.
He is hopelessly faint-hearted.

Yet one day
He will wake up.
He will wake up
And listen to the clarion call
Of his Inner Pilot.

534. THE RIPE FRUIT

When I think of God,
I become His bud.

When I pray to God,
I become His tender flower.

When I concentrate on God,
I become His unripe fruit.

When I meditate on God,
I become His ripe fruit.

535. THE MASTER-KEY

Life has two significant aspects:
A changeful aspect
And
A changeless aspect.
God is undoubtedly the
master-key
To both the aspects.

Life has two stories:
The story of destruction
And
The story of perfection.
God is undoubtedly the
master-key
To both the stories.

536. I NEED

I need.
I need my Mother's Love.

I need.
I need my Father's Wisdom.

I need.
I need my Master's Light.

I need.
I need my God's Compassion.

What else do I need?
Nothing, absolutely nothing!

537. A WORLD OF DIFFERENCE

There is a world of difference
Between
Fear and doubt.
Fear is something that I treasure;
Doubt is something that treasures
me.

There is a world of difference
Between
Stupidity and absurdity.
Stupidity tells me that everybody
has surpassed me;
Absurdity tells me that I have
surpassed everybody.

538. WE ALLOW OUR MINDS

You allow your mind
To wander on unwanted things.

He allows his mind
To wander on wanted pleasures.

I allow my mind
To wander on futile thoughts.

Together we shall sing
The song of temptation.

Together we shall dance
The dance of frustration.

Together we shall die
The death of destruction.

539. FIRST THINK

First think of God
And then dine with man.
Do not proceed
In the reverse order.

First think of Compassion
And then meditate on Justice.
Do not proceed
In the reverse order.

First think of your own perfection
And then cherish the idea of
God-manifestation.
Do not proceed
In the reverse order.

540. PROGRESS

In the morning of our life,
Our true progress
Is measured
By the yardstick
Of our sense-control.

In the afternoon of our life,
Our true progress
Is measured
By the yardstick
Of our compassion-realisation.

In the evening of our life,
Our true progress
Is measured
By the yardstick
Of our oneness-manifestation.

541. LIFE

In the animal life
Competition is indispensable.
Here the struggle for existence,
itself,
Is a constant battle.

In the human life
Co-operation is indispensable.
Here collective peace and security
Give birth to progress and
prosperity.

In the life divine
Self-dedication is indispensable.
Here universal oneness and
love-revelation
Are God-manifestation.

542. TOGETHER STAY, TOGETHER PLAY

The murmuring of the life-river
dies
When it reaches the peace-ocean.

The functioning of the unlit mind
ceases
When the soul embraces the
mind.

The dancing of the heart begins
When meditation and dedication
Together stay,
Together play.

543. WHEN THE MIND

When the mind
Thinks of silence,
It begins to solve its problems.

When the mind
Speaks to silence,
Half of its problems are solved.

When the mind
Sleeps in the lap of silence,
All its problems are solved.

544. WHEN HE SPEAKS

When he speaks to doubt,
He becomes a stream of faith.

When he speaks to fear,
He becomes a stream of courage.

When he speaks to insecurity,
He becomes a stream of
confidence.

When he speaks to impurity,
He becomes a stream of purity.

When he speaks to his lower self,
He becomes a stream of concern.

When he speaks to his higher Self,
He becomes a stream of
admiration.

545. I SHALL FIGHT

Until my life burns down
I shall fight.
I shall fight against
My brooding ignorance.

Until my life burns down
I shall fight.
I shall fight against
The world's roaring indifference.

Until my life burns down
I shall fight.
I shall fight against
Heaven's burning impatience.

546. SPEAKING TO MY DIFFERENT SELVES

To speak to my highest Self,
I need neither vision nor voice.

To speak to my higher self,
I need only vision.

To speak to my lower self,
I need both vision and voice.

To speak to my lowest self,
I need a sleepless vision,
I need a tireless voice,
I need a dauntless heart.

547. WHEN HE SLEEPS

When he sleeps beside faith
He enjoys a restful sleep.

When he sleeps beside doubt
He suffers a restless sleep.

When he sleeps beside fear
He dies in his endless sleep.

548. PAVILION OF THE ETERNAL BEYOND

His heart-life
Is a pavilion of earth.

His soul-life
Is a pavilion of Heaven.

His God-Life
Is a pavilion of the Eternal
Beyond.

Earth sees
Through his heart.

Heaven feels
Through his soul.

The Eternal Beyond glows
Through his God-Life.

549. STAY NOT IN THE PARADISE

O my body,
Stay not in the paradise
Of helplessness.

O my vital,
Stay not in the paradise
Of wilderness.

O my mind,
Stay not in the paradise
Of forgetfulness.

O my heart,
Stay not in the paradise
Of ungratefulness.

O my soul,
Stay not in the paradise
Of carelessness.

550. JUST A HABIT

Why do I speak to God?
It is just a habit
Of my perfection.

Why do I adore myself?
It is just a habit
Of my imperfection.

Why do I love man?
It is just a habit
Of my obligation.

551. ABSENCE

In man's absence
My fondness-tree proudly grows.

In God's absence
My life-tree helplessly dies.

O man and God,
I tell you
My supreme secret:
Ignorance misses my absence,
Earth cherishes my absence,
Heaven terminates my absence.

552. WHAT IS IT?

Abstinence, what is it?
The best medicine.

Persistence, what is it?
The surest crown.

Surrender, what is it?
The highest goal.

553. WITH MUCH SWEAT

Without sweat
I acquired teeming doubts.
Without regret
I threw them away.

Without sweat
I grabbed ignorance-night.
Without regret
I killed its life.

With much sweat
I have acquired an iota of faith.
If I ever lose it
My life-boat shall sink.

With much sweat
I have discovered an iota of Light.
If I ever lose it,
I shall become a soulless creature.

554. DIFFICULTIES

A woman
Finds it difficult
To admit her insecurity.

A man
Finds it difficult
To admit his impurity.

Poor earth
Finds it difficult
To brave its sufferings.

Rich Heaven
Finds it difficult
To hide its Treasures.

The Supreme
Finds it impossible
To overrule His Compassion.

555. THE UNDIVINE AND THE DIVINE

The undivine flourish,
The divine die young:
This is what we hear,
This is what we think,
This is what we know.

My soul wants to add
Something to this lofty theory:
The undivine flourish
In the closed coffin of Death.
The divine die young
In the Lap of Immortality.

556. HIS BOOKS AND HIS LOOKS

His books lead me
To the sage inside him.

His looks draw me
To the animal inside him.

His books deserve immediate
recognition.
His looks need gradual
transformation.

557. NOTHING MORE, NOTHING LESS

To keep the doctor away
I need sound health.

To keep sound health
I need nature's blessing.

To have nature's blessing
I need God's Grace.

To have God's Grace
I need the strength of surrender.

To have the strength of surrender
I need just one thing:
Faith, only faith.
Nothing more,
Nothing less!

558. I ASSOCIATE

I associate with God
To enjoy my natural realisation.

I associate with Man
To enjoy my regular aspiration.

I associate with Earth
To enjoy the universal Emptiness.

I associate with Heaven
To enjoy the absolute Infinitude.

559. BOYS AND GIRLS

Boys will be boys;
Girls will be girls.
Boys will reach their Goal
Singing and running.
Girls will reach their Goal
Dancing and diving.

Boys will be boys;
Girls will be girls.
Boys will realise God,
The Highest Realisation.
Girls will manifest God,
The Absolute Perfection.

560. BEFORE

Duty before pleasure,
Compassion before justice,
Offering before receiving,
Heart before mind,
Faith-flame before doubt-net,
God-realisation before
world-perfection.

561. COME AND GO, COME AND STAY

Fear, the timid guest,
Comes and goes.

Doubt, the bold guest,
Comes and goes.

Jealousy, the clever guest,
Comes and goes.

Compassion, the kind guest,
Comes and stays.

Light, the beautiful guest,
Comes and stays.

Bliss, the sweet guest,
Comes and stays.

God, the silent Guest,
Comes, stays and never goes.

562. FEAST AND FAST

A desiring vital
Feasts today,
Fasts tomorrow.

An aspiring heart
Fasts today,
Feasts tomorrow.

What does a desiring vital eat?
It eats fear and doubt,
It eats hope and despair,
It eats impurity and futility.

What does an aspiring heart eat?
It eats Compassion and Concern,
It eats Peace and Bliss,
It eats Salvation and Illumination.

563. A WILL AND A WAY

There is a will,
And that will is in the soul.

There is a way,
And that way is in the heart.

There is a will,
And that will is of God.

There is a way,
And that way is for God.

There is a will,
And that will is leading me to the
Supreme.

There is a way,
And that way has made me love
the Supreme.

564. GOD FEELS SAD

The doctor fails;
And God feels sad.
He feels sad
That He did not give the doctor
The life-saving medicine.

The patient dies;
And God feels sad.
He feels sad
That He did not give the patient
The message of immortal life.

The relatives weep;
And God feels sad.
He feels sad
That He did not tell them
That Heaven is the second floor
And earth is the first floor
Of the same building.
God feels sad
That He forgot to tell them
Even the name of the building.
Love is its name.

565. CARRIERS

Doubt, don't come to me!
If you come
I shall carry you to Faith.
Faith and I shall kill you.

Fear, don't come to me!
If you come
I shall carry you to Will.
Will and I shall kill you.

Faith, do come to me!
Carry me to the real starting point.

Will, do come to me!
Carry me to the ultimate Goal.

566. THEY DO NOT BELIEVE IT

Haste is waste:
The vital does not believe it.

Suspicion is frustration:
The mind does not believe it.

Insecurity is futility:
The heart does not believe it.

Hesitation is destruction:
The body does not believe it.

567. THE BRAIN APPRECIATES

An idle brain
Appreciates
The long nose of the devil.

An ignorant brain
Appreciates
The face of bondage.

A man-liking brain
Appreciates
The discoveries of man.

A God-loving brain
Appreciates
The omnipresence of God.

568. HE NEEDS MORE

The more an earth-bound man
has,
The more he needs.

He has doubt;
He needs more.

He has despair;
He needs more.

He has failure;
He needs more.

The more a Heaven-soaring man
has,
The more he needs.

He has faith, faith in himself;
He needs more.

He has courage, courage to brave
ignorance;
He needs more.

He has love, love to feed the
world;
He needs more.

569. SATAN AND GOD

When the human "I" enters,
Satan enters, too.

When the divine "I" enters,
God enters, too.

Who is Satan?
Satan is the grandson of
imperfection
And
The son of destruction.

Who is God?
God is the Grandfather of life
And
The Father of love.

570. GOD ENTERS

God's Compassion enters;
The animal in me departs.

God's Illumination enters;
The human in me departs.

God's Perfection enters;
The finite in me departs.

Finally God enters
And I quickly bolt the door
So that He can never depart.

571. MADE AND MEANT

Laws are made
To be executed.

Doubts are meant
To be avoided.

Ignorance is made
To be transcended.

The heights of God are meant
To be realised,
Revealed,
Manifested.

572. IT IS NEVER TOO LATE

It is never too late to learn.
I have offered this message
To my ignorant friend, Ignorance.

It is never too late to cure.
I have offered this message
To my diseased friend, Disease.

It is never too late to attain
perfection.
I have offered this message
To my imperfect friend,
Imperfection.

573. TOMORROW DOES NOT COME

Tomorrow does not come.
Why?
Because
Yesterday was enough
And
Today is more than enough.

Tomorrow will never come.
Why?
Because
God has not given birth
To tomorrow
And
He does not want
To change His Plan.

574. NO NEWS

No news is sad news
When I expect
My God-realisation news
From God,
My negligent correspondent.

No news is good news
When I expect
My endless bondage news
From ignorance,
My forgetful correspondent.

575. SUFFICIENT

A word to the surrendered heart
Is sufficient.
A million words to the searching
mind
Are sufficient.
A billion words to the striving
vital
Are sufficient.
A trillion words to the sleeping
body
Are NOT sufficient.
A sleeping body, what is it?
Doubt, man's doubt:
His teeming doubts,
His brooding doubts.

576. PASSPORTS

Money is the superlative passport
In the country of
Deception and corruption.

Conscience is the most effective
passport
In the country of
Truth and justice.

Surrender divine is the only
passport
In the country of
Realisation and Perfection.

577. ROME WAS NOT BUILT IN A DAY

Rome was not built in a day.
I have been telling this all along
To my impatient son,
Impatience.

Rome was not built in a day.
I have been telling this constantly
To my despondent daughter,
Despondency.

Rome was not built in a day.
I have been telling this year after
year
To my doubting friend,
Doubt.

Rome was not built in a day.
I have been telling this tirelessly
To my mocking enemy,
Mockery.

578. PRACTICE MAKES PERFECT

Practice makes perfect.
God believes in this theory;
Therefore
He practised Compassion.
Lo, He has become Compassion,
Unconditional Compassion.

Practice makes perfect.
God believes in this theory;
Therefore
He practised surrender.
Lo, He has become perfect
Surrender,
Surrender to man's countless
desires.

579. EARLY AND LATE

I went to see God
An hour early.
He welcomed me
And
Shook hands with me.

I went to see God
Two hours early.
He welcomed me
And
Embraced me.

I went to see God
Three hours early.
He welcomed me
And
Made me sit on His
Transcendental Throne.

I went to see God
A minute late.
He thoughtfully hesitated to
welcome me.

I went to see God
Two minutes late.
He simply ignored my arrival.

I went to see God
Three minutes late.
He refused to open the door.

580. ASK ME ANY QUESTION

O man,
Ask me any question.
I shall answer
According to your sense of
perfection.

O earth,
Ask me any question.
I shall answer
According to your sublime
satisfaction.

O God,
Ask me any question.
I shall answer
According to my insignificant
realisation.

581. THEY ASSERT

Fear asserts
Its strength.

Doubt asserts
Its certainty.

Ignorance asserts
Its wisdom.

Death asserts
Its life.

I assert
My Lord Supreme.

582. NOT ENOUGH

Not enough to aim;
You have to strike.

Not enough to aspire;
You have to realise.

Not enough to start;
You have to reach.

Not enough to have faith in God;
You have to know that God
Has faith in you.

583. MANY THINGS

Many things I have received
For the asking.

Many things I have lost
For want of asking.

Many things I have said
Only to feed my ego.

Many things I have not said
Only to hide my ignorance.

Many things I have done
At the request of ignorance.

Many things I have not done
Even at the express request of God
Himself.

584. THEY WAIT

Time waits for nobody;
Truth waits for everybody.

Peace waits for earth;
Heaven waits for human love.

God waits for man's smile;
Man waits for God's Assurance.

585. ONLY TO BE

I touched his feet
Only to be kicked.

I struck his head
Only to be blessed.

I breathed his heart
Only to be ridiculed.

I braved his soul
Only to be embraced.

586. CHANGE! CHANGE!

Change! Change!
If not, you will suffer.

Change! Change!
You will prosper.

Brave, brave the old!
If not, you will die.

Brave, brave the new!
You will fly.

587. DON'T BE

O patient,
Don't be a rank fool!
Don't make the doctor
Your heir.

O client,
Don't be a rank fool!
Don't make the lawyer
Your heir.

O dreamer,
Don't be a rank fool!
Don't make the non-idealist
Your heir.

588. HE TOLD ME

He told me
The forgotten truth:
I pray to God.

He told me
The undiscovered truth:
God needs me.

He told me
The impossible secret:
God fasts in the morning
Because I cannot afford
To eat Light in the morning.

He told me
The open secret:
God starves in the evening
Because I have consumed
All His patience-food.

589. IS IT TRUE?

"A great talker
Is a great liar."
I asked God
If this statement is true.
God said, "No!
Son, every second I speak
To My countless children,
And I never tell a lie."

"A great saint
Can never be a liar."
I asked God
If this statement is true.
God said, "No!
Son, your great saint
Has convinced his mind
That he has surpassed
My creation, which is nothing
Other than Myself, in purity.
Can anybody surpass Me in
purity?
Son, what else is he
If not a liar?"

590. FOR GOD NO RETURN

Doubt came to him on horseback
And went away on foot.

Faith came to him on foot
And went away on horseback.

Hate came to him on foot
And went away on foot.

Love came to him on horseback
And went away on horseback.

Truth came to him dancing
And went away limping.

God came to him running
And exhausted all His Energy.
God is dead tired;
He needs a long rest.
Therefore
For God, no return.

591. HE GAINS WHO LOSES

He gains love
Who loses might-power.

He gains peace
Who loses doubt-power.

He gains bliss
Who loses calculation-power.

He gains divinity
Who loses animal-power.

592. A FRIEND TO EVERYBODY

My outer body, Earth,
Is a friend to everybody.

My inner body, Heaven,
Is a friend to everybody.

My divine faith, Confidence,
Is a friend to everybody.

My highest Self, God,
Is a friend to everybody.

593. THEY FORGET

The old forget
That they have an unpardonable
past.

The young do not know
That they have an
insurmountable future.

The old do not know
That God has decided to forgive
them,
Their sordid past.
Today, this very day.

The young forget
That God is eager to help them
Surmount the heights of their
future.
Today, this very day.

594. A NEW HEAVEN, A NEW EARTH

A new friend is not quite
dependable.
A new enemy is quite forgivable.

A new patient is a real
problem-maker.
A new doctor is an immediate
grave-digger.

A new client learns the art of
surrendering.
A new lawyer learns the art of
losing.

A new Heaven I shall create for
God on earth.
A new earth God will create for me
in Heaven.

595. GOD AND I

God is a good example.
Therefore,
He needs no sermon.

I am a bad example.
Therefore,
I carry long sermons with me.

God works.
He finds
That it is not necessary to speak.

I speak,
Ignoring the fact
That I have to work.

596. CONVERSATIONS

God said to me:
"Son, you deserve God-realisation today
And I am now granting it."

Satan immediately said to God:
"No, not today, God.
Tomorrow You may grant him realisation,
If You are so consumed with that desire.
Tomorrow will be the best time,
I tell You, God."

God said to me:
"Son, of late I have not been pleased with you.
Therefore, I want to delay your God-realisation."

Satan immediately said to God:
"God, I tell You once and for all
That delaying will not satisfy You.
Please cancel Your promise, God, for God's sake.
I am telling You that if he is not ready by this time,
In spite of Your infinite Compassion,
He will never be ready.
This is not only my unmistakable conviction,
But also my immutable realisation."

597. THE GUESTS

A gold possessor
Is a welcome guest.

A silver possessor
Is an acceptable guest.

A man with no gold
And no silver
Is an unwanted guest.

But
When I went to visit God,
He asked me,
"Son, do you have gold with you?"
Sorry. No, Father.

"I am so happy, son, that you do
Not have gold.
Son, do you have silver with you?"
Sorry. No, Father.

"Son, I am so happy that you do
Not have silver.
Son, what actually have you brought for Me?"
Father, unfortunately, nothing.

"Son, you do have something for Me.
You have brought Me
Your bold nothingness-pride.
Son, give Me your pride
And I give you My All."

598. MY ADVOCATES

Doubt says to me:
"I want to be your advocate.
When happiness tortures your heart,
I shall bravely defend your cause."

Faith says to me:
"I wish to be your advocate.
When wild miseries torture your mind,
I shall unreservedly defend your cause."

God says to me:
"I shall be your advocate.
When nothingness saddens your mind
And plenitude puzzles your heart,
I shall immediately defend your cause."

599. PRIVILEGED LIARS

Poets are privileged liars.
Without even seeing the truth,
They tell the world
That they have realised the truth.

Lovers are privileged liars.
After having realised the truth
In fullest measure,
They tell the world
That they are doubtful about the existence of truth.

Seekers are privileged liars.
God repeatedly tells them
That He has His Omniscience, His Omnipotence
For them, only for them.
They tell the world
That they desperately need
What God outwardly has
And
What God inwardly is.

600. THEY ARE KNOWN

By the servant's submissiveness,
The master is known.

By the lover's oneness,
The beloved is known.

By the wife's unhappiness,
The husband is known.

By the disciple's aspiration,
The Guru is known.

By man's perfection,
God is known.

601. THE CONNECTING LINK

Master, God has blessed me with
money;
You now bless me with
realisation.

Son, God has not only blessed you
with money,
But also with realisation –
The realisation of temptation and
frustration.
Your money is the connecting link
Between
God the temptation
And
God the frustration.

602. PROCESSIONS

Insecurity is a one-man
procession.
It comes back to the place where it
started.

Fear is a ten-man procession.
It comes back to the place where it
started.

Jealousy is a twenty-man
procession.
It comes back to the place where it
started.

Doubt is a hundred-man
procession.
It comes back to the place where it
started.

But
Love is a ten million-man
procession.
Once it reaches its destination,
Illumination,
It never returns.

603. I BECOME

I become
Two souls in one body
When I think of aspiration-light.

I become
One soul in two bodies
When I think of
manifestation-light.

I become
The God-Soul in the God-Body
When I think of Perfection-Light.

604. I FEAR

I fear his silence.
His silence-sea shall drown me.

I fear his voice.
His voice-tornado shall destroy
me.

I fear his smile.
His smile-tree shall not bear fruit.

I fear his love.
His love-train shall leave without
me.

605. I LOVE

I love his silence.
His silence is my heart's pole-star.

I love his voice.
His voice is my life's only nectar.

I love his smile.
His smile is my divinity's life.

I love his love.
His love is my Eternity's All.

606. MY DREAMS AND MY REALITIES

When I am compelled to live with
dreams,
I try hard to get rid of them,
Soon.

When I am compelled to live with
realities,
I try hard to get rid of them,
Soon.

Why? Why?
Because my dreams
Are nothing but false hopes.

Why? Why?
Because my realities
Are nothing but barren deserts.

607. THEY ARE GREAT

They are great
Not because
They love their God
  unconditionally.

They are great
Not because
They serve their God
  unconditionally.

They are great
Because they rightly claim
Their God as their very own.

They are great
Because their God knows
They are His Voice,
They are His Light.

608. LENGTHEN AND LESSEN

To lengthen your aspiration,
Lessen your meals.

To lengthen your experience,
Lessen your sleep.

To lengthen your perfection,
Lessen your doubts.

609. HE NEEDS

In the human world
He needs little of everything.

In the animal world
He needs less of everything.

In the mineral world
He needs least of everything.

In the aspiration world
He needs much of everything.

In the realisation world
He needs more of everything.

In the perfection world
He needs most of everything.

610. WHY DO I TEACH HIM?

Why do I teach him?
I teach him
Because
I want him to see God
Soon.

Why do I teach him?
I teach him
Because
I want him to claim God
Soon.

Why do I teach him?
I teach him
Because
God is sleeplessly for him.

611. I NEED

Inspiration
I need
To run my Race.

Aspiration
I need
To win my Race.

Realisation
I need
To feel God's Grace.

612. FRIENDS

A blind man
Has a friend:
Light.

A poor man
Has a friend:
God.

An aspiring man
Has two friends:
Joy and Conscience.

A God-realised man
Has two friends:
Heaven's Pride and earth's
Gratitude.

A rich man
Has no friend,
Not even his soul.

613. THE MIND

Don't force the mind.
If you force the mind
It will bite you.

Don't kick the mind.
If you kick the mind
It will strangle you.

Don't hate the mind.
If you hate the mind
It will confuse you.

Don't cherish the mind.
If you cherish the mind
It will delay you.

614. RESISTANCE AND ASSISTANCE

Resistance to falsehood,
Assistance to truth.

Resistance to hate,
Assistance to love.

Resistance to fear,
Assistance to courage.

Resistance to doubt,
Assistance to faith.

Resistance to ignorance,
Assistance to wisdom.

Resistance to death,
Assistance to Immortality.

615. WHATEVER

His mind says
Whatever it likes.

His vital does
Whatever it wants.

His heart becomes
Whatever it treasures.

His body fears
Whatever it desires.

His soul owns
Whatever it has.

616. WHAT HE IS

Peace has made him
What he is:
Beautiful.

Joy has made him
What he is:
Soulful.

Love has made him
What he is:
Dutiful.

Light has made him
What he is:
Fruitful.

617. I FORGET, I REMEMBER

I forget
All my sad failures.

I remember
All my great triumphs.

By forgetting
All my failures,
I empty my mind.

By remembering
All my triumphs,
I feed my plenitude.

618. FREEDOM

No, freedom is not
Realisation.

Yes, freedom is
Revelation.

No, freedom is not
Manifestation.

Yes, freedom is
Divine Compassion
And
Human Perfection.

619. GOD'S LIGHT AND SATAN'S NIGHT

He went to Heaven
To praise God's Light.

He went to hell
To praise Satan's night.

God's Light
Raised his life
In return.

Satan's night
Erased his heart
In return.

620. ONLY ONE THING

My body needs
Only one thing: motion.

My vital needs
Only one thing: caution.

My mind needs
Only one thing: illumination.

My heart needs
Only one thing: union.

My soul needs
Only one thing: perfection.

621. A CHANGED MAN

A changed man
Is a changed world.

A changed world
Is a changed God.

A changed God
Is a changed Dream.

A changed Dream
Is a changed Silence.

622. PROMISE

You are proud
That you are God's first promise.

He is proud
That he is God's last promise.

I am proud
That I am God's concealed
promise.

God is proud
That He is far above His Promise.

623. GIVE THEM A CHANCE

Give peace a chance.
It will do everything for you.

Give bliss a chance.
It will do everything for you.

Give the world a chance.
It will ask you to do
Everything for it.

Give me a chance.
I shall make you do
Everything for yourself.

624. A BRIGHT FUTURE

There is a bright future
For the man of faith.

There is a bright future
For the man of self-control.

There is a bright future
For the man of peace.

But
There is no need for a future
For the man of God.
His present is the complete
Fulfilment of Eternity.

625. WHAT IS IT?

Nonviolence, what is it?
His heart knows.

Violence, what is it?
His vital knows.

Nonexistence, what is it?
His ego shall know.

Existence, what is it?
His surrender shall know.

626. THE LIVES OF THE MULTITUDES

Concern can awaken
The lives of the multitudes.

Love can strengthen
The lives of the multitudes.

Peace can illumine
The lives of the multitudes.

Bliss can immortalise
The lives of the multitudes.

627. PURE AND SURE

You are pure;
Therefore, you are sure.

You are sure;
That does not mean
That you are pure.

In the heart of man's purity
God grows and glows.

In the vital of man's surety
His own destruction flows.

628. FAITH AND SIGHT

When I walk by faith,
I walk in the world
Of Light and Delight.

When I walk by sight,
I struggle in the world
Of night and fight.

My faith is of God the Dreamer.
My faith is for God the Fulfiller.

My sight cherishes the animal in
me.
My sight perpetuates the human
in me.

629. GOD, MANIFEST YOURSELF

Doubt, kill yourself.
Faith, build yourself.

Fear, change yourself.
Courage, know yourself.

Hate, examine yourself.
Love, reveal yourself.

Man, perfect yourself.
God, manifest Yourself.

630. WHO ARE CALLED? WHO ARE CHOSEN?

Who are called?
Who are chosen?

Those are called
Who need God.

Those are chosen
Whom God needs.

Those who need God today
Will be chosen tomorrow by God
Himself.

Those whom God needs today
Will be made Gods tomorrow by
God Himself.

O let my heart be called today!
O let my life be chosen tomorrow!

631. WHEN LOVE-POWER TALKS

When money-power talks,
Truth-power remains silent.

When mind-power talks,
Heart-power remains silent.

When doubt-power talks,
Love-power remains silent.

When truth-power talks,
God triumphantly smiles.

When heart-power talks,
God unreservedly smiles.

When love-power talks,
God unconditionally smiles.

632. ULTIMATELY EVERYTHING BECOMES BORING

Ultimately everything
Becomes boring.

Even great miracles
Become boring.

Even the tremendous powers of
the cosmic gods
Become boring.

Even God the Omniscient
Becomes boring.

Even God the Omnipotent
Becomes boring.

But, but, but
God the All-Love
Never becomes boring.
Never.

633. WHAT HE KNOWS

His physical world
Knows one thing:
How to sleep.

His vital world
Knows two things:
How to boast,
How to sigh.

His mental world
Knows three things:
How to doubt,
How to criticise,
How to fear.

His psychic world
Knows four things:
How to free divinely,
How to give unreservedly,
How to love unconditionally,
How to fulfil eternally.

634. THEY NEED HIM

Earth
Needs his assurance.

Heaven
Needs his assistance.

Man
Needs his smile.

God
Needs his eye.

You
Need his compassion
And
Perfection.

I
Need his meditation
And
Liberation.

635. A DREAM-POET

A dream-poet
Sows gold for others
And collects silver for himself.

A reality-poet
Sows lead for others
And collects diamonds for
himself.

A God-poet
Sows fulfilment-smiles for others
And collects futility-cries for
himself.

636. SATAN EMBRACES ME

When I accuse God,
Satan embraces me
With his glorification-power.

When I accuse Satan,
Satan embraces me
With his condemnation-power.

When I accuse ignorance,
Satan embraces me
With his confusion-power.

When I accuse myself,
Satan embraces me
With his destruction-power.

637. YOUR FUTURE IS LOST

He cannot be bribed.
He cannot be fooled.

He cannot be shaken.
He cannot be broken.

He cannot be ignored.
He cannot be misunderstood.

Bribe Him,
And your future is lost.
Fool Him,
And your future is lost.

Shake Him,
And your future is lost.
Break Him,
And your future is lost.

Ignore Him,
And your future is lost.
Misunderstand Him,
And your future is lost.

Where is your future?
In His Heart.

What is your future?
His Will.

638. MY PERMISSION AND AUTHORITY

I went to two spiritual Masters
And begged them to grant me
some peace.
I needed peace so desperately.

One Master said to me:
"Go deep within."
The other said to me:
"Pray to God."

I said to the first Master:
"Can't you go deep within
On my behalf?"

"Certainly I can,
But you have to give me
permission."

To the second one I said:
"Can't you pray on my behalf?"

"Certainly I can,
But you have to give me the
authority."

I gave them
My permission and authority.
Lo, I am now swimming
In a sea of peace.

639. I SEE

I see tears in his eyes.
They *look* so beautiful.

I see tears in his heart.
They *prove* so soulful.

I see tears in his soul.
They *are* so fruitful.

I see his eyes smiling.
I enjoy it.

I see his heart smiling.
I value it.

I see his soul smiling.
I treasure it.

640. HIS COMPASSION

His words
Entertain my vital.

His silence
Inspires my heart.

His smile
Energises my soul.

His sadness
Instructs my mind.

His compassion
Awakens my body.

641. THEY ADD

Peace adds
Years to his life.
Love adds
Life to his years.

Light adds
Perfection to his height.
Delight adds
Height to his perfection.

642. A POSITIVE THOUGHT

A positive thought
Is a task performed
And
A treasure-land acquired.

A positive thought
Is a choice Hour of God
And
A song of Perfection-Dawn.

643. I AM GREAT

I am great.
Therefore
I have recognised ignorance.

I am great.
Therefore
I have accepted ignorance.

I am great.
Therefore
I shall illumine ignorance.

I am great.
Therefore
At the Feet of God
I shall offer my illumined
ignorance.

644. MY MIND IS ENTIRELY MINE

My mind is entirely *mine*!
When I am displeased with it,
I simply starve it.
When I am pleased with it,
I devotedly feed it.

My mind is entirely *mine*!
I control it to please my Lord
Supreme.
I expand it to house the Infinite.

645. HIS LIFE IS A MIRACLE

His life is a miracle, itself.
He turns everything
Into a wave of delight.

Even the tiniest event
He transforms into
A song of ecstasy.

His generous hand
Is the love-manifestation
Of his pure diamond-heart.

646. THEY WORK FOR YOU

Conscience works for you
Only after you have worked for it.

Victory works for you
Only after you have worked for it.

Happiness works for you
Only after you have worked for it.

But
God works for you
Only after you have worked for
yourself.

647. TODAY AND TOMORROW

Today never begins,
Tomorrow never ends.

Today is a birthless story,
Tomorrow is an endless story.

Today if you do not
Discover yourself,
Tomorrow you will not be able
To recognise yourself.

648. PROMISE OF GOD, PROMISE OF MAN

A promise
Pronounced
Is valuable.

A promise
Fulfilled
Is invaluable.

The promise of God
For man
Is Now
And
Here.

The promise of man
For God
Is Never
And
Nowhere.

649. CAN AND MUST

With a child
You can be another child.

With a man
You needs must be a Superman.

With God
You can be another God.

With death
You needs must be Eternity's Life.

650. NO FAILURE

No failure, no failure.

Failure is the shadow
Of success.

No failure, no failure.

Failure is the changing body
Of success.

No failure, no failure.

Failure is the fast approaching
train
Of the greatest success.

651. NO SUCH THING

I took a closer look.
There is no such thing as
ignorance.
Ignorance is nothing
But my limited knowledge.

I took a closer look.
There is no such thing as defeat.
Defeat is nothing
But the inspirer
Of my increasing will.

I took a closer look.
There is no such thing as death.
Death is nothing
But my strengthening
And
Dreaming rest.

652. SELF-DEFEAT, SELF-CONTROL, SELF-REALISATION

Self-defeat is but
A human child of self-deceit.

Self-control is but
A divine man of self-will.

Self-realisation is but
An eternal representative
Of the Absolute Supreme.

653. TIME

I have some consideration
For my time.
Therefore, I am happy.

I have much consideration
For others' time.
Therefore, I am happier.

I have most consideration
For my Lord's Time.
Therefore, I am happiest.

I have no consideration
For ignorance-night.
Therefore, I live in Eternal Day.

654. WHY AM I SO UNHAPPY?

Why am I so unhappy?
I am unhappy
Because I am ungrateful to my
highest Self,
God.

Why am I so unhappy?
I am unhappy
Because I am not willing to teach
my lowest self,
Temptation,
How to swim in the Sea of
Illumination.

655. HE FORGETS

He forgets.
He forgets that anger
Is a passer-by.

He forgets.
He forgets that doubt
Is a passer-by.

He forgets.
He forgets that jealousy
Is a passer-by.

He forgets.
He forgets that bondage
Is a passer-by.

Alas, he touches their feet
And asks them to be
His bosom friends.

656. SIX CONFIDANTS

The body takes comfort
As its confidant.

The vital takes arrogance
As its confidant.

The mind takes pride
As its confidant.

The heart takes happiness
As its confidant.

The soul takes calmness
As its confidant.

God takes Oneness
As His confidant.

657. TO ERR IS HUMAN

To err is human:
You knew it yesterday.
Therefore,
God blessed you yesterday.

To err is human:
He knows it today.
Therefore,
God is blessing him today.

To err is human:
I shall know it tomorrow.
Therefore,
God will bless me tomorrow.

To love is divine:
You knew it yesterday.
Therefore,
God embraced you yesterday.

To love is divine:
He knows it today.
Therefore,
God is embracing him today.

To love is divine:
I shall know it tomorrow.
Therefore,
God will embrace me tomorrow.

658. THREE INCORRIGIBLES

Who asked you, O World,
To find fault with me
Constantly?

Who asked me
To make mistakes
Repeatedly?

Who asked God
Not to illumine us
Compassionately?

You, God and I:
Indeed,
Three incorrigibles.

659. SOMETHING QUITE EXTRAORDINARY

Nowadays I do
Something quite extraordinary.

I bless my head
And feel that I am blessing
The entire creation of God
Most compassionately.

I touch my feet
And feel that the entire world
Is adoring me
Cheerfully,
Devotedly
And
Unconditionally.

660. THANK YOU

The world knows
How to ask me
For favours.

God immediately
Tells me:
"Thank you."

The world's helplessness
Makes me feel
That I am supremely great.

God's loving gratitude
Makes me feel
That I am divinely good.

661. TWO SERIOUS DEFECTS

He has two serious defects:
Weakness and wickedness.

His heart is weakness;
His vital is wickedness.

His body says to his heart:
"I am your eternal slave;
I am at your command."

His mind says to his vital:
"I am your eternal friend.
I shall feed you,
I shall please you."

662. DON'T BE AFRAID

Don't be afraid of doubt.
Doubt is just temporary defeat.

Don't be afraid of fear.
Fear is just a weak force.

Don't be afraid of jealousy.
Jealousy is just a slow riser.

Don't be afraid of insecurity.
Just take a closer look;
There is absolutely nothing in it
to fear.

663. GOSSIP

Gossip, gossip, gossip!
What is it?
A wild jungle.

Gossip, gossip, gossip!
What is it?
A poisonous ocean.

Gossip, gossip, gossip!
What is it?
A deliberate reputation-killer.

Gossip, gossip, gossip!
What is it?
A shameless ignorance-grower.

664. WHY DID HE FAIL?

He failed to reach his Goal.
Why?
Because he did not know
That such a thing existed.

He failed to reach his Goal.
Why?
Because he never cared for it,
Even unconsciously.

He failed to reach his Goal.
Why?
Because he forgot
To stretch out his hand.

665. THREE THINGS GOD AND I TAKE FOR GRANTED

Three things I take for granted:
God's infinite Compassion,
Earth's ceaseless patience,
Man's sleepless surrender.

Three things God takes for
granted:
Earth's thoughtful life,
Man's helpless life,
My shameless life.

666. HE IS A CRITIC

He is a critic
Who knows absolutely nothing.

He is a critic
Who hates practically everything.

He is a critic
Who thinks that perfection
Is his sole monopoly.

He is a critic
Who thinks that he alone
Can be the Teacher of mankind.

667. O EARTH, O HEAVEN!

O earth!
For God's sake,
Do not throw your
  ignorance-weight around.
I want to proceed.

O Heaven!
For God's sake,
Do not throw your
  indifference-weight around.
I want to succeed.

668. THREE FRAGILE THINGS

Only three things
Are fragile
On earth:

Human love,
Human appreciation,
Human success.

Knowing this,
He handles them
With utmost care.

669. THREE BRIDGES

Not one, but three bridges
He burnt behind him.

He burnt the first bridge:
Lo, God stood before him.

He burnt the second bridge:
Lo, God blessed his devoted head.

He burnt the third and last
  bridge:
Lo, God embraced his surrendered
  heart.

670. THE DIVINE CHINA SHOP

Simplicity
Sincerity
Humility
Purity

He sells in his divine China Shop.
His prices are very low.

Alas,
Doubt, the cosmic bull,
Very often
Upsets everything,
Breaks everything,
Destroys everything.

671. TWO THINGS I KILL

I kill two things to survive:
My useless doubt
And
My hopeless fear.

God loves two things to survive:
His ceaseless Compassion
And
His sleepless Forgiveness.

672. TOUCHY SUBJECTS

After all,
These are all touchy subjects:

What God does
With my vital emotion.
What God does
With my mental depression.
What God does
With my psychic frustration.

673. HE IS A DREAMER

He is a dreamer.
His vital dreams of constant
success.

He is a dreamer.
His heart dreams of lasting
progress.

When success dawns on him
His soul sweetly smiles at him.

When progress touches his life
His soul proudly dances around
him.

674. THEY ALL EXPORT

My heart exports
Delight
To my mind.

My mind exports
Light
To my heart.

My vital exports
Determination
To my body.

My body exports
Enthusiasm
To my vital.

My God exports
Pride
To my soul.

My soul exports
Gratitude
To my God.

675. HIS MIND

His mind has squeezed
The enthusiasm of his vital
So hard
That there is no inspiration
Left in it.
Alas! Alas!

His mind has squeezed
The joy of his heart
So hard
That there is no aspiration
Left in it.
Alas! Alas!

676. THE GREATEST MAN

Is the strongest man
The greatest man in the world?
No!

Is the purest man
The greatest man in the world?
No!

Who then is the greatest man in
the world?
The greatest man is he
Who sleeplessly
Loves and claims God
As his very own.

677. BEFORE THE DAWN OF ACHIEVEMENT

Before the dawn
Of achievement,
Everything is fruitful.

Before the dawn
Of achievement,
Everything is invaluable.

Before the dawn
Of achievement,
Everything is indispensable.

After the achievement,
Everything is useless.

After the achievement,
Everything is common.

After the achievement,
Everything is unnecessary.

678. TWO DIFFERENT MOMENTS

The unguarded moment
Secretly
Dragged me to hell
And
Prevented my return.

The guarded moment
Openly
Carried me to Heaven
And
Offered me God's eternal Throne.

679. WHEN

When my desires
Were not fulfilled,
I thought my world-boat would sink.

When my aspiration
Was not fulfilled,
I thought my world-plane would crash.

When my realisation
Was not fulfilled,
I thought my world-goal would perish.

680. MY RIGHT HAND AND MY LEFT HAND

When my left hand
Wants to do something,
I deliberately do not inform
My right hand.

When my right hand
Wants to do something,
I immediately inform
My left hand.

Why? Why am I so unjust?

I am not unjust, I tell you,
I am not unjust!
I and my justice
Are eternal friends.

To you I offer my realisation:
My left hand just talks and talks;
My right hand devotedly and
constantly acts.

681. MY FIVE TEACHERS

My poetry teacher taught me
How to cry.

My philosophy teacher taught me
How to dream.

My religion teacher taught me
How to bind life.

My yoga teacher taught me
How to find Love.

My liberation teacher taught me
How to create Peace.

682. HE WILL REACH AND MANIFEST

He will reach the Goal,
Not because he knows
How to reach the Goal,
But because
He wants to reach the Goal.

He will manifest God,
Not because he knows
How to manifest God,
But because
God wants *him*
To manifest God.

683. QUIET, PLEASE!

Quiet, please!
I wish to listen to Heaven.

Quiet, please!
I wish to speak to earth.

Quiet, please!
I wish to worship God.

Quiet, please!
I wish to love humanity,

684. FOUR TIMES I PRAYED

I prayed to God four times.

First time I prayed
For my liberation.
He most compassionately granted my prayer.

Second time I prayed
For God's Revelation.
He most cheerfully granted my prayer.

Third time I prayed
For God's Manifestation.
He most proudly granted my prayer.

Fourth time I prayed
For man's consideration.
He most vehemently denied my prayer.

685. HE

He cried;
He was denied.

He smiled;
He was rejected.

He threatened;
He was ridiculed.

He failed;
He was acknowledged.

686. WHEN HE SAYS

When he says,
"I am sorry,"
He unconsciously cherishes
The idea of repeating
The same mistake.

When he says,
"I beg to be excused,"
He insincerely offers
Condemnation to his mistake.

When he says,
"From now on I am determined
To do only the right thing,"
His determination
Is immediately blessed
By Illumination.

687. HE TRIED

He tried.
Therefore,
God gave him
Another chance
To discover the Truth.

He tried.
Therefore,
God granted him
Another weapon
To fight against ignorance.

He tried.
Therefore,
God made him
Another God
To take part in His Cosmic Play.

688. WHO LEARNS?

Who learns?
He who knows;
He who knows something.

Who knows?
He who gives;
He who gives something.

Who gives?
He who is;
He who is something.

689. AS

As
Humanity's instrument,
I aspire.

As
Divinity's instrument,
I offer.

As
Immortality's instrument,
I inspire.

690. CONVERSATIONS HUMAN AND DIVINE

Human conversations
Are
Usually
The tireless recitals
Of the heart's insecurity,
The vital's restlessness,
The mind's uncertainty
And
The body's stupidity.

Divine conversations
Are
Always
The actual performances
Of the heart's love,
The vital's determination,
The mind's intensity
And
The body's willingness.

691. PROGRESS

He makes no progress.
Why?
Because he wants to change
The Face of Reality.

He makes constant progress.
Why?
Because he surrenders
To the Heart of Reality.

692. THEY ALL DISAPPEAR

Darkness disappears
When dawn appears.

Hate disappears
When love appears.

Ego disappears
When oneness appears.

Ignorance disappears
When perfection appears.

693. MASTER OR SLAVE

Time, are you my Master
Or
Are you my slave?

Seeker, I am your powerful Master
And
I am your devoted slave.

I am your Master
When you surrender to me.

I am your slave
When you utilise me.

694. THEY TALK

He talks.
He talks to others;
He does not listen.

He talks.
He talks to himself;
He does not listen.

The world talks.
The world talks to him;
He does not listen.

God talks.
God talks to him;
He does not listen.

Doubt talks.
Doubt talks to him;
He unconditionally listens.

695. HIS EXPECTATIONS

He expects others
To work for him.
Alas,
He sees that nothing is being done
And
Nothing will ever be done for him.

He expects his surrender
To work for him.
Lo,
Everything is already done
And
Will always be done for him.

696. HIS EGO AND HIS REALITY

His personality
Feeds his ego.

His individuality
Betrays his reality.

His integrity
Illumines his ego.

His universality
Immortalises his reality.

697. CAUTIOUS, CONSCIOUS AND CONSTANT

He is cautious.
Therefore,
Nobody can deceive him.

He is conscious.
Therefore,
God utilises him.

He is constant.
Therefore,
He fulfils God.

698. HIS CORRECTION AND HIS MANIFESTATION

He corrects
His countless shortcomings
By thinking of God's Perfection.

He manifests
God's Transcendental Perfection
By becoming the Soul of God's
Aspiration.

699. HIS THREE TEACHERS

He has three teachers:
Doubt, jealousy and fear.

Doubt has taught him
How to judge
Ruthlessly.

Jealousy has taught him
How to kill
Immediately.

Fear has taught him
How to die
Helplessly.

700. MY THREE WEAPONS

I shall use
My three ultimate weapons:
Love, Devotion and Surrender.

With my Love-weapon,
I shall cheerfully love
My Lord's human life.

With my Devotion-weapon,
I shall devotedly serve
My Lord's human life.

With my Surrender-weapon,
I shall unconditionally fulfil
My Lord's human life.

701. MORE IS NEEDED

Intention is good,
But
Something more is needed.
And what is that thing?
Action.

Action is good,
But
Something more is needed.
And what is that thing?
Realisation.

Realisation is good,
But
Something more is needed.
And what is that thing?
Perfection.

702. THREE SUPREME THINGS

Three supreme things
Have made him immortal:

His Aspiration,
His morning Aspiration.

His Vision,
His afternoon Vision.

His Liberation,
His evening Liberation.

703. TWO SIDES TO EVERY STORY

Indeed,
Two sides to every story!
But
Quite often
One side is of God-realisation
And
For God-manifestation,
The other side is of
ignorance-hunger
And
For ignorance-feast.

704. GOD IS STILL MY BOSS

Darkness, you want me
To help you.
Therefore
You have come to me.
Alas,
You have more freedom
Than I have;
I have no freedom at all.
God is still my boss.

Ignorance, you want me
To serve you.
Therefore
You have come to me.
Alas,
I tell you my only secret:
I have no freedom at all.
God is still my boss.

705. I NEED YOU

O deathless Beauty's Core,
I need you.
Oh, I need you.

O sleepless Divinity's Door,
I need you.
Oh, I need you.

O blue Infinity's Shore,
I need you.
Oh, I need you.

O red Eternity's Roar,
I need you.
Oh, I need you.

O green Immortality's Life,
I need you.
Oh, I need you.

706. A HUNDRED EMPTY CRIES

A hundred empty cries
His heart is.

A hundred barren smiles
His soul is.

A hundred useless duties
His life is.

A hundred deathless necessities
His will is.

707. DO NOT GIVE UP

O my clouded efforts,
Do not give up.

O my frustrated defeats,
Do not give up.

O my unrealised centuries,
Do not give up.

O my untransformed lives,
Do not give up.

708. I COMMAND AND I OBEY

I command
My will,
I obey
My thought.
Why?
Because my will
Is brave,
Because my thought
Is helpless.

I command
My heart,
I obey
My body.
Why?
Because my heart
Is pure,
Because my body
Is insecure.

709. THE PROUD SONS

The proud sons
Of Father Heaven:
Where are they?
They are dreaming.

The proud sons
Of Mother Earth:
Where are they?
They are striving.

The proud sons
Of Father Eternal:
Where are they?
They are illumining.

The proud sons
Of Mother Eternal:
Where are they?
They are fulfilling.

710. MY TASKS

I have only four tasks
To perform:
Smile, fly, dive and run.

I have only three tasks
To perform:
Smile, fly and dive.

I have only two tasks
To perform:
Smile and fly.

I have only one task
To perform:
Smile.

711. WHEN I PLAY

When I play
In the physical world
With sleep,
I lose.

When I play
In the vital world
With depression,
I lose.

When I play
In the mental world
With doubt,
I lose.

When I play
In the psychic world
With fear,
I lose.

712. SHE LISTENS

She listens to her sincerity.
Therefore,
She is great.

She listens to her purity.
Therefore,
She is good.

She listens to her duty.
Therefore,
She is divine.

She listens to her reality.
Therefore,
She is immortal.

713. THE HOUR CAME

The hour came.
I was not ready.

God descended,
Smiled
And
Departed.

The hour came again.
I was not ready.

God ascended,
Pushed
And
Barked.

The hour came not.
I was ready.

God slept.
I cried.
Ignorance sang.
Satan danced.

714. HIS MIND AND HIS HEART

His mind thinks
God-realisation
Is something
Necessary,
But to long
For it
Right now
Is too soon.

His heart feels
God-realisation
Is something
Indispensable,
But to cry
For it
Right now
Is too late.

715. IN THE ASSEMBLIES

In the assembly
Of the lower gods,
His love-presence
Was welcome.

In the assembly
Of the higher gods,
His devotion-presence
Was necessary.

In the palace
Of the absolute Supreme,
His surrender-presence
Was indispensable.

716. IN ME

God saw in me
A poet.
Therefore
I loved nature's beauty.

God sees in me
A real man.
Therefore
I fulfil life's duty.

God shall see in me
A divine lover.
Therefore
I shall become Truth's
Immortality.

717. I AM SMILING TODAY

Centuries of my totally
Forgotten hopes
Are reborn.
Therefore
I am smiling
Today.
My God is the witness;
My despair is the witness.

Centuries of my unconsciously
Sealed inner treasures
Are unsealed.
Therefore
I am dancing
Today.
My God is the witness;
My inner penury is the witness.

718. MY MIND AND MY HEART

My mind is my life's
Slowest train
Because
It carries black doubts,
Red jealousies,
Grey fears
In boundless measure,
Along with me.

Alas, God alone knows
If ever we shall reach our
destination.

My heart is my life's
Fastest train
Because
It carries none
But me alone.

Lo, I have reached my Goal.

719. TEARS

I like the tears
That flow from the depth
Of my helpless despair.

I love the tears
That flow from the depth
Of my dawning aspiration.

I adore the tears
That flow from the depth
Of my Liberation-sea.

720. HE SINGS

He sings and sings and sings
In the physical world.
He sings with his snoring nose.

He sings and sings and sings
In the vital world.
He sings with his biting tongue.

He sings and sings and sings
In the mental world.
He sings with his suspicious eyes.

He sings and sings and sings
In the psychic world.
He sings with his orphan heart.

721. I SAW, I FELT, I CLASPED

I saw the Face
Of the Suffering Christ.
I cried and cried.

I felt the Heart
Of the Forgiving Christ.
I smiled and smiled.

I clasped the Soul
Of the Illumining Christ.
I danced and danced.

722. O RAMA!

O Rama! O Rama!
Tell me,
Why
Were you so unkind
To Sita, your consort?
Why? Why?

"I wanted
To prove
To the world
At large
That my Sita's
Sacrifice-Light
Far surpassed
My morality's
Judgement-Might."

723. O KRISHNA!

O Krishna! O Krishna!
Tell me,
Why
At times
Were you so cruel
To Radha, your partner divine?

"I wanted
To show
Humanity
That my Radha's
Unconditional Love-Light
For me
Far surpassed
My Examination-Right."

724. O BUDDHA!

O Buddha! O Buddha!
Tell me,
Why
Were you so cruel
To Yashodhara, your beautiful
wife?
What made you
Escape
From her sleeping net?

"I wanted
To tell the world
That I was totally
Unfulfilled
In my human life.
I escaped from my wife's
Love-Prison
Because
Her larger self, the world,
Needed
My immediate service."

725. O RAMAKRISHNA!

O Ramakrishna! O Ramakrishna!
Tell me,
Why
On very rare occasions
Were you a little unkind
To Sarada Devi, your devoted
wife?
She wanted to accompany you
To various places.
What made you offer her
Reluctance and rejection?
Why? Why?
Why did you torture her?

"Stop! Stop!
For my Kali's sake, at least!
Public mockery
Is merciless.
I wanted
To avoid it
Always."

But it was you
Who instructed
Your disciples:
"Man or worm."

"I see, I see.
Now listen,
Once and for all.
My wisdom
Did not permit me
To help the puny ignorance
Of the tiny worm
Grow into elephant-ignorance.
Therefore, I avoided
Sarada's and my joint appearances
In the assembly
Of lightless society."

726. I KNOW WHAT YOU NEED

O perishing pleasures
Of man,
What you need
Is
The Wisdom-Sun.

O lasting joy
Of man,
What you need
Is
The Confidence-Sea.

O illumining Compassion
Of God,
What You need
Is
The Transformation-Man.

727. BECAUSE OF HIS FEAR

Because of his fear
His black ignorance became
 blacker,
In the physical world.

Because of his fear
His red fight became redder,
In the vital world.

Because of his fear
His heavy darkness became
 heavier,
In the mental world.

728. I LOVE

Strong is the day;
I love his arms.

Sweet is the night;
I love her heart.

Bright is the noon;
I love his eyes.

Soft is the evening;
I love her feet.

729. SILENCE, POWER AND LIGHT

Silence is Bliss,
And I have it
In boundless measure.

Power is Creation,
And I have it
In measureless measure.

Light is Perfection,
And I have it
In endless measure.

730. BE THOU

Be Thou
My hands,
That I can give.

Be Thou
My ears,
That I can receive.

Be Thou
My eyes,
That I can dream.

Be Thou
My heart,
That I can achieve.

731. THE SAMADHIS

What is *savikalpa* samadhi?
Savikalpa samadhi
Is
The experience
Of Purity-sea
And
Integrity-sky.

What is *nirvikalpa* samadhi?
Nirvikalpa samadhi
Is
The experience
Of loftiest
Self-transcendence.

What is *sahaja* samadhi?
Sahaja samadhi
Is
Reality's message simplified:
Ignorance lost
Forever
And
Immortality won.

In the Cosmic Game
You discover
That you eternally and supremely
are
What all along,
From time immemorial,
You have been
Helplessly and desperately
Aspiring to become.

732. WHEN

When
I look through
The eyes of life,
I feel cheerful.

When
I look through
The eyes of death,
I feel peaceful.

When
I look through
The eyes of earth,
I feel meaningful.

When
I look through
The eyes of Heaven,
I feel soulful.

Finally,
When
I look through
The Eyes of God,
I feel fruitful.

733. TOUCHES

God-Touch
Has given me
The wings of morn.

Man-touch
Has given me
The wings of eve.

Faith-touch
Has given me
The breath of life.

Doubt-touch
Has given me
The buffets of death.

734. WORRY

Worry! Worry!
Why do you worry?
Just pray in the morning,
Concentrate at noon,
Meditate in the evening,
Contemplate at night.
That's all!
Look, your worries are buried
In oblivion-hush.

Worry! Worry!
Why do you worry?
Turn around:
Look, God is looking at you.
Enter into your mind:
Look, God is devotedly thinking
of you.
Enter into your heart:
Look, God is all for you.
Enter into your soul:
Look, God has already done
Everything for you.

735. UNAFRAID

Unafraid
Of fear:
Therefore, cheerfully I feel.

Unafraid
Of doubt:
Therefore, effectively I think.

Unafraid
Of darkness:
Therefore, clearly I see.

Unafraid
Of death:
Therefore, bravely I live.

Unafraid
Of life:
Therefore, supremely I enjoy.

736. HE IS SURPRISED

He is surprised
That his ignorance
Is still alive.

He is surprised
That his vital life
Is still strong.

He is surprised
That his inner cry
Is still feeble.

He is surprised
That his God
Is still unfed.

He is surprised
That his God
Is still compassionate.

737. WHEN HE DIED

When he died,
Both earth and Heaven
Held condolence meetings.

Earth-Children said:
"Alas, we shall miss
Our sweet brother,
The real God-distributor
Whose heart cried to illumine us."

Heaven-Members said:
"Alas, he is coming back,
The real rascal, the shameless
God-seller on earth.
Let us protest his arrival
At the inner Palace
Of our Heaven."

738. HEAD OR HEART

The hour has struck.
You are obliged
To make your final choice:
Head or Heart.

If you choose the head,
Then get ready.
For you there is no transportation
To God's Palace.
I must warn you:
God's Palace is farther
Than the farthest point.

If you choose the heart,
Then rest assured
That God has already started
flying
On His divine Jet Plane
To reach you
And
Embrace you.

739. WAIT A WHILE

Wait a while.
Don't risk a big mistake;
Don't go back to your old life.

Wait a while.
Your heart is going to win;
Your mind is going to surrender.

Wait a while.
Your inner cry is the divine
 magnet;
It will draw and draw everything
 divine
Towards you,
Towards you.
Wait a while,
Wait a while.

Wait a while.
Your sad failure is ending;
Lo, God-Light is descending.

740. LET US BE FRIENDS AGAIN

O Faith, sweet Faith,
Let us be friends again.

O Assurance, clear Assurance,
Let us be friends again.

O Promise, Promise Divine,
Let us be friends again.

O Father, Father Supreme,
Let us be friends again.

741. SOMEWHERE AND SOMEONE

Somewhere
There is someone
To think of you.

Somewhere
There is someone
To love you.

Somewhere
There is someone
To please you.

Somewhere
There is someone
To claim you.

Somewhere
There is someone
To inherit you.

742. SIX LITTLE ONES

Two
Little ears
Hear the news
Of the whole world.

Two
Little eyes
See the beauty
Of the whole world.

One
Little heart
Houses the love
Of the whole world.

One
Little head
Understands the meaning
Of the whole world.

743. BLESS ME

A sky of frustration
I have.
A sea of turmoil
I am.
An island of peace
I need.

O world, present me not
With your garland of constant
frowns.
O Lord, bless me, bless me
With your sunny summits.

744. THE OLD ROAD AND THE NEW ROAD

At the end of the old road
He was warned by God:
"No entry!
One way only!
Go back, go back!"

At the beginning of the new road
He was inspired by God:
"Son, run,
Always run.
Prove your worth.
If not, the Goal Itself
Will come and touch you
And thus embarrass you."

745. WHEN I WAS A PROPHET

When I was a prophet
I made four
Proud prophecies:

I shall have to touch
The feet of man.
I shall have to treasure
The dust of his feet.
I shall have to destroy myself
To grant man a new life.
I shall have to transform him
Into tomorrow's God.

My prophecies are coming true.
At least,
So I think.

746. I AM FOLLOWING YOU.

O good intentions,
I am following you all
With good deeds.

O good deeds,
I am following you all
With a good life.

O good life,
I am following you
With God-Manifestation.

O God-Manifestation,
I am following you
With God-Perfection.

747. O GOD, TRY TO UNDERSTAND ME

O God,
Try to understand me
When I go away
From You.
I do not think less of You,
I do not assail You,
I do not wish to dethrone You.

Now
Let me tell You
Why I leave You.
I leave You
Because
I feel that Your
Other children
Also
Must be given a chance
To love You,
To please You,
To claim You.
You, only You.

748. WHEN THEY NEAR THEIR END

When December-life
Nears its end,
Christmas comes.

When Doubt-fight
Nears its end,
Faith blossoms.

When Fear-night
Nears its end,
Courage roars.

When ignorance-sea
Nears its end,
Perfection glows.

749. EACH DAY

Each day
Is
The birthday of either my fear
Or
My courage.

Each day
Is
The birthday of either my doubt
Or
My faith.

Each day
Is
The birthday of either my failure
Or
My victory.

Each day
Is
The birthday of either my vital Satan
Or
My psychic God.

750. ONE DAY

One day
Everybody will turn against him.
He knows it,
Yet he loves them.

One day
Everybody will hate him.
He knows it,
Yet he loves them.

One day
Everybody will leave him.
He knows it,
Yet he loves them.

One day
Everybody will try to end his life.
He knows it,
Yet he loves them.

One day
Everybody will destroy his breath.
He knows it,
Yet he loves them.
And after that
Everybody
Will love him dearly,
Adore him unreservedly
And
Claim him soulfully.
Alas, this is the common story
Of this uncommon world.

751. WHAT TO LOOK FOR

What to look for
In God –
A sweet smile.

What to look for
In man –
An iota of gratitude.

What to look for
In Heaven –
A flood of compassion.

What to look for
On earth –
An island of peace.

What to look for
In life –
A particle of satisfaction.

What to look for
In death –
A song of immortality.

752. SURPRISING NEWS

God has
Surprising news for him.
God will give him
Aspiration today
And
Realisation tomorrow,
Far beyond his expectation
And
Far beyond his imagination.

He has
Surprising news for God.
At last he is ready to offer
Ignorance, his best friend, to God.
He is even prepared to offer
His own self, the desire incarnate,
to God.

753. SIGH NO MORE

Father,
Sigh no more,
I shall be Yours.

Son,
Sigh no more,
I am yours.

Father,
I assure You,
I shall love You.

Son,
I assure you,
I love you.

Father,
I wish to replace You.

Son,
You have already replaced Me.
Don't you see that you
And your friend, Ignorance,
Have been ruling My Kingdom
For a long time?

754. MY SONGS

My desire-song
Began.
But I do not know
When I stopped it.

My aspiration-song
Began.
But I do not know
How it began
Or
How I am
Continuing it.

My realisation-song
Began.
Who began it? God.
Who continues it? God.
Who listens to it? God.
Who is enamoured of it? God.

755. TWO INSTRUMENTS OF DEATH

Two instruments of death:
Fear and doubt.
I employed them
For a long time
To serve me
And
Please me.

They served me
Day in and day out.
I was really and truly
Pleased with them
And
Proud of them.

Recently faith, an instrument of God,
Came to me
Looking for a job.
I immediately employed faith.

To my wide surprise,
Faith chased away
My previous workers.
Now faith alone
Does everything for me,
From morn to eve
And
From eve to morn.

756. THREE TIMES

Three times
I looked for a hiding place.
Alas, each time
I failed.

First time
I looked for a hiding place in God.
God did not allow me
To hide inside Him.

He said
I am too restless,
I would not stay inside Him
For good.

He said to me
That I have to
Hide inside Him either
Forever or never.

He knew that I would not
Be able to stay inside Him forever.
Therefore, He did not care
To fulfil my prayer.

Second time
I looked for a hiding place in man.
Alas, it all ended in vain.

Man said to me,
"I shall allow you to hide inside
 me
On one condition.
You have to offer me daily
A sea of gratitude
And
A sea of plenitude."

I immediately told man
That his demands were
 extravagant,
Impossible and unthinkable.
I left man with my transcendental
 disgust.

Third and last time
I looked for a hiding place
Inside Ignorance-sea.
Lo, I have done it.

And nothing need I
Offer my Ignorance-sea in return.
Here I shall hide,
I shall eternally hide.

757. HE AND FEAR, HE AND DOUBT

He and fear
Together began their adventure.
Their adventure ends
As it began.
It began with helplessness
And ends in helplessness.

He and doubt
Together began their adventure.
Their adventure ends
As it began.
It began with confusion
And ends in confusion.

758. TWO STRANGERS CAME

One stranger came.
I showed him my compassion,
I gave him my protection.
Soon I came to know
That this stranger was
My Father, God, in complete disguise.

Another stranger came.
I showed him my incapacity,
I gave him my ignorance.
Soon I came to know that
This stranger was
My brother, man, in complete disguise.

759. I LIVED

I lived in the cottage
Of Dreams
To see the Face of Reality.

I live in the house
Of Dreams
To shake hands with Reality.

I shall live in the Palace
Of Dreams
To become the Soul of Reality.

760. HOMESICK

My soul is homesick.
It wants to go back
To its Fulfilment-Home.

My heart is homesick.
It wants to go back
To its Oneness-Home.

My mind is homesick.
It wants to go back
To its Vastness-Home.

My vital is homesick.
It wants to go back
To its Dynamism-Home.

My body is homesick.
It wants to go back
To its Ignorance-Home.

761. STAND UP!

Stand up!
Lo, half the battle is over.
Quick march!
Lo, all the battle is over.

Smile bright!
Lo, half the battle is over.
Laugh wide!
Lo, all the battle is over.

Aspire today!
Lo, half the battle is over.
Surrender tomorrow!
Lo, all the battle is over.

762. SOME PEOPLE

Some people
Are grateful to God
Because they feel He is so kind,
Because He fulfils their desires.

Some people
Are grateful to God
Because they think He is so blind,
Because He sees not what they do.

Some people
Are grateful to God
Because God does not fulfil
Their earth-bound desires,
Because He feeds
Their Heaven-free aspiration,
Because He evolves in them,
Because He evolves through them,
Because He is all for them.

763. THE DAY HE MET GOD

The day he met God
For the first time,
God said to him:
"Don't look back.
Forgive your past.
And be careful.
Play no more with desire-wings;
They will carry you to their
source:
Ignorance.
Play and play,
Dance and dance
With aspiration-wings.
They will carry you to their
Source:
Infinity's Delight."

764. AT LAST

At last my heart-wound
Is healed.

At last my mind-spot
Is sealed.

No problem now weighs
On my soul.

Sleepless and fearless
I see my Goal.

765. HOW CAN HE BE HAPPY?

How can he be happy
When wild storms are ahead of
 him?
How can he be happy
When red dangers are beside him?
He can be happy,
He can be happy
Because his Master has said:
"Be happy."

How can he be happy
When he knows that he has failed
In his life-examination?
How can he be happy
When he knows that he has
 fought
Against the compassion-warriors
 of Light?
He can be happy,
He can be happy
Because his Master has said:
"Be happy."

766. HE IS SUFFERING

He is suffering
Because
He knows not
His Mother's voice.

He is suffering
Because
He knows not
His Father's choice.

He is suffering
Because
He knows not
Where God is.

He is suffering
Because
He knows not
Who he is.

767. WHEN I SAY

When I say
"I wish,"
I am worthless.

When I say
"I need,"
I am meaningful.

When I say
"I have,"
I am fruitful.

When I say
"I am,"
I am the perfection
Of human aspiration
And divine satisfaction.

768. I ESCAPED

I escaped
From the Embrace of God.

I escaped
From the sea of ignorance.

I escaped
From the perdition of despair.

I escaped
From the den of destruction.

I know not why.
I know not how.

And now I see,
No escape, no escape.
I am caught by my own
Choice of freedom.

769. WHY IS SHE CHOSEN, WHY IS HE CHOSEN?

Why is she chosen?
She is chosen
Because
She cries and cries
In her heart.

Why is he chosen?
He is chosen
Because
He dares and dares
In his mind.

Why is she chosen?
She is chosen
Because
She knows what surrender is.

Why is he chosen?
He is chosen
Because
He knows what service is.

770. PRAYER

Prayer
Is the youngest brother.
He cries and cries
To see Father's heights.

Meditation
Is the eldest brother.
He smiles and smiles
To house Father's heights.

Prayer
Tells me
Where to go.

Meditation
Tells me
How to live.

771. WHO IS MY GOD?

My God is the Farmer
Who cultivates my life.

My God is the Doctor
Who cures my mind.

My God is the Lover
Who loves my heart.

My God is the Warrior
Who strengthens my vital.

My God is the Forgiver
Who forgives my body.

My God is the Liberator
Who liberates my soul.

772. GOOD AND EVIL

Good and evil –
They belong to my mental world,
They belong to my external life,
They belong to my moral
summits.

Good and evil –
I see them not
Because
I am in God,
God is in me.
Father has made Son
Far beyond the domain
Of duality's dance.

773. REALISATION

Realisation,
What is it?
It is nothing other than illusion.
For whom?
For him who wants to govern the
world.

Realisation,
What is it?
It is nothing other than
satisfaction.
For whom?
For him who wants to serve the
world.

774. WHO ARE YOU?

Are you a sinner?
Then you are carrying
My ugly past.
Thank you ever so much.

Are you a saint?
Then you are carrying
My heavy present.
Thank you ever so much.

Are you a spiritual Master?
Then you will be carrying
My Dream-Boat
To
The Reality-Shore.
Thank you, thank you
A million times, my Master sweet.

775. DEVOTION

When you love
With devotion,
You are divinely great.

When you surrender
With devotion,
You are divinely good.

When you pray
With devotion,
You are supremely great.

When you meditate
With devotion,
You are supremely good.

Devotion, devotion, devotion.

776. ARE THERE ANY GURUS IN AMERICA?

Are there any Gurus
In America?
There are.

Where are they?
They are right
In front of your nose.

Who are they?
Those who tell you
That you are a future God.

777. CHOOSE YOUR MASTER

Silence your mind
To choose your Master.
Ask your heart
To choose your Master.
Ask your Master
To show the Light.
Ask your ignorance
To end the fight.

778. WHERE IS GOD?

Where is God?
In Heaven?
"Perhaps."

Where is God?
On earth?
"Perhaps."

Where is God?
Within you?
"Perhaps."

Where is God?
Without you?
"Perhaps."

Where is God?
He is inside the "Yes"
Of your heart.
He is inside the "No"
Of your mind.

779. SON AND FATHER

Son speaks to Father
On thought waves:
Father, I wish to pay a short visit
To You.
When can I come?

"Son, at any time."

Father, do You have
Any presents for me?

"Son, I have three presents for
you:
A beautiful present,
A precious present,
An immortal present."

Father, Father,
Please, please tell me
What they are.

"A beautiful boat,
A precious pilot,
An immortal Shore."

780. IF I AM TO LEAD

If I am to lead,
I must touch others' feet first.

If I am to guide,
I must wash others' feet first.

If I am to lead,
I must kiss others' feet first.

If I am to guide,
I must become others' feet first.
And then alone
Can I be the Leader
And Guide of Divinity's Smile
And Humanity's pride.

781. COMMON SENSE

Common sense is
Always
Needed
When you are of the world
And in the world.

Common sense is
At times
Needed
When you are transcending
The low heights of morality.

Common sense is
Never
Needed
When you are in
The Heart of Light.

782. DON'T TRY, BUT DO

Try and fail:

This was the discovery
I made
While I stayed
In the mind's hesitation-world.

Do and succeed:

This is the discovery
I have now made
Since I have been staying
In the heart's confidence-world.

783. WHO IS CALLED, WHO IS CHOSEN?

Who is called?
He alone is called
Who is ready
To fight,
Fight against teeming ignorance.

Who is chosen?
He alone is chosen
Who wants
To win,
Win the Victory supreme.

Who is called?
He alone is called
Who is prepared
To love,
Love the entire world.

Who is chosen?
He alone is chosen
Who embraces,
Embraces the life
Of universal oneness.

784. WHO IS NORMAL?

Who is normal?
Is it the one who is intelligent and
sincere?
No!
Who is normal?
Is it the one who is just and pure?
No!
Who is normal?
Is it the one who always hates and
curses the world?
No!
Who is normal?
Is it the one who sincerely likes
and enjoys the world?
No!
Who is normal?
Is it the one who is in God,
Who is for man?
Yes!

785. OUR CROWNS

You wear your crown
On your unbending head.

He wears his crown
In his aspiring heart.

I wear my crown
Far above my ignorance-life.

God wears His Crown
In the heart of earth-love.

786. THREE TALKERS

You speak.
You speak too much,
Too long,
And
Your contribution is fruitless.

He speaks.
He speaks too little,
Too briefly,
And
His contribution is senseless.

I speak.
My speech is all worthless,
All useless.

God does not speak.
He spontaneously acts,
He constantly becomes,
He eternally is.

787. MY FOUR INVENTOR-CHILDREN

My great progress
Invented my yesterday.

My strong will
Invented my today.

My sweet hope
Invented my tomorrow.

My clear faith
Invented my day after tomorrow.

788. KIND AND UNKIND

O Himalayan Fear,
Because
You are kind,
You have left me.

O Himalayan Doubt,
Because
You are kind,
You have left me.

O Himalayan Faith,
Because
You are unkind,
You are still away from me.

O Himalayan Aspiration,
Because
You are unkind,
You are still hiding inside me.

789. MY FOUR HOMES

I have four homes:
Earth, Heaven, Death and God.

Earth is my frustration-home,
Heaven is my imagination-home,
Death is my oblivion-home,
God is my expectation-home.

790. WHEN I WALK DOWN THE YEARS

When I walk down the years
With fear,
Death embraces me.

When I walk down the years
With courage,
Life embraces me.

When I walk down the years
With surrender divine,
Light blesses me.

When I walk down the years
With Perfection supreme,
God utilises me,
God treasures me,
God immortalises me.

791. A STUDENT FROM GOD'S SCHOOL

He studied at God's school;
God was his main teacher.
God taught him
Only one thing: necessity.

"Son, if you want to live
Only in the soul's world,
Then
I am your only necessity.
But if you want to live
In the body's world,
Then everything is your necessity,
Everybody is your necessity,
I am your necessity,
Countless, yet countless more.
Now that you have completed
your studies,
Time has come for you to go home
And begin your life."

792. A MERE WASTE OF TIME

He finds
It is a mere waste
Of time
For him to pray.
God never listens to his prayers.

He finds
It is a mere waste
Of time
For him to desire.
God never fulfils his desires.

He finds
It is a mere waste
Of time
For him to dethrone and replace
God.
God is not so weak as to be
dethroned and replaced.

793. A JOINT SMILE

What is aspiration?
Confidence.
What is confidence?
Success.
What is success?
Progress.
What is progress?
Manifestation.
What is manifestation?
A smile,
A joint smile
Of God and man.

794. A SECRET PLACE AND AN OPEN PLACE

There is a secret place
Where I see my God.
Do you want to know where?
Look, my secret God is deep inside
My Faith-safe.

There is an open place
Where I see my God.
Do you want to know where?
Look, my open God is just before
My Love-light.

795. FROM A DISTANCE

You are kind
From a far distance.

He is pure
From a farther distance.

I am brave
From the farthest distance.

Truth shines divine
From a near distance.

Love shines perfect
From a nearer distance.

Surrender shines supreme
From the nearest distance.

796. I DO NOT KNOW

I do not know
How to run
Alone.
Therefore my friend, Faith,
Accompanies me.

I do not know
How to dive
Alone.
Therefore my friend, Courage,
Accompanies me.

I do not know
How to fly
Alone.
Therefore my friend, Aspiration,
Accompanies me.

I do not know
How to go to God
Alone.
Therefore my friend, Surrender,
Accompanies me.

797. UNVEIL

Unveil the face of simplicity.
Lo, Beauty appears.

Unveil the face of sincerity.
Lo, Reality appears.

Unveil the face of purity.
Lo, Divinity appears.

Unveil the face of humility.
Lo, Immortality appears.

Unveil the face of integrity.
Lo, the Absolute Himself appears.

798. HOPE

Hope
Is kind.
Therefore
I mix with hope.

Hope
Is swift.
Therefore
I run with hope.

Hope
Is brave.
Therefore
I collect boundless strength
From hope.

Hope
Is sincere.
Therefore
I invite hope
To accompany me
To the Golden Shore.

799. THINKER, BELIEVER, SEEKER AND SERVER

O Thinker,
Indeed you are great.
But
I wish to mix with the believer,
Because he is good.

O Believer,
Indeed you are good.
But
I wish to offer my love to the seeker,
Because he is divine.

O Seeker,
Indeed you are divine.
But
I wish to live with the unconditional server,
Because he is perfect.

800. MY DAUGHTER HAS NO EQUAL

Doubt says to God
"God, why do You love
Your daughter, Faith, so much?"

"I love My daughter
Because she does not argue with Me,
Because she does not question Me,
Because she always believes in Me,
Because she does not ask Me to make her understand
What I say to her.
She accepts My Will devotedly,
She executes My Will unconditionally.
I tell you, Doubt,
Here on earth, in My vast creation
My daughter has no equal."

801. GOD GAVE ME

God gave me patience
To wait for Him.

God gave me sight
To look for Him.

God gave me love
To claim Him.

God gave me Bliss
To distribute Him.

802. SAVE ME, EXPOSE ME

Sweet Lord,
Save me from myself.
Save me from my inner conflicts.
Save me from my bold distrust.
Save me from my sleepless
  complaints.

Master Lord,
Expose me.
Expose my blind weaknesses.
Expose my giant failures.
Expose my shameless ingratitude.
Expose my undying ignorance.

803. I AM TIRED

Lord,
I am too tired to meditate,
Yet
I meditate.

Lord,
I am too tired to dedicate,
Yet
I dedicate.

Lord,
I am too tired to surrender,
Yet
I surrender.

Why? Why?
What makes me meditate?
What makes me dedicate?
What makes me surrender?
My unfulfilled promise
To You, my Beloved Supreme.

804. I KNOW YOU WILL THINK OF ME

Lord,
I am going to pray.
I know
You will bless me.

Lord,
I am going to meditate.
I know
You will teach me.

Lord,
I am going to serve.
I know
You will strengthen me.

Lord,
I am going to sleep.
I know
You will think of me.

805. TAKE ME INTO YOUR ROOM

Lord, if You are my Brother,
Come and visit my room *now*.
I shall thank You.

Lord, if You are my Sister,
Come and visit my room
immediately.
I shall thank You.

Lord, if You are my Father,
Come and visit my room at Your
sweet will.

Lord, if You are my Mother,
Come and take away everything
From my room.

Lord, if You are my Friend,
Come and take me,
Take me into Your Room.

806. ONLY FOUR TIMES

Lord, I wish to come
To Your Palace
Only four times.

Do tell me what You
Are going to give me
Each time.

"Son, first time you come
I shall give you
My Forgiveness-Sea.

"Son, second time you come
I shall give you
My Compassion-Sea.

"Son, third time you come
I shall give you
My Justice-Sea.

"Son, fourth time you come
I shall give you
My Thunder-Sea."

807. IS THERE ANYTHING FORBIDDEN?

Lord, is there anything forbidden
In Your creation?
"Yes, My son,
Forgiveness is forbidden."

Lord, how strange.
Why is forgiveness forbidden?
"Because forgiveness is not
valued."
Lord, why is it not valued?
"Because the world is ignorant."
Lord, why is the world ignorant?
"Because the world wanted
ignorance."
Lord, why did the world want
ignorance?
"Because Satan wanted to sell it
And was successful in selling it."
Lord, who is Satan?
"Ah, Satan!
Son, don't you know
Who Satan is?
He is just a clever fool,
An impossible friend of Mine."

808. FOUR MEMBERS IN MY FAMILY

I have four members
In my family:
Fear and doubt,
Love and surrender.

Fear takes me
From nothing-chasm
To
Nowhere-palace.

Doubt takes me
From nowhere-sea
To
Nothing-shore.

Love takes me
From fulfilment-land
To
Perfection-sky.

Surrender takes me
From God-vision-seed
To
God-Reality-Tree.

809. NOTHING FROM GOD

My prayer needs
Sincerity from me
And
Bounty from God.

My meditation needs
Silence from me
And
Infinity from God.

My perfection needs
Everything from me
And
Nothing from God.

810. NOT EVEN ONCE

Not even once
Did my inner life take me away
From the outer world.

My inner life is kindness
incarnate.
It made me aware of the needs
Of the outer world.

My inner life taught me
What to love in God –
Everything.

My inner life taught me
Whom to serve in the outer
world –
Everyone.

811. I AM PROUD

O my America,
I am proud of your dollar-power
In India,
But
Not in England.

O my England,
I am proud of your
politeness-power
In America,
But
Not in India.

O my India,
I am proud of your love-power
In England,
But
Not in America.

812. O MY CANADA

O my Canada,
You are very vast.
Can you not be very high, too?
Try, you can.

O my Canada,
Why do you always follow?
Can you not lead from now on?
Try, you can.

O my Canada,
You think the world does not
admire you.
Can you not demand the world's
admiration?
Try, you can.
You certainly can.

813. MY GOD IS WORRIED AND CONFUSED

O my China and Japan,
My God has not forgotten you.

O my Germany and Russia,
My God remembers you.

O my India and Pakistan,
My God is worried about you.

O my Ireland and Scotland,
My God is confused about you.

814. I THINK I LOVE YOU

God, I think I love You.
"Daughter, what is the proof?"

God, this is the proof:
You know, God,
I do not live with ignorance
Any more;
I do not play with doubt
Any more;
I do not cry with fear
Any more;
I do not eat with jealousy
Any more;
I do not dance with despair
Any more.

"Daughter, enough.
You love Me
And
I love you.
Be happy. Remain happy."

815. O MY FRIENDS

O my English friend,
Smile.
Let me see your smiling face.

O my Canadian friend,
Dare.
Let me see your daring heart.

O my Indian friend,
Think.
Let me see your thinking mind.

O my American friend,
Rest.
Let me see your resting life.

O my other friends,
I think of you, too.
I love you, too.
I adore you, too.

816. HE WHO REASONS

He who reasons
Is not a lover
Of happiness.

He who suspects
Is not a lover
Of love.

He who denies
Is not a lover
Of Truth.

He who delays
Is not a lover
Of Light.

817. HE WHO THINKS

The philosopher in me speaks:
He who thinks
Is a stupid seeker.
He who fears
Is a sick seeker.
He who hesitates
Is a lame seeker.
He who doubts
Is not a seeker
At all.

818. THREE OPINIONS

What others think of me
I perfectly know –
"I am useless."

What God thinks of me
I always know –
"I am perfect."

What I think of myself
I do not know,
I shall not know,
Never.
Alas! Alas!

819. IF YOU WANT ME

My Lord and God,
If You want me
To live in the physical world,
Then command me to sleep.

If You want me
To live in the vital world,
Then command me to dare.

If You want me
To live in the mental world,
Then command me to learn.

If You want me
To live in the psychic world,
Then command me to surrender.

820. LIFE CAN BRING

Life can bring failure.
Life can bring frustration.
Life can bring destruction.
Life can offer many sad stories.
But work can offer
Only one thing: perfection,
The life of perfection.

821. YOU DOUBT GOD

You doubt God,
Although you are afraid of
Doing this wrong thing.

You shun Light,
Yet you are afraid of
Staying alone in darkness.

You do not listen to God,
Although you are afraid of
Appearing a fool before the world.

822. LORD, MAKE ME WORTHY

Lord,
Make me worthy
Of serving the world.
Of course
In Your own way.

Lord,
Make me worthy
Of loving the world.
Of course
In Your own way.

Lord,
Make me worthy
Of pleasing the world.
Of course
In Your own way.

Lord, Lord, Lord,
Make me worthy
Of living my life.
Of course
In Your own way.

823. WHY IS SURRENDER SO GREAT?

Why is surrender so great?

Surrender is great
Because it accepts
Cheerfully
What it does not understand
Remotely.

Also,
It does not care to understand
Vaguely
Anything whatsoever.
It only believes and obeys,
And
Obeys and believes.

Surrender is by far the greatest
Because it alone is the glowing ascent
Of the aspiring heart
And
The proud descent
Of the Absolute.

824. HOROSCOPE

He believes in horoscopes,
But his horoscope is the Supreme.
There was a time
When his Supreme
Commanded him to play
With the planets,
Volleyball in the morning
And
Football in the afternoon
And
Table tennis in the evening.
But
Now his Supreme has commanded him
To be their Instructor,
Manager
And
Referee.

825. YOU ARE GOD, YOU ARE MAN

You are at once
God and man.
You play the role of God
In man
When you give,
And
You play the role of man
In God
When you receive.
Truth to tell,
Both the roles
Are of equal
Importance.

826. I KNOW

I know definitely
That a strong body
Is the Body of God.

I know unmistakably
That a daring vital
Is the Vital of God.

I know clearly
That a doubtless mind
Is the Mind of God.

I know devotedly
That a kind heart
Is the Heart of God.

I know soulfully
That a pure life
Is the Life of God.
I know, I know.

827. ATTACHMENT

O seeker,
You want to know
What attachment is.
Attachment is when
You love one
And do not love all.

Attachment is when
You feel
That God has appointed only you
To fulfil His Vision,
And not others.

Attachment is when
You think
Of the creation first
And
Not the Creator.

Attachment is when
The spirit of bargain
Haunts you
Powerfully
And
Triumphantly.

828. SON, GIVE ME SOME TIME

Sweet Lord,
Do tell me once and for all,
Why is Your world
In such a horrible state?
Don't You care for the world any
  more
Or
Have You lost all Your control
Or
Have You deliberately forgotten
  the world
Or
Do You want to create a new world
With nice people
With Your profound Wisdom,
With Your divine Light
And
With Your supreme Power?

"Son,
Give Me some time.
If I answer your questions
Immediately,
I am afraid I shall commit
Himalayan blunders."

829. TELL ME WHY

Tell me, Father,
Why has the young generation
Taken to drugs?

"Son, let Me start telling you why.
They want to belong,
They want to be loved,
They want to be understood.

"Son, now let Me tell you
Absolutely
The main reason:
They want to invent
Something
Which I, God,
Have not yet
Invented."

830. SAVE ME, SAVE ME

O Lord Supreme,
Save me, save me
From hell.
It is so dangerous.

O Lord Supreme,
Save me, save me
From Heaven.
He is so callous.

O Lord Supreme,
Save me, save me
From earth.
She is so treacherous.

O Lord Supreme,
Save me, save me
From myself.
I am so precarious.

O Lord, O Lord,
Give me, give me a smile.
It is so precious,
It is so precious.
It is my Saviour,
It is my All.

831. ARE YOU?

Are you insecure?
Then say that
My Courage is all yours.

Are you full of doubts?
Then say that
My Assurance is all yours.

Are you always jealous?
Then say that
My Compassion is all for you.

Now
Are you thinking of becoming
perfect?
If so,
My Transcendental Perfection
Is all yours.

832. PRAYER

The prayer of the timid is:
"Shelter, eternal shelter."

The prayer of the strong is:
"Joy, immediate joy."

The prayer of the joyous is:
"Gratitude, soulful gratitude."

The prayer of the grateful is:
"Surrender, unconditional
surrender."

833. HE IS THE GOD OF POWER

He is the God of Power.
Therefore
I admire Him.

He is the God of Peace.
Therefore
I like Him.

He is the God of Compassion.
Therefore
I love Him.

He is the God of Love.
Therefore
I need Him.

834. GOD IS KIND TO ME

God is kind to me.
Therefore
He has made me deaf.

God is kind to me.
Therefore
He has made me blind.

God is kind to me.
Therefore
He has made me lame.

He has made me deaf
So that I will not hear
World-gossip.

He has made me blind
So that I will not see
World-imperfection.

He has made me lame
So that I will not dare to kick
World-ignorance.

835. COMPASSION, JUSTICE AND TRUTH

Christ applied yesterday
The quintessence of yesterday's
Lofty Gospel: Compassion.

He applies today
The quintessence of today's
Sublime Gospel: Justice.

He shall apply tomorrow
The quintessence of tomorrow's
Outstanding Gospel: Truth.

836. WHEN HE TAKES

When he takes his life
Too seriously
He suffers in the prison
Of futility.

When he takes his life
Too lightly
He suffers in the prison
Of absurdity.

When he takes his life
Too humanly
He suffers in the prison
Of temptation.

When he takes his life
Too divinely
He suffers in the prison
Of isolation.

837. CAN YOU NOT GIVE ME?

God, can You not give me
Some better disciples?
"Son, I can.
But you do not deserve them."

God, can You not give us
A better Master?
"Children, I can.
But you do not need one."

God, my disciples are most
ungrateful.
"Is that so,
Is that so, My dear son?"

God, our Master is most
inconsiderate.
"Is that so,
Is that so, My sweet children?"

838. FATHER, FATHER, DO ME A FAVOUR, PLEASE

Father, Father, do me a favour,
please,
Will You?
"What kind of favour,
What kind of favour, son?"

This thoughtless world has made
me sick.
I want to die, I want to die.

"Son, your case is not serious at
all.
If and when your sickness
becomes serious, fatal or
incurable,
I shall let you know
And
Also grant your prayer."

839. INVENTION AND DISCOVERY

What God invented
My faith discovered.

What my faith invented
My heart discovered.

What my heart invented
My mind discovered.

God invented Bliss,
Faith invented confidence,
Heart invented love.

840. ANYBODY

Anybody can deceive you,
But
Deception is usually
The profession of a rogue.

Anybody can criticize you,
But
Criticism is usually
The profession of a fool.

Anybody can love you,
But
Love is usually
The profession of a seeker.

But nobody can perfect you,
Save and except God.

841. IT'S ME, FATHER

It's me, Father.
For God's sake,
Do not be so alarmed.

It's me, Father.
For God's sake,
Do not be so disturbed.

"Son, I am not alarmed,
I am not disturbed.
I am only happy and amazed
That you are knocking at My Door
At long last.
Come in, My son, come in."

842. TELL ME WHAT YOU ARE

Tell me what you are.
I will tell you something
Most special about yourself.

"I am a doctor."
Ah, you are a doctor!
That means you are
The restorer of life
And
Feeder of death.

Tell me what you are.
I will tell you something
Most special about yourself.

"I am a scientist."
Ah, you are a scientist!
That means you are
The searcher of life
And
Runner after death.

Tell me what you are.
I will tell you something
Most special about yourself.

"I am a seeker."
Ah, you are a seeker!
That means you are
The lover of Life
And
The destroyer of death.

843. ARE ALL YOUR DEBTS PAID?

"Son, are all your debts paid?"

Father, I was heavily indebted
To my friends
For their sublime
Appreciation and admiration.
But I have paid all my debts
With my ceaseless gratitude.

Father, I was deeply indebted
To Ignorance-Night
For her constant
Attacks and confusion.
But I have paid all my debts
With my adamantine certitude.

"Son, such being the case,
I welcome you
To share
My Infinitude."

844. LETHARGY, VIOLENCE, DOUBT AND FEAR

Lethargy is the pastime
Of my unprogressive body.

Violence is the pastime
Of my unsympathetic vital.

Doubt is the pastime
Of my unbelieving mind.

Fear is the pastime
Of my unillumined heart.

845. BEAUTY, PURITY, DUTY AND DIVINITY

Beauty glows
In the eyes of the man
Who sees.

Purity flows
In the heart of the man
Who feels.

Duty sings
In the arms of the man
Who works.

Divinity dances
In the soul of the man
Who loves.

846. DO YOU SPEND?

Do you spend more than you earn?
"Yes."
Why do you do that?
Who taught you to do that?
"My ignorance-friend."

Do you spend less than you earn?
"Yes."
Why do you do that?
Who taught you to do that?
"My wisdom-friend."

Do you spend all that you earn?
"Yes."
Why do you do that?
Who taught you to do that?
"My God-friend.
He said to me:
'You fool.
Why do you have to think of the future?
Let the future take care of itself.
What I want from you
Is to take care of today,
Only today.'"

847. HER LIFE

When she does not get
Her Father's usual smile,
Her life comes to a comma.

When she sees
Her Father's angry face,
Her life comes to a semi-colon.

When she sees
Her Father's indifference,
Her life comes to a full stop.

848. NOWADAYS

Father, Father,
Why are You
So unkind to me
Nowadays?
"Daughter, not true!"

Father, Father,
Why do You
Ignore me so much
Nowadays?
"Daughter, not true!"

Father, Father,
Why are You
Not taking my services
Nowadays?
"Daughter, not true!"

Father, Father,
Why don't You
Care for me at all
Nowadays?
"Not true, not true, not true,
My daughter sweet!"

849. INFINITY

When I say:
"Infinity is this,
Infinity is that,"
I decrease Infinity's Length
With my binding mind.

When I say:
"Infinity is something more,
Infinity is something deeper,"
I increase Infinity's Life
With my expanding heart.

850. I AM YOURS, ONLY YOURS

Father, Father,
You are ignoring me incredibly.
I think this is enough.
Please, please
Give me another chance.
This time I shall please You.

Father, Father,
Every day I see You
Deliberately kicking me
Farther and farther
Away from You.
I think this is enough,
More than enough.
Please, please,
Give me another chance.
This time I shall please You.

Father, Father,
Still I think
I am Yours,
Only Yours.

851. THE BUDDHA'S PROBLEMS

Lord Buddha,
Your first problem was suffering.
Your second problem was desire.
Your third problem was
 ignorance.
Your fourth problem was the
 absence of inner light.
All your problems
You solved
Eternally for yourself.
And now the Heart that
You left behind on earth
Is trying and crying,
Crying and trying
To solve the same
Giant problems.
As you succeeded,
So also your Heart
Will succeed,
Without fail.

852. LET US UNITE OUR POSSESSIONS

Lord, since I am unable
To give up my desiring mind,
Is there any way I can get
Some benefit from this mind?
"Real benefit? No!
Real progress? No!
Take your present mind as unreality.
Then you will get
Whatever you want."

What is real, Lord?
"Daughter, your aspiration is real."
What else is real?
"My Compassion is real."

Lord, what are we supposed
To do with my aspiration
And Your Compassion?
"Daughter, we are supposed
To unite our possessions
So that we can sing the song
Of perfect Perfection
Together."

853. DO NOT CONVERT AND DO NOT BE CONVERTED

Do not convert.
Let him go in his own way.

Do not be converted.
You must go in your own way.

Do not convert.
His resistance-night
Will devour your inner joy.

Do not be converted.
Your resistance-night
Will devour his inner joy.

God will ask His Freedom
To love you.

God will ask your freedom
To feed Him.

Do not convert,
Do not be converted.

854. I SILENCED

I silenced
My mind with light.

I silenced
My vital with might.

I silenced
My heart with purity.

I silenced
My body with duty.

855. I AM TIRED, I AM READY

I am tired.
I am ready
To surrender to Ignorance.
But my Lord goes on
Asserting my cause.

I am fatigued.
I am ready
To surrender to earth.
But my Lord goes on
Asserting my cause.

I am exhausted.
I am ready
To surrender to Heaven.
But my Lord goes on
Asserting my cause.

856. MODERN AND ANCIENT

Modern art
Is not as bad as you think.
Ancient art
Was not as good as you think.

The modern world
Is not as unaspiring as you feel.
The ancient world
Was not as aspiring as you feel.

Modern man
Is not as undivine as you believe.
Ancient man
Was not as divine as you believe.

Like ancient art,
Modern art embodies its beauty
In its own way.

Like the ancient world,
The modern world reveals its
divinity
In its own way.

Like ancient man,
Modern man manifests his
immortality
In his own way.

857. WE ARE ALL INSECURE

You are insecure
Because
You are not loved.

He is insecure
Because
He is criticised.

I am insecure
Because
I am misunderstood.

Poor God is insecure
Because
He is not yet
Completely
And
Universally
Manifested.

858. FIRST LOVE GOD

First love God,
Then accept Him
Or
Reject Him.

If you accept Him,
He will surrender Himself
To your constant needs.

If you reject Him,
He will wait for you.
He will wait for you
To give Him another chance.

859. OUT OF PITY AND OUT OF COMPASSION

When
Persistence deserted him,
Defeat-King came to him
Out of pity
And embraced him.
Otherwise, Defeat-King would have remained
Quiet, absolutely quiet.
Therefore it is not proper
To curse the poor well-intentioned
Defeat-King.

When
Devotion deserted him,
Ignorance-Queen came to him
Out of compassion
And garlanded him.
Otherwise, Ignorance-Queen would have remained
Silent, absolutely silent.
Therefore it is undivine
To accuse the poor well-intentioned
Ignorance-Queen.

860. FATHER, BE CAREFUL!

Father, be careful!
I am going to expose You
This time.
You have repeatedly told me
That in fifteen years' time
I would realise You
And also far surpass You.
I have been with You
For thirty long, slow years,
Yet for me God-realisation
Is a far cry,
Not to speak of surpassing You.
Father, You are an impossible liar,
And I am going to expose You
Definitely,
Mercilessly,
This time.

861. MY DAUGHTER

My daughter,
Of late I have been thinking and
thinking
Of granting you a Transcendental
Boon.
Just tell Me what you want.
"Father, my Eternally Beloved
Father,
This is the Boon I would like
To have from You:
Please never, never dream
Of making me equal to You.
You know, Father,
There is only one thing on earth
That gives me infinite joy,
And that is to sit at Your Feet
And drink the Nectar-Delight
Of Your Eyes.
Your Feet are my only
Heaven and Haven.
If I equal You
My life of devotion will die,
My life of surrender will die.
To me, my devotion is everything;
To me, my surrender is
everything.
Father, I pray and pray to You
To live above me at least a trillion
miles
Forever
So that I can, through eternity,
Live at Your Feet
And
Treasure Your Feet."

862. NOTHING AND EVERYTHING

Noise proves nothing,
Fame proves nothing,
Triumph proves nothing,
Supremacy proves nothing.
Love proves something,
Oneness proves everything.

863. SOMETHING

Say something,
Do something,
Become something
At least.

I have already said
That I have realised
God fully.

I have already done
The work of total transformation
In myself.

Don't you see
That I have become another God,
A real God?

864. A REAL DISGRACE

My soulful sincerity speaks:
I know nothing
Save and except
The history of ignorance.

I do nothing
Save and except
Wallow in the endless pleasures
Of ignorance-night.

I am nothing
Save and except
A real disgrace
To the aspiring world,
To my soul,
To my inner Pilot.

865. CHOSEN CHILDREN OF GOD

We are the chosen
Children of God.
We agree in everything.
Therefore,
We are harmonious.

We are the chosen
Children of God.
We believe in all religions.
Therefore,
We are unified.

We are the chosen
Children of God.
We feel the divinity in all.
Therefore,
We are precious.

866. ABILITY, NECESSITY AND REALITY

My only ability
Is that I have recognised
God's capacity.

My only necessity
Is that I see the Supreme Lord
Smiling at me.

My only reality
Is that my soul is of God
And
My heart is for God.

867. HIS PRESENCE AND HIS ABSENCE

His absence
Is the death of the feeble world.
His presence
Is the birth of the loving world.

His absence
Is the opportunity of the desiring world.
His presence
Is the reality of the aspiring world.

868. WE CAN AND WE CANNOT

We can
Imitate him.
Certainly we can,
Any time
We want.

But
We cannot
Resemble him.
Not even
An iota of him.
No, never!

We can imitate him
Because
His heart-smile is for us,
Only for us.
We cannot resemble him
Because
His soul-treasure is infinitely more
Than ours.

869. NOBODY IS WRONG

Nobody can be wrong
All the time.
Are we worse than
A dead clock?
No, never!
Even a dead clock
Is perfectly right
Twice a day.

Nobody can be right
All the time.
The cosmic gods are
Far better than us
And
Much higher than us.
Yet, I tell you,
They, too,
Make deplorable mistakes
Once in a while.

870. HE

His actions
Interpret God.

His silence
Represents God.

He has reached
The Highest.
He stands beside
The Highest.

And you know
Where he started from.
He started from
The lowest,
The very
Lowest.

871. AS GOD'S DAUGHTER

You were born
As God's daughter.

You are living
As God's daughter.

You shall teach the world
As God's daughter.

You can and you shall
Transform
The face of the whole world
As God's daughter.

872. WASTED LOVE

When
You talk about
Your wasted love,
You just increase
Your blind ignorance.

Love
Is never wasted.
Love
Can never be wasted,
For love is Infinity's Life.

873. I NEVER MET

I never met a human being
Whom
I did not like.

I never met a cosmic god
Whom
I did not love.

I never met a hostile force
Whom
I did not destroy.

I never met a grateful soul
Whom
I did not adore.

874. THEY BLOW OUT

A restless man
Blows out
The lamp of his vital.

A careless man
Blows out
The lamp of his mind.

A senseless man
Blows out
The lamp of his body.

A useless man
Blows out
The lamp of his heart.

875. EXPECTATION

Expectation
Knows not how to stop.

Expectation tells
His poor friend, Disappointment:
"Let us start again."

Expectation tells
His fortunate friend, Success:
"Let us continue."

The train of expectation
Never stops.

876. THE TWENTIETH CENTURY

Unknowable
Is twentieth-century art.

Unknown
Is twentieth-century love.

Knowable
Is twentieth-century imagination.

Known
Is twentieth-century frustration.

877. SHE

The equality of souls
She likes.

The liberty of hearts
She loves.

The divinity of human beings
She adores.

The immortality of Life
She is.

878. PLEASE COME BACK TOMORROW

Father, please
Come back tomorrow.
I shall give You
Everything You want:
Pure love,
Sweet devotion,
Unconditional surrender.

I am not ready today.

Daughter, please
Come back tomorrow.
I shall tell you
What you eternally are:
Aspiration-tree,
Realisation-flower,
Perfection-fruit.

You are not fit today.

879. IN LOVE WITH GOD

In Heaven her soul
Is in love
With God's Dream.

On earth her life
Is in love
With God's Beauty.

In her heart
She is in love
With God's Infinity.

In God's Heart
She is in love
With God's Reality.

880. I SAW HIM, I FELT HIM, I KNEW HIM

I saw Him
When He was building
Castles in the air.

I felt Him
When He was crying
For a piece of bread.

I knew Him
When I gave Him
An iota of authority.

881. THE WAYS OF CONVERSING WITH GOD

Blaming is Satan's way
Of conversing with God.

Doubting is man's way
Of conversing with God.

Begging is earth's way
Of conversing with God.

Dreaming is Heaven's way
Of conversing with God.

Dancing is the fairy's way
Of conversing with God.

Self-giving is God's Way
Of conversing with us all.

882. INCOMPLETE, COMPLETE AND PERFECT

A fighting vital
Is an incomplete animal.

A doubting mind
Is an incomplete animal.

A loving heart
Is a complete man.

An all-giving life
Is a perfect man.

883. WE BELIEVE

You believe in everything.
Therefore
You are lucky.

He believes in nothing.
Therefore
He is lonely.

I believe in God only.
Therefore
I am safe.

God believes in everything.
Therefore
He is great.

God loves everything.
Therefore
He is good.

884. I LISTEN

I listen
To the little voice within.
It is soulful and truthful.

I listen
To the loud voice without.
It is awful and hurtful.

I listen
To the loving Voice of God.
It is powerful and fruitful.

885. LOVE, DEVOTION AND SURRENDER

Love
Is the key of life.

Devotion
Is the safe of the heart.

Surrender
Is the treasure of the soul.

Love
Is the Smile divine of God.

Devotion
Is the Cry eternal of God.

Surrender
Is the Pride absolute of God.

886. WHAT YOU WANT, WHAT YOU NEED

What you want
Is an admirer.
What you need
Is an instructor.

What you want
Is a life-giver.
What you need
Is a life-liberator.

887. NEXT TO GOD

Next to God, of course,
I love you most,
O my unconditional surrender
To God's Will!

Next to my unconditional
surrender, of course,
I love you most,
O my God-discovery!

Next to my God-discovery, of
course,
I love you most,
O my aspiration-light!
With you I started my journey;
With you I shall eternally
continue.

888. HONEST AND DISHONEST

The body is drowsy,
But not dishonest.

The vital is clever,
But not dishonest.

The mind is wise,
But not always honest.

The heart is pure,
And always honest.

The soul is far beyond
Dishonesty's net
And
Honesty's heights.

889. MY FRIENDS

Striking Success
Befriends the hero in me.

Illumining Progress
Befriends the seeker in me.

Fulfilling Perfection
Befriends the traveller in me.

Glowing Immortality
Befriends the lover in me.

890. HE WAS AND HE IS

The world fell
Beneath his sway.
Autocrat supreme
He became.

Now homeless he roams,
Friendless he cries.
He has now become
The Beggar-Emperor.

891. JOY

Dogs get joy
By barking and biting.

Men get joy
By fighting and stabbing.

Earth gets joy
By struggling and suffering.

Heaven gets joy
By dreaming and smiling.

Seekers get joy
By loving and surrendering.

God gets joy
By illumining and fulfilling.

892. WHEN HE SPOKE THE TRUTH

He lived in a peculiar world.
When he spoke the truth
Nobody believed him,
For truth was not spoken
In that particular world.
Bewildered, everybody stood
against him.

And when he told lies
Nobody cared for him,
Nobody appreciated him,
Nobody loved him.
For he was not doing
Anything new
To add to their world.
Disgusted, everybody deserted
him.

893. THEY ARE ONE

Truth and God are one,
God and Love are one.

Love and life are one,
Life and cry are one.

Cry and height are one,
Height and progress are one.

Progress and delight are one,
Delight and perfection are one.

894. GREAT SINGERS

Swans sing
Before they leave the world.

Men sing
After they have left
Ignorance-sea.

Human doubt sings
Before the dawn of faith.

Human despair sings
After it has embraced
The life of Light.

895. HIS PASSPORT

He forgot
To feed his aspiration-flame.
Therefore,
His passport to Paradise
Was confiscated.

He has started now
To feed his aspiration-flame
Regularly and devotedly.
Therefore,
The Passport Officer Supreme
Has granted him
A new passport.
Also,
The Passport Officer,
On His own,
Has endorsed the names
Of all the higher worlds
For him to visit.

896. SHE LIVED AND DIED

She lived.
She lived with despair
And
Died with hope.

She lived.
She lived with fear
And
Died with courage.

She lived.
She lived with doubt
And
Died with faith.

She was sure to discover in death
Everything that life
Denied her.

897. O HOW FRUITFUL YOU ARE

Inspiration! Inspiration!
O how meaningful you are.

Aspiration! Aspiration!
O how powerful you are.

Realisation! Realisation!
O how soulful you are.

Perfection! Perfection!
O how fruitful you are.

898. THE DIFFERENCE

The difference
Between
Liking and loving
Is the difference
Between
The tiny drop and the mighty
ocean.

The difference
Between
Loving and surrendering
Is the difference
Between
A tiny hill and the Himalayas.

899. GOD DESCENDS

With the knowledge
Of the mind
Doubt enters.

With the wisdom
Of the heart
Faith appears.

With the might
Of surrender
Man ascends.

With the Light
Of Power supreme
God descends.

900. DO YOUR DUTY

Do your duty.
If you do your duty well,
God will be proud of you.

Do your duty.
If you succeed,
Heaven will garland you.

Do your duty.
If you fail,
The world will embrace you.

Do your duty.
Do your duty,
And thus
Awaken your divinity.

901. IN MY OWN WAY

Father, I think of You so much,
Do You ever think of me?
"Daughter, I do think of you.
But I think of you in My own
Way."

Father, I meditate on You so
much.
Do You ever meditate on me?
"Daughter, I do meditate on you.
But I meditate on you in My own
Way.

Father, I love You so much.
Do You love me?
"Daughter, I do love you.
But I love you in My own Way."

Father, what will happen
If You once please me in my own
way?
"Daughter, if I please you
In your own way,
Your little 'I' will be overfed and
fall sick
And die before it gets its own
Illumination,
And
Your divine Self will starve,
And remain unmanifested.
Further, this will engender
My immediate death."

902. TODAY'S MAN OF ACTION AND LIGHT

Today's man of Action
Was Yesterday's Dreamer.
Today's man of Action
Shall be Tomorrow's Path-finder.

Today's man of Light
Was Yesterday's Seeker.
Today's man of Light
Shall be Tomorrow's
earth-Transformer.

903. THE ESSENCE

Desire is the essence
Of a desiring man.
Doubt is the essence
Of a blinding man.
Fear is the essence
Of a bound man.
Aspiration is the essence
Of an aspiring man.
Bliss is the essence
Of a serving man.
Surrender is the essence
Of a God-man.

904. DIFFERENCE

Difference of ideas is good.
I say this
Because
Other things are bad.

Difference of convictions is better.
I say this
Because
Other things are worse.

Difference of realisations
Is by far the best.
I say this
Because
Other things are absolutely the worst.

905. FAILURE AND SUCCESS

Defeat
Is a bad failure.
Despair
Is a worse failure.
Not to try again
Is the worst failure.

Victory
Is a good success.
Progress
Is a better success.
Surrender
Is the best success.

906. YOUR PROMISE

Your promise to God
Is God's highest Pride.
Your promise to man
Is man's strongest anxiety.
Your promise to Heaven
Is Heaven's nectar-delight.
Your promise to earth
Is earth's frustration-night.

907. HE HATES HIMSELF

He hates himself
Because
He finds evil in everything.

He hates himself
Because
He finds everything evil.

He hates himself
Because
He desired to deceive God.

He hates himself
Because
He desired to deceive his life.

908. HER MASTER

The eyes of her Master
Serve faster than his hands.
The heart of her Master
Serves faster than his eyes.
The trance of her Master
Serves faster than his heart.

909. EXPERIENCE TELLS ME

Experience tells me
How foolish I was.
Experience tells me
How wise I can be.
Experience tells me
How silly all my mistakes were.
Experience tells me
How I can easily be perfect
Next time.

910. HE IS LOST

He is lost.
He has no choice,
He has no voice.
He has lost
What he had:
Poise, inner poise.
He has forgotten
What he knew:
Joy, inner joy.
He has smashed
What he built:
His Palace, his inner Palace.

911. EVOLUTION AND REVOLUTION

Some call it
Cosmic evolution.
Others call it
Life's transformation.
I call it
God's transcending Perfection.

Some call it
Bitter frustration.
Others call it
Wild destruction.
I call it
God's challenging Revolution.

912. THE PALACE OF FALSEHOOD, THE PALACE OF TRUTH

Pure overstatement
Lives in the Palace
Of Falsehood.
Gross understatement
Lives in the Palace
Of Falsehood.

Self-discovery
Lives in the Palace
Of Truth.
God-mastery
Lives in the Palace
Of Truth.

913. GOD DESCENDED, I ASCENDED

I unconsciously
Ascended from a monkey.
God consciously
Descended from the skies.

I unconsciously
Offered God
My only treasure:
Cry, heart's cry.
God consciously
Offered me
His transcendental Treasure:
Smile, Goal's Smile.

914. HER VITAL, MIND AND BODY

Her vital triumphed
Over her heart,
But failed
To conquer her heart.

Her mind confused
Her heart,
But failed
To weaken her heart.

Her body forgot to love
Her heart,
But failed
To ignore her heart.

915. CHECKED AND UNCHECKED

Checked, her vital strives.
Unchecked, her vital fights.
Checked, her mind obeys.
Unchecked, her mind doubts.
Checked, her heart offers.
Unchecked, her heart rests.
But checked or unchecked,
Her body sleeps.

916. EQUALITY

Poor Equality,
I really feel sorry for you.
In the morning
You are mercilessly
Avoided by others'
Clever responsibility.
At noon
You are compelled
To dance with others'
Insincerity and futility.
In the evening
Absurdity and impossibility
Come into your broken heart
Only to destroy
Your entire existence.

917. I BELIEVE IN ONENESS

I believe in oneness.
A child adds his achievements
To his parents' achievements.
Thus the three become one.
Here I hear the song of oneness,
Here I see the dance of oneness,
Here I feel the reality of oneness.
But for me to say
A child's achievements
Equal his father's achievements
Or
His mother's achievements
Is sheer stupidity.
You are on the top of the life-tree,
He is in the middle of the life-tree,
I am at the foot of the life-tree.
How can our achievements
Be equal?
But we are one,
Undoubtedly one,
Because we have established
Our inseparable oneness
With the life-tree.

918. HE CLAIMS

He who has stark audacity,
Claims the physical world.

He who has dynamic energy,
Claims the vital world.

He who has silver dreams,
Claims the mental world.

He who has divine love,
Claims the psychic world.

919. YOUR ENEMY, YOUR FRIEND

He is your friend
Because
He hides the truth about you.

He is your enemy
Because
He tells the truth about you.

My God is your friend
Because
He teaches you
Secretly and devotedly.

My God is your enemy
Because
He examines you
Carefully, strictly, impartially,
Openly and publicly.

920. NO LITTLE ENEMY

There is no little enemy.
A wee fear
Tortures our whole existence.
A tiny doubt
Devours our entire being.
A puny jealousy
Destroys our universal oneness.

921. NO LITTLE FRIEND

There is no little friend.
An iota of faith
Energises my entire being.

A small fraction of love
Elevates my whole existence
To Heaven.

An insignificant portion of
surrender
Makes me one,
Inseparably one,
With Infinity.

922. MACHINES AND MEN

Machines
Unconsciously aspire
To become men.

Men
Consciously aspire
To become machines.

In machines,
God declares
His lofty Pride.

In men,
God declares
His sad disappointment.

923. THE STORY OF A SAINT

Is he a saint?
Catch him,
Strike him,
Kill him,
Since he is not
Adding anything
To our world's
Practical and real life.

Ah, he is gone!
He is dead!
His silent gaze
We miss so deeply.
His pure life
We miss so badly.
His heart of compassion
We miss so sadly.
His soul of illumination
We miss so unmistakably.
Alas, he is gone!
No more our saint is with us.

924. A DAUGHTER'S CONFESSIONS

Father, I confess my insecurity.
Therefore will You not bless me?
"Daughter, I am not a priest.
Therefore I am not entitled
To accept your confession.
But I shall bless you
For something else."

Father, I confess my jealousy.
Therefore will You not bless me?
"Daughter, I am not a priest.
Therefore I am not entitled
To accept your confession.
But I shall bless you
For something else."

Father, what is that thing
That You will bless me for?
"Daughter, I shall bless you
Because
You are My own
Searching and struggling,
Aspiring and evolving Self."

925. FAILURE

He fails
Because
He never tries.
I fail
Because
I hesitate to try.
Faith never fails
Because
It always tries.
Love never fails
Because
It constantly does.

926. HELPLESSNESS AND DESTRUCTION

O self-confessed Failure,
Do you know your other name?
Your other name is
Deplorable helplessness.
O self-confessed Doubt,
Do you know your other name?
Your other name is
Deplorable destruction.

927. O DOUBTER

Doubter,
Flatter me not.
You
Are a thief in disguise.

Doubter,
Inspire me not.
You
Are a rogue in disguise.

Doubter,
Love me not.
You
Are a butcher in disguise.

928. I CALL HIM A FOOL

I call him a fool
Because
He knows not something
Today.
Ah, I am so lucky
That God did not call me
A fool
Yesterday,
Although I myself did not know
That very thing yesterday.
The main difference
Between
God and me is this:
God illumines His world
Through loving forgiveness.
I illumine my world
Through shameless cleverness.

929. THE SONG OF FORGIVENESS

He is weak.
Therefore
He cannot afford to forgive.
You are strong.
Therefore
You can afford to forgive.
I am unwise.
Therefore
I know not how to forgive.
God is wise.
Therefore
He is all Forgiveness.

930. HE AND SHE ARE NOT FREE

He is not free,
Although
He is the King.
She is not free,
Although
She is the Queen.
He is not free
Because
He enjoys living
In the world of mental confusion.
She is not free
Because
She enjoys living
In the world of vital depression.

931. I THOUGHT OF MY FUTURE

Three times
I thought of my future
Seriously.
First time when I thought
Of my future,
My Lord said to me:
"My daughter, do not ignore
My Compassion for you."
Second time when I thought
Of my future,
My Lord said to me:
"My daughter, do not
underestimate
My Concern for you."
Third time when I thought
Of my future,
My Lord said to me:
"My daughter, do not forget
My Love for you."

932. SINCERE AND DEVOTED

She is sincere,
Therefore
She aspires more
Than she normally can.

She is devoted.
Therefore
She loves more
Than she possibly can.

933. HE BELIEVES IN GOD

He believes in God
Even though his doubts
Constantly speak against God.

He believes in God
Even though his failures
Constantly speak against God.

He believes in God
Even though God's entire creation
Constantly misunderstands him.

934. MY SURRENDER, MY SERVICE, MY GRATITUDE

My unconditional surrender
Is the only wealth
That I offer to God.

My devoted service
Is the only wealth
That I offer to man.

My soulful gratitude
Is the only wealth
That I offer
To both God and man.

935. PUNISHMENT

Doubt is self-punishment,
Faith is self-enfoldment.
Fear is self-punishment,
Courage is self-refreshment.
Division is self-punishment,
Unity is self-enlightenment.
Hate is self-punishment,
Love is self-fulfilment.

936. FOLLOW AND COMMAND

You follow;
Let me command.
God is there to watch.

You command;
Let me follow.
God is there to watch.

You shall follow;
God will command.
I shall be there to watch.

I shall follow;
God will command.
You shall be there to watch.

This is the only way
To become the seeker,
The Master,
The Supreme.

937. LOOK AT THE FOLLY

Look at the folly of his heart!
His heart feels that all men are
Helpless.

Look at the folly of his mind!
His mind thinks that all men are
Senseless.

Look at the folly of his vital!
His vital declares that all men are
Useless.

Look at the folly of his body!
His body knows that all men are
Homeless.

938. TWO PLACES TO LIVE

An injured lover
Lives in hell.
A doubtful seeker
Lives in hell.
A misunderstood Master
Lives in hell.
A demanding beginner
Lives in hell.
An unsought adviser
Lives in hell.
Let you and me
Live in Heaven.
Where is Heaven?
Heaven is just
Beside hell.

939. THE WINNER AND THE LOSER

He is the great winner
Who wins.

He is the greater winner
Who is the cheerful loser.

He is the greatest winner
Who gives equal value
To victory and defeat.

He alone is the real loser
Who separates
Defeat from victory.

940. HEART AND SOUL, TRUTH AND PEACE

Heart offers its love,
It cannot be bought.

Soul offers its joy.
It cannot be caught.

Truth reveals itself.
It cannot be demanded.

Peace spreads itself.
It cannot be commanded.

941. A REASONING ANIMAL

He is.
He is a reasoning animal.
He is not.
He is not a reasonable animal.
He has.
He has the false capacity
To admire all.
He does not have.
He does not have the admirable
capacity
To aspire at all.

942. YOUR REAL TEACHER

He who inspires you
Is your real teacher.
He who loves you
Is your real teacher.
He who forces you
Is your real teacher.
He who perfects you
Is your real teacher.
He who treasures you
Is your real teacher.

943. WHO CAN CURE?

Defects of the heart
Love can cure.
Defects of the vital
Power can cure.
Defects of the body
Compassion can cure.
Defects of the mind
Nothing can cure,
None can cure,
Only God can cure.
And
He does it cheerfully,
He does it unconditionally.

944. IF I

If I
Do not change my doubting mind
Immediately,
Then there is a safe place
For me:
A grand mental asylum.

If I
Cannot change my doubting mind
Decisively,
Then there is a safer place
For me:
An enormous coffin.

If I
Cherish my doubting mind
Deliberately,
Then there is the safest place
For me:
A vast burial ground.

945. WHEN HE LIVES

When he lives
In his heart,
He descends
Into the nature
Of a lamb.

When he lives
In his mind,
He descends
Into the nature
Of a monkey.

When he lives
In his vital,
He descends
Into the nature
Of a wolf.

When he lives
In his body,
He descends
Into the nature
Of a snake.

946. MAN'S REPUTATION

A man
With a bad reputation
Is already
Half-hanged.

A man
With a good reputation
Is already
Halfway
To Heaven.

A man
With no reputation
Is already
Half-lost
To the world
And
To Heaven.

947. GOD'S CALL

What is God's Call?
God's Call is the beginning
Of a supernal Vision.
What is a Vision?
A Vision is something
That leads us
To an immortal Decision.
What is a Decision?
A Decision is today's Kite
Of Aspiration
And
Tomorrow's Sky
Of Realisation.

948. OBEDIENCE, INNER AND OUTER

Inner obedience, inner obedience:
What is it,
If not a divine opportunity?
Outer obedience, outer obedience:
What is it,
If not a glowing beauty?
My inner obedience
Carries me to my Lord Supreme
Sooner than at once.
My outer obedience
Brings me to my Lord Supreme
Slowly, steadily and unerringly.

949. ONE MAN AND ONE WOMAN CAN SAVE THE WORLD

One man can save the world.
Who is that man?
That man is the man of
Compassion.
One woman can save the world.
Who is that woman?
That woman is the woman of
Perfection.
Where does the man
Of Compassion live?
He lives in the Abode
Of God's Transcendental Pride.
Where does the woman
Of Perfection live?
She lives in the Abode
Of God's Eternal Gratitude.

950. FATHER AND DAUGHTER

Father, how can I
Make You always happy?
"Daughter,
Think of Me more.
Think of the world more.
Think of yourself more."
Father, please tell me how.
"Daughter,
Think from today
That I am your only Thinker.
Think from today
That the world is your only
thought.
Think from today
That you are of My Heart-Dream
And
You are for My Life-Reality."

951. O LORD SUPREME

O Lord Supreme,
Why do I follow You
So closely?

"Because you love Me
So deeply."

O Lord Supreme,
Why do I love You
So deeply?

"Because you see Me
So clearly."

O Lord Supreme,
Why am I allowed to see You
So clearly?

"Because My Heart of
Compassion-Sea
Is for you, My child,
Eternally."

952. WHO IS CALLED, WHO IS CHOSEN?

Lord,
Who is called?
Who is chosen?
Who is by far the best?

Daughter,
The divine seeker in you is called.
The immortal server in you is
chosen.
The supreme lover in you
Is by far the best.

953. HELP ME, MY LORD

My sweet Lord, help me
To put You *always* first
In my life.

"Daughter, granted."

My divine Lord, help me
To love You *always*
unconditionally
In my life.

"Daughter, granted."

My supreme Lord, help me
To manifest You universally
In my life.

"Granted, My eternal daughter,
granted."

954. WHAT CAN I OFFER?

What can I offer to my Lord?
My inner beauty?
Alas, I have no inner beauty.
My outer beauty?
Alas, I have no outer beauty.

What can I offer to my Lord?
My inner love?
Alas, my inner love is insufficient.
My outer love?
Alas, my outer love is imperfect.

What can I offer to my Lord?
My inner surrender?
Alas, what is it?
My outer surrender?
Alas, where is it?

955. THEY SHALL TEACH YOU

Father, teach me how to speak
To Heaven, earth and mankind,
please.

My daughter,
My Soul of Light shall teach you
How to speak to Heaven.
My Heart of Love shall teach you
How to speak to earth.
My Life of Sacrifice shall teach you
How to speak to mankind
Cheerfully,
Devotedly,
And
Proudly.

956. DAUGHTER AND SON, FOLLOW ME

"Daughter, follow Me, follow
Me."
What will You give me, Father,
If I follow You?
"I shall give you the Nectar
Of sleepless Surrender."
Father, then my life is at Your Feet.

"Son, follow Me, follow Me."
What will You give me, Father,
If I follow You?
"I shall give You the Power
Of ceaseless Love."
Father, then I am waiting
For Your express Command.

957. MAN'S DUTY

Man's duty to earth:
Sacrifice.
Man's duty to Heaven:
Surrender.
Man's duty to man:
Purity.
Man's duty to God:
Necessity.

958. ONE FACT FOR ALL, ONE WISDOM FOR ALL

One fact for all:
All human beings are weak.

One fact for all:
All human beings are uncertain.

One fact for all:
All human beings are imperfect.

One wisdom for all:
God is Light.

One wisdom for all:
God's Hour is for all.

One wisdom for all:
God is the slave of His own
Compassion.

959. FATHER'S HAPPINESS

Father, when are You happy?
"I do not know."

Father, when were You happy?
"I do not know."

Father, when will You be happy?
"I do not know."

Father, am I responsible
For Your unhappiness?
"Of course you are."

Father, can I alone
Make You happy?
"Of course you can."

960. FATHER'S GIFTS

Father, I need a beautiful gift from
You.
"Child, I have already given you
Not one, but three
Most beautiful gifts."

Father, three gifts?
What are they?
"I gave you faithful love.
I gave you soulful devotion.
I gave you fruitful surrender.
Use My love-gift
To see Me.
Use My devotion-gift
To feel Me.
Use My surrender-gift
To manifest Me."

961. HE GOES FOR HELP

When man criticises him,
He goes to his purity for help.

When God criticises him
He goes to his sincerity for help.

When earth criticises him,
He goes to his concern for help.

When Heaven criticises him,
He goes to his silence for help.

962. FROM GLORY TO GLORY

My awakened body
Is walking from glory to glory.

My transformed vital
Is marching from glory to glory.

My illumined mind
Is running from glory to glory.

My liberated heart
Is flying from glory to glory.

My fulfilled soul
Is dancing from glory to glory.

963. MY NEEDS

Lord, from You all I need is
Love.
Man, from you all I need is
Understanding.
Heaven, from you all I need is
Concern.
Earth, from you all I need is
Patience.
Life, from you all I need is
Perfection.
Death, from you all I need is
Surrender.

964. GO AND ASK

Father, what is sin?
"Daughter, I really do not know.
Go and ask a Christian mind."

Father, what is salvation?
"Daughter, I really do not know.
Go and ask a Christian soul."

Father, what is bondage?
"Daughter, I really do not know.
Go and ask a Hindu mind."

Father, what is liberation?
"Daughter, I really do not know.
Go and ask a Hindu soul."

965. WHEN I BELONG

When I belong to God,
Satisfaction loves me.

When I belong to man,
Frustration loves me.

When I belong to myself,
Death loves me.

When I belong to nobody,
Satan not only loves me,
But also uses me.

966. FATHER, TELL ME

Father, Father,
Please tell me
The best type of service.

"Daughter, daughter,
Serve devotedly and soulfully
But do not expect
Anything in return.
Indeed,
This is the best type of service.
Try! You can and you will
succeed."

Father, Father,
Please tell me
The best type of surrender.

"Daughter, daughter,
Surrender inwardly,
Surrender outwardly,
Surrender cheerfully,
Surrender constantly,
Surrender unconditionally.
Indeed,
This is the best type of surrender.
Try! You can and you will
succeed."

967. WHEN I MEDITATE

O Lord Supreme,
When I meditate
The animal in me hates me,
The human in me ridicules me,
The world around me ignores me.
What am I supposed to do?

Daughter, you are supposed
To do three things:
Transform the animal in you,
Illumine the human in you,
Manifest the Divine in you.

968. MY THREE FRIENDS

When I try
To deliver myself
From my strong and lengthy
Self-complacency,
My ignorance-friend
Calls me
An impossible fool;
My wisdom-friend
Calls me
A great wise soul;
My Perfection-Friend
Calls me
A true lover of Light,
A true builder of Truth,
A true fulfiller of God.

969. WHEN I PRAY, WHEN I MEDITATE

When I pray
God embraces
My crying heart,
My surrendering heart,
My dreaming heart.

When I meditate
God blesses my life,
God caresses my soul,
God reveals my Goal.

970. THEY CAN TELL YOU

Three members of your family
Can tell you
How much it will cost
To become a true follower,
A pure lover of the saviour Christ.

Your searching mind
Can tell you hesitantly.
Your loving heart
Can tell you immediately.
Your illumining soul
Can tell you easily
But
Quietly,
Quietly
But
Unmistakably,
Divinely
And
Supremely.

971. YOU FOOL!

You fool!
You feel that I do not love God.
I started loving God
From the day I felt His Heart.

You fool!
You think that I do not serve God.
I started serving God
From the day I saw His Feet.

You fool!
You think that I have not yet
Surrendered my life to God.
I tell you
Once and for all:
My surrender to God is constant,
My surrender to God is complete,
My surrender to God is perfect.

972. I IMITATE GOD

In how many things
Do I imitate God?

I imitate God
In self-giving.

I imitate God
In earth-transforming.

I imitate God
In Heaven-illumining.

I imitate God
In man-immortalising.

973. IT IS TOO LATE

Her body does not want
To realise God.

Her vital wants
To realise God,
But without working for it.

Her mind wants
To realise God,
But it thinks that there is no rush.

Her heart wants
To realise God,
But it feels that it is too late.

974. FATHER, I LIVE ONLY FOR YOU

Father, I live only for You.
Daughter, live only for the Supreme in Me.

Father, I live only for You.
Daughter, live only for the Divinity in Me.

Father, I live only for You.
Daughter, live only for the Dream in Me.

Father, I live only for You.
Daughter, live only for the Reality in Me.

975. LACK OF FAITH

Lack of faith
Is
Lack of sincerity.

Lack of sincerity
Is
Lack of courage.

Lack of courage
Is
Lack of necessity.

Lack of necessity
Is
Lack of divinity.

976. DO YOU EXPRESS YOUR BLESSING?

Father, do You express
Your Blessing through material
gifts?
"Yes, I do, My daughter.
I do it to convince
Your physical mind."

Father, do You express
Your Blessing through spiritual
gifts?
"Yes, I do, My daughter.
I do it to illumine your heart,
To perfect your life,
To fulfil your soul."

977. MY FAITH, MY SURRENDER

O my inner Faith,
You are so kind to me.
You have delivered me
From my enemies:
Fear, Doubt, Bondage and
Ignorance.

O my total Surrender,
You are so compassionate to me.
You have brought me
To my Friend, my Eternal Friend,
My only Friend: God.

978. MY NEED IS MY ONLY LIMIT

At last I have come to realise
That my need
Is my only limit.
Otherwise, by this time
I could easily have become
Another God.

"My child, you are a fool.
You are already
Another God."

If I am another God,
How is it that there is
Such a difference
Between You and me?

"The difference exists
Because
Unlike Me,
You have been all along
Neglecting all your duties
And
Avoiding all your
responsibilities."

979. GOD ADMIRES HER

Her heart is open to Delight.
Therefore,
God admires her.

Her mind is open to Light.
Therefore,
God admires her.

Her vital is open to Truth.
Therefore,
God admires her.

Her body is open to Compassion.
Therefore,
God admires her.

980. FATHER, GIVE ME THREE BOONS

Father, give me three boons.
"Daughter, granted!"
But Father, I have not yet
Told You what boons I need.
"Daughter, I do not have to know.
Your boons are granted."
Father, here is the first boon:
I want You to bury all my doubts.
"Granted!"
I want You to flower my faith.
"Granted!"
Father, I want to be only Yours.
"Granted!"

981. LORD, I PRAY TO YOU

Lord, I pray to You.
Help my unbelief.
It needs Your immediate
Attention.

Lord, I pray to You.
Help my belief.
It needs Your sweet Concern.

Lord, I pray to You.
Help my faith.
It needs Your blessingful Love.

982. MY LORD, FORGIVE ME

My Lord,
Forgive me.
Forgive my body.

My Lord,
Control me.
Control my vital.

My Lord,
Warn me.
Warn my mind.

My Lord,
Illumine me,
Illumine my heart.

My Lord,
Fulfil me,
Fulfil my soul.

983. MY LORD, THE TEACHER

My Lord taught me
How to pray and expect
Good answers.

My Lord teaches me
How to pray and welcome
Sad answers.

My Lord shall teach me
How to pray and expect
No answer.

984. TWO REPRESENTATIVES

I have two representatives:
Prayer and Meditation.
Prayer goes up and speaks
To God
On my behalf.
God comes down and speaks
To my representative,
Meditation.

985. BE PREPARED!

Fear, be prepared!
I am going to leave you soon.
"Oh no, Master,
I shall not be able to live
Without you."

Doubt, be prepared!
I am going to leave you soon.
"Oh no, Master,
How can I live without you?"

Jealousy, be prepared!
I am going to leave you soon.
"Oh no, Master,
For me to live without you
Is impossible."

986. FATHER, DO TEACH ME

Father, do teach me
How to think of You.
"Daughter, I shall ask
My Illumination
To teach you how to think of Me."

Father, do teach me
How to love You.
"Daughter, I shall ask
My Silence
To teach you how to love Me."

Father, do teach me
How to obey You.
"Daughter, I shall ask
My Gratitude
To teach you how to obey Me."

Father, do teach me
How to serve You.
"Daughter, I shall ask
My Delight
To teach you how to serve Me."

987. FOUR LIVES

In animal life
There is a strong binding Rope.

In human life
There is a sweet flowing Hope.

In divine life
There is a high glowing Scope.

In immortal Life
The Rope is destroyed,
The Hope is fed,
The Scope is fulfilled.

988. THE GOAL OF THE BEYOND

Obey and trust,
Trust and obey.
Indeed, this is the short way
To the Goal of the Beyond.

Love and serve,
Serve and love.
Indeed, this is the shorter way
To the Goal of the Beyond.

Surrender and offer,
Offer and surrender.
Indeed, this is the shortest way
To the Goal of the Beyond.

989. SMILE

God will love you more,
If you smile.
God will use you more,
If you smile.
God will please you more,
If you smile.

Smile!
Lo, God is running towards you.
Smile!
Lo, God is at your command.
Smile!
Lo, God is the slave of your life.

990. LOVE

Lord, what is animal love?
Animal love is a brute instinct.

Lord, what is human love?
Human love is a striking
disappointment.

Lord, what is divine Love?
Divine Love is an illumining
Experience.

Lord, what is Transcendental
Love?
Ah, that is My Love.
Transcendental Love
Is
My fulfilled Universal Oneness.

991. I AM TELLING THE TRUTH

Your arms are long, very long.
Therefore,
You can embrace the whole
universe.
Try, you will see that I am telling
The truth.

Your eyes have the farthest vision.
Therefore,
You can see the entire length of
the universe.
Try, you will see that I am telling
The truth.

Your heart is God's largest
creation.
Therefore,
You can easily house the vast
universe.
Try, you will see that I am telling
The truth.

992. I NEED YOU

I need You, Father God,
To give me Your Silence.

I need You, Mother God,
To give me Your Light.

I need You, Brother God,
To show me Your Love.

I need You, Sister God,
To show me Your Concern.

993. KNOCK AT THE RIGHT DOOR

Father, I am doomed.
Frustration has killed me.
Nothing on earth gives me joy.
Nothing on earth will ever give
me joy.
Nothing, nothing.

"Daughter,
Do you know why you are
So frustrated?
You are frustrated
Because
You expect and expect
From the world.
"You are frustrated
Because
You expect and expect
From yourself.
"I tell you, daughter,
You are knocking
At the wrong doors.
"Knock at the right door:
My Heart-Door.
Lo, frustration out,
Illumination in."

994. HE IS ABOVE SINCERITY, HE IS ABOVE TRUTH

Lord, Lord,
Do You think of me?
"My child, I do think of you."
Lord, Lord,
How often do You think of me?
"My child, I think of you
Always, always and always."
Lord, Lord,
Only You can say this
Because You are
Far beyond the domain
Of Sincerity
And
Far above the skies of Truth.
Lord, Lord,
Do You love me?
"My child, I do love you."
Lord, Lord,
How often do You love me?
"My child, I love you
Always, always and always."
Lord, Lord,
I should have known long before
That a life of sincerity
Does not mean anything to You.
"My child, go deep within
And discover My Palace of Truth."
Lord, Lord,
Anyway, I can't make
You sincere.
You be what You want to be.
Only give me the strength
To remain sincere
ALWAYS.
To me, Sincerity and Reality
Are inseparable.
Lord, Lord,
Please answer my last question.
Who am I, after all?
"You are My universal Child
Of My Eternal Life."

995. I AM PROUD OF YOU

Lord Jesus,
This is Mother Earth speaking:
I am proud of You
Because
You showed me
Your God-Power
For three years.

I am grateful to You
Because
You suffered for me
On the Cross
For three hours.

I am full of You
Because
You stayed with me
For thirty-three years.

996. THREE CLEVER WORLD-SOULS

Krishna, Krishna,
Hurry up, hurry up!
Come down, come down!
The world needs your immediate
presence.
"Chinmoy, I am in deep
meditation.
For God's sake, don't disturb me."
Thank you, Krishna,
You have always been clever.

Thakur, Thakur,
Look, look! Earth needs
Your presence desperately.
"Chinmoy, I am sorry.
My Mother has given me
Much work to do here, upstairs.
Therefore
I simply can't think
Of going downstairs.
I am sorry."
Thank you, Thakur.
You too have become clever.

Naren, Naren,
Once more Mother Earth
Needs your warrior-heart
To fight against ignorance-night.
"Chinmoy, tell Mother Earth
That I have been fighting
More powerfully, more devotedly,
For her from here,
Against her ignorance-night.
Therefore
She does not need my
Physical presence."
Thank you, Naren.
I shall be also as clever
As you are,
When my turn comes.

997. THE MOST DIFFICULT QUESTION

Lord, please do not mind.
Today I have
The most difficult question
For You.
If You do not know the answer,
Just tell me so.
I shall understand.
But if You know the answer,
Then You have to answer me
Most sincerely
And
With no reservations whatsoever.
Lord, here is my question:
Is the world really progressing
Or
Is the world really regressing?

"Daughter, you are most proud
Of your question
And
I am most proud
Of My answer.
Here is My answer:
The world is definitely
progressing
For those who know that
I am the Creator
And
I am the Owner
Of this world,
And
The world is unthinkably
regressing
For those who think that
They are the owners
And
They are the rulers
Of this world."

998. HIS HOLINESS

His Holiness, Pope Paul,
Is a great Seeker of Truth.
Therefore
He seeks first and then speaks.

His Holiness, Pope Paul,
Is a great Lover of Light.
Therefore
He loves first and then serves.

His Holiness, Pope Paul,
Is a great Leader of mankind.
Therefore
He leads first and then fulfils.

999. NEVER COMMIT SUICIDE

Lord, sweet Lord,
I do many things to please You.
Have I done anything in this life
To displease You?
"Daughter, you have."

Father, I have displeased You!
Tell me, how?
"Daughter, time and again
You have desired
To commit suicide."
Oh that, that's nothing.
Look, I am still with You
And for You on earth.

Father, is there any punishment
 involved
When one commits suicide?
"Daughter, punishment is a gross
 understatement.
My Eye of Justice
Does not forgive the coward
Who takes her life away.
My Heart of Compassion
Ignores her.
I welcome Satan
To devour her."

1000. TWO CREATORS

Father Supreme,
I wanted to offer You
One thousand
 Love-Devotion-Surrender
 blossoms
From my heart-garden.
I am so happy that my dream
Has seen the face of Reality.
Today.
Father Supreme,
Are You not proud of me?

"Son, My praising Capacity
Is very limited.
Therefore
Either I have to praise
My creation –
You, My son –
Or
I have to praise
Your creation –
Your poetry, your child.
Son, I hope you do not mind,
I am and I want to remain proud
Only of My own creation."

PART II

THE WINGS OF LIGHT

1. THANK YOU, MY LORD

Thank you, my Lord,
For unwinding my vital life.

Thank you, my Lord,
For unlocking my mental life.

Thank you, my Lord,
For illumining my psychic life.

Thank you, my Lord,
For fulfilling my dreaming life.

2. STAY FOREVER

Love, stay on earth
Forever,
Please.

Bliss, stay in Heaven
Forever,
Please.

Gratitude, stay in my heart
Forever,
Please.

Compassion, stay in God's Heart
Forever,
Please.

3. NOT BECAUSE

I think of God
Not because I love Him.

God thinks of me
Not because He loves me.

I think of God
Not because He thinks of me.

God thinks of me
Not because I think of Him.

I think of God
Because He alone knows how to
smile.

God thinks of me
Because I alone know how to cry.

4. IN A MINUTE

In a minute
I shall meditate on God.
Lo, God is crying with joy.

In a minute
I can realise God.
Lo, God is running with joy.

In a minute
I can and I shall manifest God.
Lo, God is flying with joy.

5. MY DAILY VISIT WITH GOD AND MAN

From my daily visit with God
I learn one thing:
Surrender unconditional.
First He asks me to do something,
And then He does it for me.

From my daily visit with man
I learn three things:
Depression constant,
Frustration immediate,
Destruction total.
First man gives me
His possessions,
And then he claims them again
As his own.

6. YOU

You had what you needed:
Inspiration.

You have what you need:
Aspiration.

You shall have what you will need:
Realisation.

Inspiration made you run
To the farthest end.

Aspiration makes you fly
To the highest height.

Realisation shall make you dive
Into the deepest depth.

7. I NEED

I need an idea
To prove my life.

I need an ideal
To prove my love.

I need a Goal
To prove my perfection.

8. TO BECOME

I must defeat
My black weaknesses
To become a real God.

I must surrender
My blue love
To become a real Man.

9. MY DECLARATION

Who was I?
God's starting point.

Who am I?
Vitamin L, Love.

What do I need?
I need the declaration
Of my dependence
On God's
Reality-Light.

10. LOOK

Look ahead;
There is no black sinner.

Look behind;
There is no white saint.

Look above;
There is no grey sky.

Look below;
There is no gold joy.

11. FOUR PIONEERS

Silence
Is the pioneer-sea of Love.

Love
Is the pioneer-moon of Bliss.

Bliss
Is the pioneer-sun of Perfection.

Perfection
Is the pioneer-will of Sound.

12. THREE QUESTIONS ANSWERED

The first question:
Where from?

The second question:
Where to?

The third and last question:
How?

The first answer:
From God-sky.

The second answer:
To God-sea.

The third and last answer:
Through self-transcendence.

13. DEEPLY, STRONGLY AND UNRESERVEDLY

Yesterday I enjoyed
Fear's company.
We loved each other
Deeply.

Today I am enjoying
Doubt's company.
We love each other
Strongly.

Tomorrow I shall enjoy
Will's company.
We shall love each other
Unreservedly.

14. WHERE ARE YOU?

O Voice of Silence,
Where are you?
I need your golden wings to fly.

O Voice of Sound,
Where are you not?
I want to live there.

O Voice of God,
Where are you?
For my sake, do not hide
Any more.

15. MY THREE FREEDOMS

Thought
Was my first freedom.

Will
Is my last freedom.

Surrender
Is my eternal Freedom.

16. MY TEACHERS

God the Teacher tells me:
"Be unconditional!"
I tell God: "I am trying."

Man the teacher tells me:
"Be impartial!"
I tell man: "I already am."

Dream the teacher tells me:
"Be jovial!"
I tell Dream: "I am practising."

Reality the teacher tells me:
"Be practical!"
I tell Reality: "Alas, will I,
Can I ever be practical?"

17. LOOK AHEAD!

Look ahead!
There is no thief
To steal away your aspiration.

Look ahead!
There is no tiger
To devour your prayer.

Look ahead!
There is no man
To doubt your realisation.

18. I HAVE TWO TEACHERS

In my private room
I talk to two teachers:
God and dog.

My God-Teacher
Teaches me how to
Lead and Guide.

My dog-teacher
Teaches me how to
Follow and Serve.

My teachers
Are supremely
Satisfied with me.

My God-teacher
Has made me the
Leader and Guide
Of the cosmic gods.

My dog-teacher
Has made me the
Follower and Server
Of mankind.

19. EVERY MAN IS A PILOT

Every man is a pilot.
Like a doubt-king
He pilots his barren life
To the land of nowhere;
Like a faith-king
He pilots his dream-boat
To the Shores of Infinity.

20. SOMEBODY TO CARE FOR ME

Somebody cared for me.
Who?
My success-noon cared for me.

Somebody cares for me.
Who?
My progress-beauty cares for me.

Somebody shall care for me.
Who?
My perfection-splendour shall
care for me.

21. WHEN

When fear was in charge
Of my life-river,
The Ocean of Infinity
Was a far cry.

When doubt was in charge
Of my life-day,
The Sun of Eternity
Was a far cry.

When insecurity was in charge
Of my life-breath,
The Sky of Immortality
Was a far cry.

22. THE CLICK OF A CAMERA

The click of a camera
Brings down Immortality
Into a fragile human frame.
The soul of the Infinite
And the body of the finite
Play hide-and-seek
In the Heart-Smile
Of the Absolute Supreme.

23. GOD SMILED AT ME TWICE

God smiled at me twice:
Once when I meditated
To renounce the world;
Once when I renounced
The world to meditate.

God blessed me twice:
Once when I cried and cried
For a mounting inner flame;
Once when I offered Him
My Realisation-sky.

24. IT WILL NOT LAST

It will not last.
Your feeble insecurity-knife
Will soon stab God's
   Compassion-Heart.

It will not last.
Your black doubt-spot
Will soon breathe God's
   Perfection-Love.

25. THE IDEAL DISCIPLE

The ideal disciple
Is he who believes
Before he sees.

The ideal disciple
Is he whose mind
Is inside his heart.

The ideal disciple
Is he whose heart
Lives for his soul.

The ideal disciple
Is he whose soul
Distributes his goal.

26. SEVEN CATEGORIES

A first class disciple
Is he who sees good
In all, and everywhere.

A second class disciple
Is he who sees good
As good and bad as bad.

A third class disciple
Is he who uses his binoculars
To enlarge the bad qualities
And diminish the good qualities
of others.

A fourth class disciple
Is he who enjoys his good qualities
And enjoys others' bad qualities.

A fifth class disciple
Is he who tries to devour
Others' good qualities
And ignores his own bad qualities.

A sixth class disciple
Is he who feels that
Even God Himself is not always
Perfect, let alone his Master.

A seventh class disciple
Is he who thinks that he has made
A serious mistake
In accepting the spiritual life.

27. HIS REALISATION

His lofty realisation runs:
A hero in the physical world
Is only a zero;
A hero in the vital world
Is less than a zero;
A hero in the psychic world
Is not only a divine hero
But also the supreme pride of
God.

28. ASK ME THE RIGHT QUESTION

Ask me the right question.
"Who is God?"
God is your integral Self.

Ask me the right question.
"Where is God?"
God is inside the meanness of
your mind
And the vastness of your heart.

Ask me the right question.
"How is God?"
His Mind thinks He is sick,
His Heart feels He is weak,
His Soul announces that He needs
rest.
His Goal predicts that He will
enter
Into a new Cosmic Game.

29. GIVE THE GIVER

Give the Giver your smile.
He will increase His love-flames
And offer them to you.

Give the Giver your gratitude.
He will increase the Light of His
Power-tower
And offer it to you.

Give the Giver your snow-white
love.
He will empty Himself
And make Himself your
surrender-slave.

30. UNITY AND MULTIPLICITY

Unity is good.
Unity with multiplicity is better.
Unity in multiplicity is by far the
best.

Who owns unity?
The climbing heart.

What is unity with multiplicity?
The vision of the soul
In the manifestation of life.

Where is unity in multiplicity?
In the Silence-seeds,
Time-flowers
And
Sound-fruits of God.

31. THE RED LIGHT AND THE GREEN LIGHT

I have two intimate friends:
The red light
And
The green light.

The red light warns me
And cautions me
And finally commands,
"Stop!"

The green light inspires me
And encourages me
And finally whispers,
"Start!"

My red friend
Teaches me patience.
My green friend
Teaches me dynamism.

My red friend tells me
My life is precious.
My green friend tells me
My goal is precious.

My red friend
Perfects my will.
My green friend
Fulfils my dream.

32. REJECTION-ACCEPTANCE-EXPECTATION

I reject my hopeless fate,
I reject it totally.

I accept the world's helpless fate,
I accept it unreservedly.

I expect God's deathless Fate,
I expect it devotedly.

33. MY FAMILY MEMBERS ARE AT WAR

My faith and my fear
Are at war.

My faith and my doubt
Are at war.

My faith and my insecurity
Are at war.

What is fear?
Self-torture.

What is doubt?
Self-mortification.

What is insecurity?
Self-annihilation.

34. GOD SMILED AND CRIED

When he was consorting
With self-love,
God smiled.

When he was consorting
With self-pride,
God smiled.

When he was consorting
With self-pity,
God smiled.

But

When he was consorting
With self-transcendence,
God cried, soulfully cried.

35. A GREAT FOG

There is a great fog
Between
Human love and Pride divine.

There is a great fog
Between
Human desire and Aspiration
divine.

But

There is no fog,
No, none at all,
Between
Human surrender and Perfection
divine.

36. OUR EARTHLY WANTS AND OUR HEAVENLY NEEDS

Our earthly wants never shrink,
never.
They enormously swell
And endlessly multiply.

Our Heavenly needs shrink
And shrink
And shrink.
They become smaller than a tiny
ant,
Vaster than the vastest ocean –
To fulfil God's Will.

37. FEAR-DOUBT-INSECURITY-UNCERTAINTY

Dark fear invades my body.
Wild doubt fills my mind.

Feeble insecurity empties my
heart.
Eyeless uncertainty veils my soul.

Yet my life-river cheerfully
Wants to flow
Into the stream of the
Will-Supreme.

38. FAITH, CONFIDENCE AND ASSURANCE

Faith, sweet Faith!
Why have you forgotten me?

Confidence, bold Confidence!
Why have you denied me?

Assurance, sure Assurance!
Why have you betrayed me?

Faith, your quick forgetfulness
Tortures my heart.

Confidence, your shameless denial
Pierces my mind.

Assurance, your unpardonable
betrayal
Veils my soul.

39. SINCE NO ESCAPE

Hard I tried to escape from You
But I sadly failed.
Therefore I accepted You.
Since I accepted You
I must fulfil Your ageless Will.
Your Will alone
Shall free my mind
From the cluttered and devouring
cave
Of my wild destruction-night.

40. OUR MARATHON TALK

With my mortal comrades
I make appointments
And then we barter
Our thought-waves.
But with God, my Lord Supreme,
I make no prior appointments.
Sooner than at once
I enter into His Heart-Room
And enjoy our marathon talk.

41. GOD AND I ARE ENRICHED

I am enriched
By the laws
Of my ego-night.

God is enriched
By the loss
Of His Justice-might.

42. I DO NOT

I do not rebel against God.
I do not quarrel with God.
I do not even question God.

Why? Why? Why?
Because I know:
He who rebels remains an
  unfulfilled soul,
He who quarrels remains an
  unillumined soul,
He who questions remains an
  unsatisfied soul.

43. THEY TELL ME AND I TELL THEM

They tell me:
"Let your deeds prove."

I tell them that my deeds
Have already proved
That I cannot exist without God
Even for a fleeting second.

I tell them that my deeds
Have already proved
That the world does not need
My wise advice.

I tell them that my deeds
Have already proved
That God's Compassion-Sun
Depends not
On my aspiration-candle.

44. HE PLAYED

He played with power.
Alas, no beauty therein.

He played with speed.
Alas, no beauty therein.

He played with compassion.
Alas, no beauty therein.

He played at last
With the self-giving love.
Lo!
Beauty within,
Beauty without,
Beauty below,
Beauty above.

45. PERSIST-RESIST-SMILE-CRY

Persist,
You will succeed.
Resist,
You will succeed.
Smile,
You will succeed.
Cry,
Lo, you have already succeeded:
You have perfected your love-life,
You have manifested God's
Reality-Dream.

46. WHAT CAN GOD DO? WHAT CAN YOU DO?

What can God do?
Just give Him a chance.
He can and will make
You
Another God.

What can you do?
Ah, you have already done it.
You have made God
Your perfect slave,
Perhaps unintentionally.

47. THEY KNOW

His body knows
What quick deterioration means.

His vital knows
What sad depression means.

His mind knows
What wild frustration means.

His heart knows
What true destruction means.

And he himself knows
What death-invitation means.

48. CLAIM

Claim the darkness-shack.
Once you get it,
Ignorance will immediately
Share it with you.

Claim the Illumination-Palace.
Just claim it, that's all.
You do not have to work for it;
God Himself will gladly
Offer it to you.

49. HAPPINESS GUARANTEED!

Happiness guaranteed!
Just think of God first,
Offer your heart last
And see what happens.

Happiness guaranteed!
Just hear devotedly first,
Speak quietly last,
Stay in the middle
And see what happens
Unreservedly and
unconditionally.

50. A SLOW WALKER AND A SILENT TALKER

God I am a slow walker.
Will you wait for me
At Your Palace?

"Son, I am a silent talker.
Will you listen to Me
In the love-room of your heart?"

God, I want to live in Your Palace.
"Son, I wish to stay in your heart."

51. MY DESIRE, ASPIRATION AND REALISATION

My desire says
Although God is good
I do not need Him
Right now.

My aspiration says
Since God is good
I wish to see Him
As soon as possible.

My realisation says
Since God is good
I shall always remain
With Him.

52. DEATH DOES NOT SHORTEN

Death does not shorten,
But
Awakens life.

Truth does not destroy,
But
Enlightens life.

Love does not question,
But
Immortalises life.

53. IN HEAVEN, ON EARTH

In Heaven
When I stumbled
God came, stood beside me
And
Lifted me up compassionately and
gently.

On earth
When God starved
I came, stood beside Him
And
Fed Him devotedly and
sumptuously.

54. BIG DREAMS, SMALL DREAMS

His small head
Had big dreams.
Now
His big head
Has small dreams.
He is waiting
For his head
To become larger than the largest
So that his small dreams
Can die down
Secretly, unnoticed,
And his reality-friends
Can stand living with him
Openly and fruitfully.

55. WHEN

He is an angel
When he smiles.

He is a yogi
When he meditates.

He is a lover
When he cries.

He is a seer
When he sleeps.

He is a dreamer
When he speaks.

He is divinely great
When he is for God.

He is supremely good
When he is of God.

56. DON'T GIVE UP!

Pray and meditate;
Meditate and pray.
Don't give up!
If you give up,
Then you will be
As bad as the worst.

Pray and meditate;
Meditate and pray.
Reach the Goal.
No matter when you reach the Goal,
You will be
As good as the best.

57. HIS REALISATION

His realisation is skin-deep
Who says that the body's beauty is skin-deep.
Alas!
When will he know
That the outer beauty
Of a human being
Is a solid portion
Of God the Beauty.

His realisation is sea-deep
Who feels that man can transcend himself.
Ah! He will know,
He will know without fail
That today's man is tomorrow's God.

58. A THING

A thing of beauty
Is always a great expense.
A thing of duty
Deserves always a great reward.

A thing of necessity
Always surrenders.
A thing of surrender
Commands man to surrender
To the demand of price.

59. I BELIEVE IT

When the world says
That I am a fool,
I believe it.

When the world says
That I am a rogue,
I believe it.

When the world says
That I am a helpless,
Hopeless and useless creature,
I believe it.

But God, when *You* tell me
something,
Why do I find it so hard to believe
it?

"Son, your love
Of ignorance-night
Far surpasses your love
Of Knowledge-Light.

"Empty your experience
Inside My Heart unreservedly.
I shall flood your being
With Light and Delight
Devotedly, soulfully and
perpetually."

60. THEY WELCOME

A lazy man welcomes
Volcano-destruction.
A crazy man welcomes
Tempest-confusion.
A wise man welcomes
Wisdom-ocean.
A good man welcomes
God-Perfection.

61. THE WRITER

Before he writes a book
He reads ten books
Written by others.

After he has written his book
He stops reading altogether
Books written by others.

He reads and reads and reads
His book until he empties
His appreciation-mountain,
Admiration-ocean,
  adoration-moon
On his beloved creation-son,
A mere book.

62. BEFORE AND AFTER

You use your wise eyes
Before and after
You buy anything.

He uses his proud nose
Before and after
He buys anything.

I use my clever ears
Before and after
I buy anything.

God uses His Oneness-Heart
Before and after
He buys anything.

63. HE

He loved God
When he was
9 years old.

He judged God
When he was
18 years old.

He forgave God
When he was
27 years old.

He realised his ignorance
When he was
36 years old.

God gave him everything
When he was
45 years old.

He became God
When he was
54 years old.

The world kicked him
When he was
63 years old.

The world killed him
When he was
72 years old.

And then immediately
The world gave him
Admiration-sun,
Adoration-moon.

64. A MOTHER'S TWO GODS

Each mother has two Gods:
One is the God in Heaven,
The other is her own son.

To her God in Heaven
She prays,
To her God on earth
She surrenders.

65. A FATHER'S TWO GODDESSES

Each father has two Goddesses:
One is the Goddess in Heaven,
The other is his own daughter.

He soulfully admires
His Goddess in Heaven,
He unconditionally adores
His Goddess on earth.

66. HE HAS ALREADY WON

He who strives and dives
Will eventually succeed.

He who watches and catches
Will never succeed.

He who loves and serves
Has already won.

He who bites and blights
Has already lost.

67. THE COSMIC GAME

The donkey in him
Tries to clear the cosmic fence.

The deer in him
Wants to win the cosmic race.

The elephant in him
Wants to break down the cosmic
  palace.

The tiger in him
Wants to devour the cosmic fruit.

The God in him
Wants to enjoy the cosmic game.

68. HE THINKS

He thinks the sun shines
To please him.

He thinks God smiles
To please him.

He thinks humanity breathes
To please him.

Proudly he thinks,
Sweetly he dreams,
Quickly he sinks.

69. THE BOUNDARIES

The human in me
Has a tiny room
Bounded
On the north, south, east, west
By C. K. Ghose.

The divine in me
Has the boundless universe
Bounded
On the north, by God's
  Compassion,
On the south, by God's Protection,
On the east, by God's Aspiration,
On the west, by God's Perfection.

70. LOVE AND HATE

Love yourself.
Lo, you have begun
Your lifelong romance.

Hate yourself.
Lo, you have begun
Your lifelong battle.

Love God.
Lo, you have established
Your supremacy on earth.

Hate God.
Lo, the fool in you has caught
The fool you are.

71. WHO IS RICH?

Who is rich?
He who has peace of mind.

Where is he?
All mortals searched
And searched for him
But
Found him not.

Now God is searching for him
On Humanity's behalf.

If and when God finds him,
God will settle down
Near where he lives
To be his closest neighbour.

72. IF YOU CONTRADICT

Contradict a man:
He will tell you free
Everything he knows.

Contradict a woman:
She will tell you free
Everything she has heard about
you
And what she herself thinks about
you.

Contradict God:
He will forgive you immediately,
He will teach you unreservedly,
He will fulfil you unconditionally.

73. WHAT THEY DESERVE

Her speech deserves
Appreciation.

Her silence deserves
Admiration.

Her smile deserves
Adoration.

Her surrender deserves
Perfection:
Not man's perfection,
But God's Perfection
And
God the Perfection
Combined.

74. A VERY SLIGHT DIFFERENCE

Everyone is unrealised
Except
You
And
Me.
But there is a very slight difference
Between
Your realisation
And
My realisation.
Your realisation is
Theoretical
Partial
And
Limited;
Whereas my realisation is
Impartial
Universal
Transcendental
And even
Practical.
I mean it.
I
Repeat
It.

75. BE A LISTENER!

Be a listener!
You will be able to
Escape being a barber.

Be a listener!
Very soon you will be able to
Become a professor.

Be a listener!
Eventually you are bound to
Be the best advisor.

Be a listener!
Lo, you have become so popular
That your heights
Can easily touch
God's supernal Pride.

76. WHEN I TALK TO MAN

When I talk to man
I see that each discussion is
A public meeting
Without a microphone.

Naturally I shout,
I bark and
I do not even hesitate to bite
When necessity demands.

77. DEVOTION

Devotion:
What is it?
Devotion is the combination
Of
Love's intensity
And
Surrender's divinity.
A man of devotion
Is God's conscious and constant
  pride
In His Reality-sky
And
Infinity-sea.

78. BE CAREFUL

O descending disciples,
Be careful on your way
Down the hill.
If you kick the disciples
Who are below you
With your eyeless pride,
Then when the hour strikes
For you to ascend again,
They will not only prevent
Your upward journey,
But also extinguish
Your rekindled aspiration-flames.

79. TO AVOID

To avoid criticism,
I do nothing.

To avoid misunderstanding,
I say nothing.

To avoid competition,
I become nothing.

80. THE TIME

Awakening is the time
When the men of reason
Go to sleep.

Enlightenment is the time
When the men of amusement
Stop drinking earth-pleasures.

Perfection is the time
When the God-men and the
  God-women
Stay on earth to love supremely
And serve unconditionally.

81. DON'T DOUBT!

Don't doubt!
When you doubt God
You lengthen your
   ignorance-journey,
You diminish the flow
Of your life-energy,
You destroy your
Fast-approaching sovereignty.
Therefore, don't doubt,
Never!

82. HER BIRTHDAY, HIS AGE

She knows her birthday
But not her age.

He knows his age
But not his birthday.

But
God does not know
Either
Her birthday
Or
His age.

83. THEY TAKE US TO GOD

Doctors take us to God
Unconsciously and
   unintentionally.

Generals take us to God
Forcefully and dramatically.

Spiritual Masters take us to God
Smilingly and lovingly.

God takes us to God
Devotedly and unconditionally.

84. MY LYING, SITTING AND STANDING

Before I stand
I sit.
Before I sit
I lie.
Why? Why?

I love my lying
Because
It gives me complete satisfaction.

I admire my sitting
Because
It gives me immeasurable
   confidence.

I appreciate my standing
Because
It gives me the greatest
   competence.

85. A NEW FRIEND

I said to my friend:
"You are wrong."
Alas, I lost my friend.

I said to my enemy:
"You are right."
Lo, I gained a new friend.

86. NOW LEARN IT!

England is an island.
You knew it.
An Englishman is also an island.
Now learn it!

France is a pleasure-paradise.
You knew it.
A Frenchman is also a
pleasure-paradise.
Now learn it!

India is a degradation-life.
You knew it.
An Indian is also a
degradation-life.
Now learn it!

America is a promise-advertising
soul.
You knew it.
An American is also a
promise-advertising soul.
Now learn it!

Canada is a height-unnoticing
eye.
You knew it.
A Canadian is also a
height-unnoticing eye.
Now learn it!

87. THE INDIAN LOVE

The English language
Unites the whole world
But
Separates America from England.

The Indian love
Feeds the whole world
But
Strangles both the brothers:
Pakistan and India.

88. A SMALL FEE

A small admission fee
Takes all my enthusiasm away.
A small realisation fee
Takes all my aspiration away.
A small perfection fee
Takes all my energy away.

89. THEIR SPECIALITIES

You know everything;
That is your speciality.

He knows nothing;
That is his speciality.

I know something of everything;
That is my speciality.

Light is in everything;
That is its speciality.

Love is for everything;
That is its speciality.

God is of everything and for
 everything;
That is His speciality.

90. ATTENTION AND INTENTION

Attention he pays,
Intention he hides.
Indeed, this is the story
Of a human thief.

Attention he pays,
Intention he lacks.
Indeed, this is the story
Of a human rogue.

Attention he pays,
Intention he tries.
Indeed, this is the story
Of a sincere man.

Attention he pays,
Intention he fulfils.
Indeed, this is the story
Of a divine hero.

91. LOVE INCREASES

Love increases
By visiting friends.
Love increases more
By helping friends.
Love increases most
By loving friends.

God the Host
Loves a visiting friend.
God the Father
Loves more a helping friend.
God the Beloved
Loves most a loving friend.

92. FRIENDSHIP

Friendship between fear and
hatred
Is only a suspension of hostility.

Friendship between doubt and
suspicion
Is only a suspension of futility.

Friendship between love and life
Is only a suspension of ecstasy.

Friendship between an ascending
cry
and a descending smile
Is only a suspension of Reality.

93. THEY SAVE ME

My faith saves me
From the suspicious world.
My love saves me
From the ferocious world.
My light saves me
From the ungenerous world.
My God saves me
From the unharmonious world.

94. TOO SHORT, TOO LITTLE, TOO FAR

His life was too short
To learn yoga.
His love was too little
To see God.
His goal was too far
To value his Beloved.

95. WHEN I OFFER GRATITUDE

When I offer gratitude to God
And God alone
I secretly expect
A greater favour from God.

When I offer gratitude to man
Man immediately claims
The most legitimate favour from
me.

O God, with my gratitude
I hopefully try to fool you.
O man, with my gratitude
I unavoidably bind my helpless
self.

96. LIFE AND LOVE

Life I give,
Life I receive.
With life I bind my Heaven and
my earth.
Love I eat,
Love I feed.
With love I free my earth and my
Heaven.

97. WHAT IS WORSE, WHAT IS BETTER?

What is worse than a donkey?
Two donkeys.
What is better than a seeker?
Two seekers.
What is worse than the worst
enemy?
Two enemies.
What is better than the best
friend?
Two friends.

Two donkeys:
Doubt and Jealousy.
Two seekers:
Sincerity and Purity.
Two enemies:
Pride and Fear.
Two friends:
Faith and Courage.

98. WHEN I TALK

When I talk with God
I cramp His conversation.
When I talk with a man
We cramp each other's
conversation.
When I talk with a woman
She cramps my conversation.
And in return
The human in me strangles our
conversation,
While
The divine in me admires her
conversation.
When I talk with myself
I overfeed my conversation
And kill the real thinker in me.

99. LOVE IS ALL

The animal in me says:
Destruction is above all,
Destruction is all.
The human in me says:
Sensation is above all,
Sensation is all.
The divine in me says:
Liberation is above all,
Liberation is all.
The angel in me says:
Beauty is above all,
Beauty is all.
The God in me says:
Love is above all,
Love is all.

100. GOD'S NATIONALITY

In his dream he saw
A Russian, an American, a
German,
A Chinaman, a Japanese, an
Indian,
A Pakistani, a Frenchman, an
Englishman
and a Canadian
Fighting over the nationality of
God.
The Russian said,
"God can be of any nationality,
but not
American."
The American said,
"I shall ask God to leave me for
some time,
Change His nationality
And stay with the Russian.
Russia needs God's inner
Presence,
Whereas I can stay for some time
Without God's outer Presence.
Needless to say, God is an
American."
The German said,
"God is a clever fellow.
He changes His nationality quite
often.
When a nation becomes powerful
He adopts the nationality of that
country
Quickly and devotedly."
The Chinaman said,
"Although God's Presence does
not add
Anything to my nation,

God secretly indulges His Chinese
nationality."
The Japanese said,
"We all know that God
Most secretly and convincingly
Enjoys His sole nationality:
Japanese."
The Indian said,
"Before God started
Taking human incarnation,
He assured India that
He would assume only one
nationality,
Forever and forever."
The Pakistani said,
"We know it.
That is why we do not allow God
The eternal Hindu
To darken our country."
The Frenchman and the
Englishman
Fought bitterly
And then divided God's
nationality
Into two gigantic halves.
The Canadian saluted the
American and said,
"God's eternal American
nationality
Will one day be proved
indisputable."
The American embraced the
Canadian and said,
"Take what I have and what I am.
What I have is outer assurance.
What I am is inner gratitude."

101. DEATH-DANCE

I met God in Heaven.
He asked me
How I was.

I met man on earth.
He wanted me to tell
How he was.

I met Satan in hell.
He told me that he had
Adopted a new course of life:
He prays to God every day,
He meditates on God every day,
He even loves God every day.

I met myself in the doubt-tornado
Of my mind, lost all:
Death-dance within, without.

102. WHEN I APPRECIATE MYSELF

When I appreciate myself
Humanity ridicules me,
Divinity enlightens me.

Divinity tells me that
My appreciation-power
Is nowhere near my
achievement-height.

Humanity tells me that
My "whole" is but a big hole.

103. CAME AND LEFT

Great men came
And
Great men left.
The world was sleeping.

Good men came
And
Good men left.
The world was snoring.

Small men came
And
Lost their vision.
The world is now treating
their blind souls.

Bad men came
And
Lost their passports.
The world is now examining
their careless souls.

104. MY JOURNEY, MY GOAL

My life is my journey,
My love is my goal.

My love is my journey,
My oneness is my goal.

My oneness is my journey,
My perfection is my goal.

My perfection is my journey,
My smile is my goal.

105. TOGETHER CRY, TOGETHER FLY

A fearful man and destruction
Together cry.

A fearless man and Liberation
Together dance.

A faithless man and despair
Together sink.

A faithful man and Bliss
Together fly.

106. LEARN TO SHUT THE DOOR

Learn to shut the door.
Fear will not frighten you.

Learn to shut the door.
Doubt will not blight you.

Learn to shut the door.
Jealousy will not strangle you.

Learn to open the door.
Courage will beautify you.

Learn to open the door.
Faith will glorify you.

Learn to open the door.
Oneness will immortalise you.

107. TAKE IT EASY!

Take it easy!
Still you have many more years on
earth.

Take it easy!
Remember God has not forsaken
you.

Take it easy!
Your promise-land is God's
Dream-Dawn.

Take it easy!
God needs you more than you
need Him.

108. STOP! STOP!

Stop! Stop!
Stop starving your body.
Your body is God's sacred temple.

Stop! Stop!
Stop starving your heart.
Your heart is God's secret shrine.

Stop! Stop!
Stop starving your soul.
Your soul is God's
dream-fulfilling Deity.

109. DON'T BE AFRAID!

Don't be afraid!
He is just a man-dog
Who is barking at you.

Don't be afraid!
He is just a God-lion
Who is roaring to inspire you,
To energise you,
To immortalise you.

110. YOU HAVE A FRIEND

You have a friend.
You may not feel his love
But
He does love you.

You have a friend.
You may not recognise his help
But
He does help you.

You have a friend.
You may not believe
That he thinks only of you
But
He does think only of you.

111. ALL

My body does all the sleeping
And
All the wasting.

My vital does all the jumping
And
All the breaking.

My mind does all the thinking
And
All the doubting.

My heart does all the loving
And
All the fulfilling.

My soul does all the watching
And
All the caring,
All the tolerating,
All the sanctioning,
All the inspiring,
All the transforming,
All the perfecting.

112. HOW TO LIVE IN A TIME LIKE THIS?

How to live in a time like this?
How? Just smile.
Lo, the world-suspicion-tiger is dead.

How to live in a time like this?
How? Just smile.
Lo, the world-blindness-elephant is dead.

How to live in a time like this?
How? Just smile.
Lo, the world-autocracy-lion is dead.

How to live in a time like this?
You fool!
Don't you know that you are
The very root of the world-miseries,
The world-calamities,
The world-failures?

113. MY FOUR SERMONS

I have given only four sermons
During my entire life.

My first sermon:
"I love Heaven."

My second sermon:
"I need earth."

My third sermon:
"Heaven, my Heaven-flower,
claims me."

My fourth and last sermon:
"Earth, my earth-fruit, I sacrifice."

114. IF I AM NOT FOR MYSELF

If I am not for myself,
Who will be for me?

God will be for me.
God the Lover will be for me.
God the Beloved will be for me.

If I am for myself,
Who will not be for me?

God the dearest Father will not be
for me.
God the sweetest Mother will not
be for me.
God the eternal Friend will not be
for me.

115. A TREE WITHOUT ROOTS

Love without life
Is a tree without roots.

Life without love
Is a tree without fruits.

Beauty without purity
Is a tree without roots.

Purity without beauty
Is a tree without fruits.

116. SOME GO UP, SOME COME DOWN

Prayer goes up;
God the Compassion comes down.

Aspiration goes up;
God the Salvation comes down.

Meditation goes up;
God the Liberation comes down.

Surrender goes up;
God the Perfection comes down.

117. THEY WILL NOT LOVE YOU LESS

Truth will not love you less
Because Love loves you more.

Love will not love you less
Because Joy loves you more.

Joy will not love you less
Because Perfection loves you more.

Perfection will not love you less
Because Immortality loves you more.

118. PESSIMIST, OPTIMIST, REALIST

A pessimist is he
Who shuts his eyes
To the rising sun.

An optimist is he
Who looks up and sees
Through the teeming clouds.

A realist is he
Who faces the clouds
And adores the sun.

119. PERFECTION

Perfection, what is it?
A smile of the Beyond.

Perfection, where is it?
In the heart of the Infinite.

Perfection, who has it?
The Absolute alone.

120. MY PROGRESS

Fear and Power begin my morn.
Doubt and Light begin my noon.
Depression and Peace begin my eve.
God and I discuss my progress at night.

121. NOTHING TO DECLARE

His body has nothing to declare
Save and except
The flood of impurity.

His vital has nothing to declare
Save and except
The dance of a mad elephant.

His smile has nothing to declare
Save and except
The strength of an ant.

His heart has nothing to declare
Save and except
The constant fear of death.

His soul has nothing to declare
Save and except
The Compassion-moon of the
Supreme.

122. FAR BEYOND THE COMMAND

A poet is born,
Neither made nor paid.

A singer is born,
Not made, but paid.

An artist is born,
Destined to starve and feast.

A philosopher is made,
Paid, but ridiculed.

A thinker is made
More than paid.

A God-lover is far beyond the
command
Of life and death.
For he has what God is: Divinity's
Smile.

123. MY DEPRESSION-WINTER, MY DESTRUCTION-SUMMER

Poor God!
When He visits my home
I am not there.
When He visits my store
I am not there.
When He visits my friends
I am not there.
Where can God find me?
Ah! He can find me
In the cold-life of my
depression-winter,
In the heat-life of my
destruction-summer.

124. A CONSTANT AND A RARE GUEST

A constant human guest is
Never
Welcome, we know.

A rare human guest is
Most sincerely,
Most devotedly
Welcome, we know.

A constant guest at God's Door is
More than
Welcome, my soul says.

A rare guest at God's Door is
Always
Welcome, my heart says.

125. THE HOSPITAL OF THE INCURABLE

There is no difference
Between
The suspicion-mind
And
The hospital of the incurable.

There is no difference
Between
The depression-vital
And
The hospital of the incurable.

There is no difference
Between
The insecurity-heart
And
The hospital of the incurable.

There is no difference
Between
The impurity-body
And
The hospital of the incurable.

This is my proud earth-bound
human realisation.
Lo, my Heaven-free divine
Realisation
Laughs and laughs
At my human
achievement-heights.

126. ONLY ONE SUBJECT

His body is ignorant of only one
 subject:
Awaking!
His vital is ignorant of only one
 subject:
Arising!
His mind is ignorant of only one
 subject:
Enlarging!
His heart is ignorant of only one
 subject:
Crying!
His soul is ignorant of only one
 subject:
Illumining!

127. WHEN I REST

When I rest, I rust.
When I rust, I starve my God-life.
When I starve my God-life, death
 invites me
To dance in the desert-heart
Of tornado-night.

128. FALSEHOOD-LOAD, FALSEHOOD-NET

His soul does not know
How to tell a lie.
His heart knows
How to tell a lie
But it will not do so.

He asked God if he should
Love them equally.
God said to him he must,
For God Himself
Loves them equally.

Because of God's love for his soul,
God did not burden it
With falsehood-load.
Because of God's love for his heart,
God warns and cautions it
Against falsehood-net.

129. MY REALISATIONS

My soul's realisation:
I am a golden divinity.

My heart's realisation:
I am a silver reality.

My mind's realisation:
I am dawn's possibility.

My vital's realisation:
I am almost an impossibility.

My body's realisation:
I am a total impossibility.

130. WHEN HE HAD

When he had
World-knowledge
Everybody called him father.

When he had
Great fortune
Everybody called him brother.

When he had
Heaven-wisdom
Everybody called him friend.

When he lost
Everything
Everybody denied him
  everything.
But
God placed him unconditionally
On His transcendental Throne.

131. YOUR TRUE REALITY

Sincerity is a divine arm;
Use it or lose it.

Purity is a divine eye;
Love it or destroy it.

Humility is a divine heart;
Illumine it or blind it.

Divinity is your true reality;
Assume it or forsake it.

132. TWO MESSAGES

Lord, if what I have
Is the message of aspiration,
Then do give me the message of
  manifestation.

Lord, if what I have
Is the message of manifestation,
Then do give me the message of
  aspiration.

"My son, you have both
The message of aspiration and
The message of manifestation.

"Your aspiration-message:
I need it.
Your manifestation-message:
I treasure it."

133. MY JOURNEY

Reverence:
I started my journey's birth
With the reverence-spirit.

Perseverance:
I continue my journey's flow
With the perseverance-heart.

Omnipresence:
I shall end my journey's close
With my omnipresence-spirit.

134. PHILOSOPHY

My mind's philosophy:
I came from the nowhere-shore
To live in the nothing-sea.

My heart's philosophy:
I was of God,
I am in man.

My soul's philosophy:
I assume God's form and
I transcend my transcendental
   Form.

135. MY FUTURE SMILES

My enemies
Are my future friends.
My friends
Are my future sons.
My sons
Are my future Suns.
My Suns
Are my future Smiles.

136. THINKING

You are too lazy to think.
He knows nothing but thinking.

The human world
Knows not how to think.
Therefore
It most deplorably sinks.

The divine world
Blesses the thought-sea,
Transforms the thought-sea,
And offers the will-sun
To the thought-sea.

137. WHO HAS, IS

Who has, is.
Who is, sows.
Who sows, glows.
Who glows, liberates.
Who liberates, perfects.
Who perfects, has.
Who has, is.

138. A TIME WHEN HE SHALL SURRENDER

There was a time
When he could;
Therefore
He did.

Now he cannot;
Therefore
He cries.

There shall be a time
When he shall surrender;
Therefore
God Himself will have to do
Everything for him,
And He will.

139. MY BLUNDERS

My failure
Enlarged my blunders.
My success
Covered my blunders.
My progress
Illumined my blunders.

My illumined blunders
Have added much light
To my perfect perfection-sea.

140. SAY AND GIVE

The animal in me
Has to say something.

The human in me
Has something to say.

The divine in me
Says and gives.

The Supreme in me
Just gives and gives.

141. GOD LOVES HIM

His prayer is his lip-homage,
Yet God loves him.

His prayer is his clever deception,
Yet God loves him.

God loves him because
He is of God.

He shall be for God because
He is in God.

142. LOVE NEEDS ONE THING

Love needs no sword
To rule the world.
Love needs no cord
To bind the world.
Love needs no strength
To free the world.
Love needs no wisdom
To expand the world.
Yet
Love needs one thing:
Acceptance, your total acceptance.

143. JUST SEE

Christ
Calls us
Honours us
Remakes us
Immortalises us
Satisfies the Supreme in us.
Together, the Supreme, Christ
  and we
Shall create the Kingdom of
  Heaven on earth.
When?
Just see
If it is not already done!

144. GOD NEEDS YOU

I demand of you
Because
I love you.

I love you
Because
God needs you.

God needs you
Because
You are His glowing
And
Fulfilling Promise.

145. BEAUTY

Beauty
Is the door.
Sincerity
Is the door-keeper.
Purity
Is the door-lover.
Humility
Is the door-opener.
Divinity
Is the door-owner.

146. FOUR TRUTHS

I speak of the unfathomable truth:
Love.
I think of the immeasurable truth:
Light.
I meditate on the unsurpassable
truth:
Compassion.
I love the undeniable truth:
Perfection.

147. LOVE YOU MUST

Pray
If you want to.
Meditate
If you can.
Surrender
You must try.
Love
You must.
I repeat,
Love
You must.

148. WHAT IS IT?

Love:
What is it
If not the royal road
To Realisation?

Devotion:
What is it
If not the short-cut
To Realisation?

Surrender:
What is it
If not a bud
Of the Realisation-Tree?

149. THE STORY OF THE HUMAN WORLD

Human help
Waxes to wane.
Human love
Grows to decay.
Human life
Lives to die.
Human death
Rests to re-enter.

This is indeed the story
Of the human world.

150. YET HIS COMPASSION LOVES ME

I saw Him,
But
I forgot to ask Him his Name.
Yet His Compassion loves me.

I dined with Him,
But
I forgot to ask Him His Address.
Yet His Compassion loves me.

I sang with Him,
But
I have forgotten the Tune.
Yet His Compassion loves me.

I danced with Him,
But
I have forgotten the cadence.
Yet His Compassion loves me.

I played with Him,
But
I forgot to smile at Him.
Yet His Compassion loves me.

151. NEXT TIME I SHALL WIN

My body gives me
The consoling news:
Next time I shall win
In the battlefield of life.

My vital gives me
The exciting news:
Next time I shall win
Without fail the cosmic game.

My mind gives me
The inspiring news:
Next time I shall win
Infinity's sweetest embrace.

My heart gives me
The aspiring news:
Next time I shall win
Immortality's ever-climbing
wings.

152. THREE SONS

Three sons:
The youngest, the middle and the eldest.

The youngest son said:
"Father is in Heaven."

The middle son said:
"The Kingdom of Heaven is in your heart."

The eldest son said:
"I and my Father are one."

To the youngest son, the Father said:
"Son, thank you for your vision."

To the middle son, the Father said:
"Son, thank you for your mission."

To the eldest son, the Father said:
"Son, thank you for your union."

153. ONE DAY'S PATIENCE

One day's patience
Awakens ten days' peace.

Ten days' peace
Expedites God's Hour.

God's Hour dawns
In surrender's sky.

154. A TREE WITHOUT ROOTS

Life without love
Is a flower
Without fragrance.

Love without oneness
Is a fruit
Without taste.

Oneness without God
Is a tree
Without roots.

155. WHEN HIS BOASTING-BOAT SANK

When
His boasting-boat sank,
His dignity-shore neared.

When
His dignity-shore neared,
God accompanied it.

Now
God has given him
What He is:
Life-flower,
Love-fruit.

156. HE DOES NOT ANSWER ALL LETTERS

He
Does not answer all letters.
He
Awakens all hearts.
He
Does not awaken all hearts.
He
Feeds all souls.
He
Does not feed all souls.
He
Implores God
To feed all souls,
To awaken all hearts,
To answer all letters.

157. A BRAKE

You are afraid of Bliss.
That means
You will be using a brake
On your inner progress.

You are afraid of Silence.
That means
You are using a brake
On your soaring progress.

You are afraid of Love.
That means
You have already used a brake
On your supreme progress.

158. YOUR SMILE, YOUR JOY, YOUR LOVE

Your smile
Is your property undisputed.
Your joy
Is your prosperity unchallenged.
Your love
Is your divinity unparalleled.

159. THE SHORTEST ROUTE

Self-doubt
Is the shortest route
From the cradle
To the grave.

Self-faith
Is the shortest route
From the grave
To the cradle.

God
Is the shortest and safest route
From the earth-cradle
To the Heaven-cradle.

160. UNTIL

The world does not honour
A great man
Until he is dead.

The world does not love
A good man
Until he is dead.

The world does not claim
A god-man
Until he is gone.

161. THE ECHO

Light is the echo
Of God's Voice
Inside the Love-Kingdom
Of my soul.

Surrender is the echo
Of God's Voice
Inside the Perfection-Palace
Of my life.

162. CONTRADICT

Contradict a man,
He will tell you
Everything he knows
About himself.

Contradict a woman,
She will tell you
Everything you do not want to
know
About yourself.

Contradict your lower self,
You will be happy.

Contradict your higher self,
You will be doomed.

Contradict God,
He will definitely forgive you.

163. A ONE-WAY STREET AND A TWO-WAY STREET

Compromise is a one-way street:
Look, and then proceed
In the right direction.

Surrender is a two-way street:
No need to look,
Just proceed the fastest
Along the earth-free and
Heaven-proud Road.

164. MY HEART IS STILL RUNNING

My body NEVER
Started the race.

My vital died
Along the way.

My mind gave up
After covering half the distance.

My heart is still running
In spite of tremendous fatigue
and weariness.

My soul is watching
My poor heart.

My Supreme is beckoning
My brave heart.

165. WHEN WISDOM RESIGNS

You hurt knowledge
When you spare ignorance.

When
Knowledge is hurt,
Wisdom resigns.

When
Wisdom resigns,
God's Smile fades
Into earth-sadness,
Earth-helplessness.

166. AN EDUCATION

What is defeat?
Nothing but a continuing
education.

What is victory?
Nothing but an inspiring
education.

What is progress?
Nothing but a fulfilling
education.

What is perfection?
Nothing but a blossomed
education.

167. FOUR ROOMS

Quick instruction
Ends in the life-room.

Slow education
Ends in the school-room.

Great realisation
Ends in the heart-room.

Perfect manifestation
Begins and never ends in the
body-room.

168. BETTER

Better go than sit.
Better meditate than go.
Better surrender than meditate.

Better try than cry.
Better think than try.
Better see than think.

169. THEREFORE HE IS HAPPY

His servant-body is deaf.
Therefore
He is happy.

His master-soul is blind.
Therefore
He is happy.

His patient-mind is unreal.
Therefore
He is happy.

His doctor-heart is kind.
Therefore
He is happy.

170. NATURALLY I AM GREAT

A dumb sheep worships me;
Naturally I am great.

A blind beggar adores me;
Naturally I am great.

A poor man admires me;
Naturally I am great.

Mother Earth loves me;
Naturally I am great.

Father Heaven blesses me;
Naturally I am great.

171. INTRODUCTIONS

Your past introduced you
To bondage-night.

Your present is introducing you
To Liberation-light.

Your future will be introducing
   you
To Perfection-height.

172. RESPONSIBILITY AND OPPORTUNITY

When
Life is responsibility,
Death is opportunity.

When
Life is opportunity,
Death is futility.

When
We live in the physical,
We come to feel that life
Is man's responsibility
And
God's true opportunity.

But
When
We live in the soul,
We come to realise that life
Is God's responsibility
And
Man's constant opportunity.

173. MY HEART AND MY MIND

My heart
Lends me an immediate hand.

My mind
Gives me endless advice.

My heart
Cultivates my life-earth.

My mind
Trims my life-tree.

174. ONENESS-MOON, ONENESS-SUN

When love thinks,
Life sinks.

When life dreams,
Love reveals.

When life and love think,
Oneness starves.

When life and love dream,
Oneness-moon grows within,
Oneness-sun glows without.

175. THE FRUIT OF EARTH'S LOVE-TREE

A wise man knows that God is
Everything.

A fool feels that he has
Everything.

A seeker feels that truth is
Only in Heaven.

A lover feels that truth is
The fruit of earth's love-tree.

176. THEREFORE

Your heart is deep;
Therefore
You see the invisible.

Your mind is clear;
Therefore
You believe the incredible.

Your life is receptive;
Therefore
You achieve the impossible.

177. MY GUIDES

I use my reason to guide me,
And I stumble and stumble.

I use my faith to guide me,
And I march and march.

I use my silence to guide me,
And I run and run.

I use my surrender to guide me,
And I see my Goal where I
eternally am.

178. BE LOVING

Be wise and watch.
Be great and govern.
Be kind and feel.
Be good and act.
Be pure and spread.
Be loving and become.

179. HOW I GOVERN THE WORLD

By crying,
I govern my physical world.
By struggling,
I govern my vital world.
By thinking,
I govern my mental world.
By meditating,
I govern my psychic world.
By loving,
I govern God's inner world.
By serving,
I govern God's outer world.

180. IF I CAN

If I can,
I shall speak to God about you.

If I can,
I shall beg God
To grant you an interview.

If I can,
I shall ask God
To simplify your long and
arduous task.

If I can,
I shall ask God to grant you
His Nectar-flood.

181. HE WILL SEE

He will see,
Who saw.
He will feel,
Who felt.
He will think,
Who thought.
He will serve,
Who served.
He will give,
Who gave.
But
He will have and be,
Who surrenders.

182. MY SOUL BENDS NOT

My soul
Bends not, breaks not.
My heart
Bends and bends.
My vital
Never bends.
My body
Only breaks.

183. LOVE IS NO LABOUR

Thought is three-fourths labour.
Hope is half labour.
Joy is a quarter labour.
Love is no labour.

What

Love undertakes,
Love accomplishes
Sooner than at once.

184. MORE LASTING THAN IMMORTAL

The conqueror
Is mortal.
The asserter
Is weaker than mortal.

The God-lover
Is immortal.
The God in man
Is more lasting than immortal.

185. I SEE, I SAY AND I DO

I see and say nothing;
Therefore
I am happy.

I see not and say not;
Therefore
I am happier.

I see, I say and I do;
Therefore
I am happiest.

186. FOUR DIFFERENT GODS

God the Saviour:
For the vigilant.

God the Forgiver:
For the sleeping.

God the Beloved:
For the seeker.

God the Transformer:
For the idler.

187. HERE AT LAST

O physical world!
Here I am adored
But
Not loved.

O vital world!
Here I am bound
But
Not subdued.

O mental world!
Here I am chained
But
Not conquered.

O psychic world!
Here at last
I am loved
And fulfilled.

188. I DESIRE, I BELIEVE, I HAVE

I desire.
I desire to be free
From the assaults of desire.

I believe.
I believe I am a chosen instrument
Of the Transcendental Supreme.

I have.
I have what the Supreme is:
Surrender, surrender
unconditional.

189. I WILL NEVER QUIT

O Master-Lord,
I will never quit.
I may suffer,
Yet
I will never quit.

O Master-Lord,
I will never quit.
I may be badly misunderstood,
Yet
I will never quit.

O Master-Lord,
I will never quit.
I may be totally destroyed,
Yet
I will never quit.

190. PROSPER AND PROCEED

I prosper and prosper.
This is what
The animal in me demands.

I prosper and proceed.
This is what
The human in me wants.

I proceed and prosper.
This is what
The divine in me aspires for.

I proceed and proceed.
This is what
The Supreme in me needs.

191. BOLDNESS

Danton says:
"Boldness and more boldness,
And always boldness!"

The seeker in me whispers:
"Boldness in the life-river,
More boldness in the
service-citadel,
And always boldness
In the surrender-world."

192. STRUGGLE, EXIST AND LIVE

Darwin says:
"The struggle for existence."

The warrior in me whispers:
"I struggle to exist.
I exist for God."

God taught me secretly how to
struggle.
God teaches me openly
How to exist.
God shall teach me unreservedly
How to live.

193. ALL FOR ONE, ONE FOR ALL

Dumas says:
"All for one, one for all."

The lover in me whispers:
"All for one
In the world of my
devotion-height,
In the world of my surrender-sea.
One for all
In the world of my Love-light,
In the world of my
Perfection-sky."

194. WHAT IS THE FUTURE?

Einstein says:
"I never think of the future.
It comes soon enough."

The sincere observer
In me whispers:
"What is the future
If not my morning smiles
Fading into my evening cries?
What is the future
If not my morning cries
Growing into my evening
smiles?"

195. THEY WILL CLAIM ME

Einstein says:
"If my theory of relativity is
proven successful,
Germany will claim me as a
German and
France will declare that I am a
citizen of the world."

The realised soul in me whispers:
"If my God-realisation is proved,
Mother India will claim me
As her very own.
If my God-revelation is proved
successful,
Father America will claim me
confidently
As his very own.
If my God-manifestation is
proved victorious,
My world-sisters and brothers
Will claim me unreservedly
As their very own."

196. TIME AND MONEY

Benjamin Franklin says:
"Remember that time is money."

The practical man in me whispers:
"I deeply admire
This great discovery.
But I have also to remember that
Time is life.
Time is God the Inspiration
In our outer life;
Time is God the aspiration
In our inner life.
And what is money?
Money is something
That has the message of
possession
In the outer world
And
The message of service
In the inner world."

197. WITHOUT

No knowledge
Without power.

No power
Without love.

No love
Without the heart.

No heart
Without the soul.

No soul
Without the Goal.

198. MISUNDERSTOOD

When I love God,
I am misunderstood by man.
Man says: "You love God
To escape from the harsh realities
Of the world."

When I love man,
I am misunderstood by God.
God says: "My son,
You are not doing
The first thing first."

199. WHY DOES HE BREAK?

Whom to blame?
No one.
Why blame?
No reason.
Who is blaming?
The deliberate breaker.
What does he break?
Oneness-vessel.
Why does he break?
Because he knows not what
Glowing
Flowing
Fulfilling
Immortalising
ECSTASY is.

200. MY PLAY IS DONE

My play is done.
Nothing more to give,
Nothing more to receive,
Nothing more to grow,
Nothing more to achieve.
My play is done.

My play is done.
I have become
What I was:
Freedom-sky,
Silence-sea.
My play is done.

201. I WROTE TO YOU FOR HELP

O my soul,
I wrote to you
For help
In my God-manifestation.
Alas,
Your answer could have been
More generous.
O my heart,
I wrote to you
For help
In my God-manifestation.
Alas,
Your poor response
Fails to inspire me.
O my mind,
I wrote to you
For help
In my God-manifestation.
Alas,
Your obscure answer
Puzzles me.
O my vital,
I wrote to you
For help
In my God-manifestation.
Alas,
Your senseless answer
Frustrates me.
O my body,
I didn't write to you
Because
I didn't know
Whom to choose
Between you
And ignorance.

202. MANY HAPPY RETURNS

On my birthday
Earth-consciousness says:
"Many happy returns."
Heaven-Delight says:
"Your every happy return to
earth-life
Is also a happy step towards My
Palace."
Alas,
Life on earth
Is temptation-frustration.
Life in Heaven
Is examination-clarification.

203. HIS LOVE TAUGHT HIM

His love of God
Taught him
How to descend
Into the world-night.

His love of man
Taught him
How to forget
His Immortality's height.

204. LIFE-PASSAGE AND LOVE-MESSAGE

Where is the world-soul?
The world-soul
Is inside my blossoming vision.

What shall I do with it?
I shall give it out.

To whom?
To those who know that
Life-passage and love-message
Are one,
Inseparably one.

205. ALTERNATIVES

Choose!
God-life or man-perfection.
Choose!

Choose!
God-edifice or man-sacrifice.
Choose!

Choose!
God-power or man-love.
Choose!

206. MY PRAYERS

My doubtful prayers
Are my prayers of clay.

My soulful prayers
Are my prayers of day.

My thought-covered prayers
Are my prayers of frustration.

My silence-filled prayers
Are my prayers of destination.

207. WHERE THEY LIVE

His heart lives
In the sea of loneliness.

His mind lives
In the pool of loneliness.

His vital lives
In the pyre of depression.

His body lives
In the cave of perdition.

208. MY LOVE-TELESCOPE

When I use
My time-telescope,
I suffer from dark uncertain
night.

When I use
My love-telescope,
I build the palace of life
In the kingdom of God-Light.

209. O LIGHT, O TRANCE

O light of trance,
Where are you?
O trance of night,
Where are you not?
O night of trance,
Where can I kill you?
O Light, O trance,
I am of you.
O night, O trance,
God is there for you.

210. KNOWLEDGE-SUN, LUSTRE-MOON

I eat,
And yet I eat not
Ignorance-night.

I drink,
And yet I drink not
Ignorance-sea.

I eat not,
And yet I eat
Knowledge-sun.

I drink not,
And yet I drink
Lustre-moon.

211. WHEN HE REPRESENTS

He is one
When he represents
Truth and Light.

He is one
When he represents
Love and Life.

He is two
When he represents
His Inner Faith
And
His Outer Doubt.

He is many
When he represents
Earth-Bondage-Night
And
Heaven-Freedom-Bliss.

212. FOUR MESSAGES

The message of his vital:
Life is a self-imposed struggle.

The message of his mind:
Life is a self-exposed-bondage.

The message of his heart:
Life is a God-inviting hope.

The message of his body:
Life is a death-manifesting
ignorance.

213. MY JOURNEY

Earth is *not*
My journey's start.

Heaven is *not*
My journey's close.

My journey is
The birthless Lover on earth.

My journey is
The deathless Beloved in Heaven.

214. SAY NOT ANYTHING AGAINST ME

O life,
I love you.
I love your sound-wave.
Therefore,
Say not anything against me.

O death,
I love you.
I love your silence-peace.
Therefore,
Say not anything against me.

215. BEHOLD THE MAGIC

No goal, no goal:
Behold the magic of the mind.

No soul, no soul:
Behold the magic of the vital.

No heart, no heart:
Behold the magic of the body.

No night, no night:
Behold the magic of the heart.

No ignorance, no ignorance:
Behold the magic of the soul.

216. A TRANSACTION

The life human
Is at its best
A transaction
Between
Black depression
And
Brown frustration.

The life divine
Is at its worst
A transaction
Between
A hungry sky
And
A thirsty sun.

217. TWO DEBTS

God, let us settle
Our accounts.
God, do I owe You anything?

"Certainly you do, My son.
You owe Me
Your failure-sea
And
Your failure-sky."
God, here they are.

"Son, do I owe you anything?"
Yes, Lord, You owe me
My Eternal Now.
"Son, here it is."

218. THREE THINGS YOU CAN DO WITH GOD

Three are the things
That you can do with God:
First kill Him and then love Him
Or
First love Him and then kill Him
Or
Love His Peace devotedly,
Love His Light unreservedly,
Love His Love unconditionally.

219. THEY DO NOT BOTHER GOD

God is lazy.
Therefore
My body does not bother God.

God is weak.
Therefore
My vital does not bother God.

God is ignorant.
Therefore
My mind does not bother God.

God is shy.
Therefore
My heart does not bother God.

220. IF YOU ARE THE SON OF GOD

If you are the son of God,
Then give Him what you have:
Your cry, your constant cry,
Your endless cry.
And
If God is your son,
Then give Him what you are:
Your smile, your birthless smile,
Your deathless smile.

221. TWO ARE BETTER, ONE IS BETTER

Two are better than one.
Therefore
I always stay
With the Compassion of the Supreme.

One is better than two.
Therefore
I never stay
With my personal efforts.

222. WHAT IS IMPORTANT?

What is important in life?
A soulful smile.

What is important in death?
A fruitful silence.

What is important in Immortality?
A dutiful necessity.

223. WE CAN EASILY WORK IT OUT TOGETHER

You and I
Can easily work it out together.
You pray to God
To grant us nectar
On our behalf.
And when God grants us nectar,
Let me taste it first
On our behalf.
If it tastes good,
Without fail
I shall share it with you.
Let us try.
You and I
Can easily work it out together.

224. THE BLESSING

The blessing of your madness:
Nobody will come near you.

The blessing of your calmness:
God will come near you.

The blessing of your impurity:
You will have to walk alone
To your goal.

The blessing of your purity:
You will not have to go to your goal,
Your goal itself shall come to you.

225. HE HAS THE MOST PERFECT ANSWER

How to be a genuine fake?
Go and ask a fanatic disciple.
He has the most perfect
Answer for you.

How to be a genuine rogue?
Go and ask a self-styled busy disciple.
He has the most perfect
Answer for you.

226. I SEE NOT

The world is too much with me.
Therefore
I see not the face of God.

The world is too much within me.
Therefore
I fail to see the face of Love.

227. THE HUMAN EYE, THE DIVINE EYE

The human eye sleeps
In the room of dreams.

The divine Eye strikes
The Hour of Reality.

The human heart declares:
Love before you perish.

The divine Heart reveals:
Love and become,
Become and love.

228. THIS IS THE DISCOVERY

Tension and destruction:
This is the discovery of the animal life.

Tension without attention:
This is the discovery of the human life.

Attention without tension:
This is the discovery of the divine life.

Attention with discovery:
This is the discovery of the supreme life.

229. MY LOVE, MY FREEWILL, MY GOD

My love is
My freewill.
My freewill is
My God.
My God is
My yesterday's Silence,
My today's Sound,
My tomorrow's Kingdom.

230. SICK SOUL, STRONG SOUL AND GOD-SOUL

He is a sick soul.
Therefore
He is an earth-bound cat.

He is a strong soul.
Therefore
He is a Heaven-free lion.

He is a God-soul.
Therefore
He cries with the heart of earth
And
Smiles with the Eye of Heaven.

231. THE CAVE-LIFE

I lived a cave-life
For meditation.
I shunned all my human friends
To gain my only eternal
And immortal Friend.

He came in and said:
"Son, your cave will suffocate me.
I want to live in your palace-life.
It will give me what I admire –
Oneness with the multitudes."

232. THE ONLY THING I KNOW

God, I teach
Because
This is the only thing I know.

"Son, I learn
Because
This is the only thing I know."

God, I judge You
Because
This is the only thing I know.

"Son, I forgive you
Because
This is the only thing I know."

233. I LIKE, I LOVE

Society and sanity:
I like society,
I love sanity.

Beauty and purity:
I like beauty,
I love purity.

Generosity and humility:
I like generosity,
I love humility.

Responsibility and duty:
I like responsibility,
I love duty.

234. JUST SURRENDER!

Don't conclude,
Just watch!
Lo, God is blessing you.

Don't watch,
Just feel!
Lo, God is loving you.

Don't feel,
Just surrender!
Lo, God is embracing you.

235. AN ALL-EMBRACING GLANCE

Fear
Is a backward glance.
Cheer
Is a forward glance.
Love
Is an inward glance.
Devotion
Is an upward glance.
Surrender
Is an all-embracing glance.

236. SURRENDER

Surrender
Is the vision of my world-clock.

Surrender
Is the reality of my life after death.

Surrender
Is the bridge
Between
My pure ascent
And
God's sure descent.

237. THIS IS JUST A SUGGESTION

Father,
This is just a suggestion:
Since You are extremely tired,
Let me take care
Of Your creation
For a while.

"Son,
This is just a suggestion:
Since you are not tired at all,
You should not make friends
With death-sleep
Any more."

238. HIS FRIENDS

He has two unreliable friends:
His black fear and his brown doubts.

He has two reliable friends:
His white faith and his purple love.

He has one indispensable friend:
His blue-gold inner cry.

239. THREE BOOKS

He has studied only three books:
The book of nonsense,
The book of ignorance,
The book of innocence.

The animal in him
Was satisfied
With his nonsense-book.

The human in him
Was satisfied
With his ignorance-book.

The divine in him
Was satisfied
With his innocence-book.

240. WHY AM I HERE?

Why am I here
In the land of the Gurus?
Why am I here
In the land of the disciples?

I am in the land of the Gurus
Because
God wants to share with me
His Realisation-Light.

I am in the land of the disciples
Because
God wants to share with me
His ignorance-night.

241. THEY DO NOT CONTRADICT ME

A great man
Does not contradict me
Because
He knows
I am a senseless soul.

A good man
Does not contradict me
Because
He knows
I am a loveless soul.

A God-man
Does not contradict me
Because
He knows
I am a helpless soul.

242. JUST START

Why start?
Just start and see.

How to start?
Just start and feel.

When to start?
Just start and reach.

243. HE PAID THREE VISITS TO GOD

He paid three visits to God:

First time he went
With a beggar's humiliation.

Second time he went
With a seeker's humility.

Third time he went
With a lover's oneness.

God questioned the beggar,
God smiled at the seeker,
God caught the lover.

244. THE CROSS, THE CROWN

If you
Love the cross,
The crown will adorn you.

If you
Love the crown,
The cross may not utilise you.

What is the cross?
The cross is self-examination.
What is the crown?
The crown is self-manifestation.

245. THEIR MINDS

The mind of a fool
Knows everything.

The mind of a wise man
Asks everything.

The mind of a great man
Envelops everything.

The mind of a good man
Treasures everything.

246. THE POND, THE RIVER, THE SEA

The pond cries
For the Power of the sea.
The river runs
For the Light of the sea.
The sea sighs
For the Light within.

247. THE DIFFERENCE BETWEEN MY MIND AND MY HEART

The difference
Between
My heart and my mind
Is this:
My heart grows up
But
Does not grow old,
Never;
My mind grows old
But
Does not grow up,
Never.

248. SAYING AND DOING, GIVING AND RECEIVING

The difference
Between
Saying and doing
Is this:
Saying is man-power,
Doing is God-shower.

The difference
Between
Giving and receiving
Is this:
Giving is the stamp of the individual man,
Receiving is the stamp of the universal God.

249. WHAT THEY NEED

What my body needs
Is an endurance-contest.

What my vital needs
Is an appearance-contest.

What my body needs
Is an inconscience-conquest.

What my heart needs
Is an assurance-rest.

250. NOBODY CAME, ALL CAME

Light for sale.
Nobody came
Because
Light is too powerful.

Truth for sale.
Nobody came
Because
Truth is too hurtful.

Ignorance for sale.
All came
Because
Ignorance teaches them how to sing.

Bondage for sale.
All came
Because
Bondage teaches them how to dance.

251. NOTHING LIVES FOREVER

Nothing lives forever
Save and except
Man's inner cry for God.

Nothing lives forever
Save and except
Man's soul-love for Light.

No one lives forever
Save and except
A man of heart-sacrifice.

No one lives forever
Save and except
A man of constant God-necessity.

252. THREE TRAVELLING COMPANIONS

I travelled with a fool.
He advised me:
Break your body of yesterday,
Break your heart of today,
Break your soul of tomorrow.

I travelled with a wise man.
He advised me:
Feed your body of purity,
Feed your heart of love,
Feed your soul of duty.

I travelled with God.
He advised me:
Walk with your body-brother,
Run with your heart-sister,
Fly with your soul-friend.

253. HE IS NOT OF STONE

He is not of stone.
He loves man's body-temple.

He is not of stone.
He loves man's heart-shrine.

He is not of stone.
He loves man's soul-deity.

He is not of stone.
He loves man's God-Beauty.

254. YET MY WORRIES CONTINUE

God thinks of me,
Yet
My worries continue.
Why?

God meditates on me,
Yet
My worries continue.
Why?

God loves me,
Yet
My worries continue.
Why?
Why? Why? Why?

Because
I have not given God
My yesterday's bodiless fears,
My today's heartless doubts,
My tomorrow's soulless goal.

255. NO MORE

Light has burst forth.
No more can you sleep!

Truth has burst forth.
No more can you hide!

Peace has burst forth.
No more can you strike!

God has burst forth.
No more can you fail!

256. DISGRACE, GOD'S GRACE, GOD'S FACE

Disgrace descended on his
Tempting and tempted life.

God's Grace descends on his
Crying and striving life.

God's Face shall descend on his
Surrendering and surrendered
life.

257. A GIGANTIC CONSPIRACY

A gigantic conspiracy
Inspired by
My body-vital-mind:
They wanted to kill my heart.
But
Success could not crown them
Since
My body did not have enough
strength,
My vital enough determination,
My mind enough skill.

258. WHEN HE WENT IN SEARCH

When he went
In search of his soul,
He helplessly stumbled and
stumbled.

When he went
In search of his heart,
He hopelessly fumbled and
fumbled.

When he went
In search of his body,
He ceaselessly grumbled and
grumbled.

259. THE BODY OF A GOD-LOVER

The body of a God-lover
Is made of God's
Determination-Vital.

The vital of a God-lover
Is made of God's
Concentration-Mind.

The mind of a God-lover
Is made of God's
Contemplation-Heart.

The heart of a God-lover
Is made of God's Perfection-Soul.

The soul of a God-lover
Is made of God's
Glorification-Goal.

260. THE ONLY REAL LIFE

Peace:
What is it
If not the only real life of an
animal?

Love:
What is it
If not the only real life of man?

Light:
What is it
If not the only real life of God?

261. I SHALL OFFER

O earth-bound soul!
I love you,
I love you,
I love you.

I shall offer
The last drop of my life-blood
To light your consciousness-lamp,
To smash your world's
ignorance-pride,
To accelerate your blue-gold
journey's
Hour of God.

262. I TEACH, I LEARN

It is my duty to teach;
Therefore I teach.
What do I teach?
I teach self-examination.

It is my duty to learn;
Therefore I learn.
What do I learn?
I learn self-dedication,
Self-perfection
Plus
God-manifestation.

263. ALL EXCEPT

All are saved
Except fear.

All are loved
Except doubt.

All are illumined
Except jealousy.

All are fulfilled
Except insecurity.

All are adored
Except impurity.

264. I HAVE ACCEPTED THEIR INVITATION

I have accepted
The invitation of thought-world.

I have accepted
The invitation of will-sun.

I have accepted
The invitation of Goal-paradise.

Because
Thought-world will see me for the last time,
Will-sun will see me for the first time,
Goal-paradise will claim me for all time.

265. ALL MEN SEEK GOD

All men seek God
In their own ways.

You seek God
To please God.

He seeks God
To bless his desire-train.

I seek God
To become another God.

266. WHO IS GOOD?

Who is small?
Who is great?
Who is good?

He is small
Who thinks he is so.

He is great
Who knows he is so.

He is good
Who is nothing but that.

267. HE IS THE WISEST MAN

He is a fool
Because
He has not read any books.
Perhaps so he is.

He is a wise man
Because
He has read ten thousand books.
Perhaps so he is.

He is a wiser man
Because
He has read fifteen thousand
books.
Perhaps so he is.

He is the wisest man,
By far
The wisest man,
Who has read only two special
books:
Aspiration-height
And
Surrender-light.

268. THREE DREAMS

Last night
I dreamt of an ape
And
A banana.

Tonight
I shall dream of a deer
And
A fence.

Tomorrow night
I shall dream of a love-soul
And
The God-Goal.

269. THEY ARREST ME

Fear arrests me
Quickly.
Courage arrests me
Unconsciously.
Doubt arrests me
Abruptly.
Faith arrests me
Timidly.
Love arrests me
Slowly.
Devotion arrests me
Steadily.
Surrender arrests me
Unerringly.
God arrests me
Compassionately,
Carefully
And
Completely.

270. I WISH TO RETURN HOME

O Lord,
Follow me,
Love me,
Serve me.
I wish to leave Home.

O Lord,
Guide me,
Lead me,
Carry me.
I wish to return Home.

271. DON'T BE A FOOL

Don't be a fool.
You need aspiration
In your animal life.

Don't be a fool.
You need perfection
In your human life.

Don't be a fool.
You see frustration
In your divine life.

272. YOUR MASTER

Your Master observes
More than he admits.

Your Master loves
More than he reveals.

Your Master cries
More than you see.

Your Master gives
More than you need.

273. PARTIALITY

My God is partial;
Therefore
He always thinks of me.

My God is partial;
Therefore
He always meditates on me.

My God is partial;
Therefore
He always loves me.

"My child is partial;
Therefore
She thinks of Me only."

"My child is partial;
Therefore
She meditates on Me only."

"My child is partial;
Therefore
She loves Me only."

274. NEVER DO I THINK

I love God,
But
Never do I think of His
Goodness-Beauty.

I speak to God,
But
Never do I think of His
Greatness-Duty.

I fight with God,
But
Never do I think of our
Oneness-Reality.

275. WHAT DO YOU THINK I AM?

What do you think I am?
Am I the prince of
ignorance-night?
No, I am not. Never!

What do you think I am?
Am I the frown of
destruction-night?
No, I am not. Never!

What do you think I am?
Am I not the lord of my senses?
Certainly I am!

What do you think I am?
Am I not the future God?
Certainly I am!

276. MERCHANT OF PSYCHIC SECRETS

O merchant of vital secrets,
I love you;
Therefore
Do grant me your gracious
absence!

O merchant of psychic secrets,
I think of you alone,
I love you alone,
I need you alone;
Therefore
Do grant me your benign
presence!

277. THE COST

The cost of compassion
Is negligible.

The cost of forgiveness
Is negligible.

The cost of transformation
Is a bit high.

The cost of perfection
Is exorbitant.

278. WHAT ARE WE DOING?

What are my parents doing
In Heaven today?
Ah, they are thinking
Of inviting me for dinner.

What am I doing
On earth today?
Ah, since I have no food
In my refrigerator,
I am thinking of flying
To my parents now
To enjoy my breakfast
And luncheon as well.

279. PROGRESS YOU WANT?

Progress you want?
Remember then,
Your black doubt
Is your first and last limit.

Progress you want?
Remember then,
Your courage
Is your last limit.

Progress you want?
Remember then,
Your faith
Is your endless limit.

Progress you want?
Remember then,
Your love of Light
Is your birthless start
And your deathless limit.

280. SINCE BELIEVING IS SEEING

Since believing
Is seeing,
Then seeing
Is doing.

Since doing
Is becoming,
Then becoming
Is transcending.

281. NOTHING ASSISTS HIM

More faith assists
The believer.

More courage assists
The brave.

More love assists
The lover.

But
Nothing assists
The stupid doubter.

282. IF YOU WANT TO ADVISE ME

O asserter of truth,
If you want to advise me,
Then stay fifty miles away
From me, please.

O preacher of truth,
If you want to advise me,
Then stay forty miles away
From me, please.

O lover of truth,
If you want to advise me,
Then stay twenty miles away
From me, please.

O follower of truth,
If you want to advise me,
Then do knock at
My heart's door.

283. HIS INSECURITY, HIS CURIOSITY

His insecurity
Is stingy in teaching.

His curiosity
Is generous in learning.

His insecurity, what is it?
His tremendous attachment to dust.

His curiosity, what is it?
His storehouse of information.

284. TWO DAYS MORE

Two days more
Until I go to Heaven.
Therefore
Today I shall buy
The aspiration-ticket and
Tomorrow I shall board
The Realisation-plane
To reach my sun-vast
Destination: Heaven.

285. EXCEPT ONE THING

Everything is in the hands of
destiny
Except one thing:
My bosom's will.

Everything is in the hands of
destiny
Except one thing:
My hour of God.

Everything is in the hands of
destiny
Except one thing:
My imminent Perfection-dawn.

286. ANNOUNCE, PRONOUNCE, RENOUNCE

Announce! Announce your pride.
You will feel miserable.

Pronounce! Pronounce God's
name.
You will be happy.

Renounce! Renounce ignorance.
You will be fulfilled.

287. THE APPARENT AND THE REAL

The Apparent feels that
It is self-sufficient.
Lo, our ignorance is self-sufficient.

The Real knows that
It is God-sufficient.
Lo, our love of God is
God-sufficient.

288. THREE MOST SIGNIFICANT THINGS

Just go to sleep
And don't complain.
God will think of you.

Just go to sleep
And don't complain.
God will meditate on you.

Just go to sleep
And don't complain.
God will do everything for you.

He has already done
Three most
Significant things for you:
He calls you "son".
He has given you
The message of Liberation.
He has given you the key
To unlock the Palace of Perfection.

289. SOME INSIDE INFORMATION

True, I could not get into
God's Palace;
But I have got
Some inside information.

God will retire soon.
He has already chosen
His successor.
Do you want to know who he is?

He is your bosom friend.
I mean the first personal pronoun.
That means I,
And none else.

290. WILL YOU TALK?

Master, will you talk?
"Certainly I shall.
I shall talk on
God's Perfection-sky."

Son, will you talk?
"Certainly I shall.
I shall talk on
Your Compassion-sea."

291. THE EVENING ALCOHOLICS

The morning hippies prayed to
God
For purity's flood.
God found it difficult
To believe His ears.

The noon drug-addicts prayed to
God
For the heights of Delight.
God found it difficult
To believe His eyes.

The evening alcoholics prayed to
God
For the life of
Transformation-light.
God found that impossibility's
Measureless capacities
Had surrendered
To a facile God-possibility.

292. THE DOOR

I saw the Door.
Therefore
God loved me.

I am at the Door.
Therefore
God embraces me.

I shall be the Door.
Therefore
God and I shall claim
Each other
As our very own.

293. LET MY FANCIFUL MIND ROAM

Let my fanciful mind roam.
I shall stay with You, my Lord.

Let my fanciful mind roam.
I shall love You only, my Lord.

Let my fanciful mind roam.
I shall offer You my heart, my all.

294. HIS GOD, YOUR GOD

Can a scientist believe in God?
Yes, he can and he does.
His God is Matter.
His God is Matter.

Can a seeker believe in God?
Yes, you can and you do.
Your God is Spirit.
Your God is Spirit.

His God spreads before He flies.
Your God flies before He spreads.

295. MY BODY HATES TO BE FILMED

My vital films
My mind's insincerity.

My mind films
My vital's vanity.

My heart films
My soul's beauty.

My soul films
My heart's purity.

My body hates
To be filmed.
Therefore nobody
Dares to film my body.

296. BETTER WAIT!

Better wait!
God may come down.

Better wait!
God may ask you your name and address.

Better wait!
God may give you another chance to equal Him.

Better wait!
Don't hurry. He who hurries
Buries his soul in a goalless shore.

297. TWO GUESTS

God is an uninvited guest;
Yet
He always comes.

Immortality is always an invited guest;
Yet
She never comes.

Our heart-flower loves the uninvited guest.
Our soul-bud loves the invited guest.

298. I SHALL BE WITH GOD

Let my world sink.
I shall think of God.

Let my world die.
I shall fly with God.

Let my world achieve.
I shall stay with God.

Let my world become.
I shall *be* with God.

299. NO POINT IN RESISTING

No point in resisting.
God is bound to come in.

No point in insisting.
Your pride will leave you someday
Without fail.

No point in doubting.
God is unmistakably yours.
Yours is the birthright,
Perfection-light.

300. HE WHO WOKE UP

He who woke up
Saw the blue face of God.

He who saw the blue face of God
Became the gold heart of God.

He who became the gold heart of
God
Is Eternity's cry and Infinity's
smile.

301. IN YOU I SEE

O sobbing sighs
Of the morning star,
In you I see the Beauty
Of the Lord Supreme.

O blossoming smile
Of the morning sun,
In you I feel the Duty
Of the Lord Supreme.

302. THE GREEN VAST FIELDS

The green vast fields
Of my aspiring heart
Are waiting for God's Hour
In my surrendering heart of night.

The blue vast skies
Of my revealing soul
Are offering the power of love
In the fulfilling life of Light.

303. MY CONSCIOUSNESS-TREE

Yesterday I loved
My sapling consciousness-tree
Because
It embodied my journey's start.

Today I love
My youngling consciousness-tree
Because
It reveals my journey's speed.

Tomorrow I shall love
My climbing, glowing and
  spreading consciousness-tree
Because
It will fulfil my journey's promise.

304. SILENCE-FACE, FORGIVENESS-SMILE

Life is but a day.
Therefore
I try to finish
All my aspiring
And
All my loving
In the short span
Of one single day.

Life is but Eternity,
Therefore
I sleep and dream,
I sing and dance
And
Dance and sing
In the Silence-Face,
  Forgiveness-Smile
Of the birthless and deathless Day.

305. NO MORE!

I was my heart's
Sleeping rocks.

I was my heart's
Brooding clouds.

I was my heart's
Burning anguish.

I was my heart's
Sinking heights.

But no more!
I repeat:
No more!
Again I repeat:
No more, No more!

306. I BREATHE IN, I BREATHE OUT

Quickly and lovingly
Smilingly and triumphantly
I breathe in
The blossoming breath
Of my golden morn.

Quickly and steadily
Helplessly and unreservedly
I breathe out
The fading breath
Of my folding eve.

307. THE MUSIC OF THE HEART

The music of the heart
Is the silence-light
Of Perfection-height.
The aspiration-world has
discovered
This truth sublime.

The music of the vital
Is the elephant-ignorance
Of destruction-night.
The desire-world shall discover
This truth infallible.

308. NOT BORN FOR DEATH

Not one but three discoveries
supreme
I have already made:

My heart of redolent
gratitude-blossoms
Was not born for death.

My soul of perfect oneness-vision
Was not born for death.

My life of constant
manifestation-light
Was not born for death.

309. MY EYES NEED

My closed eyes
Need
God the Beauty.

My open eyes
Need
God the Duty.

My half-open and
half-closed eyes
Need
God the Sovereignty.

310. VITAL NIGHT AND PSYCHIC LIGHT

When my vital night
Replaces my psychic light,
I die before I sink.

When my psychic light
Replaces my vital night,
I fly before I try.

311. I LOVE

I love the dancing
Of teeming clouds
Because
Of their thunder-power.

I love the singing
Of passing clouds
Because
Of their diamond-wisdom.

I love the dreaming
Of weeping clouds
Because
Of their sacrifice-soul.

312. WHEN I WOKE UP

Before I went to sleep
I saw my death's dateless night.

During my sleep
I saw my life's endless light.

When I woke up
I found Mother Earth's
Compassion
In my aspiration-heart,
And Father Heaven's Perfection
Around my dedication-life.

313. WAIT A MINUTE, GOD, PLEASE!

Wait a minute, God, please!
I have more to tell You
About my inner pangs.

Wait a minute, God, please!
I have more to tell You
About my outer triumphs.

Wait a minute, God, please!
I have more to tell You
About my surrender-light.

314. HIS IS THE SOUL THAT LOVES

His is the vital that loves
The imperious waves.

His is the mind that loves
The spacious skies.

His is the heart that loves
The gracious sun.

His is the soul that loves
The precious moon.

315. A GOOD PRICE

The voice of a singing rivulet
I had.
I sold it at a very reasonable price.

The voice of smashing thunder
I have.
I am begging ignorance to buy it
from me.

The voice of the liberating God
I shall have.
I shall give it to Mother Earth
At a good price -
Free,
Absolutely free.

316. O PILGRIM SOUL

O pilgrim soul,
Divinity
Is in your untiring feet.

O pilgrim soul,
Infinity
Is in your unblinking eyes.

O pilgrim soul,
Eternity
Is in your unbending head.

O pilgrim soul,
Immortality
Is in your unthinking heart.

317. I AM TELLING YOU THE TRUTH

The power of poise-sky
I had.
I am telling you the truth.

The power of justice-light
I have.
I am telling you the truth.

The power of compassion-moon
I shall have.
I am telling you the truth.

318. THEY SHALL GO AND RETURN

My heart shall go to Heaven
And return.
My heart shall return with more
Compassion-power.

My mind shall go to Heaven
And return.
My mind shall return with more
Perfection-light.

My vital shall go to Heaven
And return.
My vital shall return with more
Justice-height.

My body shall go to Heaven
And return.
My body shall return with more
Patience-length.

319. THEY DO NOT WANT ME

I have wasted my time;
Therefore
Bliss does not want me.

I have neglected my duty;
Therefore
Peace does not want me.

I have rejected truth;
Therefore
Light does not want me.

320. ENOUGH!

O hope, O eyeless hope,
Cling not.
Enough of your tenacity!

O reality, O vast reality,
Sleep not.
Enough of your cruelty!

O God, O mighty God,
Demand not.
Enough of Your authority!

321. MY SILVER KEY, MY GOLDEN KEY

My silver key
Opens the door
Of my wakeful and tearful heart
For God to come in
And my ignorance to go out.

My golden key
Opens the door
Of God's Nectar-Smile
For me to talk to God,
To sit on His Throne,
To become His Crown.

322. IS IT FAIR?

God, is it fair
That I am doomed to stay
With my lifeless body?

God, is it fair
That I am doomed to walk
With my cheerless vital?

God, is it fair
That I am doomed to think
With my thoughtless mind?

God, is it fair
That I am doomed to dance
With my soulless heart?

God, is it fair
That I am doomed to dream
With my goalless soul?

323. GOD WILL BE ARRIVING SOON

O my unclean body,
Be careful.
God the Purity
Will be arriving soon.

O my unruly vital,
Be careful.
God the Power
Will be arriving soon.

O my unthinking mind,
Be careful.
God the Light
Will be arriving soon.

O my unaspiring heart,
Be careful.
God the uncompromising King
Will be arriving soon.

324. I AM A CHILD OF GRACE

I am a child of Grace
When I pray soulfully.

I am a child of Race
When I concentrate
one-pointedly.

I am a child of Peace
When I meditate silently.

I am a child of Delight
When I contemplate selflessly.

325. THE SUPREME TRUTH

God is a tiny insect.
This is a strange truth.

God is a huge elephant.
This is a normal truth.

God is a devouring tiger.
This is a peculiar truth.

God is a speedy deer.
This is an infallible truth.

God is a loving cow.
This is the supreme Truth.

326. THE SONG OF MY EMPTINESS

I need an empty body
To receive God's
  Consciousness-Love-Light.

I need an empty vital
To receive God's
  Consciousness-Love-Might.

I need an empty mind
To receive God's
  Consciousness-Love-Peace.

I need an empty heart
To receive God's
  Consciousness-Love-Bliss.

327. I TOUCHED GOD'S FEET

I touched God's white Feet.
Purity's flood I became.

I touched God's green Feet.
Beauty's field I became.

I touched God's blue Feet.
Divinity's sky I became.

I touched God's gold Feet.
Reality's sun I became.

328. THEY DECLARE

Silently
My soul declares
The Vision of the Supreme.

Tenderly
My heart declares
The Compassion of the Supreme.

Clearly
My mind declares
The Light of the Supreme.

Boldly
My vital declares
The Power of the Supreme.

Unerringly
My body declares
The Love of the Supreme.

329. DO YOU KNOW?

Do you know that my heart
Is a sacred island?
Perhaps you know.

Do you know that my mind
Is a secret island?
Perhaps you know.

Do you know that my vital
Is an ignored island?
Perhaps you know.

Do you know that my body
Is a treasure-island?
Ah, you didn't know?

Then learn it once and for all.

330. I BELIEVE

I whole-heartedly believe
God is always great and aloof.

I half-heartedly believe
God is always good and kind.

With some difficulty I believe
God cares for me.

With no difficulty I believe
God deserves my criticism.

331. MY ANCIENT DREAM

O Lord Supreme,
Teach my mind
How to sleep without a futile
dream.
O Lord Supreme,
Teach my heart
How to regain my ancient dream –
The dream that revealed
You and I are one,
The dream that distributed
Our respective tasks:
You the Monarch of Heaven,
And I the Monarch of earth.

332. THE THUNDER

The thunder of the green earth
Teaches my life.

The thunder of the blue sky
Examines my life.

The thunder of the gold Heaven
Declares my triumphant results.

The thunder of the black hell
Desires my achievement-treasure.

333. I WISH TO REMAIN A PRACTICAL MAN

I love like God.
Therefore
I am an equal partner
Of God the Lover.

I think like God.
Therefore
I am an equal partner
Of God the Thinker.

I dream like God.
Therefore
I am an equal partner
Of God the Dreamer.

But
I act not like God the Doer,
Because
I wish to remain
A practical man.

334. LIFE-ROOT, LIFE-GOAL

My life-root silently
Expands.

My life-tree confidently
Ascends.

My life-fruit slowly
Descends.

My life-goal supremely
Ascends.

335. GOD'S EYES

God's thinking Eyes
I appreciate.

God's talking Eyes
I admire.

God's dreaming Eyes
I adore.

God's illumining Eyes
I love.

God's perfecting Eyes
I fear.

336. FIVE MESSAGES

Perfection
Is the message of my soul.

Compassion
Is the message of my heart.

Determination
Is the message of my mind.

Expansion
Is the message of my vital.

Revelation
Is the message of my body.

337. THE TRANSCENDENCE

His eyes are the depths
Of the Life Divine.

His mind is the promise
Of the Life Divine.

His heart is the assurance
Of the Life Divine.

His soul is the transcendence
Of the Life Divine.

338. MY HOUSES

My soul-house
Was made by God the Dreamer.

My heart-house
Was made by God the Seeker.

My mind-house
Was made by God the Thinker.

My vital-house
Was made by God the Lover.

My body-house
Was made by God the Sufferer.

339. MY SILENCE-SOUL

My silence-soul
Sows,
My silence-heart
Grows.

My silence-vital
Receives,
My silence-body
Achieves.

340. I FORGOT AND NOW I RECALL

I forgot
And now
I recall:
God is my Reality's loving Friend.

I forgot
And now
I recall:
God is my Divinity's helping Brother.

I forgot
And now
I recall:
God is my Immortality's sacrificing Sister.

341. GOD'S SILVER LADDER, GOD'S GOLDEN WINGS

My heart and I cried.
Therefore
God gave us His silver ladder to
climb.

My life and I surrendered.
Therefore
God gave us His golden wings to
fly.

342. WHEN I SANG THE SILENCE-SONG

When God sang the sound-song,
I told Him that was not fair:
He was singing my song.

When I sang the silence-song,
God happily and unconditionally
Told me that
Since I had learnt His song
He could peacefully retire.

343. THE TINIEST DROP

The curse of Time
I can easily endure,
The strokes of the Almighty
I can easily brave.
But
The tiniest drop of ignorance-sea
Can easily destroy
The blue-gold dreams of my heart
And
The green-red realities of my life.

344. A SILENT VOICE TELLS ME

A weeping voice tells me
God does not want me.

A murmuring voice tells me
God does not care for me.

A whispering voice tells me
God always needs me.

A silent voice tells me
God proudly and eternally fulfils
Himself
Only through me.

345. YESTERDAY, TODAY, TOMORROW

Yesterday
I was a homeless soul.
Today
I have a soulless home.
Tomorrow
I shall reach the goalless shore.

346. THE PHANTOM NIGHT, THE PHANTOM DAY

When
The phantom night struck me
I lost all my Heavenly spheres
Sooner than at once.

When
I struck the phantom day
I won nothing save and except
An endless frustration-night,
A soulless and goalless fight.

347. THE MAGNET

A rich smile of God
Is the magnet
That draws my heart,
My life, my all
To God's ever-transcending
Heights.

A rich cry of mine
Is the magnet
That draws God's Heart,
God's Soul, God's Goal
To my ever-sinking nadir.

348. WILL YOU BARTER WITH ME?

O martyr-sun,
Will you barter with me
My martyr-candle?

O martyr-ocean,
Will you barter with me
My martyr-drop?

O Martyr-Immortality,
Will you barter with me
My martyr-death?

349. THE TOUCH

In my world
Light is the touch
Of a fulfilling hand,
Delight is the touch
Of a vanishing hand,
Perfection is the touch
Of a vanished hand,
Peace is the touch
Of a broken hand,
Concern is the touch
Of a weak hand,
Compassion is the touch
Of an unusual hand.

350. I SAW THE BURIAL

I saw the burial of my body.
I laughed and laughed.

I saw the burial of my vital.
I laughed and laughed.

I saw the burial of my mind.
I laughed and laughed.

I saw the burial of my heart.
I cried and cried
Because
What I really had,
What I really claimed
As my own,
Was my sole tiny heart.

351. WHEN I LOVE

When I love my physical life
My life is full of futile days.

When I love my vital life
My life is full of damaging days.

When I love my mental life
My life is full of empty days.

When I love my psychic life
My life is full of fertile days.

When I love my God-life
My life is full of service-days.

352. HE DISCOVERED, HE REVEALED, HE MANIFESTED

He discovered God the Silence
In a tiny mountain cave.

He revealed God the Sound
In the battlefield of life.

He manifested God the Peace
In the emptiness of the Universal
Heart.

353. I HAVE, I AM, I SHALL REMAIN

The blue-vast body of Light
I have.
The gold-bright body of Delight
I am.
The white-pure body of Perfection
I shall always remain.

354. I CAN'T EVEN

My heart-sea is very vast;
I can't even feel it.
My mind-sky is very high;
I can't even see it.
My vital-fort is very strong;
I can't even escape it.
My body-tiger is very fierce;
I can't even tame it.

355. THE SWORDS

The sword of wisdom cautions.
The sword of aspiration protects.
The sword of life teaches.
The sword of love perfects,
illumines and fulfils.

356. WHAT IS?

What is body
If not a soulless sleeping?

What is vital
If not a senseless craving?

What is mind
If not a useless suspecting?

What is heart
If not a constant surrendering?

What is soul
If not a compassionate
compromising?

357. MY FOUR PATHS

My body crawls
Along my lightless path.
My vital stumbles
Along my shadowy path.
My mind trembles
Along my frightening path.
My heart runs
Along my sunlit path.

358. PLEASE ADDRESS

My sweet Lord,
Please address my inner eye.
I shall immediately awake.

My sweet Lord,
Please address my inner ear.
I shall immediately respond.

My sweet Lord,
Please address my inner mind.
I shall immediately receive.

My sweet Lord,
Please address my inner heart.
I shall immediately achieve.

My sweet Lord,
Please address my inner life.
I shall immediately surrender.

359. HOW CAN I HAVE IT?

A world of diamond silence:
Where is it?
A world of golden sound:
What is it?
A world of silver bliss:
How far is it?
A world of copper peace:
Alas, how can I have it?

360. HE IS HAPPY, HE IS UNHAPPY

He is happy
Because
His soul knows no stranger,
His heart knows no foreigner.

He is unhappy
Because
His mind knows no lover,
His vital knows no transformer,
His body knows no awakener.

361. HIS SURRENDERED LIFE

His surrendered body
Was light within light.

His surrendered mind
Was peace within peace.

His surrendered vital
Was power within power.

His surrendered heart
Was delight within delight.

362. WHAT IS THERE?

What is there to see?
God's Form.

What is there to feel?
God's Love.

What is there to love?
God's Silence.

What is there to become?
God's Compassion.

363. FLOODS OF DIVINITY

Peace floods the mind.
Love floods the heart.
Life floods the vital.
Light floods the body.
Consciousness floods the soul.
Surrender floods the Goal.

364. I BECOME BY SURRENDERING

I see by thinking,
I think by feeling,
I feel by living,
I live by loving,
I love by becoming,
I become by surrendering.

365. THE HOME OF UNIVERSAL LOVE

His mind
Is the secret home of sound.

His heart
Is the sacred home of silence.

His soul
Is the blue-vast home of God.

His God
Is the home of universal Love.

366. A FEEBLE CRY, A SWEET SMILE

A little ripple
Wakes the sea.

A tiny thought
Shakes the world.

A feeble cry
Brings the Supreme.

A sweet smile
Fulfils the Supreme.

367. THE HIGHEST GOD

Truth is a higher life.
Thought is a weaker world.
Doubt is a lower joy.
Faith is a brighter day.
But
Love is not only
A higher God,
But the highest God.

368. YET GOD LOVES HIM

He sighs before he prays.
He cries before he concentrates.
He sleeps before he meditates.
He fights before he aspires.
Yet
God loves him,
Because he eventually
Does the right thing.

369. BECAUSE

Because
I have something to give,
I live.

Because
I love the whole world,
I am.

Because
God and I fulfil each other,
We grow.

370. UPWARD, ALWAYS UPWARD

My body endlessly sleeps.
My vital spreads
Its aggression in all directions.
My mind spreads
Its suspicion in four directions.
My heart spreads
Its insecurity
Only in one direction -
Upward, always
Upward.

371. CONCEALED, REVEALED, FULFILLED

There was a time
Three hundred years ago
When his finite life
Concealed Infinity's Home.

There was a time
Thirty years ago
When his finite life
Revealed Infinity's Palace.

There was a time
Three years ago
When his finite life
Fulfilled Infinity's Kingdom.

372. I SATISFY GOD

I embrace the world
To find myself.

I find myself
To satisfy God.

I satisfy God
Because
That is the only thing
I understand intimately
And do satisfactorily.

373. I SAY WHAT I HAVE TO SAY!

Either believe
Or
Don't believe,
I say what I have to say!
I am who I was:
Silence-King.
I was who I am:
Perfection-Queen.

374. BY FAR THE BEST

We are surprisingly many.
That is good.
We are unquestionably more.
That is better.
We are divinely most.
That is excellent.
We are supremely one.
That is by far the best.

375. MY FIRST CHOICE

Believing, not seeing:
My fourth choice.

Feeling, not thinking:
My third choice.

Loving, not expecting:
My second choice.

Being, not becoming:
My first choice.

376. HE DEVOURS TWO THINGS

His heart devours only one thing:
Sunlit Delight.
His mind devours only one thing:
Sunlit Silence.
His vital devours only one thing:
Sunlit Power.
His body devours only one thing:
Sunlit Compassion.
But he devours two things:
God's Height
And
God's Depth.

377. YOU WILL FLY

Push not yourself beyond
  yourself;
You will sigh.
Pull not yourself beyond yourself;
You will cry.
Live not yourself beyond yourself;
You will die.

But
Love yourself beyond yourself
In your Beloved Supreme;
You will fly.

378. SOMETIMES I THINK

Sometimes
I think I am great.
Therefore
I dare to govern others.

Sometimes
I think I am good.
Therefore
I dare to love others.

Sometimes
I think I am God's.
Therefore
I dare to claim all
As my own,
My very own.

379. WITHOUT KNOWING WHY

Sometimes
We say something
Without knowing why.

Sometimes
We do something
Without knowing why.

Sometimes
We become something
Without knowing why.

But
We never love Truth
Without knowing why.

380. TOGETHER LIVE, TOGETHER DANCE

A happy man and good things
Together run.

An unhappy man and bad things
Together sink.

An aspiring man and fulfilling
  experience
Together live.

A God-man and fulfilled
  Realisation
Together dance.

381. MY BEGINNING, MY END, MY MIDDLE

My beginning was my end
When I thought
That I could do everything all
alone.

My end was my beginning
When I felt
God's Grace act in and through
me.

My middle was fulfilling
When I realised
That my limbs were made of
God's Compassion-Light.

382. AH, THERE

Ah, where is my Dream-boat?
I hear its sinking sound.
Ah, where is my Dream-boat?
I feel its dying silence.

Ah, there is my Reality-shore.
I see its flying banner.
Ah, there is my Reality-shore.
I drink its nectar-love.

383. TO YOU I OFFER TIME

O my body
To you I offer Time the forgiver.

O my vital
To you I offer Time the
transformer.

O my mind
To you I offer Time the silencer.

O my heart
To you I offer Time the lover.

O my soul
To you I offer Time the preserver.

384. FOR YOUR SAKE

O Lord,
For Your sake
I am doing the right thing.

For Your sake
I am loving everything and
everyone.

For Your sake
I am becoming the pride of
Heaven and earth.

I want nothing,
I need nothing
For myself
Either from Heaven-city
Or from earth-village.

385. SURPRISE DIES

Love the earth-soul;
You will surprise the Heaven-goal.

Love the Heaven-soul;
You will surprise the earth-goal.

Love the life of God-perfection,
You will surprise the birthless and
deathless bondage-man.

Love the birthless and deathless
bondage-man;
You will surprise the life of
God-perfection.

But when you love your
surrender-light
To the world within and to the
world without,
Surprise dies in the land of
nowhere.

386. I LIVED, I LIVE

I lived in the blue of Heaven
To sail my Dream-boat
Across the Sky-ocean.

I live in the green of earth
To sing the song of Love divine,
To play the game of Truth
sublime,
On the giant heart of my
Reality-shore.

387. HIS INSPIRATION-LIGHT

His body shuns his
inspiration-light.
His vital clasps his
inspiration-light.
His mind welcomes his
inspiration-light.
His heart feeds his
inspiration-light.
His soul leads his
inspiration-light.
His God is his inspiration-light.

388. WHERE ARE YOU?

O Lamb of God,
Where are You?
My eyes say You are not on earth,
My mind says You are not in
Heaven.

O Lamb of God,
Where are you?
My heart is fed by Your
Promise-light,
My soul is fulfilled by Your
Perfection-height.

O Lamb of God,
Where are You?

389. HE JUST COMPLETES HIMSELF

His ignorance-sea
Competes with the world-music.

His knowledge-sun
Competes with the
world-philosophy.

His wisdom-light
Competes with the
world-spirituality.

But he himself
Competes not with anything.
He just completes himself
In his surrender-drop
To the Ocean-will
Of the Transcendental Father.

390. I FOLLOWED THE PATH

I followed the path
Of self-assertion.
The world around despised me.

I followed the path
Of self-examination.
The world within admired
My bold attempt.

I followed the path
Of self-dedication.
The world within
And the world without
Had nothing for me
But lofty admiration.

391. THE MERCY

Life is the mercy of love.
Love is the mercy of surrender.
Surrender is the mercy of God's
Compassion.
God's Compassion is the mercy of
His Silence-Soul
And His Sound-Body.

392. THEY OFFER

His body-temple offers
Purity's smile.
His vital-temple offers
Agility's smile.
His mind-temple offers
Sincerity's smile.
His heart-temple offers
Humility's smile.
His soul-temple offers
Luminosity's smile.
And he himself offers
Perfection's Smile.

393. PERFECTION IMMORTAL AND SUPREME

Service is love
Visible and available.
Love is oneness
Inseparable and invincible.
Oneness is perfection
Immortal and supreme.

394. WHAT IS SACRIFICE?

Duty's beauty
God alone admires.
Beauty's purity
God alone admires.
Purity's sacrifice
God alone admires.
And what is sacrifice?
When the right hand
Devotedly gives
And the left hand
Devotedly receives.

395. GOD'S CALENDAR: MONDAY

Sweetest Father, Lord Supreme,
What was wrong with You on
Monday?
Why didn't You come on Monday
To teach us, Your children,
At our cosmic school?
Did anything happen in the
family?
Is everyone all right in Your
family?
Has anything serious happened?

"No, nothing of the sort.
What actually happened on
Monday was this:
I just over-ate My ignorance-food
On Sunday.
Therefore, I felt inexplicably
sick."

396. GOD'S CALENDAR: TUESDAY

Sweetest Father, Lord Supreme,
What was wrong with You on
Tuesday?

"On Monday night in Heaven
The cosmic gods and the hostile
forces
Had a terrible fight.
Therefore, My immediate
presence was demanded
By the cosmic gods."

397. GOD'S CALENDAR: WEDNESDAY

Sweetest Father, Lord Supreme,
What was wrong with You on
Wednesday?

"On Tuesday night
Heaven and earth bitterly fought
Over their supremacy.
I had to become their arbitrator.
Neither Heaven nor earth
Was satisfied with My decision.
Therefore, they are exceedingly
Displeased with Me.
Now neither Heaven nor earth
wants Me.
Friendless, sonless, daughterless,
I roamed in the world of
nowhere."

398. GOD'S CALENDAR: THURSDAY

Sweetest Father, Lord Supreme,
What was wrong with You on
Thursday?

"On Thursday your sweetest
Mother Divine,
Your dearest Mother Supreme,
Wanted to play with Her
Children, grandchildren and
great-grandchildren.
Therefore, I had to do all the
cooking
For our dearest and sweetest
ones."

399. GOD'S CALENDAR: FRIDAY

Sweetest Father, Lord Supreme,
What was wrong with You on
Friday?"

"On Friday Heaven tempted Me
With a much higher salary –
Love, devotion and surrender –
Infinitely more than I have been
Receiving from earth.
I was seriously considering
Whether I should accept
Such a lucrative offer."

400. GOD'S CALENDAR: SATURDAY AND SUNDAY

Sweetest Father, Lord Supreme,
What was wrong with You on
Saturday?

"On Saturday
Mother Earth phoned Me
Early in the morning
And insulted Me ruthlessly.
She has come to learn of My secret
plans,
And to My sorrow She has
dispensed
With My job here on earth.

"Sweetest children, this is Sunday.
Today I have come to see you all
For the last time,
And to offer you
My Compassion-Sea, My
Concern-Sky,
My Love-Moon and My
Blessing-Sun."

401. IN YOUR DAILY LIFE

Where is your temple?
Is it not in your daily life?

Where is your shrine?
Is it not in your daily life?

Where is your duty?
Is it not in your daily life?

Where is your God?
Is He not in your daily life?

Who is God?
He who sings the songs
Of self-transcendence
At each hush-gap.

402. THE OTHER DAY, THE OTHER NIGHT

I played with Eternity the other day.
Neither Eternity nor I won the game,
Neither Eternity nor I lost the game.

I sang with Infinity the other night.
Indeed, we two are the singers
Of the transcendental Heights.

I danced with Immortality the other day.
At the end we bartered our lives.

I walked with God the other night.
When He felt tired, I carried Him along
On my shoulders.
When I felt tired, He carried me along
Inside His Heart.

403. WITH NO DIFFICULTY AT ALL

With difficulty I discovered
The face of the earth.

With greater difficulty I
discovered
The life in the world.

With greatest difficulty I
discovered
A sun on earth.

But with no difficulty at all
I discovered the transcendental
Silence-Height
Of the Absolute Supreme.

404. I SLEEP WITH GOD

From the golden morn
To the fiery noon
I pray to God.

From the fiery noon
To the retiring eve
I meditate on God.

From the retiring eve
To the starry night
I contemplate on God.

From the starry night
To the Golden Dawn
I sleep with God.

405. THEY MAKE THEIR OWN SELECTIONS

The soul selects
Its own members.

The heart selects
Its own brothers and sisters.

The mind selects
Its own mentors.

The vital selects
Its own admirers.

The body selects
Its own fellow-dreamers.

406. HERE IS THE DIFFERENCE

Here is
The difference between
A doleful cry
And
A soulful smile:
A doleful cry
Is a human query;
A soulful smile
Is an answer divine.

407. O MESSENGER

O Messenger of death,
I feel your universal hunger.

O Messenger of life,
I know your universal Truth.

O Messenger of love,
I am, I am Your universal Light.

408. O MY WORLD

O my world,
Sleep not with a groaning age.

O my world,
Stay not with a moaning age.

O my world,
Live, live with a climbing face.

O my world,
Love, love with the dawning
grace.

409. YOU, ONLY YOU!

O orphan hope,
Who were your parents?

O infant love,
Where are your parents?

O constant fear,
Who are you?

O instant joy,
You, only you!

410. ALL ARE BORN TO TRANSCEND

All are not born to see.
All are not born to feel.
All are not born to run.
All are not born to dive.
All are not born to fly.
But
All are born to love,
All are born to serve,
All are born to progress,
All are born to perfect,
All are born to transcend.

411. THEY HAVE GIVEN ME

Earth has given me
What it has: lasting cry.

Heaven has given me
What it has: lasting smile.

Doubt has given me
What it has: lasting torture.

Faith has given me
What it has: lasting confidence.

God has given me
What He is: lasting Love.

412. THE FAVOURITE

He is Heaven's favourite lover.
Therefore
He loves the world
Devotedly.

He is earth's favourite server.
Therefore
He serves the world
Soulfully.

He is God's favourite hero.
Therefore
He defends the world
Gratefully.

413. TO PLEASE GOD, TO PLEASE MAN

To please God
I offer my life's little lamp.
And God is unreservedly satisfied.

To please man
I offer my soul's vast sun.
Yet man is unquestionably
dissatisfied.

Who can please God?
Whoever wants to.

Who can please man?
No one, not even God.

414. I AM KNOWN TO SURRENDER

You are happy
Because
You are unknown to doubt.

He is happy
Because
He is unknown to failure.

Heaven is happy
Because
It is known to tomorrow.

Earth is happy
Because
It is known to joy.

Finally, I am happy
Because
I am known to surrender,
constant surrender,
unconditional surrender.

415. DANCE AND DINE

When my weary night
Struggles into day,
God and I together dance
In the garden of Love-light.

When my fiery day
Slips into night,
Satan and the King of death
Together dine in the Kitchen of
Surprise.

416. THE SECRETS OF TRANCE

Morning the teacher
Teaches him the secrets
Of beautiful trance.

Noon the teacher
Teaches him the secrets
Of powerful trance.

Evening the teacher
Teaches him the secrets
Of silent trance.

God the teacher
Teaches him the secrets
Of natural trance.

417. TWO WATCHMEN

Man the watchman tells me:
"Stop, stop! Show me your
identification."

God the Watchman tells me:
"Come in, come in.
Look, here is my identification."

418. SILENCE AND SOUND

The sound in silence
Talks much,
Says less.

The silence in sound
Talks less,
Says more.

The God in sound
Speaks first,
Then acts.

The God in silence
Speaks not,
Just acts.

419. LET US WAGER

Lord, let us wager
Our kingdoms.
Let Thy Kingdom come down,
Let my kingdom go up.
Let us see whose kingdom
Has a faster speed.
Lord, if You win
I shall give you immediately
My only wealth: surrender-light.
Lord, if I win
Will You give me
Your Perfection-height?

420. A PRINCE OF LOVE

When I was a Prince of gloom
I thought I could do
Everything
In the twinkling of an eye.

When I was a Prince of Light
I discovered that patience and I
Eventually
Would do everything.

When I was a Prince of Love
I realised that God and I
Had already
Done everything.

421. ACHIEVE AND STOP NOT

O Lord of my body,
Awake.

O Lord of my vital,
Build and break not.

O Lord of my mind,
Receive.

O Lord of my heart,
Achieve and stop not.

422. HOW HARD I WORK

O beloved pride,
How hard I work
To build you up.

O beloved doubt,
How hard I work
To defend your cause.

O beloved fear,
How hard I work
To treasure your body.

O beloved depression,
How hard I work
To fathom your realisation.

423. MY LAST GOAL

My human goals
Have fooled me
Quickly,
Abruptly,
Ruthlessly.

My divine goals
Are ignoring me
Slowly,
Steadily,
Unerringly.

I shall now try my last goal:
The goal of God-becoming.

424. MY HEART SHALL GROW WITH YOU

O sleeping night,
Don't be so frightened.
My body shall sleep with you.

O whistling wind,
Don't be so restless.
My vital shall play with you.

O murmuring river,
Don't be so proud.
My mind shall run with you.

O lonely garden,
Don't be so depressed.
My heart shall grow with you.

425. FLYING

He was flying sweetly and divinely
From the mortal dream-world
Into the immortal Reality-world.

He is flying consciously and
supremely
From the Reality-world
Into the Perfection-sun.

He shall be flying swiftly and
unerringly
From the Perfection-sun
Into the Source:
The Silence of the
Ever-transcending Beyond.

426. DANGER-RED, DANGER-WHITE

Danger-red challenges
Human courage.

Danger-blue welcomes
Human faith.

Danger-green defies
Earthly time.

Danger-white strengthens
Our prayer.

427. THE RULER OF NIGHT

Protection, what is it?
Man's spontaneous belief in a
higher power.

What is a higher power?
Man's unmanifested Light.

What is Light?
Light is the ruler of night
And
Nourisher of Delight.

428. GOD, STAY NOT ALONE!

God, stay not alone!
I am more than eager
To stay with You.

God, use not Your Will alone!
I am more than willing
To use my will with Yours.

God, govern not alone!
Since two heads are better than
one
I am ready to offer You my
service-light
So that You can govern
Your worlds supremely well.

429. NO RECOGNITION, NO REWARD

His pride
Deserves no response.

His humility
Requires no recognition.

His ignorance
Deserves no reward.

His wisdom
Far transcends human
appreciation.

430. GOD AND I MEET TOGETHER

In the morning
God and I meet together
To appreciate our beauty's birth.

In the evening
God and I meet together
To admire our duty's end.

At night
God and I meet together
To immortalise our necessity's
life.

431. THREE SONGS

I know only three songs:
Heart-song,
Soul-song,
Life-song.

With my heart-song,
I reveal God the Lover.

With my soul-song,
I manifest God the Beloved.

With my life-song,
I fulfil God the Supreme.

432. HE AND HIS EXPERIENCES

He and his eyes
Stood against the blue-vast sky.

He and his nose
Stood against the green-brown
earth.

He and his arms
Stood against the gold-white
Heaven.

His victories were followed
By giant defeats.

His defeats were followed
By Himalayan victories.

He and his experiences
Breathe Immortality's Life.

433. EVEN SO

As I conceal
Death's proud capacity,
Even so, death
Reveals my stupendous capacity.

As I ask death
To delay its final arrival,
Even so, death demands
My supreme authority.

434. O SWEET OBLIVION, O GREAT REMEMBRANCE

O sweet oblivion,
To you I bow and bow.
You have made me forget
All my yesterdays,
My yesterdays' bitter failures.

O great remembrance,
To you I bow and bow.
You have granted me the capacity
To remember all my sublimely
significant conversations,
My conversations with the Lord
Supreme.

435. HIS MIND-CLOUD

His mind-cloud
Appreciates the teeming clouds
Of the sky.

His vital-pleasure
Enjoys the teeming pleasures
Of the world.

His body-sleep
Knows nothing save the embrace
Of ignorance-sleep.

His heart-surrender
Is all surrender to the God
In humanity.

436. WHO HAS BROUGHT ME?

Who has brought me
To the old familiar hell?
Ah, my desire-thief.

Who has brought me
To the old familiar Heaven?
Ah, my aspiration-chief.

Who has brought me
To my old familiar Lord?
Ah, His Compassion supreme.

437. YOU HAVE

O fortunate star,
You have the capacity to give.

O fortunate earth,
You have the necessity to receive.

O fortunate human-soul,
You have the divinity
To see the glory of Light,
To drink the life of Delight,
To become the Goal of Oneness.

438. GOD WENT HOME EMPTY-HANDED

To darkness
He has sold his light.

To bondage
He has sold his freedom.

To ignorance
He has sold his wisdom.

To deception
He has sold his conscience.

Alas, when God came
To buy something from him,
Nothing was left.
Poor God went home
empty-handed.

439. GOD FORGIVES

When the mind hesitates,
The vital postpones.

When the vital postpones,
The body sleeps.

When the body sleeps,
The heart weeps.

When the heart weeps,
God forgives.
He forgives all the members.

440. NOTHING ENTERS INTO ME

Nothing enters into me.
Humility does not enter into me
Even when I eat my blades of
grass.

Devotion does not enter into me
Even when I place my head at the
feet of my Master.

Sincerity does not enter into me
Even though every morning I go
to church.

Purity does not enter into me
Even though I wash myself for
hours.
Am I not something?

441. AN ABIDING AND CONQUERING NAME

When I lost the cosmic game
Centuries suffered in me.
Yet
When I won the cosmic game
Nobody cared.
Nobody was happy
Save my Lord Supreme,
My eternal friend.
He congratulated me
By giving me an abiding
And conquering name:
Love.

442. SUCCESSFUL AND HAPPY WAS I

Successful was I
When I did business
With God and God alone.

I gave Him my centuries'
possession:
Ignorance.
He gave me His Eternity's
possession:
Love.

Happy was I
When the all-forgiving
Compassion
Of the Lord Supreme
Married the extremities of my
ceaseless pride.

443. TWO PROPOSALS

Two proposals:
Humanity's inner duty needs me.
When I am needed,
I feel my life
Is divinely meaningful
And supremely fruitful.
Therefore,
I gladly accept the proposal
Of Divinity's inner duty.

444. YOUR FIRST WISH AND YOUR LAST WISH

Your first wish will be granted
This year.
You will be able to cry
Soulfully, divinely,
Supremely and unconditionally.

Your second and last wish will be
granted
Next year.
God will smile in you, through
you,
Around you and for you
With His supernal Pride.

445. MY TWO OLD FRIENDS ARE ENGAGED

My two old friends, fear and
doubt,
Are engaged.
At their wedding
I shall give them
My best smile and best embrace,
For I may not see them any more
Since they are planning to move
away
After they get married.
When my friends, fear and doubt,
go away
I will try to have two new friends:
Faith and courage.

446. IF I HAD TIME ENOUGH

Lord, I tell You,
If I had time enough
I would definitely
Help You in Your manifestation.

Lord, I tell you,
If I had time enough
I would unmistakably prove to be
Your most perfect instrument.

Alas, time is my worst enemy.
How hard I try to make friends
with time
So that I can use her
At my sweet will.

Lord, just give me the time.
A little more, I tell You,
And I shall love You,
Please You and fulfil You,
Even in Your own way.
Is it not an astonishing bargain?

447. FOUR SUPREME SECRETS

Lord Supreme,
All my life I have treasured
Three supreme secrets.
Today I shall share them with
You:
I love myself
Infinitely more than I love You.
I think I could have created
A creation infinitely better
Than Yours, Lord. I absolutely
mean it.
And Lord, third but not least,
For a long time I have
Been trying to dethrone You,
But with no success.
Alas, now that I have told You
My supreme secrets,
Will You give me something?
"Certainly I shall.
I am giving you My supreme
secret:
I love you. I love you
Infinitely more than I love Myself.
Little heart, I love you infinitely
more
Than I love My entire creation."

448. FOUR PROMISES

I made three promises
To the Supreme:
I shall appreciate the outer beauty
Through my inner eye,
I shall love the outer world
Through my inner heart,
I shall be the bridge
Between the hunger of the
earth-body
And
The fulfilment of the
Heaven-soul.

The Supreme made
One promise to me:
No matter how many times I fail,
He will come to me in His form of
Compassion-sky
And
Patience-sea.

449. MY TWO FRIENDS

I have only two friends:
God and man.
In the world of ignorance,
Man is my friend.
In the sky of Light,
God is my friend.

My man-friend secretly whispers
I need him more than he needs
me.
My God-friend openly declares
He needs me more than I need
Him.
He adds: He is ready to wait
indefinitely
For my arrival.

450. A HIGHER POSITION, A HIGHER SALARY

Lord, will You not give me
A higher position and raise my salary?

"Your salary: Peace, Light and Delight
I can and shall easily increase.
But I am afraid I shall
Not be able to give you a higher position.
A few years ago,
When I accepted you,
I accepted you as an instrument of Mine.
Then I raised your position.
I declared you as a chosen son of Mine.
Now you want to be My representative on earth.
I am sorry! For that you have to work very hard.
I am afraid it may take a few incarnations
For you to represent Me on earth."

451. TOMORROW

Tomorrow I shall get up
Early in the morning,
Since today I am dead-tired.

Tomorrow I shall meditate on God,
Since today my impure vital, jealous mind
And insecure heart
Are bothering me far beyond my
tolerance-might.

Tomorrow I shall definitely love God,
Since today I feel a kind of inner obligation
To please my body, vital, mind and heart.

After all, they comprise my own poor little life.
But tomorrow without fail
I shall love God.

452. YOU HAVE TO PROVE

You have to prove
That you are sincere.
You have to prove
That you are pure.
You have to prove
That you are real.

How can you prove
That you are sincere?
Just see everything rightly,
Feel everything timely,
And say everything soulfully.

How can you prove
That you are pure?
Just feel that your inner purity's
 beauty
And your soul's immortal duty
Are inseparable friends.

How can you prove
That you are real?
Just tell yourself today, tomorrow
 and every day
That you are of God alone
And you are for God alone.

453. MY JOURNEY

Alas,
My Heavenward journey
Is quite challenging.

My hellward journey
Is quite frightening.

My journey towards the
 Perfection-shore
Is quite discouraging.

But
My journey towards my Inner
 Pilot
Has always been encouraging,
most encouraging
And
rewarding,
most rewarding.

454. NEEDLESS TO REPEAT

In my family
There are only three members:
My father, my mother and I.
Father thinks and says
He is great,
Which he actually is.
Mother feels and says
She is good,
Which she obviously is.
And I just know and declare
I am perfect,
Absolutely perfect.
Needless to repeat,
Since everyone knows it.

455. FOUR DINNER INVITATIONS

I have received dinner invitations
From God and man,
From Heaven and earth.
Earth will feed me
With earth's food: doubt and fear.
Heaven will feed me
With Heaven's food: faith and courage.
Man will feed me
With man's food: depression and frustration.
God will feed me
With God's Food: Light and Delight.
Doubt and fear will not be able to feed me regularly;
Therefore I don't need them.
Faith and courage may be a bit slow in feeding me,
But I shall gladly wait.
Depression and frustration will poison me
With their food. No harm!
I know perfectly well
That I shall not remain always dead.
For I clearly see that God's Food,
Light and Delight,
Is fast approaching my eternally real hunger.

456. THEY ARE GOING BACK

My Lord Supreme,
You say that I have made
Tremendous improvements
In various areas of my life.

You say that I am losing
Fast, very fast,
My heart's insect-insecurity,
My mind's elephant-doubt,
My life's uncertainty-dream.

I know You are telling me the Truth,
My Lord Supreme.
But tell me, where are they going
After they have left me?

"Ah, My child, they are going back
Slowly and quietly
To their source: Ignorance."

457. WHEN I WANTED TO MARRY GOD

When I wanted to marry God
For His occult power,
He insulted me mercilessly
For my stark stupidity.

When I wanted to marry God
For His spiritual power,
He scolded me privately
For my absurd greed.

When I wanted to marry God
To empty my ignorance-night,
He said in public:
"I am more than eager
To marry you."

458. A SEA OF SMILES

Divine Lord Supreme,
How is it that You have given me
Trouble after trouble,
An endless series of troubles?

"Child, since you think and feel
That I am the only and real
culprit,
Then the best thing is
For you to offer them back to Me.
I shall gladly accept them."

Divine Lord Supreme,
How is it that I smile and smile
And have become a sea of smiles?
Who made me so?
For God's sake, You have to tell me
the truth!

"Child, for God's sake,
I am telling you the absolute
truth.
Ah, don't you know that your
divine smiles
Are the great and unchallenged
contributions
Of your devoted heart and
surrendered life?"

459. IT IS SO EASY

Lord Supreme,
You have given me
A smart mind, a sweet heart and
A kind-hearted soul.
How can I best use them
In my day-to-day life
And become a perfect instrument
of Yours?

"Ah, it is so easy, My son.
Just ask your mind not to see
Ignorance in mankind,
Including yourself.
Just ask your heart to feel
That the hearts of others are
unquestionably
As sweet as yours.
Just ask your kind-hearted soul
To show you the real Face
Of the real God."

460. THREE COMPLIMENTS

God has offered you
Not one, but two compliments.
His first compliment is:
You are His chosen child.
His second compliment is:
Your cry is of Him,
Your smile is for Him.
Man's first and only compliment
To you is this:
He can perfectly live his life
without you.
He is more than self-sufficient.

461. REGAIN AND REDISCOVER

You inherited Heaven's property:
Conscious, constant and
inseparable oneness
With the Supreme.
Alas, you have lost it.

You now inherit earth's property:
Frustration in depression.
No curse, soon you will lose it, too.

You shall in the process of your
fast-evolving fate
Inherit God's property:
Perfection.

Once you achieve Perfection
You will not only regain
Your conscious oneness with the
Supreme,
But also you will rediscover and
unearth
Your long-buried constant and
inseparable oneness
With the Supreme.

462. A GREAT UNDERSTATEMENT

God, I just thought of You.
Let us resume our old friendship.
Let us not quarrel,
Let us not fight.
After all, we are no longer kids.
After all, once upon a time
We were not only good, but best friends.
And in the hoary past
Not only did we love each other,
But also we made tremendous sacrifices for each other.
So, God, let us resume our old friendship,
Since I cannot brook any further delay.
I am sure Your sufferings, too,
Are unbearable.
"Daughter, I loved and still love
And will always love you
Infinitely more than you have ever loved Me.
Therefore, for you to say my sufferings are unbearable
Is a great understatement."

463. LORD I NEED YOU MORE

Lord, I need You more than You need me.
I love You more than You love me,
At least on the physical plane,
Or at least that is what my proud discovery is.
So Lord, don't make a fool of Yourself
By cherishing unhealthy thoughts
That I do not care for You at all.
I do care for You, hundreds of times,
But what actually happens is this:
Sometimes my old friends,
Fear, doubt, insecurity and anxiety
Make me feel that they need me
More than I need You.
Therefore, my ever-sympathetic heart
Overflows to them with diamond-concern.
Alas, at that time I forget You,
I don't love You and I even ignore You.
Lord, since I love You and need You
More than You love and need me,
I am bound to return to You
And to You alone, without fail.

464. I ALMOST

I almost saw God
When I was three years old.

I almost talked to God
When I was seven years old.

I almost embraced God
When I was thirteen years old.

I almost became God
When I was thirty-three years old.

465. IN MY CASE

Everybody needs something.
Therefore,
In my case I need
My old friend, the Himalayan
cave.

Everybody needs someone.
Therefore,
In my case I need
God the dream-boat Sailor.

466. LEAD AND FOLLOW

Sometimes I want to lead,
Sometimes I want to follow.
It entirely depends on
Whose company I am in.
If it is God, then I want to lead;
If it is man, then I want to follow.
Why? Why?
While leading God,
If I go astray,
He will correct me and perfect me
And guide me to my destination.
While following man,
If he makes a deplorable mistake,
My pure and sympathetic heart
Will want to share half the
penalty,
If not more.

467. WHAT SHALL I DO?

What shall I do
For the rest of my life?
I shall build and break,
And break and build.

I shall build my Lord's Palace
In the depths of my heart.
I shall break my giant ego
Right in front of my Lord's Palace.

I shall break the bridge
Between the Bondage-Queen
And the Ignorance-King.
I shall build the bridge
Between the compassion-sky
Of my Father Heaven
And the perfection-sea
Of my Mother Earth.

468. THE DIFFERENCE

The difference between
Your emptiness and your Infinity
is this:

Your emptiness embodies,
Your Infinity expands.

The difference between
My emptiness and my Eternity is
this:

My emptiness listens,
My Eternity talks.

The difference between
His emptiness and his
Immortality is this:

His emptiness welcomes the
universe,
His immortality serves the
universe.

469. TEMPTATION

Man tempts him
With his world of pleasure.
God tempts him
With His sea of Delight.

He tempts man by saying
That he will give man
His future realisation.

He tempts God by saying
That he will help
In His future manifestation.

470. THE HEART OF FORGIVENESS

The Hand of blessing:
How far is it?
Very near.

The Eye of compassion:
Where is it?
It is in your self-giving.

The Heart of forgiveness:
What is it?
Perfect self-extension.

471. WHEN I WEEP

Sometimes I wake to weep,
Sometimes I weep to wake.
My heart loves me
When I weep to wake.
My life loves me
When I wake to weep.
And I love myself
When I weep, only weep.

472. SMILE, MY BODY!

Learn, my heart, learn!
Lo, your Lord is teaching.

Unlearn, my mind, unlearn!
Lo, your Lord is commanding.

Cry, my vital, cry!
Lo, your Lord is crying
Because of your misdeeds.

Smile, my body, smile!
Lo, your Lord is smiling
Because you are sleeping no more.

473. THE BLOSSOMING OF MY WORLD

Lord, batter my heart
To see the face of
detachment-light.

Lord, better my heart
To see the smile of oneness-might.

Lord, repair my dream-boat
To see the shore of beauty.

Lord, perfect my reality-sun
To see the blossoming of my
world.

474. MY TEACHER

My soul of light was determined.
Therefore,
My heart of love dared.

My heart of love dared.
Therefore,
My life of duty did.

But I must tell the world
How I did all this.
I did it
Because
I had my teacher: God.

475. WHERE IS IT?

Heaven's compassion:
Where is it?
It is inside my morning eyes.

Earth's patience:
Where is it?
It is inside my evening heart.

God's Perfection:
Where is it?
It is inside my undying surrender.

476. I OWE GOD, I OWE MAN

Do I owe God?
Yes, I do.
Do I owe man?
Yes, I do.

I owe God because
He has made me the
compassion-root.

I owe man because
He has made me the
aspiration-tree.

477. I BEHOLD

Quickly and thoughtlessly
An angel ascends.
I behold her beauty's wings.

Slowly, steadily, gracefully and
soulfully
An angel descends.
I behold her beauty's light,
Offering's might and duty's
height,
And something more:
God's Compassion.

478. THEY HAVE THE POWER

Our desire-cave has the power
To encage God.

Our aspiration-palace has the
power
To liberate God.

Our realisation-country has the
power
To fulfil God.

Our perfection-universe has the
power
To own God.

479. WHEN TIME CAME BACK

When Time was away
I played with man,
I danced with man,
I dined with man.

When Time came back
I remembered to think of God,
I remembered to invite God,
I remembered God's Will.
Also, I remembered who I was:
God's sole representative on earth.

480. ONLY A GRAIN

Only a grain of faith
Can perfectly house
God, the universal Light.

Only a grain of surrender
Can shake hands with
God, the universal Power.

Only a grain of perfection
Is enough for God
To admire His Capacity in
Humanity.

481. WHEN I AM CONSCIOUS

When I am conscious
Of my vast and sublime
inadequacy,
God feeds my soulful heart,
Heaven illumines my searching
mind,
Earth fortifies my striving vital,
The devil leaves my wakeful body.

482. WHY DO YOU HIDE?

Lord, I seek and You hide.
I seek because without You
My life-flames do not and cannot
burn.
Now Lord, tell me,
Why do You hide?

"Daughter, I hide because
My hiding intensifies your
seeking.
It gratifies your loving,
Glorifies your achievement
And immortalises your
enlightenment."

483. HIS LIFE WAS INDISPENSABLE

His birth was a drop
In the sea of time.
His death shall be a drop
In the sea of time.
Yet God felt and declared
That his life was indispensable,
For he thought of God, prayed to
God,
Fought for God and fulfilled God
In the battlefield of life.

484. FOR HIS PRIVATE USE

I have only two hands
Which I have used
Millions of times
To give and receive
While I was doing business with
God on earth.

I have only two eyes
Which I have used
Millions of times
To admire and be admired
While I was playing with God
In the garden of Paradise.

I have only one heart.
I never use it,
But I always keep it clean
So that if ever God comes in,
I can offer it to Him
For His private use.

485. I WRESTLED

I wrestled with God
To make myself strong.

I wrestled with man
To make him strong.

I wrestled with Heaven
To capture its transcendental
Beauty.

I wrestled with earth
To remind it of its long-buried
duty.

486. YOU WILL BE LOVED

Bind not!
You will be bound.
Lo, even the boundless time
Is bound by a tiny clock.

Love!
You will be loved.
Lo, even a tiny dew drop
Is loved by the morning God.

487. GOD'S COMPASSION-SUN

When I see my actual presence in
God,
I hate myself and want to crucify
myself.
How weak and feeble
My aspiration-flames are!

When I see God's actual Presence
in me,
I love myself and want to glorify
myself.
How strong and powerful
God's Compassion-sun is!

488. MY LIFE-BOAT AND MY SOUL-BOAT

O failure's life,
Although your existence
Is grief in reality,
Yet you live so long.

O victory's heart,
Although your existence
Is abiding reality,
Yet you seem so brief.

O failure's life,
I need you
To make my life-boat
Strong and solid.

O victory's heart,
I need you
To make my soul-boat
Undeniable and unmistakable.

489. UNDER CONTROL

Your fear is under control.
Therefore
God the omnipotent Power loves
you.

Your doubt is under control.
Therefore
God the transcendental Light
loves you.

Your impurity is under control.
Therefore
God the supreme Pride loves you.

Your insecurity is under control.
Therefore
God the boundless Delight loves
you.

490. THE TRUTH

My imagination
Visions the Truth.

My aspiration
Nears the Truth.

My realisation
Reaches the Truth.

My perfection
Becomes the Truth.

My smile
Is the Truth.

491. ALONE I LIVE

I avoid God
When I want to lead
My animal-pleasure life.

I avoid my lower self
When I want to drink
God's ambrosial Light.

Alone I live to dig my mortal
grave,
Alone I live to quench my eternal
thirst.

492. JUST LOVE AND LOVE MORE

No remedy for black hate?
Who says?
Just love
And love more,
That's all.

No remedy for helpless fear?
Who says?
Just love
And love more,
That's all.

No remedy for blind darkness?
Who says?
Just love
And love more,
That's all.

No remedy for lengthy bondage?
Who says?
Just love
And love more,
That's all.

493. THEY DO NOT BELIEVE IT

My body is ignorance.
Alas,
My body does not believe it.

My vital is arrogance.
Alas,
My vital does not believe it.

My mind is pretense.
Alas,
My mind does not believe it.

My heart is indulgence.
Alas,
My heart does not believe it.

My soul is impatience.
Alas,
My soul does not believe it.

494. LEAVE YOURSELF TO ME

Leave yourself to me, Heaven.
I shall serve you devotedly.

Leave yourself to me, earth.
I shall guide you relentlessly.

Leave yourself to me, God.
I shall please You unconditionally.

Leave yourself to me, man.
I shall glorify you unreservedly.

495. I SEE NO DIFFERENCE

When I obey my heart,
I see no sovereign on earth
Save me.

When my heart obeys me,
I see no beggar on earth
Save me.

When I obey God,
I see no difference
Between God the Head
And God the Feet.

When God obeys me,
I see no difference
Between my frustration-height
And my destruction-length.

496. THEY BELONG

Rest sublime belongs to work,
And not to the worker.

Delight endless belongs to love,
And not to the lover.

Peace immense belongs to service,
And not to the server.

God Himself belongs to the
search,
And not to the searcher.

497. GOD'S WILL IN ME

God's Will in me
Is to sing.
Therefore
I sing
Before I even pray to God.

God's Will in me
Is to dance.
Therefore
I dance
Before I even meditate on God.

God's Will in me
Is to play.
Therefore
I play
Before I even love God.

498. I JUST WANTED TO REMIND YOU

Earth,
I just wanted to remind you,
Heaven's compassion
Is an honoured guest.

Heaven,
I just wanted to remind you,
Earth's patience
Is an honoured guest.

God,
I just wanted to remind You,
You once told me
That my surrender
Is Your honoured guest.

499. I TAUGHT

I taught my soul
What to speak:
The power of love.

I taught my heart
How to speak:
Devotedly and soulfully.

I taught my life
Where to speak:
In the garden of Love-light.

500. I GIVE

I give
My thoughts no voice.
I give
My mind no choice.
I give
My unaspiring life no nest.
I give
My aspiring life no rest.

501. YOUR IDOL

Your idol was doubt-king.
Lo, he has not only gone,
But he is shattered.

Your idol was jealousy.
Lo, she has not only left,
But she is shattered.

Your idol was hatred-prince.
Lo, he has not only departed,
But he is shattered.

502. WHEN I OBEY YOU NOT

O Faith, when I obey you not
My earth becomes
The land of the departed sunset.

O Joy, when I obey you not
My life becomes
The cage of the departed soul.

503. YOU WILL BE HAPPY

Minimise your wants,
You will be happy.

Fulfil your needs,
You will be happy.

Divinise your thoughts,
You will be happy.

Immortalise your faith,
You will be happy.

Rectify your mistakes,
You will be happy.

Intensify your cry,
You will be happy.

504. THE EMBRACE

The embrace of bondage
Demands and commands.

The embrace of freedom
Offers and showers.

The embrace of passion
Entangles and strangles.

The embrace of faith
Beholds and unfolds.

505. HIS LIFE CLOSED THREE TIMES

His life closed three times
Before its final close:
Once when he entered
Into the private chamber
Of the fear-queen,
Once when he entered
Into the cave
Of the doubt-monster,
Once when he threw himself
Into the flow
Of the insecurity-river.

506. COME, COME

Come my heart, come.
I shall gladly unburden
The great burden of your tears.

Come my mind, come.
I shall cheerfully empty
The heavy load of your
information.

Come my soul, come.
I shall immediately expedite
Your unprecedented dream
Of God-manifestation on earth.

507. GOD COMES

Faith comes,
Doubt goes.

Courage comes,
Fear goes.

Truth comes,
Falsehood goes.

Love comes,
Hate goes.

God comes,
Oneness lasts.

508. ADAMANTINE WILL

When God-freedom
In me was crucified,
I fought life.
I received from God
His adamantine Will
Which now pulsates
From life to life.
It goes from start to start,
It runs from Vision to Reality.

509. DO IT AGAIN

Do it again.
This time you will be able
To build the Palace of Truth.

Say it again.
This time you will be able
To tell the secrets of God.

Play it again.
This time you will be able
To say you are not God's sleeping
partner
In the fight against darkness and
ignorance.

510. YOU CAN ALSO HELP

You can help if you want.
Here are shining examples:
God wanted my unalloyed faith
And I gave it.
God wanted my dauntless love
And I gave it.
God wanted my constant
surrender
And I gave it.
Likewise, if you want to help
He will give you the opportunity.
Just knock and ask;
God becomes yours.

511. ALAS, HOW CAN I?

I want to be happy.
But alas, how can I,
When others are surpassing me?

I want to be happy.
But alas, how can I,
When others are governing me?

I want to be happy.
But alas, how can I,
Since I have not pleased my Inner
Pilot,
Not even once?

I want to be happy.
But alas, how can I,
Since I know I can never be
What I want to be?

512. LIFE IS WHAT WE MAKE IT

Life is what we make it.
Since I have realised this truth,
How can I fail
In the battlefield of life?

Life is what we make it.
Since I have realised this truth,
How can I forget
To keep my life a chance to
embody the Real,
And manifest the transcendental
Truth?
After all, it is I who shall share
Its matchless triumph.

513. THIS TIME I SHALL NOT FAIL YOU

Lord, can You love me again?
This time I shall not fail You.
This time I shall become
The breath of Your Heart.

Lord, can You love me again?
This time I shall not fail You.
This time I shall become
The message of Your Tongue.

Lord, can You love me again?
This time I shall not fail You.
This time I shall become
The light of Your Eye.

514. WHO AM I?

Who am I?
I asked God.
He said
I am His Dream-boat.

Who am I?
I asked Satan.
He said
I am his destruction-night.

Who am I?
I asked Heaven.
Heaven said
I am Heaven's Reality-shore.

Who am I?
I asked earth.
Earth said
I am earth's constant cry.

515. WHEN THEY STOLE AWAY MY TIME

When impatience stole away my time,
I cried and cried.

When anxiety stole away my time,
I cried and cried.

When insecurity stole away my time,
I cried and cried.

When fear stole away my time,
I cried and cried.

When Satan stole away my time,
I fought and failed.

When death stole away my time,
I unreservedly and unreservedly cried.

516. I KNOW TWO THINGS

I really don't know
What to tell God when I see Him.

I really don't know
What to give God when I see Him.

But I undoubtedly know two things:
God will forgive my stark ignorance;
God will immortalise my feeble inner flame.

517. GOD NEVER LEARNS FROM ME

God never learns from me
My ignorance-lessons.
I never drink from God
His Wisdom-light.

God never learns from me
My heart-labour achievement.
I never care for God's
All-fulfilling Perfection.

518. THE LAST THING ON MY MIND

To deceive mankind
Is the last thing on my mind;
Yet God does not trust me.

To replace God
Is the last thing on my mind;
Yet humanity does not trust me.

To bridge the distance between
   man and God
Is the last thing on my mind;
But neither Heaven nor earth
   trusts me.

To kill earth's night and sow
   Heaven's Delight
Is the first thing on my mind;
But my heart's sincerity does not
   trust me.

519. EVERYONE I MEET

In the world of aspiration-sun,
Everyone I meet is from God.

In the world of desire-height,
Everyone I meet is from Satan.

In the world of self-giving-sky,
Everyone I meet is from
   Perfection-height.

In the world of
   self-possessing-sea,
Everyone I meet is from
   destruction-night.

520. LOVE ME FOR WHAT I AM

O Lord, love me for what I am.
I am an insignificant creature.

O Lord, love me for what I am.
I am a helpless child.

O Lord, love me for what I am.
I am a hopeless seeker.

O Lord, love me for what I am.
I am a useless lover.

521. EMPTY

His future, empty of reality;
His present, empty of humility;
His past, empty of fecundity;
His life, empty of breath;
His soul, empty of goal;
His God, empty of love.
Yet he sleeps,
Yet he breathes.

522. THE SEA THAT ALWAYS ROARS

His faith is the train
That never starts.

His doubt is the train
That never stops.

His courage is the soldier
That never fights.

His fear is the wrestler
That ever struggles.

His life is the sky
That ever lives.

His death is the sea
That ever roars.

523. ANY TIME

Any time of the year
I can see God.

Any time of the month
I can love God.

Any time of the week
I can please God.

Any time of the day
I can own God.

Any minute of the hour
I can become God.

Any second of the minute
I can unburden myself
Of my self-imposed responsibility.

524. WHY DO WE WASTE OUR TIME?

O Beauty, you and I
Belong to Heaven.
Why do we waste our time
Here on this ugly earth?

O Joy, you and I
Belong to Heaven.
Why do we waste our time
Here in this world of sorrows and
pangs?

O Freedom, you and I
Belong to Heaven.
Why do we waste our time
Here in this night of bondage?

O Perfection, you and I
Belong to Heaven.
Why do we waste our time
Here on this dark-spotted planet?
Let us go, let us run
Towards our Heaven-free life!

525. GOD ASKED ME, MAN ASKED ME

The other day God asked me
What I was aspiring for.
I said, "I would like
To offer infinite praises to man."
He immediately granted my
prayer.

The other night man asked me
What I was aspiring for.
I said, "I would like
To become the dead dust of God's
Feet."
Man's answer: "How dare you
think
God would condescend to grant
you
Such a mighty prayer?"

526. ONLY WHEN I WAS LIBERATED

I thought of God
Only when I was liberated
From stealthy fear.

I prayed to God
Only when I was liberated
From strangling jealousy.

I meditated on God
Only when I was liberated
From dragon doubt.

I realised God
Only when I was liberated
From self-imposed inadequacy.

527. I DIED FOR LIGHT

I died for beauty,
But beauty came not.

I died for joy,
But joy came not.

I died for peace,
But peace came not.

I died for Light,
Light came,
Love followed,
Oneness blossomed.
Divinity's Reality
And Reality's Divinity
Are in everlasting embrace.

528. LISTEN

Listen to inner Light;
It will guide you.

Listen to inner Peace;
It will feed you.

Listen to inner Power;
It will energise you.

Listen to inner Truth;
It will glorify you.

Listen to inner Love;
It will transform you,
It will divinise you,
It will immortalise you.

529. WHAT REMAINS

The sweet rainbow comes and goes,
But its beauty remains.

The dear sun comes and goes,
But its duty remains.

The faithful day comes and goes,
But its sound remains.

The restful night comes and goes,
But its silence remains.

530. A SOUL ABOVE ALL

She is a soul above doubt;
Therefore she sows.

She is a soul above fear;
Therefore she triumphs.

She is a soul above jealousy;
Therefore she governs.

She is a soul above all;
Therefore she sows and grows
And grows and sows.

531. REVELATION

I have come into the world to offer
You revelation.
My first revelation:
Earth's pangs and penuries
Shall transcend Heaven's Light
and Delight.
My second revelation:
I shall bind God in a moment's
hush-gap;
I shall go beyond the future Goal,
The Goal unhorizoned by God's
Vision-light.

532. TRANSFORMATION

Birthless and deathless I was,
And then I was raised above
The throes of birth and the buffets
of death.
This was my first transformation.

Across the river
Of life and death
I sang only one song: uncertainty.
This was my second
transformation.

My third transformation will take
place
When the animal in me
Surrenders to the divine in me
And Immortality embraces the
divine in me.

533. INTEGRALITY

My life-tree has four branches:
Sincerity, purity, humility,
divinity.

These four branches bring me
The message of integrality
From far Heaven.

When sincerity offers me
The message of life divine,
Purity, humility and divinity
together dance.

When purity offers me
The message of self-dedication,
Humility, divinity and sincerity
together dance.

When humility offers me
The message of
world-illumination,
Divinity, sincerity and purity
together dance.

When divinity offers me
The best message of
God-perfection
Here on earth, there in Heaven,
Sincerity, purity and humility
together dance.

The dance of sincerity, purity,
humility and divinity
Is the highest flight of God,
The integral Universal Self.

534. COURAGE

The animal in me
Showed the animal courage
By fighting and strangling.

The human in me
Showed the human courage
By snubbing and belittling.

The divine in me
Shows the divine courage
In accepting and loving.

The Supreme in me
Shows the supreme courage
In transforming, widening,
deepening
And finally transcending.

535. MUSIC

When I play music
I know for sure someone is there
To listen to my music.
No matter what music I play,
Whether Heavenly or earthly,
Sublime or deadly,
There is someone to listen to my
music.
There is God.

When God plays His Cosmic
Music
Day in and day out from time
immemorial,
I enjoy and fulfil
The strongest adamantine
demands
Of my inconscience-deep.
I sleep and snore and snore and
sleep,
Nadir of universal futility.

536. EXALTATION

The other night I was exalted
When I dined with God the
Supreme.

The other day I was exalted
When I breathed the excruciating
pangs
Of earth-penuries.

From this life of mine
Only two more exalted
experiences I need,
I most desperately need.

I need the experience
unprecedented
Of seeing two human shoulders
Carrying the burdens of hell-fire,
Earth-water and Heaven-wine.

I need the experience
Of seeing Heaven-Beauty's
glorious Transcendence
Fulfilling earth-beauty's
splendour-light.

My journey's start was the
exaltation
Of God-man in me,
And my journey's close will be the
exaltation
Of man-God in the Absolute
Supreme.

537. DEVOTION

I offered my purest devotion to
God.
He accepted my devotion only to
increase
Its height and depth in boundless
measure.

I offered my surest devotion to
man.
He accepted my devotion
Only to criticise and belittle
My sincerity's heart.

I offered my blue-gold devotion to
Heaven.
Heaven accepted my devotion
With a smile, a half-knowing
smile.

I offered my devotion to the
green-brown earth.
Earth suspected, rejected,
Strangled and buried my
devotion-life.

538. AWAKENING

In my body's awakening,
I saw God as a sweet dreamer.

In my vital's awakening,
I saw God as a dauntless warrior.

In my mind's awakening,
I saw God as a peerless seer.

In my heart's awakening,
I saw God as an unconditional
lover.

In my soul's awakening,
I saw God as the sovereign
And absolute Liberator.

539. LIFE

In this rare incarnation of mine
I decided and planned to see the
lives of God,
Heaven, earth and man.

I have already seen man-life.
It is nothing but a song
Of deathless destruction-night.

I have already seen the life
Of earth, too.
It is nothing but teeming clouds.

I am now seeing the life of
Heaven,
Which is building my life-altar
To reach the transcendental
Heights.

I shall soon be seeing the life of
God,
Which will discover the
Zenith-perfection-light
Founded on my
acceptance-might.

540. GRATITUDE

When I offered my feeble
gratitude to God,
He immediately said,
"Ah, what is it? I have never seen
Such a beautiful thing in all My
life
Either in Heaven or on earth.
Can I use it for a purpose divine?"
I smilingly said,
"Certainly You can.
It is for Your daily and constant
use."
When I offered my powerful
gratitude to man,
He immediately blurted out,
"You know your deception
Has touched the topmost bough
of the earth-tree.
I have given you my silver advice,
my golden promise
And my diamond assurance.
Although they were the products
Of the world of fury,
I certainly deserve infinitely more
Living and fulfilling gratitude
Than what you have given me
today.
Take it back,
Take it back,
You rogue, you beggar-woman!
From now on my life of
compassion
Shall barter nothing
With the bones of a
beggar-woman."

541. ADORATION

I adored my Lord Supreme
With my fear-fever.
Furious he became.
He bolted His Golden Gate from
  inside
With all the power at His
  command.

I adored my Beloved Supreme
With my heart-flames.
Self-enamoured He became.
In a twinkling, sooner than at
  once,
He opened His Golden Gate wide;
He offered me His trance-bound
  emerald throne.

I adored my Eternal Friend
With my surrender-light.
Perfection-Infinity He
  immediately donned.

O Lord Supreme,
Your Forgiveness I implore.
O Beloved Supreme,
Your Love-sea I shall eternally
  treasure.
O Eternal Friend,
Your Heart's ever-widening
  Magnanimity
Has made my life
The Voice of transcendental
  Silence.

542. PROGRESS

Lord Supreme,
I want You to be
Totally frank with me.
Have I made any progress
In my three years
Of spiritual life?

"Certainly, My son, you have.
Let Me tell you about
Your great progress:
You now love Me
Infinitely more than
You love yourself.

And here is your greater progress:
Nothing will satisfy you
Unless and until
You have become the
  unconditionally
And supremely surrendered
  instrument
Of Vision-nourished Reality-Will.

Lo, your greatest progress:
You claim Me as your own,
Your very own."

543. TRANSCENDENCE

Self-transcendence
And
God-transcendence
Are the Self-form
Of the same transcendental
Reality.

When I endeavour to fathom
My self-transcendence
With my human comatose eyes,
I see the radical transformation
Of the devouring tiger in me
Into the fast-running,
sure-winning deer.

And when I plead with the
Supreme
To elucidate the signification
Of transcendence, He just smiles
And declares:
"Yours is the transcendence-task
To touch the feet of My creation
For its fire-pure transformation.
Yours is the transcendence-goal
Where the comity of souls have
discovered
Their only haven."

544. UNIVERSALITY

Sound is the universality
Of the created universe.

Silence is the universality
Of the unborn universe.

Love is the universality
Of the progressive universe.

Delight is the universality
Of the deathless universe.

545. HEART-ESSENCE

Father, my Father,
I have now caught You tightly.
Just tell me in brief
The actual meaning of
heart-essence,
And then I shall let You go.

"Child, My child,
The heart-essence
Of the aspiring earth
Is the surrender-tree
Of the Supreme's Nectar-delight.

The heart-essence
Of the sailing Heaven
Is the silence-tree
Of the Supreme's Nectar-delight.

The heart-essence
Of the liberating Supreme
Is the
surrender-silence-perfection
Tree
Of the Absolute Supreme's
Nectar-delight."

546. LUSTRE-DROP, LUSTRE-SEA

O sweet Lord of my
unconditionally
Surrendered heart,
O sweet Pilot of my life-boat,
O sweet Speed of my soul-river,
O sweet Smile of my Goal-shore,
Just tell me the difference
Between
My lustre-drop and Your
lustre-sea.

"O sweet child of My Vision's
Immortality,
The difference is very simple and
clear.
With your lustre-drop I body forth
And feed the birthless and
deathless hunger
Of the entire universe;
And within My lustre-sea I claim
you,
I own you as My only
Fulfilling and manifesting
All."

547. STILL IT IS NOT TOO LATE

O heart, my heart,
Do not cry.
Still it is not
Too late to heal.

O mind, my mind,
Do not cry.
Still it is not
Too late to expand.

O vital, my vital,
Do not cry.
Still it is not
Too late to surrender.

O body, my body,
Do not cry.
Still it is not
Too late to start.

548. I STAND STILL

The whole world moves on,
But I stand still.

The whole sky descends,
But I stand still.

The whole earth aspires,
But I stand still.

With my outer stillness,
I see the Feet of God.
With my inner stillness,
I become the Heart of God.

549. LOVE, DEVOTION AND SURRENDER BIRD

Love is a circling bird,
Devotion is a climbing bird,
Surrender is a transcending bird.

The circling bird protects me,
The climbing bird inspires me,
The transcending bird
immortalises me.

550. WHAT HE NEEDS AND WANTS

In the inner world
What he needs and wants
Is Immensity's rest.

In the outer world
What he needs and wants
Is the sea of pleasure.

In the world of the Supreme
What he needs and wants
Is the Perfection-throne.

551. DIFFICULTIES

Patience is hard
To achieve.

Sympathy is hard
To offer.

Sacrifice is hard
To make.

Fear is hard
To conquer.

Doubt is hard
To transcend.

Humility is hard
To treasure.

Surrender is hard
To become.

552. LET ME

O my body, since nobody loves
you,
Let me love you.
O my vital, since nobody
disciplines you,
Let me discipline you.
O my mind, since nobody widens
you,
Let me widen you.
O my heart, since nobody inspires
you,
Let me inspire you.
O my soul, since nobody fulfils
you,
Let me fulfil you.
O my Goal, since nobody speaks
highly of You,
Let me speak highly of you.

553. A PERFECT DAUGHTER

No man can ever have a daughter
Who always thinks of her father's
height.

No woman can ever have a
daughter
Who always thinks of her
mother's light.

No world can ever have a daughter
Who always feels its excruciating
pangs.

No truth can ever have a daughter
Who always adores its inevitable
victory.

554. LET US TALK ABOUT OURSELVES

O soul, you and I
Have come into the world
To speak of God.
Since nobody
Wants to hear us,
Let us talk
About ourselves.
O soul, I think that
Without God's guidance
I can teach His world.
"O seeker, I think that
I can manifest God
Without your assistance."

555. GOLDEN MYSTIC SUN

The descending fire descends;
The ascending fire ascends.
The smile of Light
Watches their tasks divine
From across the empty space
Where the hands of ether
Salute the golden mystic sun.

556. THE SAINT AND THE SINNER

The saint was about to fall
When he saw not the Face of God
In the mind of darkness
And
In the heart of impurity.

The sinner was about to rise
When he felt the life
Of love within, without,
And
When he sang the song
Of life-transforming Light.

557. HE KNELT, HE WEPT, HE PRAYED

He knelt, he wept, he prayed.
He quietly knelt,
He throbbingly wept,
He unreservedly prayed.

He knelt when he discovered
That God is All-might.
He wept when he discovered
That God is All-love.
He prayed when he discovered
That God is All-giving.

558. TIME, YOU DO YOUR OWN WORK!

Time, you do your own work!
Let me play and let me sing.

Time, you do your own work!
Let me jump and let me run.

Time, you do your own work!
Let me dive and let me fly.

And when I am tired
Of playing and singing,
Jumping and running,
Diving and flying,
I shall invite you
To offer me your wise
Advice,
Without fail.

559. SUDDENLY

Suddenly I shall wake.
Suddenly I shall have
Flying wings.
Suddenly the sky will give me
What it has: freedom.
Suddenly I shall once more
Consciously become
What I was before:
God.

560. MONEY DIVINELY ACQUIRED

Money is the joy of the poor.
More money is the joy of the rich.

Joy is the money of the budding
seeker.
More joy is the money of the
blossomed seeker.

Money divinely acquired and
used,
Joy divinely achieved and
distributed
Can alone
Touch the very Heart
Of God.

561. WHAT OTHERS SEE

On his path
What others see
Is the world of sorrow.

On his path
What others see
Is the dance of despair.

On his path
What others see
Is the hunger of destruction.

But
He unmistakably knows
That his path
Is the sunlit path.

562. I AM TIRED AND DISAPPOINTED

I am tired.
I am tired of eyeless days
And
Eyeless nights.

I am disappointed.
I am disappointed
In my earth-ascending pilgrimage
And
God's Heaven-descending pilgrimage.

563. FOR YOU

O Lord Supreme:
For You I see,
For You I feel,
For You I give,
For You I receive,
For You I can,
For You I become,
For You I am.

564. LET ME FINISH!

Let me finish
My unfinished life-story!
Let me finish
If possible
By tomorrow.

Let me finish
My unfinished God-story!
Not tomorrow,
Not today,
But here and now,
Before I allow myself
To worry about God
And me.

565. IF YOU DARE

Desire-king,
Stop me if you dare,
Smite me if you dare,
Break me if you dare.

Aspiration-prince,
Love me if you dare,
Build me if you dare,
Fulfil me if you dare.

566. I HAVE MUCH NEWS

Faith, my faith,
Since you left
I have no news,
None at all.

Doubt, my doubt,
Since you left
I have much news.
God has come
And
Is staying with me.
He is even thinking of hiring me
To look after His vast creation.

567. THAT'S ALL

Lord, I just don't have the time
To think of You.
That's all.

"Daughter, I just think of you
Unreservedly.
That's all."

Lord, I just forget to love You
From time to time.
That's all.

"Daughter, I just happen to know
How to forgive you,
How to love you,
How to illumine you.
That's all."

568. SLAVE AND MASTER

Who is the slave?
Who is the master?
Ah, you don't know?
Just learn it from me
Once and for all:
The slave is the one
Who sincerely feels he is a slave;
The master is the one
Who foolishly thinks he is a
master.

569. TWO PATHS

I loved the path of silence
Because
My God was All-silence.
I tell you, this was the only reason.

I love the path of sound
Because
My life is all-sound.
I tell you, this is the only reason.

570. I LOVE YOU, AMERICA

Because
You are thoughtful
I like you, America.

Because
You are powerful
I admire you, America.

Because
You are fruitful
I congratulate you, America.

Because
You are soulful
I love you,
I love you,
And
I love you, America.

571. HOW IMPOSSIBLE YOU ARE!

O self-congratulation,
How powerful you are!

O self-examination,
How weak you are!

O self-perfection,
How slow you are!

O self-degradation,
How impossible you are!

572. LET US BE WHAT WE WERE BEFORE

Let us be really great,
For
That will give us joy.

Let us be divinely good,
For
That will give God joy.

Let us be supremely divine,
For
That will make us once more
What we were before:
Immortality's Silence-sound.

573. BELIEVE IT OR NOT

I am an angel.
Believe it or not,
I am a real angel.
Alas, nobody believes it.

I am a Yogi.
Believe it or not,
I am a real Yogi.
Alas, nobody believes it.

I am God.
Believe it or not,
I am really God.
Alas, nobody believes it.

Since nobody believes me
I shall no longer remain
An angel, a Yogi or God.

I shall go back
To my old life,
A simple and ordinary life.

574. I BELIEVE YOU

My Lord,
You think I could forget Your
Love.
Impossible!

My Lord,
You think I love ignorance
More than I love You.
Impossible!

My Lord,
You think my love for You
Is not enough.
Possible.
I believe You.
I do believe You.

575. THE EVOLUTION OF MY POSSIBILITIES

Yesterday
My desire-life played
With small possibilities.

Today
My aspiration-life plays
With great possibilities.

Tomorrow
My realisation-life shall play
Only with God-Realities.

576. HIS CONCENTRATION

When he lies down
And concentrates,
Sleep-queen garlands him.

When he sits in his easy chair
And concentrates,
Pleasure-king garlands him.

When he eats voraciously at the
 dining table
And concentrates,
Death-giant embraces him.

577. LIBERATION-SEA, PERFECTION-SUN

A divine love-life
Is the Liberation-sea,
While living with humanity.

A divine light-life
Is the Perfection-sun,
While living in humanity.

578. MY COMPANIONS

I am not alone.
The dead weight of centuries
Is hanging heavy
On my two small shoulders.

I am not alone.
The love-sun of God's
birthless and deathless Life
Is smiling, singing and dancing
In the cave-light of my heart.

579. THE KNOWLEDGE

The knowledge of world-sorrow:
Renunciation.
The knowledge of God-Will:
Liberation.
The knowledge of man-love:
Confusion.
The knowledge of God-love:
Perfection.

580. THE ONLY REALITY

Death, be not proud!
Who am I,
If not the Child of Immortality?

Life, be not stupid!
You and God
Each other need.

God, be not indifferent!
Your Smile is the only Reality
Of the universe.

581. WHO FEEDS MY LIFE?

My prayer feeds
My orphan life.

My meditation feeds
My infant life.

My realisation feeds
My simple life.

My perfection feeds
My sincere life.

582. HIS LIFE SINGS FOUR SONGS

His life sings
The song of beauty.
Therefore
Heaven loves him.

His life sings
The song of duty.
Therefore
Earth loves him.

His life sings
The song of Divinity.
Therefore
God loves him.

His life sings
The song of Immortality.
Therefore
He loves himself.

583. ONLY ONE IS BORN

Some are born
To dark suffering.
My vital friend is one of them.

Some are born
To constant delight.
My psychic friend is one of them.

Only one is born
To love and become God.
My aspiration friend is the one.

584. MY LORD

Sleep, sleep,
My child-Lord, sleep.

Wake up, wake up,
My man-Lord, wake up.

Guide, guide,
My God-Lord, guide.

Fulfil, fulfil,
My Supreme-Lord, fulfil.

585. MY NAME

I am just three minutes old.
I have no name.

I am just three days old.
I have three names:
Desire, Aspiration, Perfection.

I am just three weeks old.
I have two names:
Aspiration, Perfection.

I am three months old.
I have just one name:
Perfection.

Since Perfection is what I have
And what I am
I am going back to Heaven to rest.

586. HE ACCEPTS

He accepts;
He accepts the sloth of his body.

He fears;
He fears the strength of his vital.

He doubts;
He doubts the discovery of his mind.

He surrenders;
He surrenders to the insecurity of his heart.

587. HE LIGHTS THE GLOBE

He lights the globe
With his Love divine.

He loves the globe
With his Light divine.

He perfects the globe
With his Will supreme.

His Will supreme
Immortalises the globe.

588. I LOVE MANY DIFFERENT GODS

When I am wrong
I love the God of Right.

When I am weak
I love the God of Might.

When I am dark
I love the God of Light.

When I am sad
I love the God of Delight.

When I am empty
I love the God of Plenty.

When I am dreaming
I love the God of Reality.

589. I FORGOT

O Earth, how are you this
morning?
"I am fine, thank you.
Just one thing:
This morning I forgot to pray to
God."

O Heaven, how are you this
morning?
"I am fine, thank you.
Just one thing:
This morning I almost forgot to
love the world."

O God, how are You this morning?
"I am fine, child, thank you.
Just one thing:
I just forgot through oversight
To perfect you,
To fulfil you
And thus
To glorify you."

590. NOT YOU, BUT I

It was not you
Who thought of God!
It was I who thought of God.

It is not you
Who love God!
It is I who love God.

It will not be you
Who will realise God!
It will be I who will realise God.

Of course, I shall share with you
All my possessions.

Since I shall share with you,
You can assist me
Secretly and unreservedly at least,
If not unconditionally.

591. HER THREE SURPRISES

Goddess Supreme
Has sprung not one, not two,
But three surprises.

Her first surprise:
God claimed Her
As His best friend.

Her second surprise:
God seeks only Her advice.

Her third surprise:
God is visionless without Her.

592. O SILENCE

O silence of my life-desert,
I love your intensity.

O silence of my life-forest,
I love your fecundity.

O silence of my life-sea,
I love your enormity.

O silence of my life-sound,
I love your immortality.

593. HIS INCARNATIONS

In his warrior incarnation,
God Himself supported him.

In his musician incarnation,
God Himself instructed him.

In his philosopher incarnation,
God Himself perfected him.

In his poet incarnation,
God Himself glorified him.

In his Yogi incarnation,
God Himself served Him.

594. CALAMITY

Calamity after calamity:
He fell in love with darkness,
He shook hands with falsehood,
He dined with bondage,
He embraced ignorance,
He became the colossal pride of
Satan.

595. THE COLLECTOR

I collect fame,
The dust of time.

I collect pride,
The foot of time.

I collect truth,
The pride of time.

I collect love,
The life of time.

596. HE IS MYSTERIOUS

He is a mysterious runner;
He runs while he is sleeping.

He is a mysterious singer;
He sings while he is eating.

He is a mysterious lover;
He loves while he is doubting.

He is a mysterious liberator.
He liberates while he is
strangling.

597. I LOVE HIS EYES

I love his dawn-eyes
Because
They are beautiful.

I love his noon-eyes
Because
They are powerful.

I love his eve-eyes
Because
They are fruitful.

598. THEY ARE SICK

His body is sick.
Therefore
He sleeps day and night.

His vital is sick.
Therefore
He is depressed day and night.

His mind is sick.
Therefore
He doubts day and night.

His heart is sick.
Therefore
He is jealous day and night.

599. HE HAS NOT YET DISCOVERED

Do you know
What he has invented?
He has invented God.

Do you know
What he has not yet discovered?
He has not yet discovered
That love is life.

600. HIS TREASURE

God's Beauty is his hidden
treasure.
God's Duty is his revealed
treasure.

His Love of God is his only
treasure.
God's love for him is his endless
treasure.

601. A HERO WITH SOME DEFECTS

I got up late,
I made friends with
ignorance-king,
I dined with darkness-prince,
I sang with imperfection-princess,
I danced with weakness-queen.

I must say,
These are all my little
indulgences.
Yet
I am not what I was.
Alas,
I am now a hero with some
defects.
Of course, these are all minor
defects.

602. INTEGRITY

You struggle and struggle
For integrity.
Yet
You have no integrity,
You say.
I tell you,
You don't have to cry
For integrity!
Integrity will run
To embrace you
If you just request
Your heart-friend
To look after it.
Just speak to your heart-friend.
Lo, all integrity is yours.

603. TWO NEW REALITIES

Your high conceit-horse
And
Your low vanity-bull
Were your only realities.
But
Now your aspiration-deer
Has offered you two new realities:
Faithfulness-dog,
Service-cow.

604. HIS FOUR LIVES

When he lives
In his heart,
His heart-life is exemplary.

When he lives
In his mind,
His mind-life is literary.

When he lives
In his vital,
His vital-life is arbitrary.

When he lives
In his body,
His body-life is perfunctory.

605. WHAT IS IT?

Human revolt, what is it?
It is something that strikes and
breaks.

Divine revolt, what is it?
It is something that soars and
glows.

Human surrender, what is it?
It is something that fears and dies.

Divine surrender, what is it?
It is something that loves and
lives.

606. ANCIENT ROOTS AND MODERN FRUITS

The dark disputes of the ancients
And the moderns
Over their supremacy,
Who can settle?
None, save and except
The surrendering and fulfilling
oneness
Of the ancient roots
And the modern fruits.

607. EXISTENCE AND NECESSITY

Religion proved
The existence of his home,
And also
The necessity of his sincere
And searching life.

Yoga proved
The existence of his
Conscious oneness with God,
And also
The necessity of his pure
And elevating life.

God proved
The existence of his divinity
And also
The necessity of his sure
And ever-transcending life.

608. A DIAMOND UNIVERSE

Science-prince had
A silver universe.
His mind used it and used it.

He has now
A golden universe.
His heart is now trying and trying
  to use it.

He soon shall have
A diamond universe.
Once achieved,
His soul will use it
Smilingly,
Lovingly
And
Unreservedly.

609. REASON AND CERTAINTY

Reason and certainty
Always each other need.
Yes, they do!
But I know and I tell you
Truth-life is
Far beyond the reason-sky
And far above the certainty-sea.

610. ATTACKS ON HIS AUTHORITY

His attacks on his past authority
Made him sincerity-sky.

His attacks on his present
  authority
Make him purity-moon.

His attacks on his future authority
Will make him reality-sun.

611. THEREFORE THEY LOVE ME

I am insecure.
Therefore
God's Compassion loves me.

I am inadequate.
Therefore
Man's kindness loves me.

I am insufficient.
Therefore
My consideration loves me.

612. ANOTHER REASON

Another reason for his physical
collapse:
He ate too much.

Another reason for his vital
collapse:
He fought too much.

Another reason for his mental
collapse:
He thought too much.

Another reason for his psychic
collapse:
He slept too much.

613. THE BEAUTIES OF NEW YORK CITY

The beauties
Of New York City:
It does not sleep
At night.
It has forgotten how to walk;
It just runs and runs.
It uses little of its necessity
To endear,
And much of its capacity
To steer.

614. TWO KINGDOMS

You are the King
Of two kingdoms:
Self-discovery
And
Life-mastery.

You are the King
For two kingdoms:
God-manifestation
And
World-perfection.

615. WHEN HE LIVED IN THE WORLD

When he lived
In the world ruled by Satan,
He was simply shocked
By its madness.

When he lived
In the world ruled by Death,
He was simply shocked
By its stark coldness.

When he lived
In the world ruled by Hope,
He was simply shocked
By its orphan sadness.

616. LOVE HAS REALISED HIM

Love, true I have not
Realised You,
But
What can I do?

"Child, be happy
That I have realised you
On your behalf.
You are your forgotten Infinity,
You are your remembered
nothingness."

617. MY DESIRE STAYS ON

Morning comes and morning
goes,
Evening comes and evening goes.
My aspiration comes,
My aspiration goes.
But
My desire neither comes
Nor goes;
It just stays on and on.

618. BEFORE HE DIED

Before he died
He told the world
That the world was unconscious.

Before he died
He told Heaven
That Heaven was inconsiderate.

Before he died
He told God
That God was indifferent.

619. MY GOD-HUNGER

When I lived in the desert,
My God-hunger was simply
beautiful.

When I lived in the forest,
My God-hunger was really
soulful.

When I lived in the mountain
cave,
My God-hunger was divinely
fruitful.

When I lived in my Inner Pilot,
My God-hunger was supremely
useful.

620. THEY LOVE NOT

The talker
In me loves not silence.
The listener
In me loves not sound.
The lover
In me loves not delay.
The beloved
In me loves not reserve.

621. TEARS IN GOD'S EYES

I saw tears of Light
In God's Eyes
When I fought with Him.

I saw tears of Night
In God's Eyes
When I fought with myself.

I saw tears of Delight
In God's Eyes
When I transcended myself.

I saw tears of Fulness
In God's Eyes
When I defeated Him.

622. FOR THE TIME BEING

For the time being
I shall think only of God,
To love the Real in me.

For the time being
I shall love only God,
To manifest the Immortal in me.

623. THE FUNCTION

The function of inspiration
Is to start quickly.

The function of aspiration
Is to continue steadily.

The function of realisation
Is to reach unconditionally.

624. THE SCARCITY

My mind
Is the scarcity of ideas.
My heart
Is the scarcity of ideals.
My life
Is the scarcity of dreams.
My soul
Is the scarcity of goals.

625. THE ONLY SON OF GOD

He is *a* son of God,
Who thinks God is great.

He is *the* son of God,
Who feels God is good.

He is *the only* son of God,
Who knows that
God is all surrender
To our desire-night
And
To our aspiration-light.

626. ALSO

Truth for truth alone.
Justice for justice alone.
Life for life alone.
Love for love;
Also
For hate.
Light for light;
Also
For darkness.
God for God;
Also
For Beauty's nest
And Beauty's rest.

627. GOD'S ASSISTANCE

He said quite a few things,
But what did he actually mean?
He actually meant that
He is always flooded
With God's Assistance
Even though his resistance to
    God-Light
Is endlessly persistent.

628. THE LIFE THAT YOU SAVE

The money that you save
May be God's.
The time that you save
May be humanity's.
The life that you save:
Not only God's and man's,
Definitely yours, too.

629. HE DIED FOR BEAUTY

He died for beauty.
Alas! Beauty was not to be found.

He died for purity.
Alas! Purity was not to be found.

He died for magnanimity.
Alas! Magnanimity was not to be
found.

He died for divinity's Reality
and reality's Divinity.
Lo! Nothing was missing.
Everything shone perfectly
In its God-ordained place.

630. GOD DOES EXIST

Two are the things besides God
That make us feel and realise
That God does exist:
The smile of an infant
And the tears of a bereaved
mother.

And how do we prove
The existence of God?
We prove the existence of God
By becoming the bridge
Between His silver Boat
And His golden Shore.

631. I BECAME

When Love-light was needed in
My life, I became a student.

When Compassion-height was
needed in
My life, I became a teacher.

When Perfection-delight was
needed in
My life, I became God.

632. IN THIS AGE

In this age of anxiety
What we need is the wisdom of
God the Father.

In this age of insecurity
What we need is the love of God
the Mother.

In this age of war
What we need is the embrace of
God the Brother.

633. THEY ASSURED ME

Finally Mother Earth assured me
That I was not sick.

Finally Father Heaven assured me
That I was not undivine.

Finally the Supreme assured me
That I was indispensable.

Finally I assured myself
That I was the surrender-bridge
Between man and God.

634. GOD WAS PROUD

When I was a rock,
God was proud of my adamantine
will.

When I was a tree,
God was proud of my untiring
compassion.

When I was an animal,
God was proud of my unyielding
striving.

When I was a human being,
God was proud of my heart's
crying.

When I was a divine being,
God was proud of my accepting
and rejecting,
And my becoming and being.

635. YOU DO CARE

Who says that you do not care for
God?
You do care for God;
Therefore you stay on earth.

Who says that you do not care for
Heaven?
You do care for Heaven;
Therefore you embody Heaven's
Light.

Who says that you do not care for
earth?
You do care for earth;
Therefore earth is still alive.

636. WHO CAN TELL ME?

Who can tell me
Where God-Light is?
Perhaps my aspiration-friend can.

Who can tell me
Where God-Power is?
Perhaps my prayer-friend can.

Who can tell me
Where God-Delight is?
Perhaps my surrender-friend can.

637. BE CAREFUL!

O insincere seeker,
You may swerve
From the path of truth.
Be careful! I tell you
It can easily happen.

O impure seeker,
You may drown
In the sea of ignorance.
Be careful! I tell you
It can easily happen.

638. BE CHEERFUL

O sincere seeker,
You may realise God
Even in this lifetime. Who knows?
So be cheerful. I tell you,
This can easily happen.

O pure seeker,
God may choose you to be
His matchless instrument
To fulfil Him on earth. Who knows?
So be cheerful. I tell you,
This can easily happen.

639. AN OUTSTANDING ATHLETE

You are indeed
An outstanding athlete.
You ran all the way
From your home to God's Palace
In spite of the fact
That the distance defies
All human calculations.

Of course, you had
God's Compassion-Heart
To protect your head
From ignorance-rain
And
God's Protection-Arms
To protect your feet
From ignorance-heat.

Ah, now you even have the capacity
To run every day to God's Palace
From your home, the earth,
And back again.
You are indeed
An outstanding athlete.

640. I AM READY

O earth,
Do you need any help?
I am ready to help you
With my two powerful arms.

O Heaven,
Do you need any help?
I am more than ready
To help you
With my genuine and pure heart.

O God,
Do You need any help?
I am eagerly ready
To serve You
With my unconditional life.

641. MY FAVOURITE

God is my favourite
Because
He hides all my blind and wild
  weaknesses.

Man is my favourite
Because
He admires most generously
My great and high valour.

Earth is my favourite
Because
She alone shares with me
My weakness-sea and valour-sun.

642. HOW DID IT HAPPEN?

How did it happen?
How is it that you allowed
Ignorance to steal you
From your Heavenly Palace?

How did it happen?
How is it that you have not
Informed God the Policeman
To make inquiries?
Well, still there is time.

Just go and inform God
The Policeman Supreme.
He will without fail catch the thief
And save you.
I assure you, He will.

643. LOOK AND SEE

Look and see
If you have criticised God.

Look and see
If you have deceived man.

Look and see
If your proud mouth has
overestimated yourself.

Look and see
If your timid heart has
underestimated yourself.

If you have criticised God,
Don't worry. He will illumine you.

If you have deceived man,
Don't worry. He will deceive you
back.
Therefore you will not owe him
anything.

If you have overestimated
Or underestimated yourself,
Don't worry. Just dive within
And you will unmistakably know
Where you really stand.

644. THREE SERIOUS FAULTS

He has just three
Serious faults,
That's all.
He can't stop talking,
He can't start listening.
He can,
But he does not want to
Learn the art of loving God
And thus perfect
His own human life.

645. NOW YOU TRY IT

I have told you
How to pray to God.
Now you try it.

I have told you
How to touch God's Feet.
Now you try it.

I have told you
How to speak to God.
Now you try it.

I have told you
How to become God's real
favourite.
Now you try it.

646. WHO DO YOU THINK YOU ARE?

Who do you think you are?
If you really think
That you are God's son,
Then undoubtedly your brother
Is also God's son.

Who do you think you are?
If you really think
That you are none but God,
Then I tell you
Once and for all
That I am another
God,
Plus
A far superior
God.

647. THE INNER CRY-DEVOURING TIGER

God is not pleased with me;
He does not cherish me any more.
Never mind, I shall bravely
Face all that.

I am not pleased with myself
either;
I don't cherish myself either.
Alas, I do not know
How I can ever
Face myself,
The inner cry-devouring tiger in
me.

648. I AM A CHILD

I am a child of Heaven.
Therefore
I dream.

I am a child of earth.
Therefore
I serve.

I am a child of sound.
Therefore
I grow.

I am a child of silence.
Therefore
I glow.

I am a child of God.
Therefore
I really am.

649. HE IS

He is near,
Although
I see Him not.

He is dear,
Although
I feel Him not.

He is perfect,
Although
I examine Him not.

He is my all,
Although
I know Him not
At all.

650. GOD KNOWS THE ART OF COMPENSATION

Because
I am a timid deer,
God has granted me
The message of speed
To reach speedily my goal.
I told you, my world,
God knows the art
Of compensation.

Because
I am a timid man,
God has granted me
The message of love
To found His Kingdom on earth.
I told you, my world,
God knows the art
Of compensation.

651. YOUR PROPHETIC EYES

Your prophetic eyes
Tell me that you are
The only God in Heaven.
But I suspect you.

Your prophetic heart
Tells me that I am
The only God on earth.
Therefore
I love you
And I shall always love you.

652. O MY SILENCE

O my silence-heart,
I love you and love you.

O my silence-life,
I need you and need you.

O my silence-soul,
How near are you, how near?

O my silence-goal,
How far are you, how far?

O my silence-God,
Where are You, where are You?

653. YOUR TURN

Willing or unwilling,
You must go to God.

Willing or unwilling,
You have to realise God.

Willing or unwilling,
God will make you
Another God
Before long.
Ah, He has already resigned.
Now yours is the undisputed turn.

654. I HAVE EVERY RIGHT

Since my soul
Is so weak,
I have every right to leave
This soul and look for another.

Since my goal
Is so uncertain,
I have every right to leave
This goal and look for another.

Since my God
Is so blind and deaf,
I have every right to leave
This God and look for another.

655. MY MYSTIC INSPIRATION

My mystic inspiration
Starts in my Determination's
silence-green.

My mystic aspiration
Starts in my Purity's
silence-white.

My mystic realisation
Starts in my Expansion's
silence-blue.

My mystic manifestation
Starts in my Perfection's
silence-gold.

656. MY WISHES

My dear wish
Is to love God.
My heart is the witness.

My dearer wish
Is to serve God.
My soul is the witness.

My dearest wish
Is to fulfil God.
I have two witnesses:
Heaven and earth.

657. MY NEWBORN LIFE

My newborn tongue
Only speaks of God.

My newborn heart
Only lives for God.

My newborn life
Only lives in God.

My newborn soul
Only reveals God.

My newborn Goal
Only manifests God.

658. LOOK AT THEIR STUBBORNNESS

Look at this stubborn shore!
It refuses to receive my boat.

Look at this stubborn boat!
It refuses to be a little more
Devoted to the shore.

Look at these stubborn
passengers!
They just refuse to thank
The boat and shake hands with
the shore.

Alas, I am lost in the confusion
Of indifference-sea.

659. OUR MASTER

He is our hopeful Master,
For what we can do.

He is our mournful Master,
For what we have already done.

He is our soulful Master,
Because
He knows and tells us
That we all are destined to be
The direct representatives
Of God on earth.

660. BETWEEN

My life is between
The sea and shore
Of God's unwritten Compassion
And unfailing Love.

My soul is between
The earth and Heaven
Of God's unseen Cries
And manifested Smiles.

661. DON'T BE SO SAD

O my Boatman,
Don't be so sad.
I am not as useless
As you think.

O my Boat,
Don't be so sad.
I am not as heavy
As you feel.

O my Shore,
Don't be so sad.
I am not as irresponsible
As you imagine.

662. SILENCE

What you can do:
You can criticise silence,
You can ignore silence.

What you cannot do:
You cannot sit even one fleeting
minute
In silence.

Yet one day
It is you and you alone
Who will marry silence
And become inseparably one
With silence-sky.

663. WHAT SHALL I DO WITH THEM?

What shall I do
With my stupid mind?
It is afraid of vastness.

What shall I do
With my stupid heart?
It is afraid of oneness.

What shall I do
With my stupid life?
It is afraid of duty.

What shall I do
With my stupid soul?
It is afraid of earth-reality.

664. WHO WILL READ MY POEMS?

Who will read my poems?
Man? Never!
Since he has so many
Important things to do,
I just forgive him.

Who will read my poems?
God? Why not?
He has to,
Since it is He who
Has written all these poems
In and through me.

Naturally He has to
And
He always does,
Carefully,
Lovingly,
Cheerfully.

665. I KNOW NOT WHY

To be exact,
God loves you more than
He loves me.

To be accurate,
God has all eternity for you
But
For me He does not have
Even a minute to spare.

To be precise,
God is always and ever
Partial to you,
Yet I love God.
Why?
I know not why,
And never shall I know.

666. IN HIS CHILDHOOD

In his childhood
He slept.
Therefore
He does not sleep now.

In his childhood
He smiled.
Therefore
He does not smile now.

In his childhood
He saw
The face of darkness.
Therefore
He now sees the face of Light.

In his childhood
He played
With ignorance and its brood.
Therefore
He now plays with God and His
children.

667. THE LIFE OF GOD-BEAUTY

The life of outer beauty
Is an expensive force.
The life of God-Beauty
Is an all-loving,
all-illumining,
all-fulfilling force.

668. HIS YOUTH REMAINS

His youth remains,
Although
He is ninety years old.

His youth remains,
Because
He loves the quintessence of life:
Oneness-light.

His youth remains,
Because
God has always much work
To accomplish in him,
Through him, on earth.

669. A SHORT NOTE

I went to visit my original Home.
Alas, my parents were not there.
I missed their presence badly.

I was told by the sun,
The moon and the stars
That my parents left their Home
To visit my home on earth.

I came back home hurriedly
Only to find a short note:
"Son, your father, God,
And your mother, Goddess,
Need you here on earth
And nowhere else."

670. HERE ON EARTH

I am not alone.
I am with the mists
Of brooding doubts
There on earth.

I am not alone.
I am with the snows
Of blossoming faith
Here on earth.

I am not alone.
I am with the heaving sighs
There on earth.

I am not alone.
I am with the illumining smiles
Here on earth.

671. THE PATIENT

When a patient goes to a doctor
He offers his money-power
To the doctor,
He offers his suffering-power
To God,
He offers his love-power
To his body.

672. IN PRAISE OF MARRIAGE

In praise of human marriage:
It knows how to cry.

In praise of divine marriage:
It knows how to try.

In praise of marriage to God:
It knows how to fly.

673. WHAT IS NEXT, PLEASE?

Father, I have seen Your Face.
What is next, please?
"Daughter, then love Me more."

Father, I am loving You more.
What is next, please?
"Daughter, promise you will
always take part
In My Cosmic Game."

Father, I shall always take part
In Your Cosmic Game
Cheerfully,
Devotedly,
And unconditionally.
What is next, please?
"Nothing, absolutely nothing,
My sweetest child."

674. TO SHORTEN YOUR JOURNEY

To quicken your faith,
Pray.

To frighten your doubt,
Concentrate.

To enlighten your life,
Meditate.

To shorten your journey,
Consecrate.

675. FOR GOD'S SAKE, DON'T

O my mind,
For God's sake
Don't entangle yourself.

O my vital,
For God's sake
Don't strangle yourself.

O my heart,
For God's sake
Don't torture yourself.

O my body,
For God's sake
Don't belittle yourself.

676. WHERE IS MY FRUITFUL TIME?

Days come and days go.
Alas,
Where is my God-realising
second?

Years come and years go.
Alas,
Where is my God-manifesting
minute?

Centuries come and centuries go.
Alas,
Where is my universe-perfecting
hour?

677. WHAT IS THE DIFFERENCE?

What is the difference
Between
A poor man
And
A rich man?
The poor man hurries,
The rich man worries.

What is the difference
Between
A bad man
And
A good man?
A bad man knows
What he has done for himself.
A good man knows
What he has yet to do
For both God and man.

678. THE DAY I WANTED TO SAIL

The day I wanted to sail
With doubt,
Our boat did not start.

The day I wanted to sail
With fear,
Our boat sank when the journey
Was three minutes old.

The day I wanted to sail
With love,
God immediately jumped into
our boat
And on we sailed.
Both love and I just
Slept, sang and danced in the boat.
But God did something more:
He led us all the way
With His Nectar-light.

679. I NEED

O rose-petals of joy,
I need your fragrance.

O God-secret of self-mastery,
I need your light.

O love-perfection of life-mystery,
I need your patience.

680. THE ANSWER

Beauty demands an answer.
Love commands an answer.
Duty expects an answer.
Searching needs an answer.
Oneness neither demands nor
commands
An answer;
Oneness neither expects nor needs
An answer.
For oneness itself is the
Answer of answers.

681. FOUR LOST THINGS

I have been searching and
searching
For four most precious things.
Alas, I know not when and where
I have lost them:
My childhood innocence,
My adolescent courage,
My inner poise,
My supreme smile.

682. BULL, DEER AND LION

The Bull in me
Fights for the Freedom vast.

The Deer in me
Runs for the freedom of the
Beyond.

The Lion in me
Enjoys the freedom of the
ever-transcending
Goal.

683. MY CHOICE

Whom am I going to choose: God?
Ah, He has already
Chosen me, my all.

Whom am I going to choose:
Ignorance?
Alas, I have already
Chosen her, her brooding
Darkness-cave,
Bondage-eye,
Frustration-tongue,
Destruction-arms.

684. WE LOVE EACH OTHER

I love my Master
Because
He tries within me,
He cries for me.

My Master loves me
Because
I am an infant soul,
I am an orphan life.

685. WHY THEY LOVE GOD

My mind loves God
Because
God can.
He can illumine the mind.

My heart loves God
Because
God has.
He has all love for the heart.

My soul loves God
Because
God is.
God is all.

686. RAINBOW BRIDGE

O Rainbow Bridge,
In you I see
The mounting face
Of aspiration-race.

O Rainbow Bridge,
In you I feel
The descending grace
Of Compassion-Embrace.

Your love of duty
Is your Beauty's Height.
You are the Bridge
Between
Earth-throes
And
Heaven-Delight.

687. THREE NECESSITIES

Scholarship is necessary
For those who want
To arouse the sleeping world.

Hero-worship is necessary
For those who would like
To inspire the impotent world.

Godship is necessary
For those who wish
To reach the golden Shore
of the Beyond.

688. ACHIEVE!

Achieve self-control!
At your feet
Every living soul.

Achieve God-light!
At your feet
The eternal night.

Achieve God-compassion!
At your feet
The world-salvation.

689. BECOME

Become a blossomed mind.
God's Compassion you are bound
to find.

Become a dedicated heart.
God's Delight without fail
Will play its part.

Become a surrendered ray.
God's Pride will immediately
Give you His eternal Day.

690. GOD WAS HIGHLY PLEASED

He renounced
His pleasure-life
For
His joy-life.
Therefore
God was highly pleased.
God gave him
God-competence;
God gave him
God-accomplishment.

691. NO GREATER GAIN, NO STRONGER STRENGTH

No greater gain
Than selflessness;
No greater loss
Than forgetfulness.

No stronger strength
Than forgiveness;
No stronger weakness
Than self-indulgence.

692. WHAT IS DELIGHT?

What is Delight?
Divinity's Light.

What is Divinity's Light?
Reality's Height.

What is Reality's Height?
Immortality's Right.

693. YOUR LIFE

Your life is a life
Of God's constant Grace.
Therefore
With Heavenly gods
You have your eternal place.

Your life is a life
Of unconditional surrender.
Therefore
God's Height and God's Depth
Are anxious to have you
As their peerless treasure.

694. NO HIGHER PRIDE, NO GREATER JOY

No higher pride
Mother Earth contains
Than the man
Whom Divinity maintains.

No greater joy
Father Heaven owns
Than the man
Whom ignorance disowns.

695. TWO LORDS

O body, you have two lords:
A sweet lord,
And
A silent lord.
Serve your sweet lord, heart.
Serve your silent lord, soul.
Your heart's aspiration-flame,
Your soul's illumination-joy
Will transport you
Into the world of the cosmic gods.

696. LOVE

Love is peace on earth.
Love is bliss in Heaven.
Love is God's hospitality
To man.
Love is man's dignity
In God.

697. GOD PROUDLY PLEASES YOU

Your love never failed.
Therefore
You are ever hailed.

Your peace never died.
Therefore
Doubt-clouds from you hide.

Your joy never ceased.
Therefore
God proudly pleases you
And you alone.

698. NO DISGRACE

Poverty is no disgrace;
Just face the blows of the world!

Incompetence is no disgrace;
Just face the laughter of the world!

Defeat is no disgrace;
Just face the evils of the world!

Ignorance is no disgrace;
Just face the impatience of the world!

699. AN UNFORTUNATE BIRTH

With no sincerity,
Life is an unfortunate birth.

With no humility,
Life is an ignoble birth.

With no purity,
Life is a useless birth.

With no spirituality,
Life is an unthinkable birth.

700. HE HAS NOTHING TO GIVE

He has nothing to give;
Therefore
Earth does not need him,
Heaven does not want him,
Death avoids him,
Hell ignores him.
But
God's Compassion thinks of him,
God's Love meditates on him.

701. YOUR DIAMOND CALMNESS

O whistling wind, my life
And I
Long for your silver cheerfulness.

O rising dawn, my heart
And I
Long for your golden brightness.

O resting sun, my mind
And I
Long for your diamond calmness.

702. WE NEED YOU

O quenchless aspiration-flames,
The God in me needs you,
You alone.

O endless desire-train,
The man in me needs you,
You alone.

O restless monkey-life,
The animal in me needs you,
You alone.

703. CELEBRATIONS

God celebrated Himself
Before Love was born.

I celebrated myself
Before Death was born.

Death celebrated himself
Before Love was born.

704. ONE THING I SHALL KNOW

Three things I knew:
How to announce myself,
How to multiply myself,
How to entangle myself.

Two things I know:
How to give,
How to receive.

One thing I shall know:
How to become God.

705. THE MEANING

Smile
Is the meaning of my life-poem.
Dance
Is the meaning of my life-song.
Cry
Is the meaning of my life-story.

706. WHEN I LISTENED

When I listened to all sides,
I pleased none.

When I listened to you,
And
Not to him,
You embraced me
And
He struck me.

When I listened to myself,
I poisoned my life.

When I listened to God,
I transcended my desire-life
And
God immortalised my
aspiration-sun.

707. CAN YOU, WILL YOU?

O lustrous glow
Of my sun-life,
Where are you?
How far are you?

O bounteous flow
Of my God-life,
What are you?
Who are you?

O precious rainbow
Of my earth-life,
Can you please me, can you?
Will you fulfil me, will you?

708. MY REUNION

My union with God,
God and I knew.
My separation from God,
Earth and Heaven knew.
My reunion with God,
Satan knew,
And he wept for his loss.

709. THE SMILE-WORLDS OF THE BEYOND

I lived in life's stormy night
To see the face of God-Day.
I live in life's glowing day
To export my earth-core
To the smile-worlds
Of my ever-transcending Beyond.

710. INFIDELITY

Lord, infidelity everywhere
In Your creation!
How do You account for it?
"Son, I really do not know.
Perhaps My Vital-fire knows."
Lord, fidelity everywhere
In Your creation!
How do You account for it?
"Son, I really do not know.
Perhaps my Heart-vision knows."

711. THE LOSER

Earth and Heaven fought;
Earth lost.
With earth, God the Body lost;
With earth, God the expensive Cry
lost.

Earth and Heaven fought;
Heaven lost.
With Heaven, God the Soul lost;
With Heaven, God the expansive
Smile lost.

712. TRY AND CRY

Try and try, stop not!
God-realisation is indeed
A perpetual possibility.
Cry within, cry without!
God-realisation is indeed
An immediate inevitability.

713. WHAT MUSIC TELLS ME

The sound-music tells me
God is Power.

The silence-music tells me
God is Bliss.

The God-music tells me
God is Experience.

714. YOU ARE BOUND TO

Clutch and cling;
You are bound to stumble.

Love and serve;
You are bound to run.

Wait for the Hour;
You are bound to lead.

Become and Be:
You are bound to win.

715. HIS EMPIRE'S EMPEROR

Yesterday touched my feeble heart
With his growing terrors.

Today touches my unlit mind
With his blazing errors.

Tomorrow shall touch my striving life
With his amazing labours.

Finally, God shall touch my dream-boat,
And make me His Empire's emperor.

716. HEART-SWAN

Softly
The dawn-wind
Feeds my heart-swan.

Hurriedly
The noon-wind
Feeds my vital-tiger.

Convincingly
The eve-wind
Feeds my mind-horse.

Lovingly
The night-wind
Feeds my body-lamb.

717. THE WITNESS

His mind-confusion is rising,
His life-perfection is falling.
Although he denies it,
God is the silent witness.
His heart-dedication is rising.
His God-manifestation is blossoming.
Although he hesitates
The entire world on his behalf proclaims it.

718. EMPTINESS AND FULNESS

Emptiness of the mind
Is necessary.

Emptiness of the heart
Is obligatory.

Fulness of life-sound
Is God-preparation.

Fulness of silence-life
Is God-perfection.

719. SIX COMRADE-SOULS

Six divine comrade-souls
Have decided to live together
With God's lofty Blessing-pride.
A higher communion,
A deeper union,
A stronger realisation,
A brighter perfection,
A truer Reality,
A dearer Divinity.

720. YOU ARE GREAT

You are divinely great.
Do you know why?
Because
You are unbinding love.

You are supremely great.
Do you know why?
Because
You are unattached devotion.

You are eternally great.
Do you know why?
Because
You are unconditional surrender.

721. I PITY THEM

She is an anxious, worried
woman.
I pity her.
He is a confused, disturbed man.
I pity him.
I am a frustrated, broken-hearted
life.
I pity myself.

722. MY BENEFICIAL PERFECTION

My mind
Is a superficial notion.
My heart
Is a sacrificial nation.
My life
Is an official preparation.
My God-surrender
Is my beneficial Perfection.

723. ALWAYS ONE-WAY

From the Master,
Love-message in one ear,
Out the other.
From the Master,
Devotion-message in one ear,
Out the other.
But
God's Compassion-message once
in,
No exit.
It is always one-way.

724. GOD'S THREE CIRCLES

My heart's aspiration
Is a member of God's morning
circle.

My life's dedication
Is a member of God's evening
circle.

My surrender's perfection
Is a member of God's constant
circle.

725. O QUEEN, O KING

O Queen of Heaven,
I need your Compassion-light.

O queen of earth,
I need your patience-night.

O King of Heaven,
I need your Wisdom-shower.

O king of earth,
I need your resolution-power.

726. RIGHT ACTION

Right action is God-freedom.
What else is right action?
Right action is self-giving.
What is self-giving?
Self-giving is oneness-embracing.
What is oneness-embracing?
Oneness-embracing is
God-becoming.

727. HE KNOWS

He knows.
He knows the impotence of his
brutal rage.
He knows.
He knows the importance of his
forgiveness-gaze.
He knows.
He knows what he can do:
He can criticise the omnipotent
God,
He can utilise the compassionate
God.
What he cannot do without
Is his surrender.

728. BIRTHLESS AND DEATHLESS

Bottomless was his desire-sea.
He knew it,
His vital-tiger knew it.

Topless is his aspiration-sun.
He knows it,
His heart knows it.

Birthless and deathless
Shall be the realisation
Of his Perfection-goal.
He shall know it,
His life-river shall know it.

729. HE WAS HAPPY WITH HIS LIFE

His village-life was transparent.
Therefore
He was happy.

His city-life was inconsistent.
Therefore
He was happy.

His God-life was silent.
Therefore
He was happy.

730. I LOVE YOU DEARLY

Believe it
Once and for all:
O heart of night,
I love you dearly.
O soul of day,
I love you deeply.
O Role of God,
I love you constantly.
O Goal of creation,
I love you freely.

731. GUILTY

Secretly
The guilty body hides.

Shamelessly
The guilty vital fights.

Uselessly
The guilty mind defends.

Unreservedly
The guilty heart surrenders.

732. HE LIVED TO MAKE THEM HAPPY

He lived unrevealed
To see the jealous earth happy.

He lived unmanifested
To see the callous Heaven happy.

He lived for Truth
To make God happy.

He lived for Love
To make himself happy.

733. TELL ME

Tell me mind,
Why are you not steady?

Tell me heart,
Why are you not ready?

Tell me vital,
Why are you persistent?

Tell me body,
Why are you dormant?

Tell me God,
Why are You hesitant, reluctant
yet expectant?

734. DO YOU KNOW WHO CAME TO SEE ME?

I was alone in the night.
Do you know who came to see me?
My old friend, Doubt,
venom-Doubt.

I was alone with the light.
Do you know who came to see me?
My present friend, Faith,
nectar-Faith.

I was alone with God.
Do you know who came to see me?
My bosom friend, Love, Eternity's
Love.

735. YOUR FRIENDSHIP

Your friendship with humanity
Is not secure.
Therefore you always go
Out of your way
To please humanity.

Your friendship with God
Is unimaginably secure.
Therefore quite often
You manage
To forget Him.

736. YOUR EVOLVING LOVE

You loved life's
Undivine pleasures, undeniably.

You love life's
Divine joys, unreservedly.

You shall love life's
Universal oneness,
unconditionally.

737. NOTHING IS REAL

Nothing is real!
No, not even my heart.
Therefore I do not pray.

Nothing is real!
No, not even my soul.
Therefore I do not meditate.

Nothing is real!
No, not even God.
Therefore I do not love.

738. IN THE ASSEMBLY OF COSMIC GODS

To fascinate humanity,
My heart sings God's Bliss-songs
In the assembly of human souls.

To fascinate Divinity,
My life sings man's sorrow-songs
In the assembly of cosmic gods.

739. THE GUARDIAN

God the Compassion
Is the guardian of my
  cottage-heart.

God the Liberation
Is the guardian of my earth-life.

God the Perfection
Is the guardian of my soul-reality.

740. SONGS OF PASSING TIME

Childhood sings
The songs of strange curiosity.

Adolescence sings
The songs of blind carelessness.

Youth sings
The songs of cold indifference.

Maturity sings
The songs of deepening nostalgia.

Dotage sings
The songs of orphan helplessness.

741. WHY SHOULD MY GOD LOVE YOU?

If your God is so great,
Why does He not think of me?
"As long as you allow your stupid
  mind
To think of you,
Why should my God think of
  you?"

If your God is so kind
Why does He not love me?
"As long as you treasure
Your insecure heart,
Why should my God love you?"

742. THE TOUCH

The cold touch of the earthly years
Weakens you and frightens you.

The warm touch of the Heavenly
  years
Inspires you and liberates you.

The silent touch of Eternity's years
Fulfils you and immortalises you.

743. FROM MY OWN PERSONAL EXPERIENCE

You want to know what I think of
God?
I will tell you what little I know of
Him
From my own personal
experience:
He has kindness.
He is good.
At times
He is cute, too.
Now do you want to know
something
Of my personal connection and
relation with Him?
Ah, you want to know!
Then just listen:
He is my surrendered heart's
perfect slave,
My desiring vital's compassionate
Master.

744. YOU REFUSE

You refuse to go with man
Because
He is too small.

You refuse to go with God
Because
He is too great.

You refuse to go with Heaven
Because
Heaven's soul is indifferent.

You refuse to go with earth
Because
Earth's body is malignant.

745. MY BUSINESS, GOD'S BUSINESS

My business is to spend;
My Lord's business is to send.
What do I spend
And
What does He send?
His Compassion-flood.
My business is to receive;
My Lord's business is to give.
What do I receive
And
What does He give?
His Perfection-sun.

746. I AM PROUD OF MY GOD

I have sent all my teeming
desire-thoughts
Into life-long exile.
Therefore my God is proud of me.
My God uses His birthless and
deathless Will
Most scrupulously and most
unsparingly.
Therefore I am proud of my God.
I repeat:
I am proud of my God.

747. ALL FOR YOU

His mind is dry and barren,
His heart is warm and fertile.
Indeed,
All his earthly achievements are
all for you.
His soul is dreaming and
planning,
His Goal is fulfilling and
becoming.
Indeed,
All his Heavenly achievements
Are all for you.

748. YOU ARE

O mind, my mind,
You are a life-long curiosity.

O heart, my heart,
You are a life-long obscurity.

O life, my life,
You are the dance of futility.

O God, my God,
You are my only necessity,
You are my Self-Form-Reality.

749. PERFECTION INCARNATE, DESTRUCTION INCARNATE

He is great
When the silence-sea captures
him.

He is small
When the sound-volcano captures
him.

He is perfection incarnate
When he unveils God.

He is destruction incarnate
When he veils himself.

750. MY GREED

There is no difference
Between
My mind and my unsatisfied
greed.

There is no difference
Between
My vital and my dissatisfied
greed.

There is no difference
Between
My heart and my fleeting greed.

There is no difference
Between
My body and my constant greed.

751. TRANSIENCE

Earth-life is a transient cry.
Heaven-life is a transient smile.
Death-life is a transient fear.
God-life is a transient
imagination.

752. FAITH

Courage is the eye of faith.
Love is the heart of faith.
Truth is the head of faith.
God is the soul of faith.

753. NOBODY KNEW

Nobody knew
About his taut confines.
Nobody watched
His slow decline.
Nobody believed
His great inner triumph.
Nobody sympathised
With his utter outer failure.

754. THE SUPREME SECRET

Fear cannot please
His body any more.
Depression cannot please
His vital any more.
Doubt cannot please
His mind any more.
Insecurity cannot please
His heart any more.
Why?
Because he has discovered
The supreme secret:
That he is of God-Delight
And
He is for God-Light.

755. I THANK TIME

I thank each moment
For its generous heart.

I thank each day
For its gracious life.

I thank each year
For its glorious role.

756. THEY ARE LEFT ALONE

His desire-life
And the prince of hell
Are left alone.

His aspiration-life
And the prince of Heaven
Are left alone.

His God-life
And here and now
Are left alone.

757. MY ESCORTS

Pride escorted me
To the country of orphan
humiliation.
Humility escorted me
To the country of high
glorification.
Love escorted me
To the country of blossoming
perfection.

758. THE ANSWER SUPREME

No more questions!
No more questions!
I shall drown all the questions
In the Light-sea of my heart.

No more answers!
No more answers!
I have seen God's Face,
The Answer supreme,
In the freedom-sky of my soul.

759. WHY DO I WELCOME DESIRES?

I can live my life
Without a single desire.
Then why do I welcome desires?

I welcome desires because
My unchallenging life
Wishes God always to live
His God-life above
My desire-life.

760. MY ONENESS-GOAL

Fleeting
Is my beauty's body.
Lasting
Is my duty's life.
Glorifying
Is my sacrifice-soul.
Fulfilling
Is my oneness-goal.

761. MY PEERLESS DISCOVERY

I am not God;
That all of you know.
I am the future God;
That you do not know.
But
I love you all;
Therefore
I gladly share with you
My peerless discovery.

762. PERHAPS THEY KNOW

Where is God?
I do not know.
Perhaps my heart-flame knows.

Who is God?
I do not know.
Perhaps my soul-sun knows.

Why is God?
I do not know.
Perhaps my love-life knows.

763. YOU ARE THE RIGHT PERSON

God, why do You love me?
"Son, I love you
Because
I need you."

Why do You need me?
"I need you
Because
You embody My Sound-life."

Why do You want me to embody
Your Sound-life?
"I want you to embody My
Sound-life
Because
My Silence-life needs its
counterpart.
Needless to say,
You are absolutely the right
person."

764. A LIFE OF SURRENDER

A life of surrender divine
Is the joy of Olympus-height.
A life of surrender human
Is the torture of ignorance-sea.
A life of divine surrender supreme
Is the Perfection-embrace of God.

765. ALWAYS

His heart is always new
As the morning sky.

His soul is always old
As the evening hope.

His smile is always powerful
As the blazing sun.

766. WHO AM I?

"Why do I need God?"
You need God
Because you need your real Self.
"Why do I need my real Self?"
You need your real Self
Because of your oneness with God.
"Who am I?"
You are the sound-fruit.
"Who is God?"
God is the Silence-seed.

767. THEY DO NOT HOPE

Life does not hope
To see his smile.
Death does not hope
To see his face.
Hell does not hope
To see his pangs.
Heaven does not hope
To see his heart.

768. FREEDOM-SOUL

Lord, the difference
Between
Your love and my love is this:
My love has bound Your
  Freedom-soul
And
Your love has freed my
  bondage-body role.

769. GOD IS CLEVER, GOD IS WISE

God is clever.
He does not accept
My sad but unconditional
  surrender.
Why?
Because He knows that if
  opportunity dawns
I shall challenge His authority and
  supremacy.

God is wise.
He accepts
My glad and unconditional
  surrender.
Why?
Because He knows that when the
  Hour strikes
He will turn me into another God.

770. YOUR LIFE OF LUSTRE

Smile, unreservedly smile!
Your life will be
The lustre of a rose.

Dance, unerringly dance!
Your life will be
The lustre of the moon.

Cry, soulfully cry!
Your life will be
The lustre of the Supreme.

771. WHY?

Death, why do you sleep so much?
Life, why do you cry so much?

Earth, why do you fear so much?
Heaven, why do you ignore so much?

Man, why do you doubt so much?
God, why do you forgive so much?

772. I TAKE CARE OF GOD

Do you know who takes care of me?
God.
Do you know who takes care of God?
I.

God takes care of me
With His Compassion-height.
I take care of God
With my surrender-light.

773. GOD GAVE ME

When my life was a slumbering will
God thought of me compassionately.
When my life was a conquering will
I thought of myself proudly.
When my life was a surrendering will
God gave me His Heart to smile,
God gave me His Eyes to devour,
God gave me His Face to reveal.

774. I PLAY

When I meditate
Inside a mountain cave,
I play with God's secret Soul.

When I meditate
At the foot of a banyan tree,
I play with God's vast Sky.

When I meditate
Inside my heart,
I play with God's sacred Breath.

775. WHEN WILL YOU RETURN?

Father Supreme,
When will You return?
"I shall return
Before you think of Me."

"Son, My son,
When will you return?"
I shall return
Only when You give me Your
Throne.

"Son, then take it, take it."
Father, I need it, I need it.

776. THE END OF SCHOOL

Vision:
The end of Heaven-school.

Mission:
The end of earth-school.

Frustration:
The end of man-school.

Perfection:
The end of God-school.

777. MAGICAL, RADICAL AND PRACTICAL

My vision-life is magical;
Therefore the world admires me.
My reality-life is radical;
Therefore God loves me.
My God-life is practical;
Therefore I honour and treasure
myself.

778. MY FLAWLESS LIVES

My silence-life
Is birthless and flawless.

My sound-life
Is deathless and flawless.

My perfection-life
Is endless and flawless.

779. A HOME FAR AWAY

Fear is a home
Far away from God.

Love is a home
Far away from man.

Realisation is a home
Far away from Heaven.

Perfection is a home
Far away from earth.

780. SICK OF IT

Mind, be still!
I am sick of your wild restlessness.
Heart, be pure!
I am sick of your vast impurity.
Soul, be certain!
I am sick of your constant
uncertainty.

781. GOD'S TORTOISE AND GOD'S DEER

I am God's tortoise.
I do not have to worry;
Slow and steady wins the race.

I am God's deer;
I have no time to waste.
Lo, God's silver Grace is beckoning
me.

782. O MESSENGER, WHERE ARE YOU?

O messenger of Dream,
Earth needs you.
Where are you?

O messenger of Reality,
Heaven needs you.
Where are you?

O messenger of Silence,
Life needs you.
Where are you?

O messenger of God,
Death needs you.
Where are you?

783. WATCHING

My earth is thirsty;
Alas, no nectar-sea within my
reach.

My Heaven is hungry;
Alas, no nourishing-sky within
my reach.

My human birth is crying;
Alas, no saving hand within my
reach.

Yet God is watching,
Carefully watching.

784. THE FREEDOM-SKY OF ONENESS

Human life is motion and
evolution.
Divine life is the silence-sea.
God-life is the Freedom-sky of
Oneness
Between
The body of the finite
And
The soul of the Infinite.

785. THEIR WAYS

Possession
Is the unknown way of the body.

Renunciation
Is the unappreciated way of the
soul.

Perfection
Is the misunderstood way of God.

786. MY LIFE

Lord, my life is a flute
Out of tune.

Lord, my life is a meditation
Out of practice.

Lord, my life is an accident
Out of danger.

787. I WAS DETERMINED

I was determined
In my seeking.
Therefore I am really successful.

I was determined
In my God-becoming.
Therefore I am divinely
successful.

I was determined
In my surrendering.
Therefore I am supremely
successful.

788. TO LOVE GOD IS TO BECOME GOD

To love God is to need God,
To need God is to see God,
To see God is to breathe God,
To breathe God is to become God.

789. WHAT YOU HAVE AND WHAT YOU ARE

To live with man
Is to live with what you have.
To live with God
Is to live with what you are.
What you have: God-aspiration.
What you are: God-realisation.

790. INTUITION, TRANSFORMATION AND PERFECTION

Intuition: what is it?
It is the record speed of the inner
Light.

Transformation: what is it?
It is the manifested glory of the
inner Light.

Perfection: what is it?
It is the constant
self-transcendence of the inner
Light.

791. TOMORROW'S NECESSITY

Yesterday's stupidity
Failed to love her.

Today's insecurity
Fails to reach her.

Tomorrow's necessity
Will love her and reach her,
Treasure her and manifest her.

792. SHE IS

Indeed, She is the veiled deity.
Indeed, She is the concealed
Queen.
Indeed, She is the unrevealed
Mother.
Indeed, She is the unmanifested
Godhead.

793. HER NAME

Patience-sky:
That is her secret name.

Compassion-sea:
That is her sacred name.

Perfection-moon:
That is her birthless and deathless
name.

794. O SISTER OF EARTH

O Mother of Heaven,
Thy love I implore.

O Daughter of God,
Thy smile I adore.

O Sister of earth,
Thy absence
Neither humanity
Nor Divinity
Can endure.

795. HER HEIGHTS, HER DEPTHS

Her nights are God's silver
trances.
Her days are God's golden dances.
Her heights are God's diamond
discoveries.
Her depths are God's eternal
mysteries.

796. HOW TO MAKE GOD SMILE

When I pray,
The Power of God smiles.

When I meditate,
The Light of God smiles.

When I love and serve,
God Himself smiles.

797. NOT A REPETITION

She tells the world:
Life is not a fruitless repetition.

She tells the world:
Death is not a helpless repetition.

She tells the world:
Love is not an eyeless repetition.

She tells the world:
God is not a useless repetition.

798. THROUGH HER

Through her eyes,
Earth's thousand tears burn.

Through her heart,
Heaven's thousand smiles shine.

Through her life,
God's thousand lives blossom.

799. HER OCCUPATIONS

She energises the spheres
Of divine activities.

She immortalises the realms
Of silence-trances.

To man she offers her
vision-flames
Of the emerald Beyond.

To God she offers her
promise-noon
Of Infinity's life
And
Eternity's love.

800. LOOK UP, MY LIFE!

O my life of failure-sighs,
Look up! Challenge once more
The victory of ignorance-night.
Arouse the lightning speed
Of your spirit-sky.
Lo, in you abides the Emperor
Of transcendental Triumphs.

801. THE WORLD DESPERATELY NEEDS

O Mother of seer-poets,
The blind world desperately needs
Your translucent light.

O Mother of hero-warriors,
The feeble world desperately needs
Your transcendental might.

O Mother of perfection-lovers,
The imperfect world desperately needs
Your silence-bound height.

802. ANSWER

Answer slowly
So that earth can understand you.

Answer quietly
So that Heaven can understand you.

Answer silently
So that God can perfect you.

Answer immediately
So that man can admire you.

803. THE SURRENDER-LIFE

Beautiful
Is the infant smile.

Soulful
Is the orphan cry.

Fruitful
Is the silence-heart.

Successful
Is the surrender-life.

804. O SILENCE-FLOWERS

O Silence-flowers, smile;
My inner eyes are ready.

O Silence-stars, dance;
My inner heart is ready.

O Silence-sky, come;
My inner body is ready.

805. LOST AND FOUND

Lost human child cries;
Found human child cries.
Lost divine child looks within;
Found divine child looks without.

806. SUDDEN PERFECTION

Sudden aspiration,
Beyond all hope.
Sudden realisation,
Beyond all calculation.
Sudden perfection,
Beyond all imagination.

807. WHO YOU ARE

Heart, my heart,
Let me tell you who you are.
Remember once and for all.
You are God's Dream-boat;
Something more: God's Pride.

Life, my life,
Let me tell you who you are.
Remember once and for all.
You are God's Reality-shore;
Something more: God's
Gratitude.

808. FREEDOM

Mind-freedom
Of the impure life
Crucifies.

Heart-freedom
Of the pure life
Sanctifies.

Life-freedom
Of the divine life
Multiplies.

809. HIS IS THE LIFE

His is the life
Of endless ideas.

His is the life
Of fruitless deeds.

His is the life
Of visionless soul.

His is the life
Of soulless goal.

810. PRESENT YOURSELF

O fighting thought-waves,
Calm yourself.

O illumining Volcano-will,
Arouse yourself.

O fulfilling God-Compassion,
Present yourself.

811. DUTY'S LUSTRE, HUMILITY'S HEART

Beauty's face may one day die
But
Duty's lustre never shall die.

Purity's body may one day starve
But
Humility's heart never shall starve.

812. TOGETHER

Her heart and
The calmness of the midnight
Together live.

Her life and
The boldness of the midday
Together play.

Her soul and
The sweetness of the morning
Together dance.

813. NEVER STAY AWAY

O devouring Time,
For God's sake,
Stay away.

O nourishing Time,
For God's sake,
Come and shake hands with me.

O illumining Time,
For God's sake,
Just once embrace me.

O fulfilling Time,
For God's sake, for your sake, for my sake,
Never stay away.

814. EXPECT NOTHING

Your prayer is fearful.
Therefore,
Expect nothing from your prayer.

Your meditation is doubtful.
Therefore
Expect nothing from your
meditation.

Your love is not soulful.
Therefore,
Expect nothing from your love.

815. YOU HAVE EVERYTHING

You have everything that your
Mother Divine
Wants you to have.
Therefore
You need no more.

Your Mother Supreme has
everything that you
Can afford to offer her.
Therefore
Suffer and grieve no more.

816. COME IN, MY FRIENDS

Who is around my house?
Come in my dear friend,
Inspiration.

Who is at my window?
Come in my bosom friend,
Aspiration.

Who is at my door?
Come in my eternal friend,
Realisation.

Who is in my living room?
Sit down my beloved friend,
Perfection.

817. THEY HAVE WON

His faith delayed.
Therefore
Death has won.

His love decayed.
Therefore
Destruction has won.

His life overslept.
Therefore
Ignorance has won.

818. WHO HAS THE POWER?

Who has the power to love?
My feeling heart.

Who has the power to hate?
My killing vital.

Who has the power to suspect?
My groping mind.

Who has the power to deceive?
My sleeping body.

819. DON'T BE A FOOL!

Don't be a fool!
Don't touch reason's flag;
It will break.
Don't be a fool!
Touch immediately faith's
  banner;
It will carry you
Into Infinity's
Reality-fulfilling Core.

820. LOVE HER, SERVE HER

Love the Divine Mother Supreme.
You will reach
The end of your endless Journey.

Serve the Divine Mother Supreme.
You can and you shall establish
The Kingdom of Heaven on earth.

821. ETERNITY'S SUNRISE

Eternity's sunrise,
My heart is dreaming of you.
Infinity's shore,
My mind is thinking of you.
Immortality's goal,
My life is adoring you.

822. BODY'S VICTORY, SOUL'S VICTORY

The body's victory
Is often
The soul's tremendous loss.

The soul's victory
Is always
The body's amazing progress.

823. MY EYELESS, FRUITLESS SOVEREIGNTY

God has the everlasting hunger
To love me.
I have the fleeting hunger
To love myself.
Yet
I dare to disown God
When He does not fulfil my black
  desires,
And I declare
My eyeless, fruitless sovereignty.

824. THEY LOVE OUR AGING LIFE

Our infancy, Heaven loves.
Our childhood, the angels love.
Our adolescence, God the Dream
loves.
Our youth, God the Reality loves.
Our old age, God the Necessity
loves.

825. I AM CHAINED

I am chained to Doubt.
Therefore
No joy have I.

I am chained to Faith.
Therefore
God-confidence have I.

I am chained to Mortal Time.
Therefore
Nothing havc I.

826. BE NOT

Be not lonely
Like the night.
Be lovely
Like the moon.

Be not expensive
Like a diamond-sun.
Be expansive
Like the Silence-light.

827. SHE GAVE

To the undivine
She gave her ears.

To the Divine
She gave her voice.

To man
She gave her service.

To God
She gave her light.

828. NEVERTHELESS

Roses have thorns.
Nevertheless, I like roses.

The moon has spots.
Nevertheless, I love the moon.

Heaven is not all perfect.
Nevertheless, I adore Heaven.

I am not always divine.
Nevertheless, God claims me.

829. THREE HIDING PLACES

Three are the places
Where I hide:
I hide in the night of thoughts,
I hide in the Light of silence.
I hide in the Height of God.

830. WHAT WE HAVE

You have the power that hurts.
He has the love that heals.
I have the light that sees.
God has the Compassion that
feels.

831. I THINK GOD HAS ALREADY REACHED ME

I saw below my desire-life
My own image.
I see above my aspiration-life
God's own Blaze.

I thought I could reach God
With my own efforts.
I think God has already reached
me
With His unconditional Grace.

832. DON'T BE ANGRY WITH ME

God, don't be angry with me.
I love Your earth-body
More than Your Heaven-soul.

"Son, don't be angry with Me.
I love your snow-white efforts
More than your blue-gold crown."

833. YOU WANT ME TO LOVE YOU ONLY

Life, I shall love death as well,
For God lives inside the heart
Of death, too.

Death, I shall love life as well,
Since God Himself
Is so fond of life.

Death, you want me to love you
only,
But I am hopelessly helpless.
What can I do?

834. FOUR PRAYERS

The tree prays:
O Lord Supreme, see my height.

The branch prays:
O Lord Supreme, eat my life-fruit.

The flower prays:
O Lord Supreme, appreciate my
beauty.

The root prays:
O Lord Supreme, bless my duty.

835. TWICE I ENJOY MY LIFE

Twice I enjoy my life:
I enjoy my life
When I stand
Between
My man-ascent
And
My God-descent.
I enjoy my life
When my heart cries with the
finite
And
My soul smiles with the Infinite.

836. SUCCESS SHALL BE YOURS

Although
You are surrounded
By desire-life,
You can be detached.
Although
Measureless is your doubt-life,
You can be freed.
Just try!
Success shall be yours,
For
God is all yours.

837. READY

Her beauty is ready
Only for Angel's eyes.

Her life is ready
Only for God's Heart.

Her soul is ready
Only for humanity's body.

838. DON'T MIX WITH THEM

Heart, my heart,
What has made you so dry?
I advise you,
Don't mix with your mind.

Mind, my mind,
What has made you so aggressive?
I advise you,
Don't mix with your vital.

Vital, my vital,
What has made you so lethargic?
I advise you,
Don't mix with your body.

Body, my body,
What has made you so sleepy?
I advise you,
Don't mix with your death.

839. I FEEL SO SORRY FOR YOU

Heart, my heart,
I feel so sorry for you.
You are staying with imprisoned
flames.

Life, my life,
I feel so sorry for you.
You are staying in your mind's
tiny cave.

Soul, my soul,
I feel so sorry for you.
Your God-manifestation is still a
far cry.

840. NOT YOU

Your fear is dead
And not you.

Your doubt is dead
And not you.

Your jealousy is dead
And not you.

Your insecurity is dead
And not you.

Your ignorance is dead
And not you.

Your puny "I" is dead
And not your giant "I",
The Universal "I",
The Transcendental Lord.

841. REMAIN BEYOND

O my animal life,
Remain within good.

O my human life,
Remain beyond evil.

O my divine life,
Remain beyond both
Good and evil.

842. THEIR OFFERINGS

My body thinks of me
And offers me a flood of tears.

My vital thinks of me
And offers me a night of fears.

My mind thinks of me
And offers me a sea of confusion.

My heart thinks of me
And offers me a dying flame of
insecurity.

843. THE ABODE OF INFINITY

Freedom is infinite
In the firmament.

Love is infinite
In the moon.

Light is infinite
In the sun.

God is infinite
Inside my flower-heart.

844. BEFORE LIGHT

Before Light
His courage-lion quails.

Before Night
His fear-cat glows.

Before God
His perfection-sun trembles.

Before Satan
His bondage-life triumphs.

845. IN HIS OWN WAY

His life is spiritual
At the time of serious crisis.
His surrender is unconditional
At the time of unavoidable death.
Yet God loves him.
Indeed, he too loves God,
Only
In his own way.

846. NOW I CAN RETIRE

I saw my God crying
In my play's penultimate scene.
I saw my God smiling
In my play's ultimate scene.
And now I can retire
Into the mind of my Nothingness
And
Into the heart of my Infinity's
Eternity.

847. WHAT I DO

What I do:
I sow the seeds
Of higher life;
I kill the trees
Of lower life.

What else I do:
I build the kingdom
Of brighter life;
I destroy the home
Of darker souls.

848. SMILES AND TEARS

A spark of my smile
Satisfies my God.
A drop of my tears
Manifests my God.
But
Death's endless smiles,
His endless tears,
Please me not,
Fulfil me not.
Alas, alas!

849. HEART, SOUL, GOAL

Heart, my heart,
Forever stay alive, forever.

Soul, my soul,
Forward march, forward!

Goal, my goal,
I am within your compassion,
I am for your manifestation.

850. BEAUTY

Outer beauty
Feeds the greedy eyes.

Inner beauty
Feeds the needy eyes.

Soul's beauty
Elevates the weeping eyes.

God's Beauty
Illumines the searching eyes.

851. THEY ARE PLEASED WITH MY BOOKS

I am truly grateful
To man and God,
To earth and Heaven,
Because
They are pleased with my books.

God is pleased with my books,
Because
My books devotedly manifest Him
On earth.

Man is pleased with my books,
Because
My books represent him
Adequately.

Heaven is pleased with my books
Because
My books carry many seekers
To Heaven.

Earth is pleased with my books
Because
My books embody earth-pangs
And earth-smiles.

852. SURRENDER IS THE ANSWER

Desire receives the answer
From the world of night.

Aspiration receives the answer
From the world of Light.

Meditation receives the answer
From the world of Peace.
But
Surrender receives no answer.
Surrender needs no answer
Because
Surrender itself is the Answer
Of answers.

853. WHY ARE YOU SO LATE?

Is that you, daughter?
Why are you so late?
"Father, I thought I could do
Without You.
I thought You could do
Without me.
Therefore
I found no necessity to come
Earlier."

Is that You, Father?
Why are You so late?
"Daughter, I am late
Because
You have made Me late.
Until now,
You thought your
Desire-life was all.
That is why."

854. HOW IT ENDED

My animal life,
How it ended:
It ended when mind
Knocked at its door.

My human life,
How it ended:
It ended when love
Knocked at its door.

My divine life,
How it began:
It began when oneness,
Universal oneness,
Was released from my
Transcendental Being.

855. I AWAIT YOUR COMMAND

Captain, O captain
Of my outer world,
My desire-life is waiting
For your command.

Captain, O captain
Of my inner life,
Your command is waiting
For my inner preparation.

Captain, O captain
Of my God-life,
Will you ever command me?
Will you ever guide me, will you?

856. THE CHOICE:

Whom am I going to choose
This time?

I chose Satan once,
And then we two
Fought and fought against God.

I chose man once,
And then we two
Cried and slept, slept and cried.

This time I am definitely planning
To choose God.
Let me see what we two
Together can do.

857. I SHALL OFFER

To the sun-power
I shall offer my newly acquired
power:
Aspiration.

To the moon-beauty
I shall offer my long treasured
beauty:
Heart.

To the God-light
I shall offer my ever-deepening
light:
Surrender.

858. I COULD HAVE DONE FAR BETTER

When I study my life
I see clearly
How foolish I was.
I could have done far better.
I wasted all my precious time
In the company
Of brooding fears,
Shooting doubts
And dying insecurities.
Yet
God loves me compassionately.
Yet
I love God unknowingly,
Unwillingly,
Undivinely.

859. I WROTE A BOOK

I wrote a book on Satan.
He wanted to read my book
But unfortunately,
Time was hostile to him.

I wrote a book on man.
Man had the time
But
He did not care to read it.
Unfortunately, he did not want
To waste his precious time.

I wrote a book on God.
God immediately read it,
And then
He smiled and cried.
He smiled at my moon-white
Sincerity;
He cried at my sun-vast
Stupidity.

860. WHAT HAPPENED?

When I sat at God's Feet,
What happened?
He blessed me with His infinite
Compassion-Light.

When I shook hands with God,
What happened?
He gave me His infinite Love
Freely to use.

When I embraced God,
What happened?
I totally forgot
That I was a lump of clay.

861. I THOUGHT

I thought God did not care for me.
Therefore
I paid no attention to God.

I thought only man cared for me.
Therefore
I paid all attention to man.

Although
I have changed my opinions
Totally,
Will I succeed?
Will I ever?

862. HE IS MASTER OF HIMSELF

Fear has left him.
Therefore
Once more he is master of himself.

Doubt has left him.
Therefore
Once more he is master of himself.

He is master of himself.
Therefore
He knows how God in him
  proceeds
And
How man in him succeeds.

863. BEFORE AND AFTER

Before my realisation
My inner cry
Was a loving guest of peace.

After my realisation
My divine smile
Became a fulfilling host of peace.

864. I LOVE YOU, I HATE YOU

O machine-loving man,
I love you.
I shall always love you
Because
You love something.

O God-doubting man,
I hate you.
I shall always hate you
Because
You doubt Someone.

865. GOAL

O curious traveller in me,
Your Goal is very far.
O laborious traveller in me,
Your Goal is absolutely sure.

O precious Goal,
How far are you?
O gracious Goal,
I love you.

866. THREE NEW WAYS OF THINKING

I have discovered
Three new ways of thinking:

Man can think
With his heart of love-light.

Man can think
With his life of surrender-might.

Man can think
With his soul of God-right.

867. THEY ALWAYS COME

My body knows
Darkness always comes.

My vital knows
Night always comes.

My mind knows
Evening always comes.

My heart knows
Noon always comes.

My soul knows
Thc sun always comes.

And I know
Grace from Above always comes.

868. GRACE

You want to know
The history of the world?
Grace!
I tell you, it is so simple
And
It is so clear.
The father of Grace is
all-illumining Concern.
The mother of Grace is
all-fulfilling Love.
Grace has only one brother
And
Only one sister.
Brother's name is Courage-prince,
Sister's name is Faith-princess.

869. I ASSURE YOU

You say
God does not love you.
I say
Just love God.
I assure you
He cannot and will not
Remain indebted to you.

You say
God does not care for you.
I say
Just use your concern-machine.
I assure you
God will use His
Concern-machine
To claim you today,
To fulfil you tomorrow.

870. THE GREATEST MAN

In the human world
The greatest man is he
Who dares to love
Cheerfully,
Ceaselessly
And
Selflessly.

In the divine world
The greatest man is he
Who dares to try
Soulfully,
Untiringly
And
Unconditionally.

871. A PROPOSAL

God, it is just a proposal:
Kindly come and share
With me my food, ignorance.
"Man, in My case
It is more than a proposal,
It is My most sincere request:
Just come and share
With Me My food, Light.
And I assure you, man,
My food is infinitely more
Than yours
Both in quality and in quantity.
Therefore
You can easily eat
My food with Me
Through Eternity."

872. IMAGINATION, INSPIRATION, ASPIRATION

I need imagination,
I need inspiration,
I need aspiration.

Imagination I need
To invite God.

Inspiration I need
To love God.

Aspiration I need
To serve God.

873. AN INSECURE LIFE

Who is most afraid of death?
Fear.
Who is most afraid of fear?
An insecure life.
Who is most afraid of an insecure
life?
God, God Himself.
Do you know why?
Here is the answer:
God just does not know
How to satisfy
An insecure life.

874. SINCE GOD IS KIND TO ME

For the time being
I am kind to God.

For the time being
God is kind to me.

Since I am kind to God,
Let me give Him what He has been
Asking me for all the time:
Aspiration.

Since God is kind to me,
Let me at least ask Him
For a favour:
God-realisation.

875. THE ACHIEVEMENT

Compassion, what is it
If not the achievement of concern?

Concern, what is it
If not the achievement of sacrifice?

Sacrifice, what is it
If not the achievement of love?

Love, what is it
If not the achievement of
Man in God
And God in Man?

876. THE SUPREME POWER

Inspiration is the brightest power
Of the poet in me.

Aspiration is the purest power
Of the seeker in me.

Surrender is the strongest power
Of the lover in me.

Oneness is the supreme power
Of the Yogi in me.

877. THE ETERNAL STUDENT

To you, God is a loving Teacher.
To him, God is a strict Teacher.
To me, God is a wise Teacher.
To earth, God is a compassionate
  Teacher.
To Heaven, God is a kind Teacher.
To God, God is the Eternal
  Student
Of our never-dying ignorance.

878. YOUR GOD, MY GOD

You stay with your God;
Let me stay with mine.
Your God tells you
That I am unrealised,
That I am undivine
And
That I am imperfect.

My God tells me
That I am realised;
More than realised,
That I am divine;
More than divine,
That I am perfect.
My God tells me something more:
"My son, you are My
Only successor."

879. THREE LIVES

I have three lives.
I will gladly offer
The first to the animal kingdom,
The second to the human
  kingdom
And the third to the divine
  Kingdom.

The animal kingdom
Admires my destruction-life.

The human kingdom
Admires my aspiration-life.

The divine Kingdom
Admires my dedication-life.

880. THE DIFFERENCE

The difference between your God
And my God is this:
Your God may not know
How great, how powerful
And how kind you are;
Whereas
My God does not know
And yet
Does not want to know
How stupid, how worthless
And how useless I am.

881. WHAT DO YOU MEAN?

What do you mean
When you say that God is very
kind?
"I mean that God has a big heart."

What do you mean
When you say that God has a big
heart?
"I mean that God has two big
eyes."

What do you mean
When you say that God has two
big eyes?
"I mean that
God watches me,
Examines me,
Perfects me
And
Fulfils me."

882. I FORGOT AND GOD FORGAVE

How did it happen?
How did you forget God?

How did it happen?
How did God forgive you?

"I deliberately forgot God
Because
He did not care to fulfil
My sweet and strong desires.

"God forgave me
Because
His Compassion gave Him
No other choice."

883. WHO IS GOD?

Who is God?
You asked me
The same question before.
I shall give you the answer
Lovingly and cheerfully again.

Who is God?
God is the son
Of your teeming desires.
God is the father
Of your blossoming aspiration.
God is the number-one enemy
Of your insecurity-heart.
God is the number-one friend
Of your courage-life.

884. WHEN I SURRENDERED MYSELF

When I surrendered myself
To the morning light,
God's Eyes of Beauty
Blessed me.

When I surrendered myself
To the midday light,
God's Heart of Beauty
Blessed me.

When I surrendered myself
To the evening light,
God's Hands of Beauty
Blessed me.

When I surrendered myself
To the inner light,
God the Eternal Beauty
Blessed me,
Embraced me,
Claimed me.

885. THE UNKNOWN AND THE IMMEDIATE

O silence of death,
I love you.

O sound of life,
I love you.

O silence of death,
I love you
Because
I love the unknown.

O sound of life,
I love you
Because
I love the immediacy of today.

886. BY THIS TIME

Why don't you care for God?
"Why should I?"

The reason is quite obvious.
"Did God ever care for me?"

How do you know
That God did not care for you?

"I know it,
And I tell you
From my own personal
experience,
Had God cared for me
By this time I would have
At least
Become a demigod."

887. PERHAPS I AM WRONG

Perhaps I am wrong,
Totally wrong,
When I criticise humanity.

Perhaps I am wrong,
Unmistakably wrong,
When I speak ill of Heaven.

Perhaps I am wrong,
Unpardonably wrong,
When I ridicule earth-aspiration.

O how I wish to be wrong,
Always wrong,
When I deliberately find fault
With my Inner Pilot!

888. THEREFORE I AM HAPPY

My vital is unused to tears.
Therefore
I am happy.

My heart is used to tears.
Therefore
I am happy.

My mind judges the world.
Therefore
I am happy.

My soul embraces the world.
Therefore
I am happy.

My body is the innocence-world.
Therefore
I am happy.

889. TOMORROW

Yesterday
Unwillingly your vital and mind
Fulfilled God.

Today
Willingly your heart and soul
Are fulfilling God.

Tomorrow
Your body will fulfil God
devotedly,
Your vital dynamically,
Your mind consciously,
Your heart unconditionally,
Your soul constantly.

890. MY GRATITUDE-FLAMES

Thorns die,
Roses live.

Hate dies,
Love lives.

Desire dies,
Aspiration lives.

The human in me dies,
The divine in me lives.

My gratitude-flames
In the Heart of God
Never shall die.
Eternally they breathe,
Eternally they sport,
Eternally they manifest
The Supreme,
My Supreme.

891. I DO NOT DESERVE IT

Lord, I ask You humbly:
Throw me not
Ruthlessly
Into the world again.
I do not deserve
Such severe punishment.

Lord, I ask You sincerely:
Accept me not
Compassionately
Into Heaven again.
I do not deserve
Such a high blessing.

892. WHEREVER WE ARE FREE

We never speak to God,
But we love God
Wherever we are free.

We never think of God,
But we love God
Wherever we are free.

We never serve God,
But we love God
Wherever we are free.

Where are we free?
We are free
In our sweet imagination,
In our bold declaration.

893. HIS OWN DESCENDING SELF

He likes man
But
Not men.

He likes God
But
Not the cosmic gods.

Who is his man?
His own ascending self.

Who is his God?
His own descending Self.

894. A SERIOUS COMMITMENT

Earth, my sister earth,
I cannot die with you
Because
I have made a serious
  commitment
To Heaven.
I have told Heaven
That I shall establish
Heaven on earth.

Heaven, my brother Heaven,
I cannot fly with you
Because
I have made a serious
  commitment
To earth.
I have told earth
That I shall transform
Her untold sufferings
Before I do anything else.

895. YOUR SWEET IMAGINATION AND YOUR BOLD WILL

Here is the difference
Between
Your sweet imagination
And
Your bold will:
Your imagination
Lovingly and soulfully
Speaks to God,
Speaks about God;
Your will
Consciously and unmistakably
Becomes God,
Fulfils God.

896. I AVOID MY FRIENDS

I avoid my fear-friends.
They are shameless.

I avoid my doubt-friends.
They are useless.

I avoid my jealousy friends.
They are senseless.

I avoid my insecurity-friends.
They are baseless.

Finally
I avoid myself.
Why?
Because my life is faceless.

897. LEAVE YOURSELF TO ME

Leave yourself to me.
I shall look after you.

Leave yourself to me.
I shall perfect you.

Leave yourself to me.
I shall immortalise you.

I leave myself to you
For your service.

I leave myself to you
For your pleasure.

I leave myself to you
For your consideration.

898. CAN YOU?

Lord, can You see my face?
My face is bleeding.

"Daughter, can you feel My Grace?
My Grace is working."

Lord, can You make me
Worthy of Your Compassion?

"Daughter, I shall try.
But I cannot guarantee it.
But if you want Me to make you
Worthy of My Pride,
I assure you,
I shall undoubtedly succeed."

899. LOVE SHALL BE MY PERFECTION

Lord, service was my imagination,
Service is my aspiration,
Service shall be my realisation.

Daughter, love was My
Realisation,
Love is My Manifestation,
Love shall be My Perfection.

900. YOUR PILGRIMAGE

I tell you once and for all:

Simplify your life-pilgrimage.
God will be proud of you.

Intensify your heart-pilgrimage.
God will be proud of you.

Purify your mind-journey.
God will be proud of you.

Cancel your vital-journey.
God will be proud of you.

Expel your body-journey.
God will be proud of you.

901. IS MY GOD PLEASED?

Is my God pleased with earth?
No, He is sick of earth's stupidity.

Is my God pleased with Heaven?
No, He is sick of Heaven's
indifference.

Is my God pleased with Himself?
No, He is sick of His futility.

902. I UNDERSTOOD GOD

God understood me
Totally
Only when I gave up
My animal pride.

I understood God
Perfectly
Only when He lowered
His highest Height
Compassionately and
considerably.

903. I PLAY NO MORE

I play no more
With my dying friend: fear.

I play no more
With my dead friend: doubt.

I play no more
With my strange friend:
insecurity.

I play no more
With my puny friend: ego.

904. WHO HIDES?

Who hides his presence?
God.

Who hides his absence?
Man.

God hides His presence
Because He feels
He can work better
For His children unnoticed.

Man hides his absence
Because he feels
His lack of dedication
Should not be exposed.

905. MY HAPPINESS

My thought-life
Is my false happiness.

My will-life
Is my true happiness.

My service-life
Is my lasting happiness.

My surrender-life
Is my everlasting happiness.

906. LEARNING SOMETHING MORE

I have all along known
Two things:
My Heaven is deaf,
My earth is blind.

And today
I am learning
Something more:
My God is indifferent.

907. WHAT I NEED

On earth
What I need is peace.

In Heaven
What I need is progress.

For humanity
What I need is love.

For divinity
What I need is service.

From the Supreme
What I need is a sun-vast Smile.

From myself
What I need is willingness,
And its bosom friend,
Readiness.

908. I AM A FOOL

I am a fool
When I blindly imitate.

I am a fool
When I unnecessarily hesitate.

I am a fool
When I helplessly cry.

I am a fool
When I all alone
Greedily and shamelessly fly.

909. TWO MORE THINGS

One thing you have seen:
The disappearance of God
From your vital life.

Two more things you are bound to
see:
God's sweet appearance
In your heart,
His bold emergence
From your body.

910. I CAN LIVE WITHOUT YOU

Lord, in the morning
I can live without You,
But
Not without Your Sun-smile.

Lord, in the afternoon
I can live without You,
But
Not without Your Concern-sky.

Lord, in the evening
I can live without You,
But
Not without Your
Compassion-sea.

911. YOUR FREEDOM

Your physical freedom
Has bound you;
Yet you want physical freedom.

Your vital freedom
Has crucified you;
Yet you want vital freedom.

Your mental freedom
Has blighted you;
Yet you want mental freedom.

Your psychic freedom
Is crying for you;
Yet you want not psychic freedom.

Your God-freedom
Is beckoning you;
Ah, I am seeing you in your
God-freedom!

912. PABLO CASALS

Pablo Casals:
He lived the life
Of a curious child
In the heart of Mother Nature.

He loved the life
Of a precious child
In the heart of Golden Skies.

He became the achievements
Of a stupendous child
In the heart of infinite Love.

913. GOD'S NEW DAWN

I love the eyes
Of the morning rose.
In them I see
The Beauty of God.

I love the ears
Of the evening rose.
In them I see
The Patience of God.

I love the lips
Of the dying rose.
From them I hear
The message of God's new Dawn.

914. TO PLEASE GOD

In the morning
I shall seek like a seeker
To please God the Truth.

At noon
I shall meditate like a Yogi
To please God the Liberator.

In the evening
I shall love like a divine lover
To please God the Eternal
Beloved.

915. HOW CAN I LIVE?

My Lord, how can I live
With my frustration-heart?

My Lord, how can I live
With my destruction-life?

My Lord, how can I live
With my timid soul?

My Lord, how can I live
With my indifferent Goal?

916. WHO IS HE?

Day: what is it?
Day is my hopeful life.

Night: what is it?
Night is my peaceful life.

Man: who is he?
He is my stranger-friend.

God: who is He?
He is my soul's only choice,
He is my Goal's only voice.

917. JUST LOVE THE LIGHT

My Lord,
How shall I think of Thee?
"Don't think.
Just love the Light In Me."

My Lord,
How shall I meditate on Thee?
"Don't meditate.
Just love the Light in Me."

My Lord,
How shall I love the Light in Thee?
"Ah, My child, that is My task.
Leave it to Me.
I shall do it for you, and for you
alone."

918. MOTHER OF THE UNIVERSE

Mother of the universe,
You are vaster than Your Infinity
When I place my searching head
At Your Feet.

Mother of the universe,
You are older than Your Eternity
When I place my crying heart
At Your Feet.

Mother of the universe,
You are stronger than Your
Immortality
When I place my loving soul
At Your Feet.

919. HOW SHALL I FEED YOU?

How shall I feed You,
My Lord?
I have been feeding You
For a long time
With my love, devotion and
  surrender.
You are sick of my impure love,
You are sick of my false devotion,
You are sick of my conditional
  surrender.
Therefore
I am totally lost.
"My child, feed Me with your
Sincerity's breath.
Try, you can,
You shall."

920. SUPREMACY

The human in me
Openly adores the supremacy of
  Truth.

The divine in me
Soulfully loves the supremacy of
  Love.

The God in me
Secretly becomes the supremacy
  of Compassion.

921. LOVE IS

Beauty dies,
The body lives.

The body sleeps,
The soul smiles.

The soul promises,
God fulfils.

God triumphs,
Man becomes.

Man becomes,
Love is.

922. THE SECRETS OF THE WORLD

Do you want to learn
The secrets of the world
We live in?
Then carefully listen:
Perfection: who wants it?
Nobody, practically no one.
Fulfilment: who wants it?
Everybody, without exception.

923. LIKE YOU I WISH TO BE

Matter, my dear,
Like you I wish to be explicit.

"Ah, that's easy,
Spirit dear.
Just touch my feet.
Difficult?
Then sit at my feet.
That's all!"

Spirit, my dear,
Like you I want to be implicit.

"Ah, that's very easy,
Matter dear.
Just enter into my heart
And
Live there forever.
Difficult?
Then feel my heart.
That's all!"

924. PERFECTION-PROGRESS, ACHIEVEMENT-EXPERIENCE

In the world of Light
I fly from peak to peak.
Indeed, this is my
perfection-progress.

In the world of night
I stumble from
frustration-window
To destruction-door.
Indeed, this is my
achievement-experience.

925. GOD-REALISATION

God-realisation
Is your birthright.
Fantasy, it is not.
Obstinacy, it is not.
Autocracy, it is not.
Accuracy of your life Divine,
It is.
Supremacy of your Reality,
It always is.

926. YESTERDAY, TODAY, TOMORROW

Yesterday, just yesterday
I was a Heaven-inspired dream.

Today, just today
I am a God-intoxicated life.

Tomorrow, just tomorrow
I shall touch the Supreme's
Reality-Shore.

927. EARTH-BOUND TRUTH AND HEAVEN-FREE TRUTH

Do you want to know
The difference
Between
Earth-bound truth
And
Heaven-free truth?

Earth-bound truth
Is for me today,
For you tomorrow.
Heaven-free truth
Is all balanced,
Quite impartial
And
Always just.

928. THE SAD STORY

When our eyeless body
Is in the foreground,
Our clever vital
Recedes into the background.

When our aggressive vital
Is in the foreground,
Our uncertain mind
Recedes into the background.

When our unlit mind
Is in the foreground,
Our insecure heart
Recedes into the background.
And there, there alone,
The sad story ends.

929. A DIAMOND-ONENESS

You are delighted
Because
Your puny "I"
Has at last vanished.

God is more delighted
Because
Love has taken its place.

You and God
Will be most delighted
When your gold-love is
unreservedly
Transformed into a
diamond-oneness.

930. YOU WANT, YOU NEED

Expansion you want,
Integration you need.

God-study you want,
God-living you need.

Height-projection you want,
Love-manifestation you need.

931. BEFORE THEY WERE BORN

Before my God-aspiration was
born,
My life was an unlimited
ignorance.

Before my God-realisation was
born,
My life was a limited knowledge.

Before my God-manifestation was
born,
My life was a partial wisdom.

932. UNITY

Unity in duality,
Unity in multiplicity,
Unity in diversity,
I desired.
God granted my climbing prayer.

Unity in Unity,
Unity in Divinity,
Unity in Immortality,
I desire.
God shall grant my glowing
prayer.

933. YOUR TEACHERS

Your body-teacher
Taught you how to be personal.

Your vital teacher
Taught you how to be emotional.

Your mind-teacher
Taught you how to be impersonal.

Your heart-teacher
Taught you how to be universal.

Your God-teacher
Taught you how to bc practical:
Practical in life,
Practical in death,
Practical on earth,
Practical in Heaven,
Practical in God-realisation,
Practical in Height-manifestation.

934. HUMAN WILL, DIVINE WILL

In the morning
Human will is confusion-forest.
In the evening
Human will is contradiction-sea.
At night
Human will is contention-sky.

In the morning
Divine Will is Love-realisation.
In the evening
Divine Will is
Truth-manifestation.
At night
Divine Will is God-perfection.

935. NO MORE, NO LESS

You are no more
Than a human being
When you fail to meditate.

You are no less
Than a cosmic god
When you soulfully meditate.

You are no more
And
No less than God Himself
When you divinely love and serve.

936. WHEN I DO NOT FAIL

I struggle with myself,
And I fail.
I surrender in the battlefield of
life,
And I fail.
Do you know when I
Do not fail?
I do not fail only when
My heart cries
For my self-transcendence
And my soul smiles
At my self-immanence.

937. I DEPEND

I depend on my eyes.
They don't see the Truth.

I depend on my ears.
They don't hear the Truth.

I depend on my nose.
It doesn't breathe well.

I depend on my hands.
They don't work well.

I depend on my feet.
They don't walk well.

I depend on my mind.
It doesn't think well.

I depend on my vital.
It doesn't strive well.

I depend on my body.
It doesn't cry well.

I depend on my heart.
It serves me well,
It manifests me well,
It fulfils me well,
It immortalises me well.

938. THEY TELL ME

My aspiration tells me
What compassion is.

Compassion tells me
What self-knowledge is.

Self-knowledge tells me
What self-mastery is.

Self-mastery tells me
What self-sufficiency is.

Self-sufficiency tells me
What oneness is.

939. THE DIVINE

How can anyone fail?
Do we not know
That the Divine has entered
Into the human heart?

Will the Divine remain,
Can the Divine remain
Satisfied
Without regaining
Its topless heights?
Never!

940. THE SILENCE OF THE SPIRIT'S CORE

Who says it is extremely difficult
To win the silence of the spirit's
Core?

I say it is easy,
Unmistakably easy.
Just smell your action-fragrance
And
Eat your experience-fruit.
Lo, your problem is solved,
Once and for all.

941. IT IS NOT BAD

Transformed individuality
Is not bad.
It has its own uniqueness.

Transformed personality
Is not bad.
It has its own exclusive worth.

Transformed
individuality-personality
Is not bad.
It has its own significant gift.

942. THEY TELL THE WORLD

The human in me tells the world:
"I want to help you,
But tell me how."

The divine in me tells the world:
"I wish to serve you,
And I am imploring God how."

The Supreme in me tells the
world:
"I shall please you,
And I know how."

943. HOW TO LOVE THE WORLD

You say that you know not
How to love the world.
That means you are
Already choked,
stifled,
strangled.

He says that he knows
How to love the world.
That means he is
Already accepted by Infinity,
liberated by Eternity,
manifested by Immortality.

944. NEEDS AND HEEDS

Doubt assails,
Faith prevails,
Joy sails.

Fear dies,
Courage survives,
Love flies.

Light sees,
Peace feels,
Delight feeds
And
The man in God needs,
The God in man heeds.

945. THREE MARRIAGES

The weak and the ignorant
Are married to the transient.

The strong and the wise
Are married to the permanent.

The aspiring and the loving
Are married to the Omnipotent.

946. UNSEEN LINKS

Beauty
Has its unseen links
With Heaven's smile.

Beauty
Has its unseen links
With earth's cry.

Beauty
Has its unseen links
With God's Compassion.

947. CLEVER AND WISE

If you are really clever,
Bury your lower self
In the womb of night.
God will bless you.

If you are divinely wise,
Resurrcct your higher Self
In the core of Light.
God will embrace you.

948. BEAUTY

Beauty is the window
Through which I see
The Face of Reality.

Beauty is the door
Through which I welcome
My Beloved Supreme.

Beauty is the room
Where my life becomes
Immortality.

949. FULFILLING BEAUTY

Life
Is evolving Beauty.

Truth
Is revealing Beauty.

Love
Is illumining Beauty.

Peace
Is manifesting Beauty.

Light
Is fulfilling Beauty.

950. MAN IN GOD, GOD IN MAN

Hate is the man in God;
Love is the God in man.

Self-gratification is the man in
God;
Life-dedication is the God in man.

Desire-force is the man in God;
Aspiration-light is the God in
man.

951. OUTER AND INNER

Water
We need for outer purity.
Love
We need for inner purity.

Powder
We need for outer beauty.
Humility
We need for inner beauty.

Effort
We need for outer success.
Surrender
We need for inner success.

952. MY FOUR DREAMS

I sacrificed my first dream
To fulfil my second dream.

I sacrificed my second dream
To fulfil my third dream.

I sacrificed my third dream
To fulfil my fourth dream.

To become a scholar
Was my first dream.

To become a poet
Was my second dream.

To become a Yogi
Was my third dream.

To become a God-server in
humanity
Was my fourth and last
Reality-filled dream.

953. THEY HAVE NOT FORGOTTEN YOU

Your dreams have not
Forgotten you.
Be cheerfully patient.

Your God has not
Forgotten you.
Be cheerfully and endlessly
patient.

Your perfection-smile has not
Forgotten you.
Be cheerfully, endlessly
and unconditionally patient.

954. WHO DARES TO DEFEAT YOU?

Your life is selfless;
Therefore
Earth dreams of you,
Heaven dreams for you,
God works through you.
Who dares to defeat you?
Death? Never!
Who dares to challenge you?
Satan? Never!

955. THE CHOICE IS YOURS

The choice between
Your autocracy
And
Your peace of mind
Is entirely yours.

The choice between
Your ego-foot-manifestation
And
Your Heart-dedication
Is always yours.

956. DON'T DELAY!

Don't delay!
Your Master may eat
Without you.

Don't delay!
Your Master may journey
Without you.

Don't delay!
Your Master may fulfil his dream
Without you.

Don't delay!
Your Master may not
Forgive you.

957. YOUR MASTER'S SMILE

Your efforts may win
Your Master's kind smile.
Your love can win
Your Master's sweet smile.
Your surrender will win
Your Master's sure smile.
But
Your acceptance of his path
Has already won
Your Master's shadowless smile.

958. MY ACHIEVEMENTS AND ACCOMPLISHMENTS

The inner sun
Is responsible for all
My achievements.

The outer sun
Smiles on all
My unexpected achievements.

The inner Master
Is responsible for all
My accomplishments.

The outer Master
Smiles on all
My unbelievable
accomplishments.

959. HOW CAN YOU BE?

How can you be happy
Since you want a real friend
On earth?

How can you be unhappy
Since you need no service
From others?

How can you be perfect
Since you do not cry
For God?

How can you be imperfect
Since God Himself uses
Your service-love?

960. YOU AND HE

He is losing power;
Therefore
He is trying to topple you.

He is gaining power;
Therefore
He is avoiding you.

He is selling his pride;
Therefore
He is looking for you.

He is forgetting his humiliation;
Therefore
He is dancing around you.

961. THE VOICE OF THE FUTURE

The voice of the past
Will influence you.
This influence is destruction.

The voice of the present
Will inspire you.
This inspiration is preparation.

The voice of the future
Will love you.
This love is aspiration.

962. YOU DON'T HAVE TO TELL ME

You don't have to tell me –
I myself know it.
God's absence has made me see
Whom I have consciously
neglected.

You don't have to tell me –
I myself know it.
Satan's presence has made me see
Whom I have shamelessly
accepted.

963. YOU WILL BE HEARD

You seek protection
And you will be heard.
Just wait one more day.

You seek aspiration
And you will be heard.
Just wait two more days.

You seek realisation
And you will be heard.
Just wait three more days.

I tell you the truth,
Nothing but the truth.
Lo, God is my witness.

964. UPHEAVALS

Upheavals will test you,
But cannot fail you.

Upheavals will test you,
But cannot shatter you.

Upheavals will test you,
But cannot devour you.

You are God's son,
Nothing can fail you.

You are God's Sound,
Nothing can shatter you.

You are God's Silence,
Nothing can devour you.

965. YOUR CLIMBING CRY AND SPREADING SMILE

The golden Shore
Will beckon you.

The golden Boat
Will inspire you.

The golden Boatman
Will carry you.

Just permit not time
To devour your climbing cry
And
Your spreading smile.

966. YOU WILL EMERGE TRIUMPHANT

You will emerge triumphant
From blighting doubts
Alone;
Of course with God's help.

You will emerge triumphant
From devouring ignorance
Alone;
Of course with God's help.

967. WHEN THEY KNOCK AT YOUR DOOR

When
Animal the child
Knocks at your door,
Feed him with your wisdom.
He is hungry.

When
Man the child
Knocks at your door,
Bless him with your power.
He is weak.

When
God the child
Knocks at your door,
Embrace Him with your love.
He is lonely.

968. FAITH-FRIEND, DOUBT-ENEMY

In the morning
My oldest friend reappeared.

In the evening
My oldest enemy reappeared.

My faith-friend said:
"God loves me.
Therefore
He needs me."

My doubt-enemy said:
"I love ignorance.
Therefore
I need ignorance."

969. THREE TEACHERS

"Dark days are short-lived,"
My teacher, Consolation, has
taught me.

"Bright days are long-lived,"
My teacher, Realisation, has
taught me.

"Perfect days never live,"
My teacher, Manifestation, has
taught me.

970. SOMETHING MUST BE DESTROYED

Something must be destroyed
For your happiness.
Do you want to know
What it is?
It is snoring.
Something more must be
destroyed.
Do you want to know its name?
Its name is roaring.
Something more yet to be
destroyed!
Do you want to know its name?
Its name is neglecting.

971. FROM WITHIN

Shine from within.
All will gather to love you.

Love from within.
All will gather to serve you.

Serve from within.
All will gather to fulfil you.

972. THOSE WHO ARE

Those who are before you
Will inspire you.

Those who are behind you
Will acclaim you.

Those who are around you
Will doubt you.

Those who are for you
Will devour you.

Those who are of you
Will revive you.

973. THE HAND

The hand of sincerity
Shall lighten your life.

The hand of purity
Shall widen your life.

The hand of humility
Shall brighten your life.

The hand of spirituality
Shall enlighten your life.

974. DO NOT ASK OTHERS

Do not ask others;
Doubt is its own question.

Do not ask others;
Love is its own answer.

Do not ask others;
Success is necessary.

Do not ask others;
Progress is indispensable.

975. WHEN THEY COME TO YOU

Achievement comes to you
Only when you earn.

Success comes to you
Only when you strive.

Progress comes to you
Only when you need.

God comes to you
Only when you surrender.

976. ETERNAL FRIENDS

Sanctitude and multitude
Do not mix.
Why?
Because they are not friends.

Multitude and gratitude
Do not mix.
Why?
Because they care not for each
other.

Gratitude and beatitude
Mix together.
Why?
Because they are bosom friends.

Beatitude and infinitude
Mix together.
Why?
Because they are eternal friends.

977. THE ONLY WAY

Your higher emotions sing:
Give and give;
The only way to progress,
The only way to become,
The only way to be.

Your lower emotions declare:
Possess and possess;
The only way to proceed,
The only way to succeed,
The only way to rule.

978. SOON THEY SHALL LEAVE YOU

O my wild chaos,
I tell you,
Soon my vital shall leave you.
Be prepared!

O my blank darkness,
I tell you,
Soon my mind shall leave you.
Be prepared!

O my poor insecurity,
I tell you,
Soon my heart shall leave you.
Be prepared!

979. BREATH AND BODY

O God, what do You do
With Your immortal Breath?
"With My immortal Breath
I think of perfecting you,
I think of pleasing you,
I think of fulfilling you,
I think of immortalising you."

O God, what do You do
With Your mortal body?
"With My mortal body
I carry you,
I serve you,
I inspire you,
I glorify you."

980. PAINTED DREAMS AND GOD-DREAM

O my painted dreams,
Do not magnify me.
I know who I am,
I know what I am.
I need no help from you.

O my God-dream,
Do not forsake me,
Do not ignore me.
I know how great you are,
I know how real you are.
I need help from You,
Only from You.

981. O BEAUTY IMMEMORIAL

O Beauty immemorial,
I need your holiness-height.

O Duty immemorial,
I need your kindness-length.

O Time immemorial,
I need your patience-depth.

O Love immemorial,
I need your oneness-light.

982. CAN YOU DARE DENY IT?

I told you
But you did not believe.
Look, God is all-love for you.
Can you dare deny it?
Impossible!

I told you
But you did not believe.
Look, God is making you another
God.
Can you dare deny it?
Impossible!

983. I KNOW THEM

I know them: fear and doubt.
Fear tells me
God's vastness will devour me.
I bless fear and its stupidity.
Doubt tells me
God has fed everyone else
Save and except me,
And He has no intention
Of feeding me.
I bless doubt and its absurdity.

984. ONLY ONE COMPLAINT

In the City of God
Man has only one complaint
Against God:
God does not love him any more
The way He used to.

In the city of man
God has only one complaint
Against man:
Man does not think of Him any
more
The way he used to.

985. ESSENCE OF GOD

Justice, what is it
If not the factual essence of God?

Compassion, what is it
If not the actual essence of God?

Perfection, what is it
If not the perpetual essence of
God?

986. THEY ARE PROUD OF YOU

Your mind is eminently great.
Therefore
Earth is proud of you.

Your heart is transcendentally
good.
Therefore
Heaven is proud of you.

Your soul is eternally divine.
Therefore
God Himself is proud of you.

987. I AWAIT YOUR COMMAND

O Emperor-God,
How high have I to fly?
I await Your supreme command.

O King-God,
How deep have I to dive?
I await Your good command.

O Prince-God,
How far have I to walk
On Eternity's Road?
I await Your immediate
command.

988. THE DESCENT AND ASCENT OF PERFECTION

Perfect Light descends.
Lo, perfect receptivity ascends.

Perfect Compassion descends.
Lo, perfect goodness ascends.

Perfect Delight descends.
Lo, perfect oneness ascends.

989. GOD'S MATCHLESS FAILURE

Do not magnify yourself.
You are nothing,
You can be nothing
Without Mother Earth's
Patience-light.

Do not deceive yourself.
You cannot be the height
Of human perfection;
You cannot be the depth
Of divine dedication.
You must be what you actually
are:
God's matchless failure.

990. EVEN IN HIS SLEEP

Even in His sleep
God gives you His supernal Power.
Try to believe me,
You are destined to rule the world.

Even in His sleep
God gives you His transcendental
Light.
Try to believe me,
You are destined to guide the
world.

Even in His sleep
God gives you His eternal Delight.
Try to believe me,
You are destined to immortalise
the world.

991. DON'T CONFIDE IN ME

Doubt, don't confide in me.
I no longer want to be
Your father.
Let me be my heart.

Fear, don't confide in me.
I no longer want to be
Your brother.
Let me be my arms.

Jealousy, don't confide in me.
I no longer want to be
Your friend.
Let me be my soul.

992. WHEN YOU SURRENDER

When you desire,
You do not get
What you expect.

When you aspire,
Your achievement
Far transcends
Your expectation.

When you surrender,
God gives you
What He Himself
Eternally treasures:
Smile.

993. IN THIS WORLD

In this brother-world,
I just give and give.

In this sister-world,
I give and I receive.

In this mother-world,
I receive and I receive.

In this father-world,
I just achieve and achieve.

994. LAMB-GOD, LION-GOD

In the morning
I am a lamb-god.
The Absolute Supreme
Loves me, fondles me
And tells me
I am His All.
I tell my Lord
I accept His matchless Gift
With my heart's gratitude-flame.

In the evening
I am a lion-god.
The Absolute Supreme
Energises me, perfects me
And tells me
I must feed Him in all.
I tell my Lord
I accept His supreme Command
With my heart's humility-dew.

995. AN ALL-OFFERING WOMAN

Don't act like a wailing woman!
God has no need
Of a wailing woman.
She is God's abysmal failure.

Act like an all-offering woman.
God cannot exist without her
Even for a fleeting second.
God says He needs her always;
She is indispensable.
I must say,
This time God is really sincere;
He supremely means it.
Something more:
God can stay
Even without His
  God-consciousness
But
Not without her offering-light.

996. GOD DOES NOT MIND

God does not mind
His unwashed hands
As long as he is ready
To drink with God
God's Nectar love.

God does not mind
His unwashed feet
As long as he is ready
To walk with God
Along Infinity's Road.

God does not mind
His unwashed heart
As long as he is ready
To house God and claim God
As his own, his very own,
Eternally his own.

997. CONSCIOUSNESS-SEA, LIGHT-SKY

O Consciousness-God,
I need Your Power.
Don't forget me.
If You forget me
I shall die.
I tell You,
You will be embarrassed.
For Your sake, for my sake,
Give me Your Consciousness-sea.

O Light-Goddess,
I need Your Love.
Don't forget me.
If You forget me
I shall die.
I tell You,
You will be embarrassed.
For Your sake, for my sake,
Give me Your Light-sky.

998. WHEN I MEDITATE

Mother Supreme, Father Eternal,
When I meditate
On Your Eyes
I feel Your Compassion-joy.

Mother Supreme, Father Eternal,
When I meditate
On Your Feet
I feel my Salvation-joy.

Mother Supreme, Father Eternal,
When I meditate
On Your Heart
I feel our Oneness-Joy.

999. OUR MANIFESTATION-PERFECTION HOUR

O austere Angel,
I like you
But
I don't love you.
Why?
Because God does not care
For your austerity-tears.

O smiling and dancing Angel,
I love you
Because
God loves you.
I need you
Because
God needs you.
Do you know why God and I love you?
Because you are our Power.
Do you know why God and I need you?
Because in you alone
Is our manifestation-perfection Hour.

1000. THEY MUST BE CAREFUL

Father is excellent;
The son is excellent, too.
A Christian is good.
Christianity is not bad,
But
Christianity must be careful
It does not wear out.

The Supreme is excellent;
Avatars are excellent, too.
A Hindu is good.
Hinduism is not bad,
But
Hinduism must be careful
It does not rust out.

PART III

THE GOLDEN BOAT

1. DON'T BELIEVE

My foolish heart,
Who told you
That I do not love you?
Don't believe insecurity.
I tell you,
Insecurity is a graceless liar.

My foolish mind,
Who told you
That I do not need you?
Don't believe doubt.
I tell you,
Doubt is a hopeless liar.

My foolish vital,
Who told you
That I hate you?
Don't believe impurity.
I tell you,
Impurity is a shameless liar.

My foolish body,
Who told you
That I force you?
Don't believe lethargy.
I tell you,
Lethargy is a useless liar.

2. WHEN I EXPLORED

When I explored
The frontiers of my mind,
Vastness-Light embraced me.

When I explored
The frontiers of my heart,
Oneness-Height embraced me.

When I explored
The frontiers of my soul,
My cry found its perfect home
In God's Smile
And
God's Smile found its perfect
Home
In my cry.

3. THE SONGS OF LOVE

What makes an animal an animal?
Animal love.

What makes a man a man?
Human love.

What makes God God?
Divine love.

Animal love is Eternity's
destruction.
Human love is Infinity's
suspicion.
Divine love is Immortality's
Perfection.

4. THE SONGS OF POWER

What is flower-power
If not my ever-expanding
horizon?

What is candle-power
If not my ever-climbing height?

What is incense-power
If not my ever-deepening depth?

What is my aspiration-power
If not God's unconditional love for
me?

What is my realisation-power
If not my oneness-manifestation
With Perfection-God?

5. MY FOUR POINTS

Crying
Was my starting point.
Smiling
Is my finishing point.
Loving
Shall be my ever-becoming point.
Surrendering
Shall be my ever-transcending
point.

6. THE SONGS OF EXPANSION

Expand your unaspiring
individuality.
Lo, you are a fragment
And
Totally isolated.

Expand your aspiring
individuality.
Lo, you are searching
And
Significantly fulfilling.

Expand your surrendering
individuality.
Lo, you have revealed
And
Supremely manifested
God the Dreamer in you
And
You the Lover of God.

7. THE SONGS OF UNHAPPINESS

O my unhappy old age,
I suffer with you.

O my unhappy God-face,
I suffer for you.

O my unhappy God-grace,
Where are you?
I don't see you.
I assure you,
From today
I shall love you only.
I shall fulfil you only.

8. THE SONGS OF MY INNER FAMILY MEMBERS

Aspiration is the secret life
Of my soul-seed.
Realisation is the sacred life
Of my heart-plant.
Revelation is the confident life
Of my mind-tree.
Manifestation is the inspiring life
Of my vital-flower.
Perfection is the fulfilling life
Of my body-fruit.

9. THE SONGS OF ACCEPTANCE

For the world-acceptance
I wrote my books
With the tears of my desire-eyes.

For God-acceptance
I write my books
With the tears of my
aspiration-heart.

For my own acceptance
I shall write my books
With the tears of my
perfection-soul.

10. ALAS

Alas, the twain have met:
My helpless body and my hopeless
vital.

Alas, the twain have not met:
My searching mind and my loving
heart.

Alas, will the twain ever meet?
My serving soul and my fulfilling
Goal.

11. MY DESIRE-WORLD AND MY ASPIRATION-WORLD

In my world of desire
My body and my soul
Were the dreamers of different
dreams.
My body's sleepless dream:
temptation.
My soul's ageless dream:
compassion.

In my world of aspiration
My body and my soul
Are the dreamers of one single
dream:
God-manifestation
in
Oneness-realisation.

12. HE PASSED BEYOND

He passed beyond the world
Of imitation-admiration.
Therefore
His vision-sky is divinely happy.

He passed beyond the world
Of illumination-realisation.
Therefore
God's Existence-Light is
  supremely happy.

He passed beyond the world
Of revelation-perfection.
Therefore
He and God are
Infinity's Beauty,
Eternity's Duty
And
Immortality's Reality.

13. ALTERNATIVES

You exhausted
Your Heaven-free
Alternative.
Therefore death-frown
Wanted to devour you.

You have exhausted
Your earth-bound
Alternative.
Therefore God's Crown
Shines in you,
God's Palace
Treasures you,
God's Kingdom
Embraces you.

14. BROTHER, I WARN YOU

Brother, I warn you.
Think not too much
Of your animal fire.
Think not too much
Of your ferocious life.
Brother, I warn you.
Nostalgia can be nauseating, too.

Brother, I warn you.
Think not too much
Of your human life.
Think not too much
Of your voracious life.
Brother, I warn you.
Nostalgia can be nauseating, too.

Brother, I warn you.
If you think not at all
Of your gracious Lord,
Reality-kingdom shall never
Invite you,
Immortality-king shall never
Embrace you.

15. SPEAK AND DON'T SPEAK

In your aspiration-life
Speak to faith.
Faith will strengthen your success.

In your aspiration-life
Speak to courage.
Courage will widen your horizon.

In your aspiration-life
Don't speak to doubt.
Doubt will slacken your vigilance.

In your aspiration-life
Don't speak to fear.
Fear will weaken your progress.

16. FOUR MESSAGES FROM FOUR WORLDS

"Dominate and dominate."
The animal world
Gave me this message.

"Survive to dominate."
The human world
Gave me this message.

"Offer and become."
The divine world
Gave me this message.

"Offer and offer."
The world of the Supreme
Gave me this message.

17. DOUBT-LESSON, LOVE-KNOWLEDGE AND SURRENDER-WISDOM

In our aspiration-life
Doubt-lesson is never applicable.

In our aspiration-life
Love-knowledge is always
applicable.

In our aspiration-life
Surrender-wisdom is immediately
And
Eternally applicable.

18. HE WANTED TO BECOME

He wanted to become
A great athlete.
God fulfilled his pygmy aim
And smiled at him.

He wanted to become
A great poet.
God fulfilled his pygmy aim
And shook hands with him.

He wanted to become
A great Yogi.
God fulfilled his pygmy aim
And blessed him.

He wanted to become
A true lover of humanity
And
A true server of God.
God fulfilled his giant goal
And embraced him,
Powerfully,
Proudly
And
Supremely.

19. COME IN

Come in, my Eastern friend.
Give me some advice.
Your every piece of advice
Shall accelerate
My God-realisation.

Come in, my Western friend.
Give me some advice.
Your every piece of advice
Shall expedite
My God-manifestation.

Come in, my Heavenly friend.
Give me some advice.
Your every piece of advice
Shall quicken
My life-perfection.

20. DON'T WORRY, MY FRIEND

Your vital is the victim
Of acute depression.
Don't worry, my friend.
I shall stay
With your depressed vital.

Your mind is the victim
Of wild frustration.
Don't worry, my friend.
I shall stay
With your frustrated mind.

Your heart is the victim
Of cruel desertion.
Don't worry, my friend.
I shall stay
With your deserted heart.

Your body is the victim
Of constant temptation.
Don't worry, my friend.
I shall stay
With your tempted body.

21. DON'T GO NEAR HIM

Don't go near his body.
His body houses
A blind and wild elephant.

Don't go near his vital.
His vital treasures
His conceited misanthropy.

Don't go near his mind.
His mind loves
His fabulous eccentricity.

Don't go near his heart.
His heart has lost
All its pristine purity.

22. I REFUSE

I refuse to see
The animal face
Because
It is cruel.

I refuse to see
The human face
Because
It is ugly.

I refuse to see
The divine face
Because
It is indifferent.

I refuse to see
The supreme Face
Because
It is too slow.

23. NO ONE

No one has a kind word
To tell you.
Yet
You think of them devotedly.

No one has a kind heart
To love you.
Yet
You treasure them soulfully.

No one has a kind soul
To please you.
Yet
You bless them lovingly.

I alone know
How great you are.
God alone knows
How good you are.

24. ON MY PART

On my part
It is painfully inappropriate
To speak ill of my earth-reality.
Yet
I do it.
I do it because I am a citadel
Of inconscience-night.

On my part
It is fruitlessly inappropriate
To speak ill of my Heaven-dream.
Yet
I do it.
I do it because my life
Is a dance of
frustration-annihilation.

25. YOUR UNWANTED GUEST

In the past
When God came to you
You were deeply sceptical.

This morning
God came to you again.
You doubted Him openly.

God will come to you
Again and again
Even if you go
To the length of hating Him
  ruthlessly.

Why? Why?
Because
Poor God cannot dare
To live without you.
You are His Soul.
You are His Goal.
You are His All.

26. NO DIFFERENCE

No difference
Between
A sea of thought
And
A brittle hope.

No difference
Between
A whisper of will
And
The Himalayan Silence.

27. MY OUTER SCHOOL AND MY INNER SCHOOL

My outer school
Is the perfect bridge
Between
My information-education
And
Frustration-destruction.

My inner school
Is the perfect bridge
Between
My illumination-education
And
Realisation-perfection.

28. ATTACHMENT-FONDNESS-ONENESS

Your constant attachment
To the temptation-world
Is really surprising.

God's strong fondness
For your ignorance-life
Is unbelievably surprising.

The oneness
Of your helpless cry
And
God's deathless Smile
Is eternally surprising.

29. EXPECTATION-DANCE

Don't expect
Anything
From the world.
Lo, you have become
The world's best friend.

Expect everything
From God.
Lo, you have become
God's best friend.

Expect nothing
From your earth-bound night
And
Expect everything
From your Heaven-free day.
Lo, you have become
Your own best friend.

30. YOU ARE GREAT, YOU ARE GOOD

The psychoses and neuroses
Of the outer world
Have not been able
To plague you.
Therefore
You are unmistakably great.

The realisation and perfection
Of the inner world
Have found
Their complete satisfaction
In your heart-cave.
Therefore
You are supremely good.

31. PURITY

Purity's height
Has a million torches
Flaming bright.

Purity's depth
Only God can dare
To plumb.

Purity's flood
We can expect
Only from the unconditional God.

32. MY CHALLENGE

I cannot change
Because
I do not want to change.

I can change you
And
The entire world
Because
That has always been
My soulful wish, my faithful task,
And
My bold challenge supreme.

33. BECAUSE

Because
You meditated this morning
You have once more
Become
Master of yourself today.
Don't forget this divinely adorable
discovery.

Because
You smiled this morning
You have once more
Become
The beloved friend of the whole
world.
Don't forget this highly profitable
discovery.

34. BELIEVE IT OR NOT

O greedy pleasures,
Believe it or not,
My vital does not
Want you any more.

O nourishing joy,
Believe it or not,
My heart needs you
Badly and unmistakably.

O fulfilling satisfaction,
Believe it or not,
My Lord has promised to me
That He will eventually offer me
Your Transcendental Soul
And
Universal Body.

35. GOD COMES DOWN

God comes down
To inspire
The worshipper's concentration.

God comes down
To visit
The dreamer's meditation.

God comes down
To love
The server's heart.

God comes down
To embrace
The lover's surrender.

36. BELIEVE THEM

Love-light
Tells you:
You are as sweet
As God's Heart.

Devotion-light
Tells you:
You are as pure
As God's Soul.

Surrender-light
Tells you:
You are as indispensable
As God Himself.

Believe them.
They are perfect strangers
To stark falsehood.
I repeat.
Believe them.

37. WHY I LOVE

I do not know
Why I love God.
I love God
Perhaps
Because He loves me.

I do not know
Why I love the world.
I love the world
Perhaps
Because the world loves me.
But
I do know why I love myself.
I love myself
Because
The ascending poor beggar in me
Loves me constantly
And
The descending rich beggar above me
Loves me unconditionally.

38. ALAS

I do not think of God
But
That is not what pains me,
And
My heart.

I do not love God
But
That is not what tortures me,
And
My soul.

I am not another God.
Alas,
That is what kills me,
My blue dream-boat
And
My Golden Shore.

39. GOD PERFECTS HIMSELF

Fear defends herself.
Courage expands himself.
Doubt offends himself.
Faith protects herself.
Purity transcends herself.
Impurity glorifies herself.

I destroy myself.
God perfects Himself.

40. I SHALL REMAIN THE SAME

Yesterday
You were breathless
With adoration.

Today
You are breathless
With suspicion.

Tomorrow
You will be breathless
With rejection.

But I shall remain
Eternally the same
God-lover
In the Heart of humanity.

41. I AM DISGUSTED

O Heaven,
I am disgusted
At your superiority.

O earth,
I am disgusted
At your inferiority.

O man,
I am disgusted
At your insincerity.

O woman,
I am disgusted
At your insecurity.

O God,
I am disgusted
At my stupidity.

O God,
I am disgusted
At Your futility.

42. DON'T FORGET

O my puny body,
You need me
And
My aspiration
To realise God.
Don't forget
This supremely important fact.

O my large soul,
You need me
And
My dedication
To manifest God.
Don't forget
This eternally significant fact.

43. WHERE IS THE PROMISED LAND

Where is the promised land?
Is it inside my greatness
or
Inside my I-lessness?

It is neither inside my greatness
nor
Inside my I-lessness.

The promised land
Is in man's constant
  acceptance-light
Of God's Perfection-Delight
On earth.

44. WHEN

When
I live in the body,
I discover:
Man is the future of man.

When
I live in the soul,
I discover:
God is the future of man.

When
I live in God,
I discover:
Man is the birthless Dream
Of God
And
God is the deathless Reality
In man.

45. BELIEVING OR NOT BELIEVING

Believing nothing
You go to death-world
As an invited guest.

Believing something
You stay in your own world
Of merciless caution.

Believing everything
Without concentrating
And
Without meditating
You enter into the
frustration-world
As a tempted guest.

46. MY TWO SUNS

A visible sun
Above my head
Energises my body-life.

An invisible sun
Within my heart
Fulfils my soul-life.

O visible sun,
You are so kind,
Yet
You are too far.

O invisible sun,
You are so kind,
Yet
You are too slow.

47. THE ANIMAL, THE HUMAN AND THE DIVINE IN ME

The animal in a destructive man
Wants to live unchanged.

The human in a frustrated man
Wants to die unchanged.

The divine in an aspiring man
Wants to change and live –
Wants to change for himself,
Wants to live for God.

48. HE LIVED, LIVES AND SHALL LIVE

He lived among his books.
Everybody laughed,
With the sole exception of God.

He lives among
Love, devotion and surrender.
Everybody admires him,
Including God.

He shall live with
God the Father
And
God the Mother.

Nobody will believe it.
Nobody will care for him.
Nobody will even think of him.

49. THERE WAS A TIME

There was a time
When my obscurity was my
  protection.

There was a time
When my aloofness was my
  protection.

But now
My heart of love is my protection.
And
My life of service is my protection.

50. I AM NEVER AFRAID

I am never afraid
Of hell.
Therefore
Hell always ignores me.

I am never afraid
Of Heaven.
Therefore
Heaven always examines me.

I am never afraid
Of God.
Therefore
God always
Teaches me unreservedly,
Loves me constantly,
Perfects me untiringly.

51. DON'T THINK, DON'T SLEEP

When he was a child,
One day
His father said to him:
"Don't think, my child.
God never thinks."
Since then, he never cared
To learn the art of thinking.

When he was a child,
One day
His mother said to him:
"Don't sleep, my child.
God never sleeps."
Since then, he never cared
To learn the art of sleeping.

52. INSPIRATION-SEED, REALISATION-PLANT, MANIFESTATION-TREE

Yesterday
In my soul-house
I kept my inspiration-seed.

Today
In my heart-room
I keep my realisation-plant.

Tomorrow
At my body-door
I shall keep my
manifestation-tree.

53. O SEEKER

O seeker of silence-beauty,
I long to fly with you.

O seeker of soul-smile,
I long to expand like you.

O seeker of God-Reality,
I long to be
The Son-Light of the absolute
King
Like you, with you.

54. TEARS

O clever tears
Of my eyes,
Stop descending.

O secret tears
Of my heart,
Start ascending.
God is awaiting your great arrival.

O sacred tears
Of my soul,
I love you;
I love you only.

Not because you *have* the
world-treasure,
Not because you *are* the
world-treasure,
But because you have chosen me
As your very own.

55. ALTHOUGH I SLEEP

Although I sleep
During my morning meditation,
God appreciates my attempt.
Therefore
I thank God.

Although I sleep
During my evening meditation,
I am proud of my attempt.
Therefore
I love myself.

56. IN ONE DAY

In one day
I became old:
When earth refused to accept
My help.

In one day
I became young again:
When Heaven offered me
His friendship.

In one day
I fed earth's ageless hunger:
When earth showed me
Her sunken sun.

57. GOD'S PLANS

Music that I wish to hear,
God is planning to compose.

Love that I wish to feel,
God is planning to create.

Joy that I wish to become,
God is planning to offer.

Perfection that I wish to see,
God is planning to plant.

58. A MAN OF GOD-SUBSTANCE

What was he?
A man of fabulous divinity!

What is he?
A man of imprisoned pride!

What is he going to be?
A man of God-substance,
A man of love-essence.

59. QUARRELS WITH GOD

You quarrel with God
Because
God has not granted you
Realisation.

He quarrels with God
Because
God has not given him
Aspiration-kite.

I quarrel with God
Because
God has not given me
The capacity to manifest Him
Completely on earth.

God quarrels with Himself
Because
God feels that He could have
created
A far better world.

60. THEREFORE YOU FAILED

It was a poor preparation.
Therefore
You failed.

It was a bad calculation.
Therefore
You failed.

It was an abrupt depression.
Therefore
You failed.

It was an unwarranted surrender.
Therefore
You failed.

61. YOUR INNER WEATHER

Your inner weather
Is always foul
Because
You do not dream
High realities.

Your inner weather
Is always foul
Because
You are afraid to face
Your lifeless shadow
Alone.

Your inner weather
Is always foul
Because
You are fond of living
In your puny
Imagination-temptation world.

62. EXPECTATIONS

As long as men are mortal
I expect nothing from them.
However, one thing I expect:
Their gratitude-flames.

As long as the gods are immortal
I expect many things from them.
But perhaps one thing will do:
Constant concern.

63. DO DOUBT, DO QUESTION!

O my doubtful eyes,
When I think I am
Perfect perfection,
Do doubt my unprecedented
discovery!

O my questioning mind,
When I act like a god,
Do question my authority!

64. TEACH ME

O energetic ant,
Do be my master sweet.
Teach me not to waste time.
Teach me how to walk along
The patience-road.
Teach me simple, fruitful reality,
Misnamed stupid simplicity.

65. MY FRIEND, MY FELLOW BEGGAR

When I am
With my Friend, God,
I come down
From Heaven to hell.
With my Friend
I change the face of hell.

When I am
With my fellow beggar, man,
I go up
From hell to Heaven.
With my fellow beggar
I look to see
If the sleeping God is awake.

66. YOU HAVE RUINED MY REPUTATION

Dear depression,
You have ruined my
Inspiration-reputation.

Dear frustration,
You have ruined my
Aspiration-reputation.

Dear delusion,
You have ruined my
God-perfection.

67. MY COURAGE SUPREME, MY GOD-DREAM

God needs me.
Therefore,
Today my courage supreme is reborn.

I need God.
Therefore,
Today my God-dream becomes man-reality.

68. HERE THEY ARE

Truth is where you see it,
Love is where you feel it,
Delight is where you find it,
Power is where you invoke it,
Peace is where you need it,
Light is where you claim it.

69. ALAS!

Alas!
My brave Divinity-day
Has sunk in the chasm of night.

Alas!
My years have hastened
To their destined end.

Alas!
The Teacher of all teachers,
My inner faith,
Forgets to teach me
Regularly,
Divinely
And
Supremely.

70. WHOM SHALL I SERVE?

Whom shall I serve?
A mortal master?
"Never!"

Whom shall I serve?
An immortal Master?
"Always!"

But where is He?
"He is inside your heart-cave."
Who is He?
"He is your active partner."
Who are you?
"His Eternity's sleeping partner."

71. GOD'S ATTENTION

Fear invokes
God's attention immediate.

Courage expects
God's attention immediate.

Doubt invites
God's attention immediate.

Faith treasures
God's attention eternal.

72. THEY HAVE THE ANSWER

Was God ever born?
My heart has the answer.

Did God ever die?
My soul has the answer.

Will God ever be fulfilled?
My dream-boat has the answer.

73. NEVER GIVE UP

Your life can be
Grown to perfection.
Don't give up.

Your soul
May replace God.
Don't give up.

God definitely shall make you
Another God.
Never give up.

74. UNVISITED

Human fear
Is unvisited by God.
Divine courage
Is unvisited by human fear.

Human love
Is unvisited
By the seeker's fulfilling success.
Divine Love
Is unvisited
By the seeker's animal past.

75. MY SCHOOL LESSONS

From the school
Of simplicity
I learnt:
God is simple
And within my easy reach.

From the school
Of diversity
I learnt:
Incomplete uncertainty
Is God's entire creation.

From the school
Of complexity
I learnt:
God is extremity's
Futility.

76. O MY DREAM-BOAT, O MY REALITY-SHORE

O Dream-boat of my joy,
Ultimately
You will reach the Reality-shore.

O Reality-shore of my joy,
Ultimately
You will make me another God.
Therefore
You ask me
To check my tornado-impatience,
And to enjoy
My earth-transformed
And
Heaven-born
Freedom.

77. HIS MISTAKES

He sleeps too much.
Therefore
He desires.

He thinks too much.
Therefore
He cries.

He fears.
Therefore
He fails so soon.

He doubts.
Therefore
He dies so soon.

78. GOD AND I ARE EVEN

God and I are even.
I defeated God
By outliving Him
In the world of ignorance-sea.
God defeats me
By outliving me
In the world of gnostic-sun.

79. LIFE

Harmless and noiseless life
I accepted.

Loveless and soulless life
I rejected.

Thoughtless and senseless life
I protested.

Godless and truthless life
I arrested.

80. FUTILE THOUGHTS

In the life of a desiring man
Satisfaction is a futile hope.

In the life of an aspiring man
Depression is a futile topic.

In the life of a God-realised man
Life-negation is a futile task.

81. BECAUSE

Because
Of his diseased ambition,
He is drinking pain.

Because
Of his deceased goal,
God is inspiring him
And saying to him,
"Your destiny is blossoming.
Hear the clarion call!"

82. HE HATES AND HE LOVES

He hates prosperity
Because
Prosperity harmed his humility.

He hates success
Because
Success ruined his progress.

He loves sincerity
Because
Sincerity never deserted him.

He loves humility
Because
Humility is God's universal
Oneness-light,
Oneness-might,
Oneness-flight.

83. HE DID NOT APPRECIATE

He received joy
But
Forgot to appreciate it.

He achieved success
But
Neglected to appreciate it.

He received love
But
Refused to appreciate it –
Consciously
Deliberately
Shamelessly.

84. MY FOOD

O desire-life,
Do you want
To eat my food?
Doubt-sighs are my food.

O aspiration-life,
Do you want
To eat my food?
Progress is my food.

O Realisation-life,
Do you want
To eat my food?
Oneness is my food,
My only food.

85. O EMPTINESS

O emptiness of ages,
I eat your silence-food.
Therefore
To you I offer my gratitude-heart.

O silence of Eternity's
Vision-dawn,
You fulfil your
sound-manifestation
Through my life's inner cry.
Therefore
To you I offer my certitude-soul.

86. GOD TREASURES

Your mind's unparalleled
Vastness,
God secretly treasures.

Your heart's unparalleled
Sacrifice,
God soulfully treasures.

Your life's unparalleled
Love,
God sacredly treasures.

87. O MY DESIRE, O MY ASPIRATION

O my scorching desire,
Are you not my shameless
  disgrace?
"Yes, I am.
But God still loves me."

O my burning aspiration,
Are you not my fulfilling promise
  to God,
My eternal Father?
"No, I am not.
I am the mere Grace-servant
And Reality-son of God."

88. ONLY THAT

Only what is permanent
Is free.

Only what is free
Is divine.

Only what is divine
Is fulfilling.

Only what is fulfilling
Is life-giving.

Only what is life-giving
Is God-becoming.

89. TALKERS

Body, I had no idea
That you were such a useless
  talker.

Vital, I had no idea
That you were such a great talker.

Mind, I had no idea
That you were such a secret talker.

Heart, I had no idea
That you were such a silent talker.

Soul, I had no idea
That you have never been a talker.
God bless you!

90. WORLD PLANS

Your head houses
World-shaking plans.

Your eyes contain
World-devouring plans.

Your heart embraces
World-illumining plans.

Your soul treasures
World-surrendering plans.

91. SHE LOVES THE WORLD

She loves
The ungrateful world
Because
She knows that
The gratitude-flower
Is not to be found on earth.

She loves
The imperfect world
Because
She knows that
The perfection-moon
Is not to be found on earth.

She loves
The unaspiring world
Because
She knows that
It takes time
For aspiration to come into
existence-life.

92. WHEN THEY ARE POOR

When education
Is poor,
Life is stupidity's struggle.

When illumination
Is poor,
Life is necessity's frustration.

When God-realisation
Is poor,
Life is reality's suicide.

93. THEREFORE I SHALL

Dancing makes the soul young.
Therefore
I shall dance.

Loving makes the heart soulful.
Therefore
I shall love.

Offering makes the life fruitful.
Therefore
I shall offer.

Surrendering makes the dream
real.
Therefore
I shall surrender.

94. ANOTHER NAME

Mind, don't you know
That you have another name:
Insatiable curiosity.

Heart, don't you know
That you have another name:
Destructive insecurity.

Soul, don't you know
That you have another name:
Dream-boat Reality.

95. UNWORTHY ONES

Your unworthy disciples
Give you their ignorance,
Their old and only friend of the
past.
For God's sake, bless them.

Your unworthy Master
Gives you what he has:
His old and only friend,
deception.
For God's sake, leave him and go
alone.

96. THIEVES

O sweet thief in my heart,
Do steal away not only
What I have, but also
What I am.
From now I shall have
Only one need:
You, only you.

O swift thief of the world around
Who came to rob me,
Don't act like a fool.
Don't empty
My venom-cup.
Your life of light shall die
Before it begins.

97. PERHAPS THEY WILL

Since
It is a good day to die,
Ask your old ignorance-friend
To die for you.
Perhaps he will.

Since
It is a good day to study,
Ask your knowledge-brother
To study for you.
Perhaps he will.

Since
It is neither a good day nor a bad
day,
Ask your compassion-mother
To fulfil you.
Certainly she can and she will.

98. TWO FRIENDS

When I sit
On the summits of my mind,
My old friend, Joy, leaves me
immediately.
The joyless beggar
Helpless comes down.

When I play
In the depths of my heart,
My old friend, God, appears
before me.
Two friends together drink
Nectar-light,
Two friends together become
Oneness-soul of Peace,
Oneness-goal of Bliss.

99. EXCUSES

God, we were fully awake,
But our pilot slept
All the way.
Therefore we are late.

God, our pilot was fully awake,
But we slept
All the way.
Of course he had
Our inner support
And
Outer approval
To place us
At Your Feet
On time.

100. HE SMILES AT ME

When I sleep
After my prayer,
My Lord smiles at my child-heart.

When I sleep
After my concentration,
My Captain smiles at my
soldier-will.

When I sleep
After my meditation,
My Beloved smiles at my
surrender-life.

When I sleep
After my contemplation,
My Friend smiles at my
oneness-soul.

101. ARE YOU STARVING FOR LOVE?

Are you starving for love?
My blue eyes shall feed you
Without fail.
Just wait a second,
I need permission
From my Lord Supreme.

Are you starving for love?
My white heart shall feed you
Without fail.
Just wait a second,
I need permission
From my Lord Supreme.

Are you starving for love?
My golden soul shall feed you
Without fail.
Just wait a second,
I need permission
From my Lord Supreme.

102. FOUR REALISATIONS

My body-cage has realised
Freedom's quick fame
Does not and cannot last.

My mind-cave has realised
Freedom's quick promise
Does not and cannot last.

My heart-flame has realised
Freedom's quick transformation
Does not and cannot last.

My soul-flower has realised
Freedom's quick perfection
Does not and cannot last.

103. THANK YOU

My Lord,
I saw You sailing
In my dream.
How beautiful You looked!
I must say,
You are more beautiful than I am.
"Thank you, My child."

My Lord,
I saw You as the only
Golden Shore.
How fulfilling You proved!
I must say,
You are more fulfilling than I am.
"Thank you, My child."

104. YOUR GOD

Good stars met.
Therefore
Horoscope became your God.
Who can forgive your foolish
  discovery?
No, not even God;
I mean the real God.

Good lines were born
In your palm.
Therefore
Palmistry became your God.
Who can forgive your foolish
  discovery?
No, not even God;
I mean the real God.

105. IF YOU DO NOT BELIEVE

I see God.
If you do not believe it,
That is your serious fault
And not mine.

God loves me most.
If you do not believe it,
That is your deplorable fault
And not mine.

God is going to make me
Another God.
If you do not believe it,
That is your unpardonable fault
And not mine.

106. FREEDOM

Earth-freedom:
Disastrous madness.

Heaven-freedom:
Harmonious oneness.

God-freedom:
Prosperous surrender.

107. O SELF-COMPLACENCY

O self-complacency,
Be not unconscious
Of your stark inferiority.
Lo, the phantom-hour
Is mocking you.
Terminate your groundless
Satisfaction.
Stop, stop your prolonged
Clever navigation.

108. WHEN I THOUGHT OF GOD

Fear obeyed me
When I thought of God.

Doubt surrendered to me
When I meditated on God.

Failure gave me joy
When I loved God.

Ignorance left me
When I spoke to God.

109. ONE NECESSITY

Believe it or not,
Heaven's blue smile
Is my soul's beauty.

Believe it or not,
Earth's green cry
Is my body's duty.

Believe it or not,
God's golden Promise
Has one necessity:
My surrender-reality.

110. IF I LOVE GOD

If I pray to God
Daily,
My life shall grow
Soulfully.

If I meditate on God
Daily,
My life shall run
Indefinitely.

If I love God
Daily,
My life shall be fulfilled
Eternally.

111. I CHALLENGE

Trance of the sky,
I challenge your beauty.

Trance of the night,
I challenge your ignorance.

Trance of God,
I challenge your Duty.

Trance of man,
I challenge your unreality.

112. EXILED

When I danced with doubt,
I was exiled
From God's Kingdom-Light.

When I sang with fear,
I was exiled
From God's Kingdom-Bliss.

When I spoke with jealousy,
I was exiled
From God's Kingdom-Love.

113. I CLIMBED UP

I climbed up
The ladder of ambition
Only to be caught
By the frustration-giant.

I climbed up
The ladder of aspiration
Only to be embraced
By my Realisation-Father.

I climbed up
The ladder of surrender
Only to be immortalised
By my Perfection-Mother.

114. I LIVE ONLY FOR THOSE

There was a time
When I lived
Only for those
Who told me
That they loved me only.

There was a time
When I lived
Only for those
Who told me
That they loved God and me
equally.

But now I live
Only for those,
I repeat,
Only for those,
Who love God only.

115. THEY KNOW NOT

Reason and passion
Know not how to converse.
Therefore,
Each other they hate.

Reason and faith
Know not how to love.
Therefore,
Each other they hate.

Reason and doubt
Know not how to look.
Therefore,
Each other they hate.

116. I DO NOT NEED YOU!

O black wings of death,
I do not need you!
Therefore
Don't touch my body-temple.

O red wings of hell,
I do not need you!
Therefore
Don't touch my heart-shrine.

O grey wings of ignorance,
I do not need you!
Therefore
Don't touch my soul-child.

117. CELEBRATIONS

Yesterday I celebrated
My mind's immortal extinction.
Satan was the witness.

Today I celebrate
My heart's immortal cry.
God is the witness.

Tomorrow I shall celebrate
My life's immortal surrender.
Mother Earth shall be the witness.

118. HE PLAYED

He played with
His ignorance-neighbour.
Therefore,
His name died
Before his body's death.

He played with
His knowledge-brother.
Therefore,
His name lived
Long after his body's death.

He played with
His Compassion-Mother.
Therefore,
Mother Earth claimed
His unparalleled beauty.

He played with
His Silence-Father.
Therefore,
Father Heaven claimed
His soul's fulfilled duty.

119. GOD TAUGHT ME

Before the first hour
Of my sleep,
God taught me
How to sleep.

During the second hour
Of my sleep,
God taught me
How to wake up.

In the last hour
Of my sleep,
God taught me
How to capture Him,
How to possess Him,
How to treasure Him.

120. DOUBT

Three defects of doubt:
Doubt does not see
The beauty of Truth.
Doubt does not declare
The reality of Truth.
Doubt is afraid
Of the immortality of Truth.

121. MY MOTHER

My ancient Father
Told me:
My Mother was Compassion.

My present Father
Tells me:
My Mother is Love.

My future Father
Will tell me:
My Mother is
The Universal Choice
And
The Transcendental Voice.

122. MY FATHER

My ancient Mother
Told me:
My Father was Silence.

My present Mother
Tells me:
My Father is Sound.

My future Mother
Will tell me:
My Father is
Realisation-Height
And
Perfection-Light.

123. CRY, LOVE, WIN

Although
Hell loves me,
I shall cry for Heaven.

Although
Hell tortures me,
I shall love God.

Although
Hell claims me,
I shall win God.

124. MYSELF

I saw myself
As nothing,
And beyond that nothing
There was really nothing.
I was proud of my self-discovery.

I see myself
As everything,
And beyond that everything
There is really everything.
I am proud of my God-discovery.

125. GOD-BIRD

O time-bird,
I want you
And
I need you.

O success-bird,
I need you
And
I need you.

O progress-bird,
Others may need you
But
I never need you.

O God-bird,
Where are you?
Do you not need me?

126. O MY HUNGRY ASPIRING HEART

O my hungry aspiring heart,
For you no jaws of death,
No mouth of hell.
In you is the silence
Of the hoary past.
In you is the forgiveness
For the world's blind greed.
In you is the whirlwind
Of the world's
transformation-life.

127. O LUSTRE

O nebulous lustre,
O pastime of Infinity,
When will you shine
In the heart of Eternity?

O Heaven-born lustre,
You can change
The inevitable yoke
Of human life.

O God-illumined lustre,
Yours is the life
That shines through the muddy
impurity
Of the world's burning insanity.

128. THEY CLUTCH HIM

Fear clutches him
When he thinks of man.
Doubt clutches him
When he thinks of God.

Insecurity clutches him
When he thinks of God-love.
Frustration clutches him
When he thinks of his
self-transcendence.

129. WHEN I SAW, WHEN I TOUCHED

When I saw
A flame of living love,
My life of dole
Became Divinity's Smile.

When I touched
The breathing Shrine of God,
My heart of delight
Became Immortality's Pride.

130. EFFORT

With maximum effort
I loved God
And
Realised God.

With minimum effort
I revealed God
And
Manifested God.

With no effort
I shall glorify God
And
Distribute God.

131. SURRENDER-LIFE

He aimed at Peace.
Peace came not.
He aimed at Joy.
Joy came not.
He aimed at Power.
Power came not.
He aimed at Surrender-life.
Lo and behold,
Peace came in unreservedly,
Joy came in ceaselessly,
Power came in measurelessly.
And who followed?
No human being,
No cosmic god,
But God Himself,
The Absolute Supreme.

132. POWER YOU NEED, POWER YOU GET

Action-power
Is needed.
Grace-power
Is more needed.
Surrender-power
Is most needed.

How to get action-power?
Cry within.
How to get grace-power?
Stay within.
How to get surrender-power?
Fly within.

133. NO ONE IS WITHOUT IMPERFECTION

No one is without imperfection.
No, not even God.
Am I not
An imperfect manifestation of
God?

No one is without perfection.
No, not even my worst enemy.
Who is my enemy
If not God's Manifestation-music
of Soul-Perfection?

134. MY THOUGHTS TELL ME

My mind's ready-made thoughts
Tell me
God is a far cry.

My heart's love-blossomed
thoughts
Tell me
God is nearer than my eyes.

My soul's life-fulfilled thoughts
Tell me
God is my own illumined higher
Self.

135. GOD AND I LOVE

God and I love
The white simplicity
Of the soul.

God and I love
The green purity
Of the heart.

God and I love
The blue immensity
Of the eyes.

136. IN THEMSELVES

Desire in itself is
Hurtful.

Aspiration in itself is
Fruitful.

Grace in itself is
Success-might.

Surrender in itself is
Progress-light.

God in Himself is
Perfection-Height.

137. BEYOND THE SKY

Beyond the sky
Of the puny, narrow life
Fear-kite flies not,
Doubt-dart flies not,
Opportunity-door leads not,
Man-dream breathes not,
God-Reality ceases not.

138. ATTRACTIONS

Yesterday
The nothingness of things
Attracted me, my puzzled mind.

Today
The earth-beauty of things
Attracts me, my helpless heart.

Tomorrow
The Heaven-delight of things
Shall attract me, my illumined
life.

139. A RARE ASPIRATION

A rare Indian aspiration:
Power-manifestation.

A rare American aspiration:
Peace-manifestation.

A rare earth-aspiration:
Perfection-sun.

A rare Heaven-aspiration:
Concern-sea.

140. YOU TOLERATED ME

My Lord, You tolerated me
Before I aspired.
Therefore
My vital-horse is all gratitude to
You.

My Lord, You tolerated me
Before I realised You.
Therefore
My heart-deer is all gratitude to
You.

My Lord, You tolerated me
Before I manifested You.
Therefore
My soul-lion is all gratitude to
You.

141. THEY LED THE WAY

My faith led the way
With its universal acceptance.

My aspiration led the way
With its transcendental
appearance.

My surrender led the way
With its absolute assurance.

142. COME TO ME

O morning of Infinity,
Come to me
With your Infinity's cry.
My heart shall cry with you.

O morning of Eternity,
Come to me
With your Eternity's smile.
My soul shall smile with you.

O morning of Immortality,
Come to me
With your Immortality's love.
My Goal shall be in love with you.

143. THEY CAN NEVER BE MINE

No coward soul
Can ever be mine.
No foolish heart
Can ever be mine.
No proud mind
Can ever be mine.
No wild vital
Can ever be mine.
No lazy body
Can ever be mine.
No unmanifested God-life
Can ever be mine.

144. REAL AND UNREAL

My desire-life
Made my earth-life
Unreal.

My aspiration-life
Is making my Heaven-life
Divinely and supremely
Real.

My realisation-life
Will make my death-life
Unreal.

145. THEN AND NOW

There was a time
When I was the sadness
Of a saddening thought.

There was a time
When I was the madness
Of a maddening thought.

But now
I am the vastness
Of an unhorizoned thought,
I am the brightness
Of the solar thought.

146. EASY TO ACHIEVE

God-realisation
Is actually easy to achieve.
You just cry
Like a three-year-old child.

God-revelation
Is actually easy to achieve.
You just run
Like a young athlete.

God-manifestation
Is actually easy to achieve.
You just love and become
The divine Reality Supreme
within you.

147. LOVE-FLOWER, INGRATITUDE-SOUL, DEPRESSION-LIFE

All things eventually fade
Save and except
A love-flower.

All things ultimately live
Save and except
An ingratitude-soul.

All things ultimately win
Save and except
A depression-life.

148. WHERE DO YOU EXIST?

O Fountain of constant Love,
Where do you exist?
Do you really exist?
"I exist
In the body of your heart."

O Fountain of constant Peace,
Where do you exist?
Do you really exist?
"I exist, I exist
In the heart of your mind."

O Fountain of constant Delight,
Where do you exist?
Do you really exist?
"I exist, I exist, I exist
In the life of your soul."

149. THE INHERITORS

Believe it or not,
Doubt is the inheritor
Of the body-mind's
Unfulfilled dream.

Believe it or not,
Fear is the inheritor
Of the body-vital's
Unfulfilled dream.

Believe it or not,
Anxiety is the inheritor
Of the body-heart's
Unfulfilled dream.

150. O HEAVY WEIGHT OF TODAY'S HOURS

O heavy weight of today's hours,
Tomorrow I shall meditate
And away I shall fly.

O heavy weight of today's hours,
Tomorrow I shall meditate
And make God my heart.

O heavy weight of today's hours,
Tomorrow I shall meditate
And Eternity's bird will offer me
Its wings
To fly in the soul-sky
Of Infinity's Immortality.

151. THE FUTURE OF A MAN

The future of a simple man:
Success.

The future of a sincere man:
Progress.

The future of a humble man:
Glory.

The future of a pure man:
Enlightenment serene.

The future of a concentrative,
  meditative
and contemplative man:
Perfection supreme.

152. O BEARER

O my mind,
O bearer of my human searching,
Gracious is your life.

O my heart,
O bearer of my human longing,
Precious is your life.

O my soul,
O bearer of my human receiving
  and achieving,
Magnanimous is your goal.

153. HIS DESIRE TO PLEASE GOD

His desire to please God
Ultimately failed.

His ambition to please God
Ultimately failed.

His aspiration to please God
Ultimately failed.

Finally
His surrender-heart pleased God
Openly,
Lovingly
And
Supremely.

154. SHE AND THE WORLD

She plays merrily,
Therefore
The world likes her.

She speaks sweetly,
Therefore
The world loves her.

She sings melodiously,
Therefore
The world adores her.

She blesses divinely,
Therefore
The world constantly needs her.

155. LIFE IS VELOCITY

Life is velocity.
Therefore
I want to run fast, very fast.

Love is necessity.
Therefore
I want to love more, ever more.

Truth is reality.
Therefore
I want to achieve, only achieve.

156. WHEN WILL YOU ARRIVE?

Hope, my hope,
When will you arrive
At your goal?

Faith, my faith,
Have you not arrived
At your goal?

Love, my love,
When did you arrive
At your goal?

Light, my light,
You need the expansion
Of your goal.

157. MY BEST DAYS

My best days
In hell:
When I smash the pride of Satan.

My best days
In Heaven:
When I cry for God-realisation.

My best days
On earth:
When I cry for God-manifestation.

158. VIOLATIONS

You violated
Your inner dignity.
Therefore
Reckless irresponsibility
Embraced you.

You violated
The secret teachings
Of the cosmic law.
Therefore
Even God did not near you
To save your life
Of untold deception.

159. THE SEED OF PERFECTION

Slowly grows
The seed of love.

Steadily grows
The seed of faith.

Unerringly grows
The seed of life.

Supremely grows
The seed of perfection.

160. WHAT IS IT?

Speed, what is it?
Beauty's light.

Love, what is it?
Duty's pride.

Delight, what is it?
Necessity's height.

161. A VERY SPECIAL PRAYER

Lamentation-force
Is a very special prayer.
Silence-force
Is a very special concentration.
Delight-force
Is a very special meditation.
Perfection-force
Is a very special contemplation.

162. THEE I ADORE

O Protector of poor souls,
Thee I adore.

O Saviour of wicked souls,
Thee I adore.

O Liberator of earthbound souls,
Thee I adore.

O Transformer of fallen souls,
Thee I adore.

O Fulfiller of aspiring souls,
Thee I adore,
Thee I love,
Thee I invoke.

163. HEAVY AND LIGHT

Heavy
Is the weight of failure.
Heavier
Is the weight of success.
Heaviest
Is the weight of progress.

Light
Is the weight of hope.
Lighter
Is the weight of faith.
Lightest
Is the weight of love.

164. I AM NOT ALONE

My progress is permanently
Protected by my Father's Will.

My faith is permanently
Protected by my Mother's Love.

I am not alone.
I am with my Father's
Dream-boat Reality.

I am not alone.
I am with my Mother's
Reality-fulfilled Dream.

165. DEVOTION-POWER AND SURRENDER-POWER

Insecurity's length
And
Timidity's breadth
Comprised his little world.

Then, suddenly, devotion-power
Became the light-giver
To his ignorance vast,
And
Surrender-power
Made him one
With the Transcendence-goal
Of the ever-transcending Beyond.

166. YOUR LIFE

That was your life:
You deliberately forgot to aspire.
This is your life:
You spontaneously remember to aspire.

That was your life:
Hard you endeavoured to surpass God.
This is your life:
Hard you try to please God,
Even for a fleeting moment.

167. LIKE IT OR NOT

Whether you like it
Or not,
God will tell you many things.

Whether he likes it
Or not,
God has no time to talk to him at all.

Whether I like it
Or not,
God wants to embarrass me
By placing me on
His Transcendental Throne.

168. THIS IS NOT MY BIRTHDAY

This is not my birthday.
My birthday was yesterday,
When God and I sang and played.

This is not my birthday.
O earth-pilgrims,
Why do you torture me
With earthly gifts?

I need only one Heavenly gift,
Love:
Love from God,
Love from God alone.

169. IN THE EYES OF THE SAVIOURS

In the eyes of the Saviour Christ,
The world was an
ignorance-night.

In the eyes of the Saviour Krishna,
The world was an ignorance-sea.

In the eyes of the Saviour Buddha,
The world was an ignorance-sky.

O ignorance-night,
Your futility hurts me.

O ignorance-sea,
Your insensibility hurts me.

O ignorance-sky,
Your indifference hurts me.

170. THE OPENING

Faith is the opening
Of the wisdom-eye.

Love is the opening
Of the oneness-heart.

Service is the opening
Of the immortality-life.

171. SHUN HIS COMPANY

His vital is a mixture
Of impure vanity
And
Dark superstition.
Therefore,
Shun his company.
If you mix with him
You are bound
To welcome
Your inner death.
Alas, what a troublesome world
His earth-life represents!

172. FEAR, DOUBT AND FAITH

To me,
Fear is a pardonable defect
Because it dies;
Doubt is an unpardonable defect
Because it always survives;
Faith is a radiant smile
Because it overrules
All blind human opinion.

173. SILENCE AND SOUND

When the desire
To escape captured him,
He entered
Into a Himalayan cave.
Alas, peace and joy
Cared not for him.
He came back
To the sound-life
And discovered:
Silence is embodied perfection,
Sound is revealed manifestation.

174. JOURNEY OF LIGHT AND DELIGHT

There was a time
When I endured
The indifference of
ignorance-night.
But now ignorance
Endures my indifference-light.

There was a time
When I endured
The tortures of human
boundaries.
But now they
Are no more.
They have disappeared
In my upward and inward journey
Of Light and Delight.

175. O BUILDER

O builder of my soul,
Where are You?

O builder of my Goal,
How far are You?

O builder of my heart,
How kind are You?

O builder of my mind,
How fantastic are You?

176. I AM COMING

O abyss of oblivion,
I am coming to you
With my information-mind.
Please wait.

O palace of illumination,
I am coming to you
With my aspiration-heart.
Please wait.

177. FORGETFULNESS-MONARCH

O stormy vital emotion,
From now on my name shall be
Forgetfulness-Prince.

O sombre mental frustration,
From now on my name shall be
Forgetfulness-King.

O foolish psychic destruction,
From now on my name shall be
Forgetfulness-Emperor.

Yet
I shall run,
But with a vital new,
with a mind new,
with a heart new,
Beyond the length
Of extremity's song.

178. SKY OF PERFECTION-DAWN

From his tongue
Comes every possible
Absurdity.

From his eyes
Comes every possible
Futility.

Yet his ecstatic
Love-adoration for God
Saves him and lifts his life
Into the sky of Perfection-Dawn.

179. EVERY MESSAGE

Every secret message
Is a Thought of God.

Every sacred message
Is a Will of God.

Every divine message
Is a Consciousness-Sun of God.

Every supreme message
Is a Perfection-
Manifestation-
Reality
Of God.

180. HIS BODY'S SHALLOW STRENGTH

When he thinks,
He thinks from his mind's
Pygmy height.

When he speaks,
He speaks from his vital's
Unmeasured length.

When he acts,
He acts from his body's
Shallow strength.

181. SILENCE-SKY, SOUND-SEA

My weeping heart
Teaches me
God is an indifferent King.

My singing soul
Teaches me
God is a jovial Friend.

My loving Goal
Teaches me
God gives two gifts –
Morning's silence-sky,
Evening's sound-sea.

182. CONCLUSIONS

Human life is a dream.
Indeed,
This is your philosopher's
conclusion.

Human life is a game.
Indeed,
This is your lover's conclusion.

Human life is a Reality.
Indeed,
This is your seeker's conclusion.

183. SECRETS

Top secrets
Everybody knows:
God is man's Light,
Man is God's night.

Open secrets
Nobody knows:
Man is another golden God,
Man is another black animal.

184. WHEN I LOOK AT HIM

When I look at him
I see an aura of fear
Behind his head.
When I look at him
I see an aura of death
Around his face.
A mere mortal
He can never be.
An inner pain
Gnaws at him
Constantly.
His is a life of
Ill-fortune
And
Hermit-existence.

185. THEY LEARN MORE

Children learn more
When they are loved.

Parents learn more
When they are ignored.

Humanity learns more
When it is appreciated.

Divinity learns more
When it is rejected.

186. OUR COMMITMENT

Life is our commitment
To equality.
Love is our commitment
To reality.
Peace is our commitment
To liberty.
Power is our commitment
To divinity.
God is our commitment
To Immortality.

187. HIS HUNGER FOR GOD

His body's hunger for God
Was a stupid curiosity.

His vital's hunger for God
Was a dauntless curiosity.

His mind's hunger for God
Was a cautious curiosity.

His heart's hunger for God
Was an illumined curiosity.

188. YOU ARE YOUR WILL

Always control yourself.
A moment of impatience
Is a movement of self-destruction.
You are your own adamantine
will.
In you and for you
Is your transcendental Goal.

189. A PERFECT FOOL

A perfect fool he is.
He began his life-journey
Badly and stupidly,
And it went on worse,
Strikingly worse.
Yet he fails to surrender
To reality's light
And divinity's height.

190. LUMINOUS, PRECIOUS, GRACIOUS

Luminous was she
Within her heart.
Precious was she
In the heart of her life.
Gracious was she
In the soul of her Goal.

191. YOU HAVE A PASSION

You have a passion for Truth.
Therefore
Truth is within you.

You have a passion for Light.
Therefore
Light enlightens you.

You have a passion for Love.
Therefore
Love immortalises you.

192. A GREAT COMPETITION

God and I
Entered into a great competition.
He pitted His Love
Against my teeming doubts.
Alas, He won.
I pitted my ingratitude
Against His flowing Compassion.
Alas, this time too, He won.

God, since twice I have lost to You,
I shall muster no more
Courage-light
To challenge Your superiority.

193. A COMPLETE INNOCENCE, A COMPLETE PERFECTION

A complete innocence
Signifies an awakened life.
A complete perfection
Signifies an unconditional
  surrender-light
And transcendence-height
In the heart-nest
Of the seeker.

194. HE BECAME WHAT HE WAS

With bubbling enthusiasm
He launched into the path of yoga.
With doubting uncertainty
He walked along the path.
With his destructive impatience,
With his devouring personality,
He left the path,
Only to become once again
What he was before:
A monkey with a
Sesquipedalian tail.

195. DIVINITY'S SMILE AND IMMORTALITY'S DAWN

Doubt ends
When separativity ends.
Faith begins
When consciousness ascends
And reaches the free heights
Of divinity's Smile
And
Immortality's Dawn.

196. A GOLDEN LINK

Between
His heart of fear
And
His mind of doubt
A wide chasm creeps.

Between
His vital of aggression
And
His body of suppression
A wide chasm creeps.

But
Between his soul of service
And
His God of Love
No chasm creeps.
A golden link
Unites
God the Lover Supreme
And man the server divine.

197. SMILE AND GO AWAY

Short are the hours of
pleasure-life,
Yet man wants it.
Long are the hours of
happiness-life,
Yet man wants it not.

Smile and go away
From the hours of pleasure-life.
Cry and stay within
The hours of happiness-life.

198. THREE VOICES

A deep warning voice solemnly
commanded:
"Don't speak to doubt.
Doubt is poison."

A deep loving voice smilingly
whispered:
"Mix with faith.
Faith is reality's all."

A deep illumining voice soulfully
revealed:
"Drink the fragrance of love.
Love is all."

199. THE DAWN

Silence
Is the dawn of time.

Sound
Is the dawn of will.

Man-success
Is the dawn of aspiration.

God-progress
Is the dawn of Perfection.

200. THE GOLDEN ONES

The golden Boat
Is beauty's speed.

The golden Shore
Is divinity's crown.

The golden Dream,
Reality dreams.

The golden Pilot,
Eternity claims.

201. DO THE GODS FEEL SORRY?

Do the gods feel sorry?
Yes, they do.
Why?
Because men surpass them.

Does God feel sorry?
Yes, He does.
Why?
Because most men
Do not dare to play with Him,
Let alone compete with
Or surpass
Him.

202. MOTION AND REST

Motion and rest
Complete God's Game.
Motion and rest
Are two brothers.

Rest prepares;
Motion distributes.
Rest dives deep within;
Motion flies far without.

In rest God dreams
His Reality-life.
In motion God becomes
One and inseparable
With His Dream-fulfilled Boat.

203. WHAT IS IT?

Wisdom, what is it?
Peace.
Peace, what is it?
Satisfaction.
Satisfaction, what is it?
Perfection.
Perfection, what is it?
Light,
More Light,
Abundant Light,
Light infinite.

204. AFTER THE LONG INNER STRUGGLE

There was a time
When he was far removed from Truth.
But
Now he measures
Not only
His life
But also
The immensity of God's Depth
And
The infinity of God's Height.
After the long inner struggle
He sees the meaning of life,
He feels the meaning of light.

205. CONTRADICTIONS

Human birth
And
Life-freedom
Are contradictory.

Human life
And
Love-perfection
Are contradictory.

Human goal
And
God-Smile
Are contradictory.

206. NO SIN, NO VIRTUE

When sin plagues him
He cries aloud.
When virtue plagues him
He cries aloud.
His Lord today tells him:
"No sin, no virtue, My son.
Only think that
I experience the life-breath
Of every moment
In a different way,
That's all."

207. WHEN I CONFIDE

When I confide my secrets
To my mind,
My mind betrays me
In a jungle of confusion.

When I confide my secrets
To my vital,
My vital throws me
Into a tornado of destruction.

When I confide my secrets
To my heart,
My heart takes me
To my soul
For special guidance.

And when I confide my secrets
To my soul,
My God-Goal immediately
Runs towards me.

208. WORDS

A man of strength
Is a man of few words.

A man of silence
Speaks no words.

A man of divinity
Uses words
To please God,
To bring down God,
To manifest God the Dream on earth
And
To fulfil God the Dreamer in Heaven.

209. OF YOU, FOR YOU

You have seen
What was never kept concealed.
You have found
What was never kept hidden.
You have found your God,
Who has always been
In the heart of your love-light.
No matter how sincere you are,
No matter how hard you work
To disqualify yourself for God-realisation,
You shall sadly fail.
For God's Transcendental Dream is of you,
And God's Universal Reality is for you.

210. EXPECTATIONS

I expect nothing from earth,
I expect nothing from Heaven.
My Supreme expects
In and through me
From earth's life.
My Supreme expects
In and through me
From Heaven's soul.
Earth has fulfilled our
expectation:
Service-Might.
Heaven has fulfilled our
expectation:
Light-Delight.

211. TWO WICKED SINNERS, TWO LOVING FRIENDS

Doubt and jealousy are
Two wicked sinners.

Faith and hope are
Two loving friends.

Courage and sacrifice are
Two noble souls.

Beauty and Purity are
The seeker's heart.

Truth and God are
Reality's eyes.

212. ONE WITH EXTINCTION'S SIGH

He avoided humanity
Because humanity was sick and
weak.

He avoided Divinity
Because Divinity was strong
and indifferent.

He stayed inside his fearful cave
and tearful heart
Until he become one with
extinction's sigh.

213. THREE MESSAGES

He had only three messages to
give:
One to Heaven,
One to earth,
One to hell.
"Dear Heaven,
Be careful of your
indifference-power.
Dear earth,
Be careful of your
ignorance-length.
Dear hell,
Be careful of Satan's autocracy."

214. TO RECEIVE

To receive humanity
I need an abundance of space.

To receive divinity
I need an abundance of grace.

To receive God
I need an abundance of surrender.

To receive my own lower being
I need an abundance of power.

215. ARE YOU NOT INSEPARABLE?

O truth-lover, O man-saver,
Are you not inseparable?

O love-giver, O oneness-seer,
Are you not inseparable?

O illumination-distributor,
O duty-fulfiller,
Are you not inseparable?

O landlord-man, O Tenant-God,
Are you not inseparable?

216. GOD-REALISATION DEMANDS

Austere concentration is not needed
To realise God.
Extensive meditation is not needed
To realise God.
God-realisation demands
Conscious surrender
Of the puny "I"
And expansion-perfection
Of the earthbound life.

217. NO ONE VENTURES

No one ventures
To explain
God-Truth.

No one ventures
To serve God
With surrender-light.

No one ventures
To distribute
God-vision.

No one ventures
To know the power
Of God-Invention.

No one ventures
To realise the power
Of aspiration-vision.

218. YOU ARE SPECIAL, YOU ARE DIVINE

You are gifted.
Therefore
The world appreciates you.

You are special.
Therefore
The world admires you.

You are divine.
Therefore
Both God and the world
Love you
and
Love you,
Forever
and
Forever.

219. THE DISTANCE BETWEEN

The distance
Between
Hope and despair
Is no distance.

The distance
Between
Love and hate
Is no distance.

The distance
Between
Doubt and faith
Is no distance.

But

The distance
Between
Your lower life
And
Your higher life
Is incredibly long,
Arduous and dangerous.

220. TOGETHER THEY GO

The hour of grace
And
The shower of glory
Together shine.

The hour of victory
And
The power of surrender
Together strike.

The Hour of God
And
The flower of gratitude
Together blossom.

221. NO COMPLETION

No purity,
No sanity.

No sanity,
No realisation.

No realisation,
No perfection.

No perfection,
No completion.

222. NOWHERE TO BE FOUND

The hermitage of peace
Can easily be found.

The home of light
Can easily be found.

The nest of silence
Can easily be found.

But
The room of perfection
Is nowhere to be found.

223. TO BECOME

To enjoy is
To obey.

To obey is
To shine.

To shine is
To become.

To become is
To transform
The animal in us,
To elevate
The human in us,
To fulfil
The divine in us.

224. DARKER, PURER, SURER

Darker than night
Is my mental doubt.

Purer than dawn
Is my weeping heart.

Stronger than a giant
Is my blossomed faith.

225. HE WANTS BOTH

He wants both
Humanity and Divinity:
Humanity to wash his feet,
Divinity to breathe its love.

He wants both
God and man:
God to pull him towards God,
Man to push him towards God.

226. UNLESS

Unless the child cries,
The mother brings him no milk.
Unless the disciple cries,
The Master brings him no nectar.

Unless man tries,
God gives him nothing.
Unless God forces,
Man does nothing.

227. ONLY TO OFFER

Only to rise,
He stumbled.
Only to succeed,
He failed.
Only to create,
He stopped.
Only to become,
He shunned.
Only to offer,
He is.

228. PERFECT, IMPERFECT

Doubt-pride
Is in itself imperfect.

Faith-glow
Is in itself perfect.

Fear-insecurity
Is in itself imperfect.

Love-flow
Is in itself perfect.

Satan-night
Is itself imperfect.

God-day
Is itself perfect.

229. YOUR SADNESS IMMEASURABLE

"Lord, Your sadness
Immeasurable,
How can I relieve?"

Think that I suffer,
Feel that I suffer,
Love humanity as I do.

Lo, half of My suffering-night
Has captured your oneness-love
With its Reality-Height.

230. O IMMACULATE BEAUTY

O immaculate Beauty,
God needs you.

O immaculate Purity,
God utilises you.

O immaculate Lustre,
God perfects you.

O immaculate Consciousness,
God expands Himself
In you,
With you.

231. THE AIM

The aim of all seeing
Is serving.

The aim of all serving
Is loving.

The aim of all loving
Is identifying.

The aim of all identifying
Is oneness-becoming.

In oneness-becoming
We mark the journey's close.

232. WHY DO I SUFFER

Why do I suffer,
My Lord Supreme?
Is it because
I am not careful?
Is it because
I enter into ignorance?

"No, nothing of the sort.
Your big heart
Cannot live
Without housing others' pain
As your very own."

233. THOUGHT-WORLD

The activity of a thought-wave
Fascinates me.

The reality of a thought-sea
Transforms me.

The divinity of a thought-world
Immortalises me.

234. NOW I SHINE

I died in thought.
Now
I fly with Will.

I died in time.
Now
I dance with Eternity.

I died in imperfection.
Now
I shine with God-Perfection.

235. NOW WE ARE SATISFIED

I spoke;
I was badly misunderstood.
I remained silent;
I was properly understood.

I loved;
I was suspected.
I served;
I was appreciated.

I saw;
Neither God nor I was satisfied.
I became;
Now
Both God and I are totally
satisfied.

236. WITHOUT THEE

To think without Thee
Is to cry.

To see without Thee
Is to sigh.

To work without Thee
Is to fail.

To rest without Thee
Is to die.

I know, I know,
Yet
I fail to practise.

237. HIS IMMORTAL SELF

He greets mortal breath
With his immortal grace.

He illumines mortal confusion
With his immortal face.

He transforms mortal pangs
With his immortal heart.

He consoles mortal failure
With his immortal progress.

238. HE ASCENDS AND DESCENDS

God's Hour helps him
Ascend and descend.

He ascends to pluck
The fruits of Nectar-light.

He descends to distribute
The fruits with Beauty's heart.

239. YOU WILL BE CAUGHT

Don't pretend
Without the truth;
You will be caught.

Don't expand
Without the light;
You will be caught.

Don't preach
Without the silence;
You will be caught.

Don't argue
With your inner effulgent light,
With your outer flickering candle;
You will be caught.

240. NOTHING ELSE TO THINK ABOUT

Lord, I think of You
Not because You are
Kind to me,
But because I have
Nothing else to think about.

"Son, I think of you
Not because I have
Nothing else to think about,
But because when
I think of you
I get the joy of a child,
The strength of a youth
And the wisdom of an old man."

Lord, from now on
I shall think of You
And not remain indebted to You.

241. THE DUE PRICE

Lord, when people
misunderstand me,
What shall I do?
"Forgive them."
I do that.
But again and again they
misunderstand me.
"My son, do not allow
All and sundry
To have free access to you.
Don't make your spirituality
cheap.
All must pay the due price."

242. TAKE ME TO STAY WITH YOU

A beggar stood
Before
God, man and Satan.

To God he said:
"Lord, take me to stay with You
In Your Boat."
"Your desire is granted, My son."

To man he said:
"Brother, take me to stay with you
In your boat."
"Sorry, my boat is too small."

To Satan he said:
"Esteemed Friend, take me to stay
with you
In your boat."
"Certainly, you will not only stay,
But be the boatman
And thus relieve me
Of my long and endless task."

243. TO SAY THE LEAST

"Good-bye, Father,
I shall see You tomorrow."

Good-bye, son,
I shall see you in a minute.

"Why and how, Father?
I am leaving, Father.
I am tired, really tired,
To say the least."

I am proud of you,
I am one with you.
I share your glory's light
Equally and unmistakably,
To say the least.

244. DON'T TELL A LIE!

Who has not stumbled?
You?
Don't tell a lie!

Who has not failed?
You?
Don't tell a lie!

Who has not seen
The Face of God?
You?
Don't tell a lie!

Who will not
Become God?
You?
Don't tell a lie!

245. ETERNAL SURRENDER

Lord Supreme,
Eternal surrender:
Does it exist or will it ever exist?

"My son, from time immemorial
Eternal surrender
Has walked the soil of earth.

My transcendental Silence
And
My universal Sound
To each other have offered
Their capacity-height
In the form of surrender-light.

The surrender of My Silence
To My Life of Sound
Makes earth grow
Towards the highest height.

The surrender of My Sound
To My Life of Silence
Makes Heaven descend
To feel the bleeding heartbeat
Of Mother Earth."

246. HE IS IMPORTANT

He is serene.
Therefore
God's Mind caresses his mind.

He is brilliant.
Therefore
God's Vital welcomes his vital.

He is important.
Therefore
God's Heart
With Fondness-light
Houses him,
His dream-boat,
His dream-river,
His dream-shore.

247. MANY AND FEW

Many seeds, few crops.
Many blossoms, few fruits.
Many seekers, few realised souls.
Many Masters, one God.
The self-same God
Sails His Dream-Boat
And becomes His Reality-Shore.

248. TO GET UP, TO MEDITATE

To get up early in the morning
Is one thing;
To meditate soulfully
Is something else.

If I fail to get up early
In the morning,
How can I meditate?
Again, if I get up
And do not meditate well,
I just torture my poor body.

O my body,
From now on I shall use you
Only for God's sake.
O my soul,
From now on I shall use you
Only for God's sake.

249. YOU HAVE TO SHARE MY FATE

My Lord, is it my business
To perfect the world?
"Son, who else's business is it?
If you dare to call yourself My son
You have to share
Equally My fate.
Love Me, I am yours.
Serve Me, you are Mine,
Mine alone."

250. PERFECT STRANGERS

Lord, Lord,
Save me, save me.
I am in terrible danger.
I am fighting against time
To prove to my spiritual children
That I am a poet of high
magnitude.
Father, do save me, save me.

"Son, don't insult Me.
You and I are perfect strangers
To the birth and life of defeat."

251. SLEEP

Lord, is sleep death or rest?

"Son, sleep is death; sleep is rest.
Sleep is fulfilling rest
When angels visit you
Or
You enter into the world
Of the illumining Beyond.
Sleep is death
When the vital world
Of
Destruction-night
Threatens you and frightens you.
Sleep is death
When you fail to see
The flow of Eternity's river
In
Your consciousness-realm."

252. PRECIOUS

Each thought is precious
When we live in the world
Of desire.

A precious thought blossoms
In the Garden
Of God's gracious Light.

A precious will is born
In the Heart
Of God's Intuition bright.

A precious surrender is born
When God and man
Barter their precious treasures:

Man, his agelong ignorance-sea;
God, His Infinity's Peace and Bliss.

253. COVER

My sweet Lord,
Do You cover
My falsehood-life,
Impurity-breath
And
Bondage-night?

"My sweet daughter,
I cover them not;
Again, I expose them not.
I claim your possession-world
As my reality's substance
And essence.
Therefore
I own your little world
And
I endeavour to change the face
Of your little world
To My Satisfaction-Light."

254. SMILE

Lord Supreme,
I smile to draw the attention
Of my little world around me.
But why do You smile?
What makes You smile?

"My daughter,
Nothing compels Me to smile.
Nothing compels Me to do
anything.
But yet I do and act,
For I know I am not only the Doer
But also the action;
I am not only the Speaker
But also the speech.
If I fail to unite My creation-flower
With My Creator-seed,
Nothing can breathe on earth
Even for a fleeting second.
My child, I smile
Because inside the Heart of My
Smile
Beauty's day dawns;
Inside the Body of My Smile
Duty's morn breaks."

255. GRACE

Lord Supreme,
Is there any difference
Between
Your supernal Grace
And
Reality's face?

"My daughter sweet,
No difference at all.
I tell you a secret supreme:
The outer world,
My outer creation,
Pays no attention
To the omnipotent power of
  Grace.
But I depend, on earth,
On the descending flow
Of My own transcendental Grace.
My Grace is not only My
  preparation-seed
But My Perfection-Tree."

256. SELF-FORGETFULNESS

My sweetest Lord Supreme,
Is self-forgetfulness
A divine blessing
Or
An animal curse?

"Self-forgetfulness can never be
A curse.
It can only be
A sad experience
In a seeker's ever-running and
Transcending journey
To the Beyond.
The self-forgetfulness of the puny
  "I"
Is a blessing supreme indeed,
As the self-remembrance of the
  giant "I"
Is an unparalleled blessing
On the seeker's march along the
  path
Of reality's space.
Forget the sad and the saddening
  past;
Remember the illumining and the
  illumined present.
Accelerate the birth and the
  life-flow
Of the fast-approaching
  future-noon.
Before the dawn of
  realisation-height,
Self-forgetfulness at times saves
The seeker's inner sky
And outer moon.
After the birth of
  realisation-height,
Self-forgetfulness in the heart
Of a Master divine
Is the zenith of impossibility
  remote."

257. GOD'S FIRST SECRET

Do you know
What God told me the other day?
I am telling you
In top secrecy.
If you breathe a word to God
I shall never tell you anything
again.
Remember, be careful!
Needless to say,
God has shared with me
Millions of His sacred secrets.
Now I shall share with you
His first secret:
At the end of your journey's close
Your epitaph will read
'An unfulfilled tear of God';
My epitaph will read
'A fulfilled smile of God.'
Remember, be careful!
If you breathe a word to God
I shall not share anything else
with you;
No, not even the precise hour
of your God-realisation
Which God told me
Only this morning
In top secrecy.

258. TROPHIES AND SMILES

I love the trophies
Of a world-conqueror.
They show me
What God the Beggar
Needs and gets.

I love the smiles
Of a world-lover.
They show me
What God the Emperor
Gives and is.

259. O CHILD OF THE SUN-GOD

O child of the Sun-God,
Did you ask your Father
How much Wisdom-power
He has kept aside
For you?
"I did ask my Father!
He said
He has not kept aside
Even a flame of Wisdom-power
For me.
I shall have to deserve and
acquire."

O child of the Moon-Goddess,
Did you ask your Mother
How much Love-perfection
She has kept aside
For you?
"I did ask my Mother!
She said
She has kept aside
Her Love-perfection-universe
For me.
She is eagerly waiting
For me to claim it as my very
own."

260. ECHO

Echo of my life:
Give.

Echo of Heaven:
I don't have it.
Love? I don't have it.
Perfection? I don't have it.

Echo of God:
Son, what have you done
With My Love?
What have you done
With My Perfection?
Have you squandered everything
Like an earthly fool?
No, Father, no!
Where then is My boundless Love?
Where then is My deathless
Perfection?

261. O LORD, I TRUST

Lord, I trust Your sacred Heart.
It tells me
I am all Yours.

Lord, I trust Your secret Breath.
It tells me
You are all mine.

Lord, I trust Your open Soul.
It tells me
I shall perform the things
That You Yourself have failed
To perform on earth:
God-manifestation.

262. GOD'S BOUNDEN DUTY

O my infant eyes,
Don't worry!
God is nearing
Your vision-light.

O my orphan heart,
Don't worry!
God the Father
And
God the Mother
Are totally incomplete
Without you.
Therefore
It is Their bounden duty
To blossom within you
And
For you, for you alone.

263. MY HYMNS

My mind-desert hymn:
God is dry.
My mind needs Him, His dryness,
To be away from the world.

My heart-forest hymn:
God is dense.
My heart needs Him, His density,
To be in the heart-life of the world
And
The love-soul of the world.

264. WHEN I LEFT THE BODY

My bugle grieved
When I left the body
For a future hope-life.
Do you believe it?
Well, I tell you,
God believes me totally,
And needless to say,
Unmistakably.

My bugle smiled
When I left the body
For a future surrender-love.
Do you believe it?
Well, I tell you,
God believes me unreservedly,
And needless to say,
Unmistakably.

265. O PROPHET

O prophet of my soul,
I assure you,
You shall be all victory
With your silence-life.

O prophet of my body,
I assure you,
You shall be all victory
With your sound-life.

O prophet of my Goal,
I assure you,
Your boat and my heart
Are destined to complete each
other.

266. ACCOMPLISHMENT UNPARALLELED

O my doubter-mind,
Since we need each other
So desperately
And
Since we do not need God at all,
Let us do one thing:
Let us escape from God's world
And create a world of our own.
Then we can challenge God
And
His Believer-Heart.

O my doubter-mind,
Even if we lose
To God and His Believer-Heart,
No harm!
Together we shall remain
independent
Of our Lord Supreme.
Is this not the accomplishment
Unparalleled
Since the birth of the Creator
Himself?

267. LOVE'S GIFT

When I became a voyager of Light
I gave my all to Love.
And Love gave me
Its fountain of perpetual Peace
To feed God's earth-reality
And
Expand God's Heaven-Dream.

268. O LIBERTY

O sweet Liberty,
I need your beauty's heart.

O brave Liberty,
I need your duty's pride.

O perfect Liberty,
I need your Immortality's Life.

269. NO TIME

I love and love;
No time to hate!

I build and build;
No time to break!

I promise and promise;
No time to withdraw!

I become and become;
No time to see!

I am and am;
No time to dream!

270. TWO BOONS

Two boons of my aspiration-life
I give to the world:
My transformation-body
And
My dedication-soul.

Two boons of my realisation-life
I give to the world:
My contemplation-flood
And
My oneness-blood.

271. TWO FOOLS

I have two fools in me.
They separately pray:
Lord, I need Your Love;
Lord, I need Your Light.

My Lord says:
You fool, you need love?
Don't you know that
You are My Heart's only love?
You fool, you need light?
Don't you know that
You are My Soul's only light?

272. CALLED AND CHOSEN

Many were called.
Therefore
My mind was called.

Two were called.
Therefore
My vital and my body
Were called.

Only one was called.
Therefore
My body was called;
Not only called,
But chosen;
Not only chosen,
But supremely chosen.

273. IN MY POCKET

In my silence-pocket
I keep my heart's love-power.
Therefore
I am happy,
I am fulfilled,
I am complete.

In my sound-pocket
I keep my life's power-love.
Therefore
I am complete,
I am fulfilled,
I am happy.

274. TWO UNANSWERED QUESTIONS

I asked God
Two questions.
Strangely enough,
He could not answer
Even one.
My questions were:
How and why
Am I inferior to Him?
How does He know
That I cannot perfect Him?
My Lord of Compassion
Proved that He can be
The Lord of Silence, too.

275. IN TOMORROW'S DAWN

O ashes of yesterday,
I do not need you.
Just stay where you are
In your futility's sleep.

O meshes of today,
I do not need you.
Just stay where you are
In your stupidity's dream.

I shall live in tomorrow's dawn;
I shall live for tomorrow's sun.

276. O HEART OF FIRE

O heart of fire,
Do burn me
For my purification white.

O heart of love,
Do love me
For my illumination bright.

O heart of light,
Do immortalise me
For my perfection height.

277. HE DROPPED HIS MASK

He dropped his mask and showed the world
That he was another God.
He dropped his mask and showed the world
That he was just a man.

As another God,
He revealed his Infinity's Power.
As just a man,
He revealed the insignificance of
The finite earthbound hour.

278. THEY SHALL TELL ME

A new cry shall tell me
Where God is.
A new smile shall tell me
Who God is.
A new surrender shall tell me
How I can win God.
A new perfection shall tell me
Why I am the future God.

279. MY HEART CONCEALS AND FEELS

My heart conceals
The pangs of ages.
My heart conceals
The failures of human races.
My heart conceals
The indifference of God's faces.
But
My heart feels
Only one thing:
God's Heaven-free
And
Sky-vast changes.

280. THEY LONG TO CONSUME

My heart's hunger
Longs to consume
The perfume of my soul.

My soul's hunger
Longs to consume
The Light of my Lord.

My Lord's hunger
Longs to consume
The imperfection of my bosom's
pride.

281. I LEARN AND UNLEARN

I have
God's brain and man's heart.
With God's brain I learn
The message of the infinite
vastness.
With man's heart I unlearn
The age-long pangs of
inconscience-night.

282. EAVESDROPPER

O eavesdropper,
My mind employs you
To know what
God says about me.

O eavesdropper,
My heart employs you
To know what
Death thinks of me.

O eavesdropper,
My soul employs you
To illumine the furious man in me
And
To awaken the gracious God in
me.

283. I NEED

To rend the veil of my life
I need
The help of my naked
vision-knife.

To immortalise the core of my life
I need
Eternity's patience-light
And
Infinity's immortal might.

284. HIS UNMISTAKABLE ANSWER

Is it his impatience
That scolds
The disciples of his inner circle?
Who can answer?
Not he, not he!
Perhaps God.

Is it his sense of duty
That scolds
The disciples of his inner circle?
Who can answer?
Not he, not he!
Perhaps God.

Is it his unconscious attachment
That scolds
The disciples of his inner circle?
Who can answer?
Not he, not he!
Perhaps God.

Is it his supreme promise
To the Absolute Supreme
That compels him to scold and
perfect
The disciples of his inner circle?
Ah, at least he knows how to
answer this question.
He needs no God to answer this
question,
For his very existence on earth
Is his unmistakable answer.

285. REALISATIONS

When I sleep
Inside the Heart of my God,
I realise how kind and sweet
My God is.

When I sit
At the Feet of my God,
I realise how powerful and fruitful
My God is.

When I stand
On the Head of my God,
I realise how high and tall
My God is.

When I live
Inside the Eye of my God,
I realise how perfect my God's
Vision is
And
How complete my God's Reality is.

286. BEAUTY-DREAM, BEAUTY-FLAME

My soul feeds
On the blue dream of beauty.

I feed
On the snow-flames of beauty.

God's Beauty-dream
Is His Silence-height.

Earth's beauty-flame
Is her surrender-light.

287. WHEN I LOOK

When I look up
Silence sweeps me
Like a snow-white wave.

When I look forward
Hungry gloom-fires sweep me
Like a red-hot wave.

When I look backward
I become one
With oblivion-promise.

When I look within
I see the game
Of my aspiration-height
And God's Compassion-light.

288. FULFILMENT-SUN

My soul smiled and said,
"Lord, You are all for me."

My heart cried and said,
"Lord, You are more than enough
for me."

My dream-boat
In silence-light said,
"Lord, I need You as my eternal
Companion."

My reality-shore
In perfection-dawn said,
"Lord, You are all-where, my
Fulfilment-sun."

289. SAFETY

Heart-cry is my body's
Only safe spot.

God-smile is my life's
Only safe shore.

Earth-sacrifice is my vital's
Only safe promise.

Heaven-oneness is my soul's
Only safe perfection.

290. BELIEF-ROLES

Earth's green belief
Comes and sings
Like the evening sky.

Heaven's blue belief
Appears to be devoured
By the giant hunger of earth-life.

Man's red belief
Stabs his reality
Before its journey's
perfection-start.

God's white belief
Birthless and deathless sports
In the core of man's
aspiration-flames.

291. ONLY TWO THINGS

Heaven likes only two things:
A child's dream-blue eyes
And
His flower-white heart.

A child likes only two things:
Earth-mother's concern-height
And
Heaven-father's
Compassion-light.

God needs only two things:
The Dream-boat of His
Silence-sky
And
The Reality-shore of His
Freedom-sound.

292. THE SMILE OF DESTRUCTION-SEA

Consciously I returned
To the confines of human blood
Only to be ridiculed and belittled.

Unconsciously I returned
To God's Freedom-height
Only to be enthroned and
crowned.

Soulfully hard I tried
To feed earth's hungry abyss.
Alas, I was assailed by
world-suspicion-god
And thrown into the smile of
destruction-sea.

293. SIX MESSAGES

My imagination tells me
That my God is far, very far.

My inspiration tells me
That although my God is very far,
I shall be able to reach Him
Someday, somewhere, somehow.

My aspiration tells me
That I shall ascend one step
And God will descend ninety-nine
steps,
And then we shall be together
And become one.

My realisation tells me
That I do not ascend and God does
not descend.
He just comes out of my
dream-reality
And
I just come out of His
Reality-dream.

My revelation tells me
That God and I together reveal
Eternity's cry,
Infinity's smile
And
Immortality's light.

My manifestation tells me
That we manifest only two things
on earth:
The promised land
And
A perfect life.

294. FOUR REASONS

My soul wanders.
My heart wonders.
My mind flounders.
My vital squanders.
My body wavers.
Why?
Because
My animal life I have not yet
conquered,
My human life I have not yet
transformed.
My life divine I have not yet
manifested
And
My life supreme I have not yet
glimpsed.

295. HUMAN HEART AND DIVINE HEART

A sacred heart
Is God's inspiration.
A secret heart
Is man's imagination.
A crying heart
Is man s illumination.
A self-giving heart
Is God's realisation.
A surrendered human heart
Reaches God's transcendental
Heights.
A perfect and manifested heart
Is the pride of God's
Reality-dream.
A surrendered divine heart
Is the smile of the Absolute
Supreme.

296. THE MIND'S COMRADES

The mind plays with its comrades
Fear, doubt and anxiety.
While playing,
Fear dies
Only to become
supremacy-strength.
While playing,
Doubt dies
Only to become totality-sun.
While playing,
Anxiety breaks
Only to become
confidence-mountain.

297. GUEST AND HOST

Man is a wonderful guest!
He brings with him
Nothing
When he goes to God.
He feels that since God
Has everything and is everything
He needs no gift from a poor
mortal.

God is a wonderful host!
He carries with Him
All that He has and all that He is
When He comes to man.
For He knows
That He houses within Himself
Eternity's infinite wealth.
He knows that man is helpless, if
not hopeless;
Hopeless, if not effortless;
Effortless, if not loveless;
Loveless, if not Godless.

298. TWO ROADS

No one walks along this road.
God once tried, but He failed
Because
This road is
Man's frustration-road:
destruction.

Man once walked along this road,
But failed
Because
This road is
God's perfection-road:
satisfaction.
Someday, perhaps man and God
Will together walk along this road
When
Man offers to God his surrendered
cry
And
God offers to man His
unmanifested Smile.

299. MY LIFE-PLAY

When the day of my life-play
dawned
I blamed God,
For my day was empty
Of infinite Light.
When the evening of my life-play
ended
I blamed myself,
For I had not tried to ascend
achievement's height
and I had not transcended my
reality's Goal.

300. BECOMING HAPPY

Lord, why am I suffering so much?
"You are suffering
Because you are a sleeping body."

Lord, why am I suffering so much?
"You are suffering
Because you are a demanding
vital."

Lord, why am I suffering so much?
"You are suffering
Because you are a doubting
mind."

Lord, why am I suffering so much?
"You are suffering
Because you are an unaspiring
heart."

Lord, why am I suffering so much?
"You are suffering
Because you are an unilluming
soul."

Lord, is there any way I can be
happy?
"Yes, you can.
Just tell your body
That its boss is your dynamic vital.
Just tell your vital
That its boss is your searching
mind.
Just tell your mind
That its boss is your surrendering
heart.

Just tell your heart
That its boss is your fulfilling soul.
Just tell your soul
That its boss is your
Dream-transforming
And
Reality-immortalising God."

301. FOR YOUR TRANSFORMATION

O intruding thoughts,
I know where you come from.
You come from fear-night,
You come from doubt-forest,
You come from anxiety-river.

Do you know where you will go?
You will go to courage-day.
What for?
For your unmistakable
transformation.
You will go to
certainty-mountain.
What for?
For your immediate
transformation.
You will go to assurance-sea.
What for?
For your supreme transformation.

302. FOUR WORLDS

In my heart-world,
Everything is a liberal doing
And
Everything is a happy happening.

In my mind-world,
Everything is an intentional doing
And
Everything is an unthinkable
happening.

In my vital-world,
Everything is a sensational doing
And
Everything is a short-lived
happening.

In my body-world,
Everything is a mechanical doing
And
Everything is a lifeless happening.

303. HOW TO ACQUIRE THEM

Happiness:
How do you acquire it?
Just give and give.

Peace:
How do you acquire it?
Just think you are an insignificant
creature.

Power:
How do you acquire it?
Just believe God loves you.

Perfection:
How do you acquire it?
Just feel you are of God.

304. PATHWAYS TO PERFECTION

Doubt-conquering
Is the pathway to pure perfection.
I knew it.

Love-manifesting
Is the pathway to sure perfection.
I know it.

Life-giving
Is the pathway to divine
perfection.
I shall know it.

God-becoming
Is the pathway to supreme
Perfection.
I have just learnt it from God.

305. NOTHING IS AIMLESS

Nothing walks
With aimless feet.
No, not even my stupid doubt.

Nothing sleeps
With an aimless body.
No, not even my
beggar-insecurity.

Nothing sings
With an aimless soul.
No, not even my dying life.

306. OUR NATURES

God has been
Kind and compassionate.
He has always been so.

Man is
Jealous and dangerous.
He is always so.

I will be
God-loving and man-fearing.
I will always be so.

307. THE TWO WITNESSES

O invading night,
I am not ready.
Tomorrow invade me
Right after I have dined
With God-light.
I tell you,
God will unconditionally be our witness.

O devouring night,
I am not ready.
Tomorrow devour me
Right after I have perfected
My life-reality.
I tell you,
My soul will happily be our witness.

308. THE UNIVERSAL QUESTION

The universal question:
Who is God?
Who else is God
If not I?

The universal question:
Who is God?
Definitely you are not!
Positively he is not, either!
Why? Why?
You are not God
Because
You do not dare.
He is not God
Because
He does not care.

309. I APPRECIATE

O seed of time,
I appreciate
Your God-Necessity.

O tree of time,
I appreciate
Your God-Duty.

O fruit of time,
I appreciate
Your God-Beauty.

310. TRUTH AND I ARE FRIENDS

A sleeping flower
Is my heart.
Believe it or not,
I tell only the truth.
Truth and I
Are indispensable friends.

A sleeping leaf
Is my mind.
Believe it or not,
I tell only the truth.
Truth and I
Are inseparable friends.

A sleeping lion
Is my vital.
Believe it or not,
I tell only the truth.
Truth and I
Are eternal friends.

A sleeping dog
Is my body.
Believe it or not,
I tell only the truth.
Truth and I
Are transcendental friends.

311. WHAT DO YOU WANT?

What do you want?
God?
Just look at my soulful eyes.

What do you want?
Man?
Just look at my helpless eyes.

What do you want?
Heaven?
Just look at my self-giving heart.

What do you want?
Hell?
Just look at my truth-binding
mind.

312. THREE DECLARATIONS

God-existence
Is indispensable:
Thus declares his crying heart.

God-existence
Is unnecessary:
Thus declares his unaspiring
mind.

God-existence
Is uncertain:
Thus declares his sleeping life.

313. WHY GOD LOVES US

I love you;
Therefore
God loves you:
Thus declares my self-styled,
gracious vital.

You love God;
Therefore
God loves me:
Thus declares my precious
oneness-heart.

314. NEXT TIME

God, I shall be back again.
Next time when I come
I shall give You my all:
My surrender.

Son, I shall be back again.
Next time when I come
I shall give you My All:
My Smile.

315. BROKEN BRIDGES

My hope was the bridge
Between
My earth-cry and my
Heaven-smile.
Alas, the bridge broke down
Because
I forgot to pray
This morning.

My promise was the bridge
Between
My earth-necessity and my
Heaven-immortality.
Alas, the bridge collapsed
Because
I forgot to meditate
Last evening.

316. YOU ARE AND GOD IS

You think,
Therefore
You cry.

You cry,
Therefore
You fly.

You fly,
Therefore
You love.

You love,
Therefore
You live.

You live,
Therefore
You are
And
God is.
You are of God's Promise;
God is for your love.

317. THE CHILD

True, I do not know
Where God came from,
But I do know
Where God's love came from.
It came from His Sound-necessity.
And what is His Sound-necessity?
His Sound-necessity
Is the child
Of His Silence-reality.

318. REVELATIONS

The life of love
And
The love of life
Reveal
Perpetual mutual sacrifice-height.

The life of God
And
The God of life
Reveal
Perpetual reciprocal
oneness-light.

319. BECAUSE HE BELIEVES

He lives in a dream-boat
But
He breathes in frustration-flames.
Why does he live?
He lives because
He believes in God's future Smile.
Why does he breathe?
He breathes because
He believes in the immortality
Of his earth-life.

320. TO LIVE SEPARATED

I want to live
Separated from humanity
Because
Its heart-cave is too small.

I want to live
Separated from Divinity
Because
Its soul is now empty
Of Compassion-Reality.

321. GOD'S CREATION-LIFE BLOSSOMS

I neglect God,
Therefore
My soul-life
Remains unfinished.

God loves me,
Therefore
God's creation-Life
Blossoms satisfaction-goal.

322. POSSESSORS AND SERVERS

The doubter cries
With his possessor:
Doubt.

The hater dies
With his possessor:
Hate.

The lover awakens
With his server:
Love.

The beloved fulfils
With his server:
Surrender-oneness.

323. NO DIFFERENCE

From my own experience
I tell you:
No difference
Between
Possession-sea
And
Frustration-sky.

From my own experience
I tell you:
No difference
Between
Surrender-life
And
God-oneness.

324. I NEED YOUR HEART

O God,
I need Your Forgiveness-Heart.
O man,
I need your surrender-heart.
O Heaven,
I need your fragrance-heart.
O earth,
I need your sacrifice-heart.

325. HE HAS LOST HIS CHARM

Because
Of his teeming doubts,
He has lost all his mental charm.

Because
Of his brooding fears,
He has lost all his psychic charm.

Because
Of his undying insecurity,
He has lost all his divine charm.

326. DIFFERENT WORLDS

Limitation is
In the low world.
Imitation is
In the lower world.
Frustration is
In the lowest world.

Transformation is
In the high world.
Perfection is
In the higher world.
Satisfaction is
In the highest world.

327. I USE

I use my heart
To scale the summit of excellence.

I use my soul
To transcend the acme of
excellence.

I use my God
To be His ever-transcending
Transcendence.

328. FALSE HEART

Show me your heart.
I shall immediately tell you
If it is a false heart
Or
A true heart.

Ah, I see your heart is false,
Totally false,
Because
You deliberately forgot
To include me, my great
contribution,
In your God-realisation
And
Your Perfection-manifestation.

329. TWO VISIONS

I have a vision,
And I assure you
My vision is not
A mental hallucination.
It is all God's future revelation.

You have a vision,
And I assure you
Your vision is what
We all truthfully call
A vital fabrication.
It is all this world's present
realisation.

330. FOUR VOICES

My imagination tells me
I can easily surpass God.
My inspiration tells me
I can easily equal God.
My aspiration tells me
I shall eventually see God's Feet.
My realisation tells me
I shall eternally serve God.

331. YOU DESERVE

Do you doubt?
Then you deserve the eternal
Death.
Do you believe?
Then you deserve the eternal Life.
Do you know?
Then you deserve the eternal Sun.
Do you not know?
Then you deserve the eternal
Compassion.

332. I SEE

I see the hand that leads me.
Its name is duty.
I see the heart that feeds me.
Its name is purity.
I see the soul that frees me.
Its name is beauty.
I see the God who wields me.
His name is Necessity.

333. THE RIGHT PLACE

Heaven is the right place
For my tired soul.
Earth is the right place
For my fired soul.
Hell is the right place
For my escaping soul.
Consciousness-sun is the right
place
For my aspiring soul.

334. THE STUDENT

Earth examines
The student in my mind.
Heaven illumines
The student in my heart.
Truth loves
The student in my soul.
Love fulfils
The student in my Goal.

335. HIS CONTINUOUS OCCUPATION

From morning to evening
He prays.
He makes God feel
Really great.

From night to morn
He meditates.
God makes him feel
Really good.

336. THE BURIAL GROUND

Earth
Is the burial ground of hope.
I knew it,
I know it,
I shall always know it.
Yet I cannot escape
And enter into the Reality-land.

Heaven
Is the burial ground of promise.
I knew it,
I know it,
I shall always know it.
Yet I cannot escape
And enter into the
Fulfilment-God.

337. VISIONS

Passion is the vision
Of the lower vital world.
Your vital-tiger knew it.

Salvation is the vision
Of the higher vital world.
Your vital-horse knows it.

Frustration is the vision
Of the lower physical world.
Your body-bull knew it.

Illumination is the vision
Of the higher physical world.
Your body-deer knows it.

338. WHO CAN CONQUER IT?

The whisper of temptation:
Who can conquer it?
No, not the vital man!

The torture of frustration:
Who can conquer it?
No, not the mental man!

The rapture of destruction:
Who can conquer it?
No, not the physical man!

The power of compassion:
Who can conquer it?
No, not even the psychic man!

339. HIS LIFE

His body-life
Is the life of immortal chaos.

His vital-life
Is the life of immortal destruction.

His mind-life
Is the life of immortal
  dissatisfaction.

His heart-life
Is the life of immortal surrender.

His soul-life
Is the life of immortal vision.

340. ALL THESE THINGS

All this finite nonsense!
Who wants it?
Who needs it?
No, not even my ignorance-night.

All this infinite Truth!
Who has it?
Who claims it?
No, not even the cosmic gods.

341. HE DESIRES HIS LIFE TO BE

He desires his life
To be the fruit of selected fictions.
Therefore
Happiness is compelled
To deny him its illumining
  presence.

He desires his life
To be the tree of
  imperfection-forest.
Therefore
Perfection is compelled
To deny him its nectar-presence.

342. WHEN I LIVED

When I lived in the sleeping body
My life was a million vacant cries.

When I lived in the unaspiring
heart
My life was a million heavy sighs.

When I lived in the non-giving life
My life was a million
imperfection-souls.

343. HERS

Hers is the heart
Of unplumbed beauty's core.

Hers is the soul
Of beauty's measureless shore.

Hers is the life
Of beauty's sleepless door.

344. EARTH'S POWER AND HEAVEN'S POWER

A single earth-cry
Can bring down
God's transcendental Height.

A single Heaven-smile
Can illumine
Earth's ignorance-life of
millennia.

A single earth-cry
Can empty
Eternity's Infinity.

A single Heaven-smile
Can spread
Divinity's Immortality.

345. I SEE, FEEL AND BECOME

In my repeated failures
I see God's perfecting Face.

In my repeated triumphs
I feel God's ever-increasing
Hunger.

In my unlimited progress
I become Heaven's Dream-reality
And
Earth's Reality-perfection.

346. COMMAND AND OBEY

I have commanded;
Therefore I have also obeyed.

Who has commanded?
The I-God in me.

Who has obeyed?
The I-man in me.

I have obeyed;
Therefore I shall also command.

I shall command
My Eternity's perfection
Of dedication-life.

347. WHEN I PLAY

When I play with God
Nobody loses,
For God's Heart
And my surrender
Are equally formidable.

When I play with man
I always lose,
For my lack of attention
And man's abundance of
temptation
Are equally harmful.

When I play with Heaven
We do not compete,
But complete the Game.

When I play with earth
Neither of us wins,
For we know not how to play the
Game.

348. THEY SHALL LISTEN TO YOU

The world shall listen to you.
Just give the world
A little more of your time.
Don't lose hope.
Hope shall reach God-Height
And God-Crown.

God shall listen to you.
Just give God
A little more of your heart's
love-life.
Don't lose patience.
Patience accelerates the
Goal-reality
In the immediacy of your today's
life.

349. THE HOUR

The hour came
But I forgot to invoke God.
Therefore bondage remained my
life.

The hour comes
But I forget to love life.
Therefore helplessness is my other
name.

The hour shall come
But I shall forget to become God's
Silence-seed.
Therefore I shall fail to measure
God's Sound-birth.

350. TWO WORLDS

In the world of the cosmic gods
I act like an all-conquering lion,
For God has told me who I
eternally am.

In the world of feeble mankind
I act like a lost child
In the brooding forest of time,
For I know not my incapacity-boat
And my capacity-shore.

351. THE PERFECT ONES

His life is the perfect general
Of reality's empty dreams.

His soul is the perfect soldier
Of dream's empty reality.

His goal is the perfect voice
Of Eternity's empty choice.

His God is the perfect slave
Of Immortality's empty role.

352. WHAT GOD HAS MADE ME

My body desired to be
A great runner.
But God has made me
A God-lover.

My vital desired to be
A great warrior.
But God has made me
A God-lover.

My mind desired to be
A great thinker.
But God has made me
A God-lover.

My heart desired to be
A God-lover.
But God has made me
Another God.

353. NO DIFFERENCE

No difference
Between
His earth-life
And
His arrows of dark desire-night.

No difference
Between
His Heaven-life
And
His stars of blue Perfection-Light.

No difference
Between
His God-life
And
His love-flames of
Oneness-Delight.

354. SLOW TRAINS

The world's slow train:
My love-cry.
Alas, what can I do?

The world's slower train:
My sacrifice-smile.
Alas, what have I done?

The world's slowest train:
My oneness-embrace.
Alas, what shall I do?

355. TIME

O seeker,
You are the user of Time.

O meditator,
You are the seer of Time.

O lover,
You are the fulfiller of Time.

O God,
You are the Player of time.

356. WHEN I THINK

When I think of myself
I know
What an invading pleasure is.

When I think of God
I know
What a perishing pleasure is.

When I think not,
I know not
Where pleasure-treasure is,
And
When I judge not
I know
Where perfection-satisfaction is.

357. HE AND IMPERFECTION

He and his imperfect life
Feel that they can perfect the
world.

He and his imperfect heart
Feel that God's arrival is overdue.

He and his imperfect dream
Feel that Reality-sun purposely
delays.

358. O SUFFERING CHRIST

O suffering Christ,
My heart of love
Suffers with you and for you.

O forgiving Christ,
My love of life
Enjoys with you and for you.

O illumining Christ,
My life of love
Is for you, only for you.

359. PERFECTION-TOUCH, IMPERFECTION-KEY

God has given me
His Perfection-touch;
Therefore,
Satisfaction is within my easy
reach.

Man has given me
His imperfection-key;
Therefore,
I fail to open God's
Compassion-door
And my own aspiration-door.

360. MY TWO LOVERS

Death loves me;
Therefore,
He has bandaged
My heart of bleeding experience.

Immortality loves me;
Therefore,
She has engaged
My incapacity
To blossom in her divinity.

361. NOT FOR THEM

Not for the complaining stream
The Silence-sea.

Not for the complaining lamp
The Illumination-sun.

Not for the complaining mind
The Liberation-God.

But for the complaining soul
The Compassion-Lord.

362. THE REASON IS OBVIOUS

My brave day sinks
In my darkening night.
My confident heart sinks
In my trembling fear.
Do you know why?
The reason is obvious.
When I was wearing my
victory-crown
And
When I was sitting on the
victory-throne
I consciously forgot
To place at God's Feet
My garland of
surrender-gratitude.

363. PERFECTION-MOON, SATISFACTION-SUN

O Darkness-night,
Don't spread your jealous wings.

O Effulgence-day,
Heighten your zealous heart.

O Perfection-moon,
Quicken my life-boat.

O Satisfaction-sun,
Brighten my Reality-shore.

364. SHE

He speaks,
Yet he says nothing.
She speaks not,
Yet she says everything:
The depth of God-realisation
And
The height of man-perfection.
Man adores her
Because
She is his voice.
God loves her
Because
She is His peerless Choice.

365. ONLY FROM AFAR

He is brave
From a safe distance.
She is beautiful
From a far distance.
His aspiration works
Only in distant skies.
Her realisation works
Only on foreign shores.

366. EVEN THEY KNOW IT

Man is my kingdom.
I know it.
Even my stupidity knows it.

Truth is my palace.
I know it.
Even my insincerity knows it.

Love is my home.
I know it.
Even my insecurity knows it.

God is my nest.
I know it.
Even my ambiguity knows it.

367. YOUR PRESENCE AND ABSENCE

Lord, since You know
That Your Presence is my
Himalayan delight,
Why don't You come to me
More often?

Lord, since You know
That Your absence
Is my oceanic sorrow,
Why don't You tell me
Why You are quite often,
In season and out of season,
Absent?

368. JUSTIFICATIONS

When you live
In the vital world
You justify slavery.

When you live
In the psychic world
You justify freedom.

When you live
In the physical world
You justify ignorance-frown.

When you live
In the God-world
You justify
Everything within,
Everything without.

369. TWO PERFECT STRANGERS

Human birth
And
Divine freedom
Have no liking
For each other.

Human goal
And
Divine soul
Act from dawn to dusk
Like two perfect strangers.

370. I MEASURE NOT

I measure not
My realisation-height.
It is too discouraging.

I measure not
My perfection-light.
It is too disheartening.

I measure not
My satisfaction-sun.
It is too frightening.

I measure
Only one thing:
God's Compassion-ocean.

371. WHAT WE ARE

Eternity
Is my soul-splendour.

Infinity
Is my soul-measure.

Immortality
Is my soul-treasure.

And I am
My world's morning pleasure
And
Evening pressure.

372. DREAMS

Silence-light
Is the dream
Of my earth-aspiration.

Sound-power
Is the dream
Of my Heaven-vision.

God-delight
Is the dream
Of my life-perfection.

373. THE HOPEFUL UNIVERSE

He is crying;
Therefore,
Divinity is hopeful.

He is smiling;
Therefore,
Humanity is hopeful.

He is loving;
Therefore,
God is hopeful.

He is becoming;
Therefore
The entire universe is hopeful.

374. REAL GOD, FALSE GOD

Who has made God?
He Himself.
Who has made the small gods?
Man has made them.
Who is a real God?
A silence-lover
And
A sound-performer.
Who is a false God?
A builder of temptation-palace
And
A destroyer of love-nest.

375. WHAT ELSE CAN POOR GOD DO?

His dark insincerity
Is as deep as man's weakness.
Yet God loves him.
What else can poor God do?

His fleeting sincerity
Is as shallow as man's goodness.
Yet God loves him.
What else can poor God do?

His dreaming perfection
Is as impossible as man's
immortality.
Yet God loves him.
What else can poor God do?

376. GIFTS OF THE TRUE GOD

Love-smile
Is a gift of the true God.
Don't lose it.
If you lose it,
You are undone.

Truth-cry
Is a gift of the true God.
Don't lose it.
If you lose it,
Your life will be totally destroyed.

Surrender-perfection
Is a gift of the true God.
Don't lose it.
If you lose it,
Your God-realisation will be
indefinitely delayed.

377. IT HAS ALREADY BEEN GIVEN

If you need Love in your heart,
It has already been given by God.
Just feel it.

If you need Peace in your mind,
It has already been given by God.
Just believe it.

If you need Power in your vital,
It has already been given by God.
Just distribute it.

If you need Perfection in your
body,
It has already been given by God.
Just offer it.

378. SHOWERS

My thought-life
Is a shower of blind folly.
My will-life
Is a shower of bright glory.
My surrender-life
Is a shower of perfect beauty.

379. THE DISTANCE BETWEEN

My heart-cave
Is the distance
Between
My hope and my despair.

My life-hole
Is the distance
Between
My victory and my defeat.

My love-drop
Is the distance
Between
My animal destruction
And
My divine perfection.

380. JUST BREATHE A PRAYER

Just breathe a prayer.
God shall be
Your Impurity-chaser.

Just breathe a prayer.
God shall be
Your Duty-performer.

Just breathe a prayer.
God shall be
Your eternal Partner.

Just breathe a prayer.
God shall be
Your unconditional Lover.

381. MY EXPERIENCE

To enjoy
Is to obey:
Indeed, this is
My earth-experience.

To obey
Is to enjoy:
Indeed, this is
My Heaven-experience.

To obey
And obey:
Indeed, this is
My body-experience.

To enjoy
And enjoy:
Indeed, this is
My soul-experience.

382. MY LIFE-ROAD

At one end of my life-road
Is man
With his darkening night.

At the other end of my life-road
Is God
With His illumining Light.

My life began
With Eternity's hush.
My life shall end
With Infinity's rush.

383. I CRY

I cry in the City of God
To be as perfect as God.

I cry in the village of man
To be as sincere as a villager.

I cry in the core of my soul
To be as beautiful as my soul.

384. THREE POINTS OF VIEW

God sees me
Through His beams of Love;
Therefore, He calls me
His perfection-representative.

Man sees me
Through his whims of hatred;
Therefore, he calls me
His arch adversary.

I see myself
Through my heart's
  uncertainty-door;
Therefore, I call myself
A totally lost soul.

385. FLYING

My Lord flies in me
With His wings of Beauty
When I cry and cry.

I fly in my Lord
With my wings of purity
When He smiles and smiles.

To my Lord,
Flying is His world-perfecting
Choice.
To me,
Flying is my world-conquering
noise.

386. DON'T TELL ME A LIE!

Don't tell me a lie!
There is no man
Who has never stumbled.

Don't tell me a lie!
There is no man
Who remains always on the
ground.

Don't tell me a lie!
There is no man
Who will not realise God.

Don't tell me a lie!
There is no man
Who will not become a future
God.

387. I SUPPORT THEM

I support God personally
Because
He is all love for me.

I support myself wholeheartedly
Because
I do everything perfectly.

I support man immediately
Because
His weakness pains me deeply.

388. PURCHASES

I buy God
With a throbbing cry.

God buys me
With a winning Smile.

I buy Heaven
With my aspiration-heart.

Heaven buys me
With its Vision-soul.

389. O SUNSHINE

O sunshine of Beauty,
My heart invokes
Your light.

O sunshine of Duty,
My life invokes
Your soul.

O sunshine of Love,
My soul is all
Concern for you.

O sunshine of Perfection,
In you I feel the perfect presence
Of the perfect God.

390. PULSE OF THE PAST

O pulse of the past,
I do not need you
To found my reality on earth.

O pulse of the past,
My future dreams
Are growing fast
In my today's reality.

O pulse of the past,
My animal past
Was my destruction-night;
My human past
Was my future dream;
My divine past
Has become one with the
immediacy of today.

391. WHO WILL BE MY PARTNER?

Who will be the partner of my
sorrow?
No, not even my Lord, the
Compassion-peak.

Who will be the partner of my joy?
No, not even my Illumination-sky.

Who will be the partner of my
perfection?
Long have I searched for him,
Much have I offered to him.
My life of surrender-light
Is only for him, only for him.

392. HE IS THE FOUNTAIN

He is the fountain
Of thinking.
Let him think and sink.

He is the fountain
Of feeling.
Let him feel and expand.

He is the fountain
Of love.
He spreads his wings and
becomes.

He is the fountain
Of light.
His outer life grows
And his inner life sows.

393. HIS GOD

He is a mountain of sin;
Therefore,
The Saviour has to take care of
him.

He is the sea of service;
Therefore,
The Liberator employs him.

He is the sky of error and
perfection;
Therefore,
His God is Progress
And
His God is Supreme.

394. SHE SHINES

Her glory shines
In the world of her silence-light.
Her progress shines
In the world of her
heavenward-sight.
Her perfection shines
In the world of her
surrender-might.
Her manifestation shines
In the world of God's choice
Hour-delight.

395. WHEN HE PLAYS TRUANT

When he plays truant from earth,
He fails to learn
The wisdom of sacrifice-light.

When he plays truant from
Heaven,
He fails to learn
The vision of God's
Silence-height.

When he plays truant from his
inner home,
His life becomes
A forest of ignorance-night.

When he plays truant from his
outer life,
His life becomes
The dance of destruction-fight.

396. IN THE UNIVERSE OF LIFE

In the room of life
My Lord sleeps and sleeps.

In the apartment of life
My Lord dreams and dreams.

In the house of life
My Lord struggles and struggles.

In the palace of life
My Lord dares and dares.

In the city of life
My Lord smiles and smiles.

In the country of life
My Lord sings and sings.

In the world of life
My Lord becomes and becomes.

In the universe of life
My Lord eternally is.

397. ONLY FOR YOU

Walk up to her;
She will bless you.
March up to her;
She will love you.
Run up to her;
She will claim you.
Sit at her feet;
She will proclaim you.
Bow to her;
She will garland you.
Meditate on her;
She will crown you.
Surrender your all to her;
Her life within,
Her life without,
Will be all for you,
Only for you.

398. THE HEART OF AN ORPHAN-TEAR

He hates his tired body.
He hates his fired vital.
He hates his doubting mind.
He hates his unloving heart.
He hates his dreamless soul.
He hates his useless God.
When? When?
When he feels that his life
Is the heart of an orphan-tear.

399. TOUCH YOUR GOD

Touch your God,
Touch your God.
He enjoys your touch.

Strike your God,
Strike your God.
He enjoys your torture wild.

Love your God,
Love your God.
He will feed the heights of your
inner cry.

Serve your God,
Serve your God.
He will offer you
His Eternity's Crown
And
Immortality's Throne.

400. THE DESERTER

His mother guided him and
moulded him.
His father blessed him and
protected him.
His God divinised him and
immortalised him.
But alas,
He deserted his inner life of dream
And
Negated his outer life of reality.

401. WHEN I SEE DEATH'S HAND

When I see Death's hand
On your face,
My heart just breaks.
How I wish you could stay
On earth
A few more good and God-years!

When I see Death's hand
On your heart,
My heart just breaks.
I blame, I blame God
Because He has not granted you
Even an immortal human birth.

402. TWO GREAT AMBITIONS

Two great ambitions have I.
I want to see
If God can manage to exist
On earth
And
In Heaven
Without my conscious and
constant support.
I want to see
If any soul
On earth
Or
In Heaven
Has ever displeased God
More than my demanding and
possessing life.

403. TWO UNBORN DREAMS

I long for the blossoming
Of two unborn dreams.

I wish to fly
From life to death
To change the face and fate of
earth
In the world of death.

I wish to fly
From earth-failure to
Heaven-triumph
To change the sorrows and pangs
of God
In the world of man.

404. HIS NAME

His name
Is no man's inspiration-flow.

His name
Is no man's aspiration-glow.

His name
Is no man's realisation-flood.

Yet he is one,
Inseparably one,
With God's Compassion-blood.

405. NONE TOO SMALL

No Truth too small
To illumine me.

No Light too weak
To fulfil me.

No Bliss too little
To immortalise me.

No Perfection too insignificant
To claim me.

406. O MY PARTNERS

O Silence-partner
Of my heart,
I need your silence-peace
To feel the Heart of God.

O Light-partner
Of my soul,
I need your light-liberation
To see the Soul of God.

O Power-partner
Of my life,
I need your power-tower
To clasp the Hour of God.

407. FRIEND, I AM SORRY!

Friend, I am sorry!
Your beauty-lustre is gone
Because
Earth has possessed you.

Friend, I am sorry!
Your duty-hour is gone
Because
Heaven no more needs you.

Friend, I am sorry!
Your realisation-height is gone
Because
God has discovered a new
instrument
to replace you.

408. HIS FEET HAVE NO REST

I saw the feet of a thief.
I felt sorry for them
Because
They have no rest.
Even during the night
Ignorance compels them to run.

I saw the feet of a saint.
I felt sorry for them
Because
They have no rest.
Even when he is in his own room
His followers cannot live
Without touching and polluting
his feet.

409. FATHER-CONSCIOUSNESS, MOTHER-LIGHT

Father-Consciousness,
I need You
To claim You –
Your Vision's Reality.
Without it I am lost
In ignorance-night.

Mother-Light,
I need You
To claim You –
Your Reality's Perfection.
Without it I am captured
By pleasure-snares.

Therefore,
Father and Mother,
I need You two
More than You
Can possibly think.

410. YOUR PRESENCE

Your presence manifests
God-light on earth;
Therefore,
I am safe.

Your presence manifests
God-delight on earth;
Therefore,
I am happy.

Your presence manifests
God-perfection on earth;
Therefore,
I am useful.

411. RIVERS OF SORROW

Your life is a river of sorrow
Because
Nobody loves you.

Your life is a hundred rivers of
sorrow
Because
Nobody needs you.

Your life is a thousand rivers of
sorrow
Because
Man-confidence,
Self-confidence,
God-confidence,
Are all strangers to you.

412. MY BONDAGE REIGN

My heart-pain
Has destroyed my beauty's core.

My earth-chain
Has bound my freedom-shore.

My ignorance-reign
Has forgotten my reality-door.

413. O DREAM-BEARER

O dream-bearer,
My heart needs
Your heart of Golden Dream
To see Heaven's silver fire.

O dream-bearer,
My soul needs
Your soul of Reality-Sun
To illumine earth's black mire.

414. DREAMLAND

When I first dreamt of you
I thought I loved you.
I really did.
But alas,
Reality is something else.

When I first spoke to you
I thought I had you.
I really did.
But alas,
Dreamland is the land where I
live.

415. A SERIOUS MISTAKE

O earth, you thought
You had possessed me
And I would please you
In your own human way.
Better late than never,
You have realised
That it was a serious mistake.

O earth, I thought
I had transformed you
And you would please me
In my own divine way.
Better late than never,
I have realised
That it was a serious mistake.

416. GOD'S TWO BATTLEFIELDS

Earth is God's battlefield.
Here He tries so hard
To give humanity
What He has: Perfection.
Alas, nobody knows
If ever He will succeed.

Heaven is God's battlefield.
There He tries so hard
To give divinity
What He is: Realisation.
Alas, no soul knows
If ever He will succeed.

417. MY DREAM IN YOUR EYES

My dream in Your Eyes
Offers me the realisation
That You are
My God, my only God, my eternal God.
O dream, my dream,
How soulful you are.

My dream in Your Heart
Offers me the realisation
That I am
Your own, Your very own, Your eternally own.
O dream, my dream,
How fruitful you are.

418. GOD IS GOD

God is God
Because
He dares to believe
That I am another God.

God is God
Because
He dares to transcend
What He *eternally* is.

419. I NEED BETTER THOUGHTS

I need better thoughts.
I need the thought that loves God
Unconditionally.
I need the thought that loves man
Soulfully.
I need the thought that loves
The animal kingdom
Carefully.
I need the thought that loves
The plant world
Ceaselessly.
I need the thought that loves
The stone life
Compassionately.

420. TRY AGAIN

Nowhere to progress;
Therefore,
You are unhappy.
Nothing to express;
Therefore,
You are unhappy.
No one to impress;
Therefore,
You are unhappy.
None to suppress;
Therefore,
You are unhappy.
If you progress
Your soul will love you;
If you express
Your heart will love you;
If you impress
Your mind will love you;
If you suppress
Your vital will love you.
Therefore,
Try and try again.

421. MY GREAT CAPACITIES

My sorrows are great;
They want to be distributed.

My joys are great;
They want to be perfected.

My achievements are great;
They all came from God.

My surrender is great;
It is my only real life.

422. MY MENTAL PROGRESSION

O my mental clouds,
When are you going to be thinner?

O my mental cave,
When are you going to be wider?

O my mental plant,
When are you going to be taller?

O my mental cry,
When are you going to be purer?

O my mental life,
When are you going to be wiser?

423. WHEN GOD INVENTED

When God invented Duty
He also invented Beauty.

When God invented Life
He also invented Love.

When God invented His
Dream-moon
He also invented His Reality-sun.

When God invented His
Silence-choice
He also invented His
Manifestation-voice.

424. TWO QUESTIONS

Lord, I have two childish
questions.
Why did You create the world?
Are You not a fool?

Lord, I have two child-like
questions.
Do you love me, Lord?
Will You make me as good as You
are?

Lord, I have two God-like
questions.
When will I be eternally happy?
When will I be completely perfect?

425. FATHER AND DAUGHTER

Father, give me the capacity
To count the time
I have misspent.

Daughter, give Me the capacity
To count the good things
You have done for Me.

Father, why do You make fun of
me?

Daughter, why do you make Me
sad
By dragging yourself
Back to the fruitless past?

426. THE DREAMER TELLS ME

The dreamer from the East
Tells me:
God is Peace.
I believe him
And
I shall always believe him.

The dreamer from the West
Tells me:
God is Power.
I believe him
And
I shall always believe him.

The dreamer from Heaven
Tells me:
God is an eternal child.
I believe him
And
I shall always believe him.

The dreamer from earth
Tells me:
God is an ever-descending Light.
I believe him
And
I shall always believe him.

427. AMBASSADORS OF GOD

O Ambassadors of God,
What do you need
From earth and Heaven?

"We need earth's confidence
In us
So that we can show earth
The golden Feet of God.
We need Heaven's confidence
In us
So that Heaven does not point out
to God
Our incapacities
While we strive hard
To manifest Him on earth."

428. GOD DOES NOT MIND

God does not mind
The imperfections of my face.

God does not mind
The limitations of my eyes.

God does not mind
The incapacities of my arms.

God does not mind
The endless follies of my mind.
But
God objects to even an iota of a
spot
On the hallowed tablet
Of my heart.

429. GOD IS HIS OWN FATHER AND SON

God is His own interpreter.
He interprets His divine message to man
With His Compassion-height.
God is His own boss.
He directs man to do the right thing,
To be the right thing,
With His Concern-light.
God is His own Father and Son.
As a father, He needs His Son
To manifest His life of Immortality.
As a son, He needs His Father
To supply Him with
His ever-transcending Reality.

430. DO NOT GO!

Don't go
Near that hysterical woman!
She thinks even God
Has deceived her.

Don't go
Near that neurotic man!
He feels even God
Is jealous of him.

431. BIG QUESTIONS

Big questions
With no answer:
Will death punish me
Or
Will death adore me
When I die?
Will there be another Lord
On earth
After my death?
Why is God
So insecure?
Why does He not make
Every man perfect like Him?
What is wrong with Him?

432. A BETTER WAY

A better way
To pass the morning:
I shall meditate every morning
For fifteen minutes
To love God in His own Way,
Plus cheerfully.

A better way
To pass the afternoon:
I shall meditate every afternoon
For fifteen minutes
To please God in His own Way,
Plus cheerfully.

A better way
To pass the evening:
I shall meditate every evening
For fifteen minutes
To fulfil God in His own Way,
Plus cheerfully.

433. DON'T GO NEAR HIM!

Don't go near him!
He is practising selfish holiness.

Go near him!
He is practising simple kindness.

Don't go near him!
He says God-power is on sale.

Go near him!
He says God-love cannot be described.

434. TRY, YOU SHALL SUCCEED

You may not reach Heaven
At a single bound,
But
You can reach God without fail
At a single bound.
Try, you shall succeed.

You may not please Heaven
All at once,
But
You can please God without fail
All at once.
Try, you shall succeed.

435. GOD, ARE YOU DISCOURAGED?

God, are You discouraged
When I make so many mistakes
Everyday?
God, are You displeased
That I have not made You
The first thing in my life?
God, are You disheartened
That every day I fail you?

Son, if I am discouraged
Then I shall not
Look at you.
Son, if I am displeased
Then I shall not
Smile at you.
Son, if I am disheartened
Then I shall not
Bless you.

436. I WAS BORN TO BE ALONE (I)

I was born to see alone.
Whom have I seen?
An orphan soul.
What have I seen?
An infant world.

I was born to walk alone.
Whom have I reached?
The King of frustration.
Where have I reached?
Eternity's nowhere.

437. I WAS BORN TO BE ALONE (II)

I was born to cry alone.
For whom do I cry?
I cry for my forgotten half:
God.

I was born to starve alone.
Why do I starve?
Because I fear to dine
With my absolute Lord Supreme.

438. STILL GOD WANTS YOU TO WORK FOR HIM

Although
You have fallen asleep,
God wants you to work
For Him.
Why?
God wants you to conquer sleep
So that you can be
His sleepless partner.

Although
You have told a good many lies,
God wants you to work
For Him.
Why?
God wants you to conquer
falsehood
So that you can be
His perfect partner.

439. SOMETHING REMAINS UNTOLD

Something remained untold.
What was it?
God's Compassion
For humanity.

Something remains untold.
What is it?
God's Aspiration
In humanity.

Something shall remain untold.
What is it?
God's Perfection
Of humanity.

440. A BETTER WORLD

Daughter, I have been
Looking for you everywhere.
Where have you been?
What have you been doing?
"I have been inside my mind."
Ah, that is why I have been
missing you.
What have you been doing there?
"I have been thinking
Of how to create a better world."
I see, daughter.
Please do Me a big favour.
When you create a better world,
Make Me an honorary citizen of
your world.
Not only are you disappointed
In My world,
But I am also disappointed
Far beyond your imagination's
flight.

441. WHO FEARS?

Who fears to follow?
Not the heart-man in me.
Who fears to follow?
The mind-man in me.

Who fears to lead?
Not the soul-man in me.
Who fears to lead?
The body-man in me.

Who fears to change?
Not the God-man in me.
Who fears to change?
The vital-man in me.

442. A FAVOUR

God asked me for a favour.
I gave Him not what He wanted.
Can you imagine
What He wanted from me?
He wanted to have
All my ignorance.
I said to Him,
"If I give You all my ignorance
What will I have on earth
To live with and to live for?"

I asked God for a favour.
He gave me immediately what I
wanted.
He gave me
His Infinity's Love,
Eternity's height
And
Immortality's life.
He shared with me His supreme
Secret:
That real joy is in self-giving.

443. THEIR FEES

I will tell you
What I paid for my
God-realisation:
To God I paid His Fee:
Surrender unconditional.
To my earth-teacher I paid his fee:
Love-flood.
To the Heaven-witness I paid his fee:
Smile-dawn.
To the Time-lawyer I paid his fee:
Silence-sky.

444. CARRY THEM ALWAYS

Courage: carry it always.
It will help you.

Faith: carry it always.
It will save you.

Joy: carry it always.
It will feed you.

Love: carry it always.
It will immortalise you.

445. WHAT IS THE MATTER?

What is the matter with me?
Why do I not love God?
He does everything for me.

What is the matter with God?
Why does He not ignore me?
I deserve His indifference-blow.

What is the matter with earth?
Why has it lost all its hope?
Hope is the harbinger of achievement.

What is the matter with Heaven?
Why does it promise all the time?
Promise unfulfilled is insincerity's betrayal.

446. I WARN YOU

Why are you tormenting me,
doubt?
I warn you once and for all,
I shall throw you into the
lion-mouth
Of faith.

Why are you tormenting me, fear?
I warn you once and for all,
I shall throw you into the
giant-heart
Of courage.

Why are you tormenting me,
insecurity?
I warn you once and for all,
I shall throw you into the
goal-height
Of oneness.

447. IT IS TIME TO DO MORE

True, you have realised God.
But it seems that it is time for you
To learn something more.

True, you have revealed God.
But it seems that it is time for you
To do something more.

True, you have manifested God.
But it seems that it is time for you
To please your Inner Pilot more.

448. FOR THE TIME BEING

For the time being
I shall think only of God,
Since He has promised me that
He will make me happy.

For the time being
I shall love only man,
Since I have promised man that
I shall make him happy.

For the time being
I shall adore only Heaven,
Since Heaven sincerely cares for
me.

For the time being
I shall bless only earth,
Since earth always longs for me.

449. MY NAME

Don't trap me!
My name is a moment;
I shall unmistakably free you.

Don't belittle me!
My name is a seed;
I shall eventually fulfil you.

Don't forget me!
My name is an iota of perfection;
I shall definitely immortalise you.

450. NO DIFFERENCE

Love of power:
What is the difference
Between
You and a ferocious tiger?
No difference, none!

Power of love:
What is the difference
Between
You and God?
No difference, none!

451. EARTH

It is my joy, my privilege,
To talk to you, earth.
My silver hope
And
My golden faith
Are centred inside the breath
Of your heart.
Heaven is God's Dream,
Nothing more.
You are God's Reality.
Something more:
You are God's own Progress.

452. A REAL GURU

Who is a real Guru?
A real Guru is he
Who does not call you stupid,
Undivine and useless.
A real Guru is he who says:
"You have knowledge,
But you need more knowledge.
Try, you certainly can!"

A real Guru is he who says:
"You are divine,
But you can be more divine.
Try, you certainly can!"

A real Guru is he who says:
"You are useful,
Infinitely more useful
Than you ever can imagine.
But you can be more useful.
Try, you certainly can!"

A real Guru is he who says:
"You are God's chosen
instrument.
You are useful,
You are fruitful,
You are indispensable
To the divine Vision of God."

453. THE BUILDERS

Don't forget,
You are the builders
Of tomorrow's world.
What do you have?
Inspiration-flood.
That is enough.
What else do you have?
Aspiration-blood.
That is more than enough.
God has a message for you:
Don't imitate,
But create something new
That will forever last.

454. WHY DO YOU SUFFER?

Why do you suffer?
You suffer
Because
You trust idle rumours.

Why do you suffer?
You suffer
Because
You do a lot of hasty thinking.

Why do you suffer?
You suffer
Because
You do not eschew clever
opportunism.

Why do you suffer?
You suffer
Because
You ceaselessly expect popularity.

455. DON'T YOU KNOW?

Don't you know
That your doubtful mind
Is a big blot
On your soul's fair smile?

Don't you know
That your suspicious mind
Is a big blot
On your heart's deep cry?

Don't you know
That your argumentative mind
Is a big blot
On your God's Compassion?

Don't you know
That there is no difference
Between your doubtful mind
And your militaristic mind?

Don't you know
That there is no difference
Between your suspicious mind
And your imperialistic mind?

Don't you know
That there is no difference
Between your argumentative
And your unrealistic mind?

456. BECAUSE YOU ARE GREAT

Your body loves you
Because
You are a great sleeper.

Your vital loves you
Because
You are a great warrior.

Your mind loves you
Because
You are a great debater.

Your heart loves you
Because
You are a great server.

Your soul loves you
Because
You are a great observer.

Your God loves you
Because
You are a great dreamer.

457. DON'T SPEAK ILL OF THEM

Don't speak ill of your poor body.
It regularly feeds itself;
You are just not aware of it.

Don't speak ill of your poor vital.
It regularly widens itself;
You are just not aware of it.

Don't speak ill of your poor mind.
It regularly empties itself;
You are just not aware of it.

Don't speak ill of your poor heart.
It regularly fills itself;
You are just not aware of it.

Don't speak ill of your poor God.
He regularly examines Himself;
You are just not aware of it.

458. LOOK!

You are not blind.
Look at your mind.
Your mind is a rich awakening.

You are not weak.
Look at your heart.
Your heart is a rich resolve.

You are not hopeless.
Look at your soul.
Your soul is a rich harvest.

You are not useless.
Look at your God.
Your God is all for you,
For you alone.

459. REMEMBER ONE MORE THING

Ignorance-insincerity
Is the marked feature
Of your unlit mind.

Ignorance-insecurity
Is the marked feature
Of your unaspiring heart.

Remember, God needs your mind.
Remember, God needs your heart.
Remember one thing more:
What you call life-building....
I call that very thing
God-flowering.

460. I AM SORRY

Why don't you play,
Sing and dance?
Don't you believe in
God's universal Love
Of immortal Oneness?
If you fail to believe
I am sorry.
Your heart-life
Is nothing
But
A progressive poverty.

461. HIS HAPPINESS

In his animal life
He was happy
Because
There was no human observer.

In his human life
He is happy
Because
He is always at the Feet
Of God the constant Forgiver.

In his divine life
He will be happy
Because
He will always play
With God the unconditional
Lover.

462. THIS WILL REALLY MAKE ME HAPPY

Lord, accept me
As a dreamer
In Your Heaven.
This will really make me happy.

Lord, accept me
As a striver
On Your earth.
This will really make me happy.

Lord, accept me
As a searcher
Outside Your Body.
This will really make me happy.

Lord, accept me
As a lover
Inside Your Heart.
This will really make me happy.

463. WHY GOD IS SO PLEASED WITH YOU

Do you know
Why God is so pleased with you?
He is pleased with you
Because
You have realised
That there is no stranger
In the kingdom of humanity.

Do you know
Why God is so pleased with you?
He is pleased with you
Because
You have realised
That there is no intruder
In the country of Divinity.

464. YOU DON'T BELONG TO YOURSELF

You don't belong to yourself.
You belong to humanity's hope.

You don't belong to yourself.
You belong to Divinity's Dream.

You don't belong to yourself.
You belong to Infinity's Progress.

You don't belong to yourself.
You belong to Immortality's Life.

465. IF YOU REALLY WANT TO SEE

Don't separate,
Don't divide;
Do unite,
Do reconcile
If you really want to see
God in man.

Don't hate,
Don't destroy;
Do love,
Do build
If you really want to see
Man in God.

466. BELIEVE IT OR NOT!

Believe it or not....

The Kingdom of Heaven
Is not in paper-resolutions.

The Kingdom of Heaven
Is not in mind-solutions.

The Kingdom of Heaven
Is in heart-aspiration.

The Kingdom of Heaven
Is in life-dedication.

Believe it or not....

467. WORLD-MISSION

Krishna's perfection for humanity
Was responsible for his
world-mission.

Buddha's compassion for
humanity
Was responsible for his
world-mission.

Christ's dedication to humanity
Was responsible for his
world-mission.

Your aspiration for humanity
Is responsible for your
world-mission.

My resignation before humanity
Is responsible for my
world-mission.

468. WE CAN BE ETERNALLY HAPPY

I can be eternally happy
Only when
My silence-heart is filled
With God-cries.

God can be eternally happy
Only when
His Dream-Boat is filled
With man-smiles.

469. AFTER HE IS SOUGHT

Love is not becoming,
Love is being.

Life is not hallucination,
Life is aspiration.

God is not taught,
God is caught.
Of course,
After He is sought.

470. I FEEL SO SORRY FOR YOU

O my unsafe life,
You suffer so much
From
The hurtful invasions of the vital.
I feel so sorry for you.

O my weak life,
You suffer so much
From
The doubtful invasions of the
mind.
I feel so sorry for you.

O my poor life,
You suffer so much
From
The meaningful invasions of the
soul.
I feel so sorry for you.

471. A NEW BREATH

When I think
Of my body,
I breathe a new breath
Of frustration.

When I think
Of my vital,
I breathe a new breath
Of destruction.

When I think
Of my mind,
I breathe a new breath
Of hallucination.

When I think
Of my heart,
I breathe a new breath
Of consolation.

472. I KNOW NOT, I KNOW

I do not know;
Therefore
Immortality-seed is for me,
Eternity-tree is for me,
Infinity-flower is for me,
Divinity-fruit is for me.

I know;
Therefore
Temptation-seed is not in me,
Depression-tree is not in me,
Frustration-flower is not in me
Destruction-fruit is not in me.

473. BEFORE I ACT

Before I give
I think of God's Depth;
Therefore
My life is meaningful.

Before I receive
I think of God's Height;
Therefore
My life is fruitful.

Before I achieve
I think of God's Smile;
Therefore
My life is beautiful.

474. PRESENT NAME, FUTURE NAME

Your aspiration's present name is
Uncertainty;
Its future name is
Realisation.

Your realisation's present name is
Uncertainty;
Its future name is
Revelation.

Your revelation's present name is
Uncertainty;
Its future name is
Manifestation.

Manifestation has two more
names:
Perfection and Satisfaction.

475. LIFE IS A QUEST

Life is a quest
And
Not a conquest.

Love is a conquest
And
Not a quest.

Earth is aspiration
And
Not illumination.

Heaven is illumination
And
Not aspiration.

God is a smile
And
Not a cry.

Man is a cry
And
Not a smile.

476. I KEEP SENTINEL

I keep sentinel
Over my loveless words;
Therefore
My heart is nearing
My Lord's Perfection-Door.

I keep sentinel
Over my black thoughts;
Therefore
My mind is nearing
My Lord's Perfection-Door.

I keep sentinel
Over my teeming desires;
Therefore
My vital is nearing
My Lord's Perfection-Door.

I keep sentinel
Over my Godless deeds;
Therefore
My body is nearing
My Lord's Perfection-Door.

477. GOD NEEDS YOU

God needs you.
Why?
Because you have conquered
The sluggishness of your blind
body.

God needs you.
Why?
Because you have perfected
The selfishness of your narrow
vital.

God needs you.
Why?
Because you have silenced
The clamour of your unruly mind.

God needs you.
Why?
Because you have offered
The ignorance of your unaspiring
heart.

478. YOU HAVE FREED YOURSELF

You have freed yourself
From the din and roar
Of the exterior world;
Therefore
God is offering you
His Beauty's Height.

You have freed yourself
From the ruthless desire-invasion
Of the interior world;
Therefore
God is offering you
His Duty's Pride.

479. EVERY REASON TO REJOICE

Because I do not live
In the unlit chamber of the mind,
I have every reason to rejoice;
And I constantly do so.

Because I do not breathe
In the unwidening cave of the
heart,
I have every reason to rejoice;
And I constantly do so.

480. TWO BOONS

No more hurdles
Between me and my Lord
Supreme!
He has given me two supreme
boons:
His lotus Feet belong to my heart;
The tyranny of my ego-life
From now on is His concern,
And not mine.

481. WHAT HE GAVE UP

He gave up
The path of popularity
To follow the path of spirituality.
He is really great and sublime.

He gave up
Considering himself a spiritual
orphan
To become the bridge between
God and man.
He is really wise and divine.

482. REPEATING GOD'S NAME

You repeated God's Name
With the clever tongue
Of your mind.
God was afraid of your dangerous
 deception;
Therefore
He did not dare to near you,
Let alone bless you.
But now
You repeat God's Name
With the loving adoration
Of your heart.
Look, God is not only embracing
 you,
But also claiming you,
You alone, as His very own.

483. COMPASSION LIFTS ME UP

My feet have slipped
And
I have not held out my arms;
Yet
The Compassion of my Lord
 Supreme
Lifts me up.

My life of aspiration
Has been lost in the world
Of hallucination and temptation
And
My heart is empty of cries and
 sorrow;
Yet
The Compassion of my Lord
 Supreme
Lifts me up.

484. MY LORD SAYS

I have just begun my long journey
With my first step.
Look,
My Lord says that
I have far advanced on the path.

I have just begun to meditate
In the early hours of the morning.
Look,
My Lord says that
My Goal no longer remains
A far cry.

485. DON'T YOU WORRY!

True, your mind is a rebel.
But don't you worry!
God is determined
To convert your unruly mind
Into a perfectly disciplined child.

True, your life is ignorance-reality.
But don't you worry!
God is determined
To teach you to swim
Across the sea of
   Perfection-reality.

486. THE INDISPENSABLES

Silence is indispensable,
For silence is concentrated power.

Joy is indispensable,
For joy is meditative light.

Love is indispensable,
For love is contemplative oneness.

487. PERHAPS THEY NEED IT

Who needs a disciplined life?
Perhaps my body needs it.

Who needs a purified life?
Perhaps my vital needs it.

Who needs an expanded life?
Perhaps my mind needs it.

Who needs a surrendered life?
Perhaps my heart needs it.

488. EMOTION

In the body
Emotion is self-indulgence.

In the vital
Emotion is self-temptation.

In the mind
Emotion is self-mortification.

In the heart
Emotion is self-expansion.

489. NO HAPPINESS THERE

Don't be in love with machinery.
There is no happiness there.

Don't be in love with money.
There is no happiness there.

Be in love with your heart-life.
There, only there,
Is the flood of happiness.

490. YOU FEEL, YOU HEAR, YOU SEE

You feel.
What do you feel?
You feel God's Presence.

You hear.
What do you hear?
You hear God's Voice.

You see.
What do you see?
You see God's Face.

When you feel,
God is pleased with you.
When you hear,
God is proud of you.
When you see,
God is ready to garland you.

491. WHO?

Who applauds you?
He who longs to imitate you.

Who stones you?
He who knows
That you are far beyond his
imitation.

Who loves you?
He who wants to know you.

Who hates you?
He who wants you
To be ignorant of him.

492. SPIRITUALITY

Who told you
That spirituality
Is a compartment
Totally cut off
From the activity-flow?
Who told you
That spirituality
Is not life-blossoming?
I tell you
Once and for all:
Spirituality is activity-flow,
Spirituality is life-blossoming,
Plus
Spirituality is God-becoming.

493. GURU AND DISCIPLE

What is a Guru?
A Guru is he who devours
The ignorance-sea of his disciple.

What is a disciple?
A disciple is he who swims
In the wisdom-sea of his Guru.

What is a Guru?
A Guru is he who finds himself
In the soul of his disciple.

What is a disciple?
A disciple is he who loses himself
In the heart of his Guru.

494. ARISE IN FAITH!

Arise in faith!
Earth will give you
All its love.

Arise in faith!
Heaven will give you
All its joy.

Arise in faith!
God will give you
All His Freedom.

Arise in faith!
You will realise
That you are not only in all,
Of all and for all,
But also
You are ALL.

495. YOU WILL BE STRONGER

Fight injustice.
Your soul will be stronger.
Combat wrong.
Your heart will be stronger.
Oppose doubt.
Your mind will be stronger.
Abjure domination.
Your vital will be stronger.
Serve truth.
Your body will be stronger.

496. YOUR MAIN OBSTACLE

What was your main obstacle?
Your animal hunger.
What is your main obstacle?
Your human pride.
What will be your main obstacle?
Your fear of total surrender.

497. YOUR PEERLESS TREASURE

What was your peerless treasure?
Your silver faith.
What is your peerless treasure?
Your golden love.
What will be your peerless
treasure?
Your diamond oneness.

498. A MAN OF PRINCIPLE

I was a man of ideas,
But my ideas were
Uncertain and vague.

I was a man of ideals,
But my ideals were
Blind and selfish.

Now that I have become
A man of principle,
My ideas faithfully serve me
And
My ideals soulfully elevate me.

499. GOD NEEDS ONLY YOU

Transform your desire-night
Into aspiration-light.
Do not desert your good God.
Remember, God needs only you,
And nobody else.

Transform your aspiration-light
Into Perfection-height.
Do not disappoint your good God.
Remember, God needs only you
And nobody else.

500. PERHAPS WE BOTH ARE RIGHT

You say
He has a sharpened mind.
I say
He has a darkened mind.
Perhaps we both are right.

You say
His heart is all love for humanity.
I say
His heart is all love for Divinity.
Perhaps we both are right.

You say
His soul is of God.
I say
His soul is for God.
This time no "perhaps";
We both are unmistakably right.

501. GIVE AND SURRENDER

Give! Grasp not!
You will reach far beyond
Your grasp.

Surrender! Demand not!
Your achievement will far surpass
Your imagination-sky.

502. WHEN ALL ELSE HAS PASSED AWAY

When all else has passed away
Your imagination-dreamer
Will remain with you.

When all else has passed away
Your inspiration-runner
Will remain with you.

When all else has passed away
Your aspiration-climber
Will remain with you.

When all else has passed away
Your realisation-diver
Will remain with you.

503. MY ANCIENT PROMISE

Lord, You are with me;
Therefore,
I am not afraid
Of the darkening and frightening
clouds
In my mind.

Lord, You are with me;
Therefore,
I am ready
To brave the storms
In my heart.

Lord, You are with me;
Therefore,
I shall be worthy
Of my ancient promise to You:
Love-manifestation
In the core of my body-life.

504. GOD'S DREAM-REALITY

I think
I am an animal,
And I mean it.
God declares
I am another God.
Who is right?
We both are right.

God lives in the Dream-Reality
Of His Perfection-light.
I live in the reality-dream
Of my destruction-night.

505. SLOWLY AND QUICKLY

Slowly
Descend to the level of dust.

Quickly
Ascend to the heights of Heaven.

Carefully
Run to the farthest corner of the
outer world.

Smilingly
Dive into the deepest depths of
the inner world.

506. BECAUSE OF YOU

Lord, You love me proudly;
Therefore
You are on my lips
Always.

Lord, I love You devotedly;
Therefore
I am on Your Lips
Always.

Lord, because of me
Your Boat may sink.
"Son, because of you
My Boat will sail
Steadily,
Unerringly,
And
Supremely."

507. ACCEPT WHAT COMES

Don't pick, don't choose;
Accept what comes!
If you devotedly
Accept what comes,
Then in the heart of your world
history
You unmistakably shall become
What God eternally is.

508. PROGRESSION

What isolates, divides.
What divides, tempts.
What tempts, frustrates.
What frustrates, destroys.
What destroys, fails.
What fails, conceals.
What conceals, is exposed.
What is exposed, surrenders.
What surrenders, becomes
The future God.

509. MANIFESTATION

All manifestation
In the outer world
Is an imitation-fool
And
A limitation-cave.

All manifestation
In the inner world
Is a perfection-light
And
A satisfaction-smile.

510. EXPRESS AND SUBLIMATE

Express, do not suppress.
If you suppress,
Your destruction will be drawing
nigh.

Sublimate, do not eradicate.
If you eradicate,
You may die before you reach
Your Perfection-Goal.

511. WHAT THEY TELL ME

My desire-night tells me
What I can easily do.

My aspiration-light tells me
What I can eventually become.

My Realisation-Perfection tells me
What I eternally am.

512. LOVE, SERVE AND SURRENDER

Love God.
You will be able
To go to God.

Serve God.
God will definitely
Come to you.

Surrender to God.
God will offer you
Unmistakably
His transcendental Throne.

513. WHO AM I?

Who am I?
A poor singer.
Who am I?
A poor poet.
Who am I?
A poor seeker.
Who am I?
A rich lover of God.

514. PURE THINKING

Pure thinking is not escaping
But
Self-offering.

Pure thinking is not observation
But
Self-transformation.

Pure thinking is not
experimentation
But
Self-perfection.

Pure thinking is not God-fearing
But
God-becoming.

515. WHICH MASTER DO YOU NEED?

Which Master do you need?
The one who advises you?

Which Master do you need?
The one who instructs you?

Which Master do you need?
The one who transmits Light?

Which Master do you need?
The one who liberates you?

Which Master do you need?
The one who makes you another
God?

Make your own choice.
You are at perfect liberty.

516. HELP ME, LORD

Lord, I am short
But You are very tall.
I long to reach Your Height;
So, help me, Lord.

Lord, I am weak
But You are very strong.
I long to plumb Your Strength;
So, help me, Lord.

Lord, I have a low role
But You are a very high Goal.
I long to become the Goal;
So, help me, Lord.

517. I AM NOW SO PROUD OF YOU

O my heart,
Since when have you freed
yourself
From the strains and stresses of
life?
I am now so proud of you.
You are really great.

O my mind,
Since when have you freed
yourself
From doubt and pride?
I am now so proud of you.
You are really great.

O my vital,
Since when have you freed
yourself
From dust and din?
I am now so proud of you.
You are really great.

O my body,
Since when have you freed
yourself
From fear and indolence?
I am now so proud of you.
You are really great.

518. MY LOVE OF GOD

My morning love of God
Liberates me from the frets
And fevers of life.

My afternoon love of God
Protects me from world-dangers
And world-tragedies.

My evening love of God
Inspires me to stand
On the battlefield of life
To distribute the Breath of God.

519. ALL SHOW

A simple heart knows
All show is a faded flower.

A sincere heart knows
All show is a deceased truth.

A loving heart knows
All show is a forgotten God.

520. FOUR DEATH BLOWS

Insecurity is slow death.
Pride is quick death.
Doubt is sheer death.
Ingratitude is all death.

521. WHAT AM I GOING TO DO WITH YOU?

You love noise-sea;
You fear Silence-sky.
What am I going to do with you?

You want the power-world;
You need the Love-God.
What am I going to do with you?

You shirk duty;
You want God-perfection.
What am I going to do with you?

522. I SERVE THREE FLAGS

With my love-smile
I serve the flag of humanity.

With my devotion-concern
I serve the flag of divinity.

With my surrender-oneness
I serve the Flag of the Supreme.

523. LEARN, LOVE AND BECOME

Learn more.
Grow quickly
In the Heart of God.

Love more.
Glow divinely
In the soul of man.

Become more.
Flow supremely
In the Perfection-goal of the Supreme.

524. I TELL YOU

Don't be in anguish.
I tell you,
God does care for you.

Don't be in travail.
I tell you,
God does love you.

Don't be in despair.
I tell you,
God does need you.

Don't be in stupidity.
I tell you,
God does live for you,
For you alone.

525. HUMAN NATURE

He loves
What he ignores.
He utilises
What he refuses.
He glorifies
What he challenges.
He blesses
What he breaks.
He becomes
What he devours.

526. SILENCE

Silence frightens your heart.
I feel sorry for you.

Silence awakens his heart.
I am proud of him.

Silence widens his heart.
I am all gratitude to him.

Silence illumines his heart.
I am all surrender to him.

527. THE PLACE

My heart is my secret place
To treasure God.

My soul is my sacred place
To welcome mankind.

My life is my perfect place
To flower in Divinity.

528. MIND AND HEART

Where is my mind?
Inside the wide hunger
Of one thousand miles
Of wild clouds.

Where is my heart?
On the top of Mount Everest.
What is it doing over there?
It is singing the song
Of my Lord's Compassion-light
And
My life's ingratitude-night.

529. MY LIFE CARRIES THE SUNRISE

You want to know
What my life of hope does.
My life carries the sunrise.

You want to know
What my heart of despair does.
My heart carries the sunset.

You want to know
What my mind of doubt does.
My mind carries the night.

530. MY LIFE'S REALITY-SHORE

My life's sunrise sings,
My life's sunset clings,
My life's Heaven beckons me,
My life's earth constantly needs
  me,
My life's dream-boat sails,
My life's Reality-shore smiles.

531. WHAT CAN GOD DO?

A thousand lives
And no aspiration!
What can God do?

A thousand bodies
And no service!
What can God do?

A thousand souls
And no promise!
What can God do?

532. EVERYWHERE

Everywhere
My heart cries.

Everywhere
My mind flies.

Everywhere
My vital tries.

Everywhere
My body sighs.

533. MORNING DREAM AND EVENING REALITY

My morning dream:
I can and shall see God today,
I can and shall fulfil God today,
I can and shall become
Another God today.

My evening reality:
I am the emperor of depression,
I am the king of frustration,
I am the prince of destruction.

534. I SEE THE BOATMAN FAST APPROACHING

O orphan-boat of my heart,
Do not stop;
Sail on.
I see my Lord, the Boatman
  supreme,
Fast approaching you.

O orphan-cave of my life,
Do not cry,
Do not sigh.
I see my Lord, the Saviour
  supreme,
Coming to visit you.

535. BIRD OF PERFECTION

O bird of Time,
When were you born?
O bird of Life,
Where were you born?
O bird of Light,
How were you born?
O bird of Night,
Why were you born?
O Bird of Perfection,
Will you ever be born?

536. ARE YOU SURE?

Silence, are you sure
That you are the seed of my life?

Aspiration, are you sure
That you are the plant of my life?

Realisation, are you sure
That you are the tree of my life?

Revelation, are you sure
That you are the flower of my life?

Perfection, are you sure
That you are the fruit of my life?

537. LIVING FOR HOPE

When I was living
For the body of hope,
I doubted God's Compassion.

When I was living
For the heart of hope,
I doubted God's Concern.

When I was living
For the soul of hope,
I doubted my own aspiration.

538. I AM REALLY CONCERNED

I have seen the black wings of
death.
Believe me, I was not frightened.

I have seen the white wings of
Heaven.
Believe me, I was not elated.

I have seen the red wings of earth.
Believe me, I am really concerned.

539. DO YOU WANT HAPPINESS?

Do you want happiness?
Then step out of your life's
proclamation,
Your life's shameless procession,
Your life's thoughtless
protestation,
Your life's purposeless
procrastination.

Do you want happiness?
Then step into your life's
imagination,
Your life's silver inspiration,
Your life's golden aspiration,
Your life's diamond dedication.

540. EACH SOUL HAS WINGS

Each soul has wings.
It won't stay long on earth.
But you effectively delay its
departure
With your aspiration-light.

Each soul has wings.
It won't stay long in Heaven.
But you can easily delay its
earthbound journey
With your Realisation-might.

541. ENOUGH

My body declares:
A little is enough.

My vital declares:
What is enough?

My mind declares:
Where is enough?

My heart declares:
Here is enough.

My soul declares:
Nothing is enough.

My God declares:
My child, for Me
You are more than enough.

542. TO SEE THE DANCE

I have returned
To the confines of the world.
Why?
Just to see the dance
Of my Infinity's Height
In the chasm
Of mortality's futility-night.

543. THEREFORE I AM ON EARTH

Heaven-beauty feeds me;
Therefore
I am on earth.

Earth-duty employs me;
Therefore
I am on earth.

God-necessity perfects me;
Therefore
I am on earth.

544. O BLOOM OF DAWN

O bloom of dawn,
You are so beautiful.

O gloom of evening,
You are so doubtful.

O boom of night,
You are so meaningful.

O doom of death,
You are so baneful.

545. ALL THAT WE ARE

O Lord of Compassion,
All that we are
Is because of You.

O Lord of Concern,
All that we are
Is for You.

O Lord of Love,
All that we are
Is You, is You.

546. FOLLOW THEM

Follow the stars;
They will inspire you.
You do need the stars.

Follow the moon;
She will feed you.
You do need the moon.

Follow the sun;
He will guide you.
You do need the sun.

547. YOUR SILENCE

Your silence proves
That you are either
An ignorance-sea
Or
A Knowledge-sky.

If your silence indicates
God is for others' use,
Then you are an ignorance-sea.
If your silence indicates
You want God and God alone,
Then you are a Knowledge-sky.

548. HER LIFE IS A SEA

In the morning
Her life is a sea of silence-love.
The world sits at her feet.

In the afternoon
Her life is a sea of silence-light.
The world sports in her heart.

In the evening
Her life is a sea of silence-bliss.
The world sleeps in her eyes.

549. THE ESSENCE

The essence of my yesterdays:
Old bundles of sleep.

The essence of my today:
New bundles of hope.

The essence of my tomorrows:
Heavy bundles of uncertainty.

550. WHEN FREEDOM EMBRACES ME

When the freedom of Heaven
Embraces me,
Speechless I remain.

When the freedom of earth
Embraces me,
Consciousness I regain.

When the Freedom of God
Embraces me,
Perfection I attain.

551. WAITING FOR YOU

O body, my body,
Don't sleep any more.
Look, Vision-God is waiting for
you!

O vital, my vital,
Don't remain spiritless any more.
Look, Energy-God is waiting for
you!

O mind, my mind,
Don't doubt any more.
Look, Perfection-God is waiting
for you!

O heart, my heart,
Don't cry any more.
Look, Satisfaction-God is waiting
for you!

552. THREE LESSONS

Self-abnegation teaches me
I do not need earth-life.

Self-purification teaches me
I need God's living Breath in
Heaven.

Self-realisation teaches me
Earth-life I need to please God;
Heaven-life I need to please
myself.

553. I HATE THOSE LIARS

I hate my yesterday
Because
She told me a dark lie.
She told me that God-life
Is not meant for me.

I hate my today
Because
She has told me a serious lie.
She has told me that
God-realisation
Is not meant for me.

I hate my tomorrow
Because
She is telling me a stupid lie.
She is telling me that there is
And there can be
No God
For an idle fellow like me.

554. YOU ALONE KNOW WHAT LOVE IS

Lord, Your Speech is simple.
Therefore
I like You.

Lord, Your Philosophy is sublime.
Therefore
I love You.

Lord, Your Sacrifice is constant.
Therefore
I adore You.

Lord, You alone know what love is.
Therefore
I need You, only You.

555. LIGHT IS PRECIOUS

Precious,
Light is precious.

Spacious,
Life is spacious.

Gracious,
Truth is gracious.

Voracious,
Falsehood is voracious.

Sagacious,
Heart is sagacious.

Glorious,
Faith is glorious.

Dangerous,
Hate is dangerous.

Conscious,
Love is conscious.

556. HER PRESENCE

Her presence
Is always treasured.

Her smile
Is always adored.

Her silence
Is always garlanded.

Her compassion
Is always crowned.

557. MY EGO, MY LOVE

My ego feeds
Earth-reality.
My ego binds
Heaven-dream.
My love pilots
Earth-aspiration.
My love manifests
Heaven-realisation.

558. GOD IS ALL FOR YOU

Are you a fighter?
Then God's Banner is for you.

Are you a dreamer?
Then God's Arbour is for you.

Are you a sacrificer?
Then God's Nectar is for you.

Are you a lover?
Then God is all for you,
Only for you.

559. IF YOU ARE SUPREME

If you are great,
Then show me your face.
I want to examine your face.

If you are good,
Then show me your eyes.
I want to examine your eyes.

If you are divine,
Then show me your heart.
I want to examine your heart.

But
If you are supreme,
Then examine me.
I shall definitely
Equal you.
Just give me a chance,
That's all.

560. DO ME A FAVOUR

If you are the Earth-Mother,
Then do me a favour.
Give me, please, Your
  patience-tree.

If you are the Heaven-Father,
Then do me a favour.
Give me, please, Your
  Knowledge-fruit.

If you are the Saviour-God,
Then do me a favour.
Give me, please, Your
  Oneness-banner.

561. LESSONS YOU HAVE LEARNT

Life is beautiful.
This lesson you have learnt
From your temptation-teacher.

Light is beautiful.
This lesson you have learnt
From your aspiration-teacher.

Delight is beautiful.
This lesson you have learnt
From your perfection-teacher.

562. BEGGARS

Yesterday's beggars:
Man and his greed.

Today's beggars:
God and His Needs.

Tomorrow's beggars:
God the Perfection-lover,
And
Man the ignorance-devourer.

563. MY GIFTS

Yesterday
I gave You, Lord,
My life's bitter defeat.

Today
I give You, Lord,
My soul's glorious victory.

Tomorrow
I shall give You, Lord,
My heart's oneness-goal.

564. THE HEIGHT AND DEPTH OF EARTH-LIFE

I touch the feet
Of Silence-light
To scale the height
Of earth-life.

I touch the head
Of sound-pride
To plumb the abyss
Of earth-life.

565. MY DIFFERENT FRIENDS

Doubt, do you know
Who you are?
You are my fleeting friend.

Faith, do you know
Who you are?
You are my bleeding friend.

Life, do you know
Who you are?
You are my searching friend.

Love, do you know
Who you are?
You are my illumining friend,
You are my eternal friend,
You are my God-Friend.

566. HER HEART

Green as young grass
Her heart is;
Therefore, she runs to the farthest
Beyond.

Blue as the vast sky
Her heart is;
Therefore, she flies into the
farthest Beyond.

Red as the morning sun
Her heart is;
Therefore, she illumines the
world without.

White as Himalayan snow
Her heart is;
Therefore, she feeds the world
within.

567. WHEN I LOVE

When I love desire-night,
I fail God.
When desire-night loves me,
Truth-love forgets me.

When I love aspiration-light,
God-Beauty envelops me.
When aspiration-light loves me,
God-height claims me.

568. TWO THINGS HE DOES

Two things, only two things,
He does:
He breathes in the perfume
Of God-promise
To Mother Earth;
He breathes out the odour
Of frustration-reality
To Father Heaven.

569. PERFECTION-BANNER YOU OFFER

Truth-banner you own;
Therefore
You are great.

Light-banner you hold;
Therefore
You are great.

Perfection-banner you offer;
Therefore
You are great,
You are good,
You are divine,
You are supreme.

570. MY LORD GOD IS MISSING

If you are wakeful
Then look around with me,
Help me.
My Lord God is missing.

If you are soulful
Then look within my heart,
Help me.
My Lord God is missing.

If you are blissful
Then look up with me,
Help me.
My Lord God is missing.

571. MY EVENING SONG

My morning song was:
How far to go?
Far have I to go!

My afternoon song was:
Can I reach my Goal?
I can and I shall
Reach my Goal!

My evening song is:
Have I reached my Goal?
I have not only reached my Goal
But
Far transcended my Goal!
I desired to touch His Feet
But
My Lord has made me feel His
Heart.

572. HOW IS IT?

Soul, my soul, how is it that
Your power is so mysterious?

Heart, my heart, how is it that
Your power is so soulful?

Mind, my mind, how is it that
Your power is so immense?

Vital, my vital, how is it that
Your power is so intense?

Body, my body, how is it that
Your power is so dubious?

573. WHAT I CALL IT

Some call it evolution,
While others call it
man-transformation.
I call it God-perfection.

Some call it aspiration,
While others call it man-cry.
I call it God-smile.

Some call it realisation,
While others call it reality-life.
I call it God-satisfaction.

574. WHERE ARE YOU?

Oblivion, stay where you are.
Don't come near me!

O my remembrance-friend, where
are you?
I need you immediately.

O my aspiration-friend, where are
you?
I need you constantly.

O my realisation-friend, where are
you?
I need you eternally.

575. O MORNING OF ETERNITY

O Morning of Eternity,
I love your silence-face.

O Morning of Infinity,
I love your sound-arms.

O Morning of Immortality,
I love your perfection-heart.

576. THE CALL

Yesterday
My vital enjoyed
The tempter's call.

Today
My mind enjoys
The doubter's call.

Tomorrow
My heart shall enjoy
The lover's call.

The day after tomorrow
My body shall enjoy
My Father's Call.

577. TWO SWORDS

Aspiration-flame
Is the sword
That separates Knowledge-Light
And
Ignorance-night.

Realisation-sun
Is the sword
That unites the cry of the finite
And
The Smile of the Infinite.

578. OUR DEVOTION

Your devotion-seed
Loves a holy face.

His devotion-tree
Salutes a holy life.

My devotion-fruit
Becomes a holy heart.

579. PAY MORE ATTENTION TO IT

God loves your earth-body;
Therefore
Pay more attention to it.

God loves your Heaven-soul;
Therefore
Pay more attention to it.

God loves your Immortality-goal;
Therefore
Pay more attention to it.

580. YOU ARE PERFECT, TOO

Are you calm?
Then you are confident, too.

Are you confident?
Then you are progressive, too.

Are you progressive?
Then you are instrumental, too.

Are you instrumental?
Then you are perfect, too.

581. SILENCE AND SOUND

Silence, silence,
My Lord is coming.

Sound, sound,
My Lord is going.

Silence, silence,
My Lord is returning.

Sound, sound,
My Lord is perfecting.

Silence, silence,
My Lord is enjoying.

Sound, sound,
My Lord is becoming.

582. FIRE AND WATER

O march of fire,
My heart longs for
Your determination-blood.
Do share with me
Your aspiration-height.

O march of water,
My vital longs for
Your expansion-flood.
Do share with me
Your consciousness-light.

583. I SALUTE

I salute earth
Because
She tries and cries.

I salute Heaven
Because
He dreams and smiles.

I salute man
Because
He sows and grows.

I salute God
Because
He divinely has,
He supremely is.

584. THEY LONG FOR SILENCE

My body longs for
Loving silence.

My vital longs for
Daring silence.

My mind longs for
Thoughtless silence.

My heart longs for
Soundless silence.

My soul longs for
Worldless silence.

My God longs for
Breathless Silence.

585. THE DANCE

The dance of the sea
Inspires me to be dauntless.

The dance of the sky
Inspires me to be sorrowless.

The dance of the moon
Inspires me to be guileless.

The dance of the sun
Inspires me to be selfless.

The dance of the earth
Inspires me to be sleepless.

The dance of Heaven
Inspires me to be thoughtless.

The dance of man
Inspires me to be soulless.

The dance of God
Inspires me to be deathless,
Also soundless.

586. YOU WILL BE HAPPY

Speak without words.
You will be happy.

Dedicate without proclaiming.
You will be happy.

Love without being loved.
You will be happy.

Surrender without being
  subjugated.
You will be happy.

Become without being known,
without being caught,
without being sought.
You will be happy.

587. I STAND ON THE BALCONY OF LIGHT

I stand
On the balcony of Light
To brave Satan's death-dart.

I stand
On the balcony of Peace
To devour the hungry, war-mad
  world.

588. THEY LISTEN TO ME

The morning-silence
Listens to me;
Therefore
I am so pure.

The noon-sound
Listens to me;
Therefore
I am so sure.

The evening-light
Listens to me;
Therefore
I am never obscure,
I am never neglected,
I am never rejected,
And
My heart-love has become
What my soul-life eternally is.

589. I AM PROUD

Lord, I am proud to be
Your servant.
You allow me to touch Your Feet.

Lord, I am proud to be
Your child.
You allow me to dine with You.

Lord, I am proud to be
Your comrade.
You allow me to sport with You.

Lord, I am proud to be
Your lower self.
You allow me to worship You.

590. MY BONDS ARE BROKEN

My earth-bonds are snapped;
Therefore
I can go to Heaven
And rest and dream.

My Heaven-bonds are severed.
This realisation has dawned on me
In my own way;
Therefore
I can go to earth
To please my Lord Supreme –
To please Him
In His own Way,
Unlike the Heaven-hungry souls.

591. CRY

O Compassion supreme,
I cry
When I see You.

O Tyrant supreme,
I cry
When I cannot avoid You.

O Nectar supreme,
I cry
When I love You.

O Indifference supreme,
I cry
When I cannot love You.

O Awareness supreme,
I cry
When You love me.

O Forgetfulness supreme,
I cry
When You do not love me.

592. O MY PATIENCE

O my patience-heart,
Because of you
Today I own Liberation-sky.

O my patience-life,
Because of you
Today I own Perfection-world.

O my patience-God,
Because of You
Today I own Satisfaction-goal.

593. FREEDOM

Freedom burdened:
Indeed,
This is what
My poor mind enjoys.

Freedom unburdened:
Indeed,
This is what
My serving heart enjoys.

Freedom birthless and deathless:
Indeed,
This is what
My wise soul enjoys.

594. PROMISE BLUE, PROMISE GREEN

O earth-kingdom,
Don't suffer.
To you I offer
My promise blue:
My heart shall help you ascend
And touch God's
Transcendental Height.

O Heaven-kingdom,
Don't suffer.
To you I offer
My promise green:
My soul shall help you descend
And feel God's
Bottomless Depth.

595. EARTH-DOOR AND HEAVEN-GATE

Earth-door
Naked we knock.

Heaven-gate
Nameless we knock.

Earth-door
Offers us its peerless treasure:
A ceaseless cry.

Heaven-gate
Offers us its ceaseless treasure:
The dream of the Beyond.

596. ALL ARE EAGER (I)

My deer is eager
To win for me.

My horse is eager
To dive for me.

My bull is eager
To fight for me.

My dog is eager
To wait for me.

My cow is eager
To illumine for me.

My lion is eager
To roar for me.

My God is eager
To smile for me.

597. ALL ARE EAGER (II)

My rabbit is eager
To jump for me.

My tiger is eager
To devour for me.

My giraffe is eager
To reach for me.

My turtle is eager
To die for me.

My monkey is eager
To climb for me.

My swan is eager
To realise for me.

My cat is eager
To cry for me.

My camel is eager
To carry for me.

My elephant is eager
To brave for me.

598. FOR MY SAKE

O restless mind,
When will you stop
Beating your wings?
Stop for my sake at least,
Please.

O heedless heart,
When will you start
Unsealing your ears?
Start for my sake at least,
Please.

599. WHEN SHE SMILES

When she thinks,
Teeming stars dance
With Light.

When she wills,
The Supreme sports
With His highest Height.

When she smiles,
The Creator and the creation
Are at once fulfilled.

600. A CAVE OF MY OWN

O my heart,
I have a sky of my own.
I want you to fly
From end to end.

O my mind,
I have an ocean of my own.
I want you to swim
From end to end.

O my sweet Lord,
I have a cave of my own.
I want You to walk
From end to end.

601. MY EXAMINERS

My heart of sincerity
Has examined my previous years.

My mind of clarity
Examines my present years.

My life of dedication
Shall examine my earthbound
years.

My goal of realisation
Shall examine my Heaven-free
years.

602. THEY ARE BEYOND

Her soul is beyond
Silence-Light.

Her heart is beyond
Beauty's life.

Her mind is beyond
Intuition-flight.

Her vital is beyond
Purity's goal.

Her body is beyond
Humanity's soul.

603. HOW CAN IT BE OTHERWISE?

Nothing to complain,
Nothing to criticise.
God's world is nice;
How can it be otherwise?

Nothing to suffer,
Nothing to compromise.
God's world is another paradise;
How can it be otherwise?

604. I LOVE THE FEET OF MORNING

I love the feet of morning
Because of their supernal purity.

I love the feet of noon
Because of their habitual surety.

I love the feet of evening
Because of their perpetual duty.

I love the feet of night
Because of their eternal beauty.

605. YOUR SOUL'S SPLENDOUR

Your soul's ancient splendour
Of God-revelation
Has sunk.
Yet you are quite cheerful.

Your body's modern splendour
Of ignorance-manifestation
Has arisen.
Yet you are not doleful.

606. IN MY DREAMS

In my old dream
I saw the face of beauty.

In my new dream
I feel the arms of duty.

In my forthcoming dream
I shall achieve the pride of
Divinity.

607. LOOK AT THEM!

Two greedy eyes
Want to devour
God's infinite Love.
Look at their stupid audacity!

Two speedy feet
Want to reach
God's endless Goal.
Look at their deplorable stupidity!

One needy heart
Wants to feel God's
Compassion-flood.
Look at its miserable incapacity!

608. WE HAVE FAILED

You have tried to break
Death's control.
Alas, you have badly failed.

He has tried to fathom
A love-sea.
Alas, he has sadly failed.

I have tried to build
A gratitude-cottage.
Alas, I have hopelessly failed.

609. YESTERDAY, TODAY, TOMORROW

O greedy yesterday,
Do not follow me, please.
It is not nice to follow someone
Without his permission.

O speedy today,
Do not be a deer, please.
Please be a tortoise.
Have you forgotten the
unforgettable maxim:
"Slow and steady wins the race"?

O my tardy tomorrow,
How long do you want me to wait
for you?
"Time and tide wait for no man".
Hasten your arrival, please,
If your compassion-breath at all
cares for my life.

610. GOD AND HIS DAUGHTER

My sincerity speaks:
God, I need You.
God's sincerity speaks:
"Daughter, I need you
More than you need Me."
Father, why?
Why do You need me
More than I need You?
"Daughter,
My daughter,
I need you more than you need Me
Because I know what you really
 are:
On earth you are My only hope,
In Heaven you are My only
 promise."

611. COME, MY FRIENDS

Faith, my quiet friend,
Come, let me feel your
 flower-heart.

Courage, my secret friend,
Come, let me see your
 determination.

Love, my sacred friend,
Come, let me see your
 perfection-goal.

612. WHAT GOD CAN MAKE OF ME

I saw what I could be:
God-heights.

I see what I cannot be:
World-nights.

I shall see what God can make of
 me:
A deserted soul
Or
A perfected God.

613. THREE QUESTIONS

Answer me three questions.

This is a cruel question:
How is it that you are not
Another God?

This is a friendly question:
How have you pleased God
So quickly and so completely?

This is an unanswerable question,
But I wish you to try:
Did God tell you
When He is going to make me
The first perfect man and
Another perfect God?

614. NOBODY NEEDS HIM

He is in a vast desert;
Nobody needs him.

He is in a dense forest;
Nobody needs him.

He is in a shoreless sea;
Nobody needs him.

He is in high Heaven;
Ah, everybody needs him
Or
At least wants him.

615. I SHALL MAINTAIN MY LOVE

With humanity's cry
I shall maintain
My inseparable love.

With divinity's smile
I shall maintain
My undivided love.

With God's Dream
I shall maintain
My constant love.

616. NO PEACE

My
Earth has no peace
Because
I am restless.

My
Heaven has no peace
Because
I am listless.

My
God has no peace
Because
I am faithless.

617. YES, I HAVE ONE

Yes, I have a soul,
But right now
It is all shattered.

Yes, I have a heart,
But right now
It is all battered.

Yes, I have a life,
But right now
It is worse than a sheep.

Yes, I have a God,
But right now
He is fast asleep.

618. GOOD FRIENDS

Expectation and I
Were once good friends.

Surrender and I
Have become good friends.

Eternity's Infinity,
Infinity's Immortality
And I
Are soon going to be good friends.

Who says so?
God!
Who believes it?
The God in Heaven,
The God in my heart.

619. GOD HAS DESCENDED

God the Compassion
Has descended
To rescue my soul-flow.

God the illumination
Has descended
To rescue my heart-river.

God the Perfection
Has descended
To rescue my life-boat.

620. A BRIEF OBLIVION

My earth-life:
A brief oblivion.

My Heaven-life:
A brief oblivion, too.

My earth-oblivion
Prevents me from seeing
The Face of God.

My Heaven-oblivion
Prevents me from touching
The Feet of God.

621. NO ORDINARY HUMAN BEING

You are no ordinary
Human being.
In you I see
A star of illumination blue.

He is no ordinary
Human being.
In him I see
A moon of compassion green.

And

I am no ordinary
Human being.
In myself I see
A sun of perfection gold.

622. WE WERE NOT PREPARED

You were not prepared
To meet life's shoreless sea.

He was not prepared
To meet the boat without the
pilot.

And

I was not prepared
To touch the goalless shore.

623. FALSE AND TRUE

False!
What is false?
A power-hungry life.

False!
Who is false?
A love-demanding man.

True!
What is true?
A self-giving life.

True!
Who is true?
A God-becoming man.

624. INSEPARABLE

Madness and fearlessness
Are inseparable
In the physical world.

Goodness and selflessness
Are inseparable
In the inner world.

Oneness in many-ness,
Perfection in all-ness
Are inseparable
In God's highest world.

625. ONE DAY

Your thunder-pride,
God will one day break.

Your jealousy-tree,
God will one day fell.

Your doubt-sky,
God will one day rend.

Your insecurity-sea,
God will one day devour.

626. THEY LONG TO FOLLOW YOU

O tears and beggars,
Where are you going?
My heart-life
And
My love-soul
Long to follow you.

O joys and kings,
Where are you going?
My earth-renunciation
And
My Heaven-determination
Long to follow you.

627. HOW CAN I LOVE HIM?

I have always
Longed to love.
But
Whom to love?
Man?
Not worth loving!
God?
Where is He?
How can I love Him
If He denies me
His Presence supreme?

628. PERHAPS MY OLD FRIEND CAN

I have always
Longed to live.
But where?
On earth?
It is not worth living there!
In Heaven?
Where is it?
Does it really exist?
Who can tell me
Where Heaven is?
Perhaps
My old friend,
Hope-flame,
Can.

629. CAPTURED

My earth-life
Is captured
By the ugly anger of the world
And
By the wild hunger of the world.

My Heaven-dream
Is captured
By the bitter frustration of the world
And
By the dire destruction of the world.

630. REMOVE ME

Lord, that I may near You,
Remove me from my fears.

Lord, that I may love You,
Remove me from my tears.

Lord, that I may please You,
Remove me from my desire-life.

Lord, that I may manifest You,
Remove me from my self-love.

631. THEY NEED SILENCE

Soothing silence
My body needs.

Striving silence
My vital needs.

Searching silence
My mind needs.

Illumining silence
My heart needs.

Fulfilling silence
My soul needs.

632. LIGHT AND FAITH

Darkness has vanished
But
Where is light?
O where is light?
Light is in self-giving.

Doubt has vanished
But
Where is faith?
O where is faith?
Faith is in love-becoming.

633. WHEN HE HURLED DEFIANCE

When he hurled defiance
At ignorance,
Ignorance refused to surrender.

When he hurled defiance
At darkness,
Darkness hesitated to surrender.

When he hurled defiance
At falsehood,
Falsehood ran away.

When he hurled defiance
At death,
Death immediately surrendered.

634. I NEED

Lord, I need
The Infinity of Thy Love.
I need
To feed my hungry heart.

Lord, I need
The Eternity of Thy Silence.
I need
To quench my thirsty mind.

Lord, I need
The Immortality of Thy Life.
I need
To free my world from
ignorance-dream.

635. FLOWER-SONGS OF MORNING

Flower-songs of morning
Make my life pure.

Fire-songs of noon
Make my life sure.

Rainbow-songs of evening
Make my life leap.

Star-songs of night
Make my life fly.

636. I LOVE MY SERVANT

I love my silence-servant.
Devotedly he feeds my mind.

I love my sound-servant.
Dauntlessly he feeds my vital.

I love my Heaven-servant.
Carefully he feeds my heart.

I love my earth-servant.
Unconditionally he feeds my
body.

637. GOD'S BIRTHLESS SONG

My life started
With God's birthless Song.
My life shall end
With God's endless Dance.

In God's Song
I saw man the future God.
In God's Dance
I saw God the eternal man.

638. I LONG TO BE SILENCE

Great is truth;
Therefore
I long to be truth.

Good is love;
Therefore
I long to be love.

Divine is sound;
Therefore
I long to be sound.

Supreme is silence;
Therefore
I long to be silence.

639. THE BEGINNING OF EARTH-EMANCIPATION

Your inner life
Is the island of light.
Your outer life
Is the sunshine of smile.
Your God-life
Is the beginning
Of earth-emancipation
And
Earth-perfection.

640. A KING OF PERFECTION-LOVE

You were a king
Of aspiration-flames;
Therefore,
You were a king
Of renunciation-life;
Therefore,
You were great.
BUT
Now you have become a king
Of Perfection-love;
Therefore,
You are good.

641. YOUR FLATTERERS

Earth-mirror
Flatters you, your body.

Heaven-dream
Flatters you, your vital.

Life-responsibility
Flatters you, your mind.

Death-insincerity
Flatters you, your heart.

God-necessity
Flatters you, your soul.

642. HOW THEY DIFFER

The difference
Between
My heart and my mind:
My heart is creation-light;
My mind is confusion-night.

The difference
Between
My vital and my body:
My vital wants to roar;
My body wants to snore.

The difference
Between
My God and my soul:
My God wanders;
My soul wonders.

643. A REAL SURPRISE

His earth-life
Is a real surprise.
He has made himself
Smaller than atom-life.

His Heaven-life
Is a real surprise.
He has become
The best God-dreamer.

His God-life
Is a real surprise.
He and God
Sit on the same throne;
He and God
Complement each other.

644. THEY HAVE FOUND THEMSELVES

Beauty has found herself
In love.

Love has found herself
In duty.

Duty has found herself
In necessity.

Necessity has found herself
In reality.

Reality has found herself
In perfection.

Perfection has found herself
In satisfaction.

Satisfaction has found herself
In aspiration.

645. MORNING AND EVENING

In the morning
I am an undying hope.
In the evening
I am a broken heart.

In the morning,
Short is my road.
In the evening,
Endless is my road.

In the morning
God is within my vision's range.
In the evening
God is nowhere to be found.
Indeed,
I am in the flow
Of contradiction-confusion sea.

646. O TEARS OF EARTH

O tears of earth,
I am for you,
Always for you.

O smiles of Heaven,
I think of you,
Always think of you.

O hate of man,
I am not with you,
And shall never be with you.

O love of God,
I am of you,
Always of you.

647. NEVER AND EVER

God has chosen me.
I shall not fail Him.
Never!

Man has chosen me.
I shall love him.
Ever!

Heaven has chosen me.
I shall never speak ill of Heaven.
Never!

Earth has chosen me.
I shall carry earth's burden.
Ever!

648. IN HIS OUTER LIFE

In his outer life
He is a useless abundance.
In his inner life
He is a careless abundance.

In his earth-life
He is a soulless sound.
In his Heaven-life
He is a goalless silence.

649. I NEED THE SHORE

Body, what do you need?
I need the shore of inspiration.

Vital, what do you need?
I need the shore of determination.

Mind, what do you need?
I need the shore of illumination.

Heart, what do you need?
I need the shore of liberation.

Soul, what do you need?
I need the shore of perfect
perfection.

650. GOD ALONE KNOWS

The joy of faith,
God alone knows.
The faith of joy,
Man tries to learn.

The beauty of spirit,
God alone knows.
The spirit of beauty,
Man tries to learn.

651. FOOLISH PRIDE

Yesterday
You were foolishly proud
Of your vital suppression.

Today
You are foolishly proud
Of your mental depression.

Tomorrow
You shall be foolishly proud
Of your psychic frustration.

652. WHEN YOU DOUBT

When you doubt
You are contagious.

When you believe
You are prosperous.

When you love
You are glorious.

When you surrender
You are victorious.

653. MY FAITH-FLOWER

O humanity,
Doubt is my little self.
Don't pay any attention to it.
It will die away very soon.

O divinity,
Faith is my big self.
Do not give up hope,
Be a little more patient.
My faith-flower is blossoming
Petal by petal
For your manifestation-light
Here on earth.

654. THEY ARE WEEPING

Your doubt is weeping
Because
Everybody ignores it.

Your faith is weeping
Because
Everybody suspects it.

Your world is weeping
Because
Everybody ridicules it.

Your God is weeping
Because
Everybody is wedded to stark
falsehood.

655. TO THE CORE

Use your mind.
It is empty to the core.

Use your vital.
It is false to the core.

Use your eye.
It is dangerous to the core.

Use your heart.
It is luminous to the core.

Use your soul.
It is bounteous to the core.

656. RIGHT OF ENTRANCE

Insecurity, this is my heart-home.
You don't have
The right of entrance.

Doubt, this is my mind-home.
You don't have
The right of entrance.

Depression, this is my vital-home.
You don't have
The right of entrance.

657. ALL FOR YOU

Lord, believe me
Once and for all.
Accept my silence-salutation.
It is all for You,
It is all for Your Satisfaction-light.

Lord, believe me
Once and for all.
Accept my sound-salutation.
It is all for You,
It is all for Your
Manifestation-delight.

658. DOUBT-KING, FAITH-QUEEN

O Doubt-king,
No room is left
In my mind-room;
Therefore
Go away,
Go away.
Who wants you?
Who needs you?

O Faith-queen,
Still there is room
In my heart to fill;
Therefore
Come in,
Do come in.
I need you.
God's entire creation needs you.

659. WHEN THEY SPREAD THEIR WINGS

When your aspiration-cry
Spreads its wings,
You will see God's Face
Without fail.

When your devotion-cry
Spreads its wings,
You will feel God's Heart
Without fail.

When your surrender-cry
Spreads its wings,
You will become God's Breath
Without fail.

660. MY RECOMPENSE

Heaven, I spoke ill
Of your vast indifference.
Here is my recompense.
From today on
I shall work to please you
In your own way on earth.

Earth, I spoke ill
Of your great incapacity.
Here is my recompense.
From now on I shall lift you up
Into the world of the Highest
Beyond
Although you are sleeping,
Although you are dreaming,
Although you are demanding.

661. FIRST OF ALL

God the Lover
Must be loved first.

God the Beloved
Must be served first.

God the creation
Must be perfected first.

God the Creator
Must be manifested first.

662. WE ALWAYS REMAIN HAPPY

When I see my Lord Supreme
In the Heaven of Freedom-light,
I tell Him
What I shall really do for Him
On earth.
He believes me;
Therefore
He always remains happy.

When I see my Lord Supreme
In the world of bondage-night,
He tells me
What He will really do for me
In Heaven.
I believe Him;
Therefore
I always remain happy.

663. I LOVE YOUR POWER

Lord,
I love Your Power
Because it perfects me,
My vital darkness-world.

Lord,
I love Your Light
Because it illumines me,
My mental confusion-world.

Lord,
I love Your Delight
Because it fills me,
My psychic receptivity-world.

664. CALM IT, MY FRIEND

I see no difference
Between
Your vital world
And
An angry storm.
Calm it, my friend, calm it.

I see no difference
Between
Your mental world
And
A confusion-sea.
Calm it, my friend, calm it.

I see no difference
Between
Your earthly life
And
A devouring tiger.
Calm it, my friend, calm it.

665. GOD ALWAYS BELIEVES ME

A life of compassion
Is the secret of my heart,
Believe it or not.
I must say,
Unlike you,
God always believes me, my purity.

A life of illumination
Is the secret of my mind,
Believe it or not.
I must say,
Unlike you,
God always believes me, my sincerity.

A life of dedication
Is the secret of my vital,
Believe it or not.
I must say,
Unlike you,
God always believes me, my humility.

A life of perfection
Is the secret of my body,
Believe it or not.
I must say,
Unlike you,
God always believes me, my capacity.

666. THEY WILL BE JEALOUS

I utter not my name
To Heaven's ears
Because
It will be jealous
Of my stupendous sacrifice
On earth.

I utter not my name
To earth's ears
Because
It will be jealous
Of my endless treasure
In Heaven.

667. IN THE DEPTH OF SECRECY

In the depth of earth's secrecy
Two things loom large:
Stark ignorance-night
And
False conviction-pride.

In the depth of Heaven's secrecy
Two things loom large:
Blue Compassion-sea
And
Red Perfection-sun.

668. WHAT I DID INSTEAD

Lord, the day I met You
For the first time,
You asked me
To open my heart on earth
And
Open my mouth in Heaven.
But
What I did, You know,
(Of course You know)
I opened my mouth on earth
Instead,
And I have been planning
To open my heart in Heaven
Instead.
Alas, I am now dancing
With my disobedience-ignorance
And
Deception-perdition.

669. ETERNAL TIME

Nature's total transformation:
Let me leave it
For the moment.
After all, am I not living
In Eternal Time?

God's perfect manifestation:
Let me leave it
For the moment.
After all, why worry,
Since I am living
In God's own Eternal Time?

670. WAITING FOR YOU

Don't look back!
The devouring tiger
Is desperately waiting for you.

Don't look ahead!
The challenging bull
Is dauntlessly waiting for you.

Look within!
Lo, the roaring lion
Is sleeplessly waiting for you.

671. I NEED YOU ETERNALLY

O Compassion-God,
I needed You yesterday.

O Perfection-God,
I shall need You tomorrow.

O Liberation-God,
I need You now.

O Love-God,
I need You immediately,
I need You eternally.

672. THEY WILL NOT FAIL YOU

Trust Divinity.
Divinity will not fail you.
I assure you,
Divinity will give you its heart:
Perfection-smile.

Trust humanity.
Humanity will not fail you.
I assure you,
Humanity will give you its soul:
Perfection-cry.

673. THE GIFT OF PERFECTION

Yesterday
Life-giving earth
Gave me perfection-seed.

Today
Life-transforming earth
Gives me perfection-plant.

Tomorrow
Life-fulfilling earth
Shall give me perfection-tree.

674. PAST AND PRESENT

My past is pathless;
Therefore
I cannot and do not walk
Into the past.

My present is uncertain;
Therefore
I pay no attention to it.
I cannot germinate
In the core of uncertainty.

675. NOT EVEN IN MY DREAMS

I am the seed,
You are the tree.
Who knows this?
God, our mutual lover.
But I am not jealous of you.
Never!
Not even in my dreams.

I am the sand,
You are the land.
Who knows this?
God, our mutual fulfiller.
But I am not jealous of you.
Never!
Not even in my dreams.

676. DEFEAT AND VICTORY

When I accept my defeat,
My human ego dies
And
My divine soul flies.

When I declare my victory,
My divine life fasts
And
My supreme truth starves.

677. MY BANNER-BEARERS

My inner world's
Banner-bearer
Is my ever-increasing poise.

My outer world's
Banner-bearer
Is my ever-roaring noise.

What is poise?
God-light of the Supreme.
What is noise?
Man-might of mortality's futility.

678. HUMAN BIRTH, DIVINE BIRTH

Precious
Is human birth.
A Truth-seeker knows it;
A God-lover knows it.

Gracious
Is divine birth.
An ignorance-transformer knows it;
A perfection-discoverer knows it.

679. SHE IS CONSECRATED

She is a consecrated head;
Therefore
The outer world adores her.

She is a consecrated heart;
Therefore
The inner world adores her.

She is a consecrated soul;
Therefore
The Pilot Supreme
Ceaselessly needs her.

680. O GIVE ME

O give me the heart
That sings only God's Songs.

O give me the mind
That builds only God's Palace.

O give me the vital
That spreads only God's Wings.

O give me the body
That serves only God's Feet.

681. THEN AND NOW

The love of Heaven
I received when I lived in Heaven.
The Heaven of love
I now receive here on earth.

The God of Heaven
I saw on the highest Height.
The Heaven of God
I now see here on earth.

682. REPUBLICAN AND DEMOCRAT

A republican sings:
I shall show you the way.
But you must
Follow me, me alone.

A democrat sings:
I shall walk with you
With the hope that you will carry me
When I am tired,
When I am lost
On the way.

683. O SLEEPLESS ONES

O sleepless silence,
My heart desires
Your beauty's height.

O sleepless sound,
My body desires
Your duty's joy.

O sleepless God,
My life needs
Your Perfection-light.

684. INTERROGATION

When your heart interrogates,
Everyone fails to answer.

When your mind interrogates,
No one cares to answer.

When your eyes interrogate,
Everyone can and does answer.

685. ADVERSITY AND PROSPERITY

Adversity tells me
God has to be sought,
God has to be caught.
How?
By becoming more vigilant.

Prosperity tells me
God has come to me;
I don't have to go to God.
God has already fed me;
I am sure
He does not expect
Anything in return.
What He really wants from me
Is a satisfaction-smile
From Perfection-sun.

686. A MAN OF DIGNITY

You are a man of dignity.
I desire your Himalayan heights.

You are a man of purity.
I desire your moon-white purity.

You are a man of duty.
I desire your ever-unparalleled
responsibility.

687. I NEED YOU

O face of time,
Do not hide.
I need you desperately.

O heart of love,
Do not hide.
I need you constantly.

O vision of God,
Do not hide.
I need you ceaselessly.

O Perfection of God,
Do not hide.
I need you immediately.

688. THE TRUTH

You love Heaven.
Indeed,
This is a partial truth.

You love earth.
Indeed,
This is an inconceivable truth.

You love God.
Indeed,
This is an undeniable truth.

You love yourself.
Indeed,
This is the eternal truth.

689. VIEWPOINTS

A little soul says
God is good.

A big soul says
God is great.

A divine soul says
God boundlessly has.

A supreme soul says
God eternally is
Plus
God eternally proceeds.

690. O SAVIOUR

O Lover-saviour,
My heart desires Your Love.

O Dreamer-saviour,
My mind desires Your Dream.

O Soldier-saviour,
My vital desires Your Strength.

O Server-saviour,
My body desires Your Dedication.

691. I GLORIFY EARTH

I glorify earth
Because
Its body knows how to endure,
Because
Its heart knows how to aspire,
Because
Its soul knows how to wait
For God, for God's choice Hour.

692. I GLORIFY HEAVEN

I glorify Heaven
Because
Its Dream-Reality is illumining,
Because
Its Divinity-Immortality is
fulfilling,
Because
Its Compassion-Infinity is
all-embracing.

693. KING AND QUEEN

You are Heaven's King;
Therefore
You are sure.

You are Heaven's Queen;
Therefore
You are pure.

You are earth's King;
Therefore
You have tried everything.

You are earth's Queen;
Therefore
You are everything.

694. THEY ENJOY

His body enjoys
Inequality.

His vital enjoys
Charity.

His mind enjoys
Clarity.

His heart enjoys
Necessity.

His soul enjoys
Divinity.

His God enjoys
Reality.

695. YOUR PHILOSOPHY AND MINE

Your philosophy is
Mortal sin: ignorance,
Immortal sin: ingratitude.

My philosophy is
Mortal failure: imperfection,
Immortal failure: doubt.

696. SHELTER

Love shelters my heart;
Therefore
I am safe.

Clarity shelters my mind;
Therefore
I am safe.

Joy shelters my vital;
Therefore
I am safe.

Purity shelters my body;
Therefore
I am safe.

697. WHEN SOUND WAS MY LORD

When God
Was my Lord,
I was misunderstood.

When I
Was my Lord,
All alone I stood.

When Silence
Was my Lord,
I was deified.

When Sound
Was my Lord,
I was crucified.

698. RUN EVERMORE

Sigh no more.
Your brave days
Are dawning fast.

Cry no more.
God's Smile
Is drawing nigh.

Run evermore,
Dive evermore,
Fly evermore.
Why?
Because God the Inspiration
Has Himself become your
aspiration,
And
God the Aspiration
Has Himself become your
realisation.

699. DON'T BE

O mind, my mind,
Don't be a busy old fool.

O heart, my heart;
Don't be a tortured weakling.

O vital, my vital,
Don't be a ruthless tyrant.

O body, my body,
Don't be a marathon sleeper.

O soul, my soul,
Don't be a fruitless dreamer.

700. NEVER LOVE

Never see
Unless you give.
Never give
Unless God inspires you.

Never,
Never,
Never love
Unless your heart
Devotedly can,
Unless your soul
Unconditionally can.

701. WARRIORS

Life is a battle
Between
Desire-warriors
And
Aspiration-warriors.

God
Does not want
Desire-warriors
To win
Because
They want to dominate
The world.

God
Desperately wants
Aspiration-warriors
To win
Because
They want to liberate
The world.

702. MY HAPPINESS

Yesterday
My happiness
Was my God-acceptance.

Today
My happiness
Is my life-transformation.

Tomorrow
My happiness
Shall be my God-manifestation
In the core of perfection.

703. I AM GRATEFUL

Lord,
I am grateful to You
Not because all my needs
Are supplied by You,
But because You have chosen me
To love You and cry to You,
To reveal You and manifest You,
To claim You and treasure You.

704. STAY WITH THE PRESENT

Do not dig into the past
Unless
You have something nice
To say about your past.

Do not peep into the future
Unless
You are sure that
You will welcome your future
Unreservedly and
unconditionally.

Stay with the present.
Stay with your eternal Now.

705. SO WHAT

Just laugh!
If the world has disappointed you,
So what?

Just laugh!
If your best friend has deserted
you,
So what?

Why do you need the world?
Why do you need a friend?
Is God not enough for you?
God can never disappoint you;
God can never desert you.

706. LOOK FOR THE GOOD

Look for the good:
Everything is God,
Everyone is God.

Look for God:
Everything is good,
Everyone is good.

Look for the good in me;
I shall not confuse you.

Look for the God in me;
I shall not disappoint you.

707. PATIENCE

Patience
Is my confidence-light
In God's choice Hour.

Patience
Is my perfection-life
To reveal God-tower.

Patience
Is my Immortality-smile
On earth to flower.

708. READY

I was ready;
Therefore
God-Compassion accepted me.

I am ready;
Therefore
God-Concentration accepts me.

I shall be ready;
Therefore
God-Perfection shall accept me.

709. RENUNCIATION

Yesterday
You renounced
Your wild animosity;
Therefore
Heaven is unmistakably proud of
you.

Today
You have renounced
Your blind stupidity;
Therefore
Earth is divinely proud of you.

Tomorrow
You will renounce
Your proud necessity;
Therefore
Both God and I
Will be supremely proud of you.

710. CONGRATULATIONS!

Congratulations, my brave
Heaven!
You have at last loved earth
Once in your entire life.

Congratulations, my brave earth!
You have at last smiled at Heaven
Once in your entire life.

Congratulations, my wise God!
You have at last liberated me
Once in Your birthless and
deathless creation.

711. MY ONLY REALITY

In Heaven
My only reality is Light.

On earth
My only reality is might.

In God
My only reality is Love.

In me
My only reality is surrender.

712. APPOINTMENTS

Accept God lovingly.
He will surely give you
An appointment some day.

Accept God devotedly.
He will surely give you
An appointment tomorrow.

Accept God unconditionally.
Lo, you have already had
The most significant interview
with Him.

713. TRY

Try to see God
In every human being.
Indeed, that will be your supreme
invention.

If you cannot do that,
Try to see God
In yourself, at least.
Indeed, that will be your supreme
discovery.

If even that you cannot do,
Then try to feel
That you are for God
And God alone.
Indeed, that will be your supreme
choice.

714. UNION AND RE-UNION

You want to know
The difference
Between
Man-realisation
And
God-realisation.

The difference is very simple:
Man-realisation is the union
Of illumining Light
And
Devouring darkness
In your mind-search.

God-realisation is the re-union
Of Universal Love
And
Transcendental Truth
In your heart-cry.

715. DONKEY, MONKEY AND LION

Are you a donkey?
No, you are not.

Are you a monkey?
No, you are not.

Are you a lion?
Yes, you are.

Why are you not a donkey?
You are not a donkey
Because
You and dark ignorance-life
Are perfect strangers.

Why are you not a monkey?
You are not a monkey
Because
You and restless sound-life
Are perfect strangers.

Why are you a lion?
You are a lion
Because
You are roaming divinely and
 supremely.
For what?
Earth-transformation and
 God-manifestation.

716. NO BEGGING

No begging, no pleading,
But dreaming and achieving.
Your Lord Supreme
Treasures this adventure of yours
Far beyond the vision
Of your imagination's flight.

717. WHAT IS FAITH?

What is faith?
Your divinity within you.

What is faith?
God's supreme Pride in you.

What is faith?
Your eternal Immortality in God.

718. YOU DON'T BELIEVE

You say you don't believe
In the liberating God-goal.
To me, it is quite unimportant.

You say you don't believe
In the searching world-soul.
To me, it is quite unimportant.

But when
You say you don't believe
In your loving heart-cry,
To me, it is a serious matter.
Utter destruction is going to
 embrace you
Sooner than at once.

719. READY TO WAIT

Since my purity
Needs God's Heart,
It is ready to wait
For God's choice Hour.

Since my patience
Needs God's Smile,
It is ready to wait
For God's choice Hour.

Since my perseverance
Needs God's Blessing,
It is ready to wait
For God's choice Hour.

720. HE IS STILL ALIVE

His life is based on hope-joy;
Therefore
He is still alive.

His mind is based on plan-might;
Therefore
He is still alive.

His heart is based on
  surrender-light;
Therefore
He is still alive.

721. ALWAYS SLOW

His body is slow,
Always slow,
In serving.

His vital is slow,
Always slow,
In striving.

His mind is slow,
Always slow,
In learning.

His heart is slow,
Always slow,
In loving.

His soul is slow,
Always slow,
In manifesting.

722. PROMISES AND HOPES

My past promises
Are important.

My future hopes
Are more important.

My present cries
Are infinitely more important
Than my unfed promises
And
My hungry hopes.

723. WHEN

When she concentrates,
The Sun-king gives her
Power infinite.

When she meditates,
The Moon-queen gives her
Love immortal.

When she contemplates,
The Sky-princess gives her
Concern eternal.

724. LEAVE ME ALONE

O world,
Leave me alone
With my searching mind.
My mind is my Immortality's
friend.

O world,
Leave me alone
With my aspiring heart.
My heart is my Eternity's All.

725. SILENCE

Silence is God's Vision.
My heart knows it
Unmistakably.

Silence is Heaven's illumination.
My mind sees it
Proudly.

Silence is earth's perfection.
My life discovers it
Unconditionally.

726. CAN AND CANNOT

He who can, does.
God is a shining example.

He who cannot, preaches
Plus barks.
Alas, I am that deplorable
example.

727. THEREFORE

I love;
Therefore, I have:
I have Eternity's Peace.

I serve;
Therefore, I am:
I am Infinity's Bliss.

728. HUMANITY MISUNDERSTOOD

Humanity
Misunderstood me
When
I stood an inch higher.

Humanity
Misunderstood me
When
I stood an inch lower.

Humanity
Misunderstood me
When
I stood parallel.

Therefore
My frustration-life
Is pining to enter
Into the world-chasm of nowhere.

729. A PEERLESS MASTERY

Ignorance
Is a helpless slavery.
My mind knows it.

Knowledge
Is a shadowless discovery.
My heart knows it.

Love
Is a peerless mastery.
My soul knows it.

730. I APPRECIATE

I appreciate
Prayers without words.

I admire
Meditations without thoughts.

I adore
Realisation without sound.

I love
Perfection without expectation.

731. PASS IT ON

Heaven
Has shown you Heaven's
compassion.
Pass it on.

Earth
Has shown you earth's patience.
Pass it on.

God
Has shown you God's Confidence.
Pass it on.

732. I NEED YOU ONLY

O morning of beauty!
I love you.
I always love you.

O evening of silence!
I love you.
I always love you.

O time of Compassion-perfection!
I need you.
I always need you.
I need you only.

733. DISCOVERIES

My body's discovery:
Death is strong.

My heart's discovery:
Love is stronger.

My soul's discovery:
Smile is stronger than the
strongest.

734. WE STUMBLE

Who has never stumbled?
You?
Let your sincerity speak.

Who has never stumbled?
He?
Let his sincerity speak.

Who has never stumbled?
I?
Let my sincerity speak.

Why do we stumble?
We stumble
Because
God in us is experiencing
An ever-transcending-Reality.

735. BECAUSE GOD

You are beautiful
Not because
You love God sincerely,
But because
God loves you unconditionally.

You are divine
Not because
You need God desperately,
But because
God needs you eternally.

736. ALAS! ALAS!

Your insincerity-drop
Has poisoned
Your spirituality-sea.
Alas! Alas!

Your insecurity-second
Has eclipsed
Your reality-sun.
Alas! Alas!

737. HUNGRY

You were hungry
For earth-beauty.
It was necessary then.

You are hungry
For Heaven-duty.
It is customary now.

You shall be hungry
For God-necessity.
It will be compulsory then.

738. NO MEDICINE, NO ENEMY

Alas! Alas!
No medicine
To cure my self-deception.

Lo and behold!
No enemy
To obstruct my God-realisation.

739. GOD WILL GIVE YOU

Love,
God will give you more love.

Serve,
God will give you more light.

Surrender,
God will give you
Not only more perfection
But all His Perfection.

740. SKY AND SUN

Compassion-sky
Shelters all souls together
Under its canopy.

Perfection-sun
Embraces one soul at a time
On ecstasy's blue-gold heights.

741. JOY-FRUIT

The fear-cat in him
And
The doubt-dog in him
Were disputing over
Their claims to Joy-fruit.

The faith-deer in him
Smiled and carried away
The Joy-fruit.

742. HE WHO GIVES

He who obeys,
Commands.

He who teaches,
Learns.

He who gives,
Not only has
But eternally is.

743. HIS INVOCATIONS

His sickness needed God;
Therefore
He invoked God.

His cleverness needed Satan;
Therefore
He invoked Satan.

His insecurity needs ego;
Therefore
He invokes his ego.

744. THE SEED AND THE TREE

The soul
Is the seed.
The body
Is the tree.

Love the tree
For its all-spreading beauty.
Serve the seed
For its all-illumining duty.

745. MONEY-POWER

You must know
What you *can* buy
And
What you *cannot* buy
With your money-power.

With your money-power
You can buy physical strength,
You can buy vital strength,
You can buy mental strength.
But
You cannot buy psychic strength.

What is psychic strength?
Love, Infinity's Love.
Oneness, Eternity's Oneness.

746. COMPLAINTS

You complain
Because
Your greatness
Is not acknowledged.

He complains
Because
His smallness
Is well exposed.

God complains
Because
His goodness
Is not claimed by humanity.

Alas,
I know not what to do
With you people.

747. I KNOW GOD

My love knows
Where God is.
My devotion knows
Who God is.
My surrender knows
Why God is.

Where is God?
Inside my heart-cry.
Who is God?
God is my Life-Lover.
Why is God?
God is for my satisfaction-smile.

748. I SPEAK

I speak to God
Because
God understands me.

I speak to Heaven
Because
Heaven appreciates me.

I speak not to man
Because
Man neither understands me
Nor appreciates me.
To my wide surprise,
He does not even recognise me.

749. CALL NOBODY YOUR OWN

Call nobody your own.
Look, your own doubt-son
Has deserted you.
Look, your own jealousy-daughter
Has strangled you.
Look, your own
impurity-husband
Has buried you.
Only call God your own:
Look, He has resurrected you:
He is feeding you,
He is energising you,
He is immortalising you.

750. I

I was defeated
Because
I stayed with my little I,
Ignorance-eye.

I am defeated
Because
I do not feed
My big I,
Universal I.

I shall succeed
Because
I shall claim God-I
As my only I.

751. NO DIFFERENCE

No difference
Between
Heaven-grace
And
Earth-gain.

No difference
Between
Earth-sacrifice
And
Heaven-victory.

752. DON'T BE ALOOF

Don't be aloof.
God does not want that.

Don't be aloof.
The world cannot brook that.

Don't be aloof.
Your soul does not understand
that.

Don't be aloof.
Your life may revolt
Against
Man, the future God.

753. TELL ME THE DIFFERENCE

Tell me the difference
Between
Love divine
And
Permanent liberation.

Tell me the difference
Between
Expansion divine
And
Lasting perfection.

Tell me the difference
Between
Truth-discovery
And
Bliss-reality.

754. APPRECIATION

I appreciate my heart
Because
It deserves appreciation.

I appreciate my mind
Because
It wants appreciation.

I appreciate my vital
Because
It cries for appreciation.

I appreciate my body
Because
It needs appreciation.

755. DREAMS

Bad dreams frighten me,
My helpless vital.

Good dreams enlighten me,
My fearless heart.

Earth-dreams discourage me,
My infant mind.

Heaven-dreams illumine me,
My orphan-body.

756. SOUND-BOAT, SILENCE-BOAT

When the sound-boat
Touches the Silence-shore,
I see the glorification
Of the finite
In the core of the Infinite.

When the Silence-boat
Touches the sound-shore,
I discover the perfection
Of the Infinite
In the core of the finite.

757. THE KINGDOM OF GOD'S SOUL

O dark cave of my mind,
Do not feel sorry.
My Lord Supreme
Shall visit you tomorrow,
Without fail.

O vast palace of my heart,
Lo, who is at your gate?
Don't you recognise Him?
He is your Beloved Supreme.

"O boundless kingdom of My
Soul,
Do you not remember
That you embody My Dream-sky,
That you reveal My Reality-sea
And
That you manifest My
Divinity-height?"

758. STAY WITH THE PRESENT

Stay with the past.
You will receive
Thunder-kicks from death.

Stay with the future.
You will see
The destruction-frown
Of measureless temptation.

Stay with the present.
You will eat
The Reality-fruit
Of Divinity-dawn.

759. OUR DIFFERENT OCCUPATIONS

Earth speaks untiringly.
Heaven dreams ceaselessly.
The seeker in mankind seeks rarely.
The lover in mankind fails miserably.
God pilots unconditionally.
And I sleep in ignorance eternally.

760. GOD HONOURS ME

When I aspire
God honours me.
He tells the world
That I am His fond child,
I am His choice instrument.

When I do not aspire
He also honours me.
He tells the world
That I am His future Choice,
I am His future Voice,
I shall embody His future Race,
I shall reveal His future Face.

761. TWO UNLUCKY SOULS

Lord, how long
Can we endure our separation?
Let us settle our dispute
Once and for all.
I shall share with You
What I have: ignorance-night.
You shall share with me
What You have: Nectar-light.

Daughter, I try and cry,
Cry and try,
To share with you.
But
You neither receive
My cherished treasure,
Nor do you share
Your treasure with Me;
Therefore
We play the role of
Two unlucky souls
And two helpless lives.

762. THE BARRIER OF NEARNESS

The barrier of nearness
At times does exist.
But why?
Because
The seeker does not surrender
His earthbound fondness to
The Master-leader;
Because
The seeker builds a paradise of his
own
Where he wants to possess
The Master ceaselessly
Before the Master
Claims and proclaims him
Compassionately and proudly
As his own, very own.

763. BECAUSE HE IS WEAK, BECAUSE HE IS COMPASSIONATE

Because he is weak,
I love and support man
Personally
Against the denizens
Of the other worlds.

Because He is compassionate,
I love and support God
Unconditionally
Against me, my life
And my world.

764. TO BUY A BLESSING

I have spent
All my aspiration-wealth
To buy a smile
From the face of Heaven.

I have spent
All my dedication-wealth
To buy a cry
From the heart of earth.

I have spent
All my surrender-wealth
To buy a blessing
From the Feet of God.

765. AT THE APPOINTED HOUR

At the appointed hour
Humanity said to me:
"Give me, give me.
This is the only way
For you to become great."

At the appointed hour
God said to me:
"Accept Me, receive Me.
This is the only way
For you to become good."

766. THREE CHEERS

At long last
I have conquered
Ignorance-night.
I share the good news
With earth, Heaven and God.

Earth said: "Not true, not true!"
Heaven said: "When? How?"
God said: "Three times three
cheers
For My son! Bravo!"

767. THREE DANGEROUS THINGS

I warn myself
Against three dangerous things:
My indulgence-capacity,
Earth's preference-capacity,
Heaven's indifference-capacity.
My Lord Supreme
Loves and blesses me
For my great discovery.

768. DO YOU LOVE?

Do you love man?
Then give him a cheerful smile.

Do you love God?
Then give him a soulful cry.

Do you love yourself?
Then give yourself a powerful
assurance.

769. HEAVEN IS PUZZLED

World-publicity
Declares him a great man.

Earth-sagacity
Declares him a perfect rogue.

Heaven-necessity
Is totally puzzled.
It knows not whether to accept
  him
Immediately
Or to reject him
Unreservedly.

770. AFTER HE HAD CONQUERED

After he had conquered earth,
He discovered
That he had conquered nothing.

After he had conquered Heaven,
He discovered
That he had conquered
  something.

After he had conquered himself,
He discovered
That he had conquered not only
  much,
But everything,
Even the monstrous things that
  he thought
He would never be able to
  conquer.

771. WHO COMES HERE?

Who comes here?
God?
Please wait.

Who comes here?
Man?
Why are you so late?

Who comes here?
Satan?
I am sorry.
This is the wrong place.

772. YOUR MIND, YOUR HEART

Yours is the mind
That sees everything
And
Knows everything;
Therefore
God tells me that you arc
Divinely great
And that He will utilise you
In the distant future.

Yours is the heart
That feels everything
And
Loves everything;
Therefore
God tells me that you are
Supremely great
And that He is using you
Proudly and incessantly.

773. WHAT DO YOU WANT?

What do you want?
God's Infinity?
It is inside the smile
Of your eyes.

What do you want?
God's Eternity?
It is inside the cry
Of your heart.

What do you want?
God's Immortality?
It is inside the silence-beauty
Of your soul.

774. WHAT DO I LIKE?

What do I like?
The simplicity of your life.
What do I like?
The sincerity of your heart.
What do I like?
The luminosity of your soul.

Do I like anything more?
Yes, I do.
I like the stupidity
Of your mind,
Although not much.

775. MY HEART, MY SOUL

I am my heart.
I do not need
Anything more
Since my heart is soulful in itself.

I am my soul.
I do not need
Anything more
Since my soul is fruitful in itself.

776. GOD IS

God is my Way;
Therefore
I like him.

God is my Home;
Therefore
I need Him.

God is my Room;
Therefore
I love Him.

777. GIVE WHAT YOU HAVE

Do you want
Himalayan joy?
Then give to God
What you have:
Your heart's aspiration-cry.

Do you want
Pacific peace?
Then give to man
What you have:
Your life's dedication-smile.

778. WHEN I MEASURE GOD

When I measure
Your God,
I laugh and laugh
Because
Your God is not great.

When I measure
His God,
I laugh and laugh
Because
His God is not good.

When I measure
My God,
I smile and smile
Because
My God is trying,
My God is striving.

779. ON EARTH, IN HEAVEN

On earth
I am the frustration-silence
Of hunger.

In Heaven
I am the hunger-cry
Of silence.

780. HIS BODY'S SLAVERY

His vital justifies
His body's slavery.

His mind ignores
His body's slavery.

His heart suffers
His body's slavery.

His soul liberates
His body's slavery.

781. HUMAN BIRTH, DIVINE FREEDOM

Human birth
Needs divine freedom
For its perfection-height.

Divine freedom
Needs human birth
For its manifestation-smile.

782. WHAT I NEED

What I need
Is duty's body.

What I need
Is humility's vital.

What I need
Is serenity's mind.

What I need
Is purity's heart.

What I need
Is beauty's soul.

783. DIVINELY GREAT AND SUPREMELY GOOD

You have commanded
temptation;
Therefore
You are great.

You have demanded perfection;
Therefore
You are good.

You have obeyed compassion;
Therefore
You are divinely great
And
You are supremely good.

784. ONLY ONE

Only one need:
God-satisfaction.

Only one deed:
Perfection-manifestation.

785. HEART'S PUNISHMENT, MIND'S PUNISHMENT

Both
My mind and my heart
Punish me.
Yet I love my heart
And hate my mind.

Why?
My heart's punishment
Is reformatory.
My mind's punishment
Is vengeful.

My heart punishes me
Because
Of my own immediate necessity.
My mind punishes me
Because
Of its own constant necessity.

786. THE VEDIC SOUL, THE VEDIC BODY

My heart loves
The Vedic Soul
Because
It is Silence-unity.

My life loves
The Vedic Body
Because
It is Sound-multiplicity.

787. RIGHT FROM TODAY

Right from today
I shall not permit
My desire-cry
To make me a certified expert
In only one branch of the life-tree
And thus doom me to remain
Totally oblivious of the rest.

Right from today
I am invoking
My aspiration-might
To help me climb up
Every branch of the life-tree
And thus make of me
An integral, whole and complete man.

788. A BIG FAVOUR

Can you believe
What God has asked me to do?
He has asked me
To do Him a big favour.
From today on,
He wants me to practise
God-love;
He wants me to demonstrate
God-compassion.
I must tell you,
This is not an easy task.
Perhaps you already know it.

789. THE CREATION, THE CREATOR

The creation in me
Is perfect
Only when it undyingly cries
For self-emancipation.

The creator in me
Is perfect
Only when it untiringly smiles
At self-manifestation.

790. MY EXPERIENCE

Indulgence:
That is my earth-experience.

Indifference:
That is my Heaven-experience.

Preference:
That is my human experience.

Ignorance:
That is my devastating
experience.

Love:
That is my ever-illumining
and
Ever-transcending experience.

791. YOUR WHOLE WORLD

Your whole world
Has gone to rack and ruin,
Not because you know not
Who God is,
But because you have not
Tried to discover
Who God is,
Where God is,
Why God is,
Finally,
How God is.

792. EVERYTHING HAPPENS TO PLEASE ME

When the time is ripe,
Everything happens to please me.
Lo and behold!
Earth-cry needs me,
My dedicated service,
To realise God.
Heaven-smile needs me,
My dedicated service,
For its manifestation
On earth.

793. GOD WILL DO IT

Try your best;
Do your best.
Leave the rest
At God's Compassion-Feet.

Devotedly
He will, without fail,
Do and fulfil
What is left undone,
Unconditionally.

Do you know
Who God is?
He is your desire's Lord
And
Your aspiration's Slave.

794. YOU HAVE BECOME

Choose carefully,
Love unreservedly,
Surrender unconditionally.
Lo, you have become
Earth's safe journey
And
Heaven's sure goal.

795. GOD-CENTRED LIFE

His is the God-centred life;
Therefore
Earth needs him to carry her
To God-Light.
His is the God-centred life;
Therefore
Heaven needs him to stay
On earth eternally
For its dream-manifestation.

796. EARTH-SORROW, HEAVEN-JOY

Earth-sorrow
Is time-born;
Therefore
It cannot last.

Heaven-joy
Is beyond the snares of time;
Therefore
It will not only last
But also
Invoke the past,
Energise the present,
Expedite the future
Into the immediacy of today.

797. I HAVE THE TIME

I have no time
To think of great possibilities.

I have no time
To think of grand opportunities.

I have the time
Only for dedicated activities
And blossoming necessities.

798. MY LOVE, MY SURRENDER

My love of God
Tells me what I can be:
God's perfect instrument.

My surrender to God
Tells me what I already have
become:
God's Satisfaction-smile,
God's Perfection-pride.

799. HIS VERY OWN

If you lead
An irresponsible life,
Earth may not like you,
Heaven may not need you,
And
God will definitely
Not
Claim you as His own,
His very own.

800. THE PRIDE

In my animal life
When I was at my zenith,
I was the pride
Of earth's destruction-power.

In my human life
When I am at my zenith,
I am the pride
Of Heaven's aspiration-power.

In my divine life
When I shall be at my zenith,
I shall be the pride
Of God's Perfection-power.

801. YOU ARE AN ANGEL

You are an angel of the tongue.
I do not need you.

You are an angel of the heart.
I need you.

You are an angel of God.
I love you,
I need you,
I acknowledge you as my divine
superior,
I claim you as my very own.

802. THE COSMIC TASK

A human life neglected,
A cosmic plan unfinished.

A human life regulated,
A cosmic task that has reached its
zenith goal.

He who neglects
Is a failure in God's Eye.
He who leaves his task unfinished
Again and again must come
To the earthly shores to complete
his task:
The task of earth-transformation
And his own body-perfection.

803. VISION DOES NOT DIE

Fear does not die with its
possessor.
It dies long before.

Doubt does not die with its
possessor.
It dies long before.

Jealousy does not die with its
possessor.
It dies long before.

Hope dies with its possessor.
Promise dies with its possessor.
Achievement dies with its
possessor.
But
There is another thing
That does not die with its
possessor.
What is it?
Vision, God's cosmic Vision.

804. YOU AND I

Lord,
You and I are two.
This is the eternal falsehood.

Lord,
You and I are one.
This is the eternal Truth.

Lord,
I am of You;
Therefore
The divine in me
Is invoking You
And expecting Your express
arrival.

805. TWO REASONS

God loves you
For two significant reasons:

Your voice is pure.
He loves purity.

Your choice is sure.
He loves surety.

806. LOST CHARMS

You have lost all your physical
charms;
Therefore
You are no longer called a man of
temptation.

You have lost all your vital
charms;
Therefore
You are no longer called a man of
danger.

You have lost all your mental
charms;
Therefore
You are no longer called a man of
awakening
beauty.

You have lost all your psychic
charms;
Therefore
You are no longer called a man of
enlightening
duty.

807. MESSAGES OF IMAGINATION AND INSPIRATION

Imagination tells me
I am of God.

Inspiration tells me
I am for God.

Imagination tells me
My nest is very far.

Inspiration tells me
No matter how far,
I can and shall
Fly to my nest.

808. HE CAN BE WITH ME

Mine is a vision, a God-Vision.
Mine is a mission, a God-Mission.
Mine is a satisfaction, a
God-Satisfaction.
Mine is a perfection, a
God-Perfection.

He who has a simple heart
Can be with me in my vision.

He who has a sincere life
Can be with me in my mission.

He who has a dauntless soul
Can be with me in my
God-Satisfaction.

He who has perfect beauty, inner
and outer
Can be with me in my
God-Perfection.

809. YOU DESERVE

Do you love God?
If you do not love God,
Then you deserve the eternal
Death.

Do you love humanity?
If you love humanity,
Then you deserve the eternal
Light.

Do you love the unreal in you?
If you love the unreal in you,
Then you deserve the eternal hell.

Do you love the real in you?
If you love the real in you,
Then you deserve the eternal
Heaven.

810. THE WHISPER

The whisper of temptation
Is dangerous.
Your vital knows it.

The whisper of aspiration
Is advantageous.
Your heart knows it.

The whisper of realisation
Is prosperous.
Your soul knows it.

811. ONLY ONE

Only one need:
Aspiration-flight.

Only one seed:
Perfection-light.

Only one deed:
Surrender-might.

812. NO ONE CAN LOSE

God says:
No one must lose.

God says:
No one shall lose.

God says:
No one can lose.

No one must lose in the battlefield
of life.
No one shall lose in the
Heaven-winning race.
No one can lose in Eternity's
cosmic Game.

813. SON, YOU MUST WIN

He wants his victory's crown,
He wants his victory's throne,
For the searching mind of
humanity,
For the crying heart of humanity,
For the self-giving life of
humanity.
Therefore
God says to him:
Son, you must win.
If not, your loss is My loss;
Your defeat is My defeat.

814. THEY SHALL LISTEN

The outer world shall listen to you
If the inner world guides you.

The inner world shall listen to you
If the outer world loves you.

815. THE HOUR

The hour came
When God blessed me
And sent me down to earth.

The hour has come
When I have to tell the world
What the world is,
And what the world will be.

What is the world?
A self-giving seed.
What will the world be?
A God-fulfilling tree.

816. GOD SAW IN ME

God saw in me a soldier;
Therefore
He allowed me to make friends
With His Mission's Might.

God saw in me a poet;
Therefore
He allowed me to make friends
With His Beauty's Height.

God saw in me a lover;
Therefore
He allowed me to make friends
With His Duty's Right.

817. THREE TRAINS

Earth's slow train
Is progress sure.

Heaven's fast train
Is perfection sure.

God's fastest train
Is Satisfaction sure.

Sweet is progress.
Divine is satisfaction.
Immortal is perfection.

818. GO TO HIM

Although your desire-friend
Is staying all alone,
Don't go to him.
He will spoil you;
He will ruin you.
He will spoil your character;
He will ruin your life.

Although your aspiration-friend
Is weak and not helping you,
Go to him and stay with him.
One day he will become strong;
One day he will become rich;
One day he will become immortal.
When he becomes strong
All his power will be yours.
When he becomes rich
All his wealth will be yours.
When he becomes immortal
All his Immortality will be yours.

819. I DO NOT MIX WITH YOU

I do not mix with you,
Not because
You are past correction.
No, that is not true.

I do not mix with you
Because
Perfection is not your goal.

I do not mix with you,
Not because
You are ignorant of God-Light.
No, that is not true.

I do not mix with you
Because
You are not for God-Light.

I do not mix with you,
Not because
Of what you are.
No, that is not true.

I do not mix with you
Because
You do not want to be
What I want you to be.
What do I want you to be?
Another God.
That's all.

820. EXEMPTIONS

True sincerity
Is exempt from earth-fear.
True purity
Is exempt from
world-imperfection.
True humility
Is exempt from
ignorance-embrace.
True luminosity
Is exempt from failure-cry.

821. WHEN I LOOK AT HIM

When I look at him
With my eyes open,
I see nothing but
His frightening eyes.

When I look at him
With my eyes closed,
I see nothing but
His compassionate heart.

822. THE DIFFERENCE

The difference between God and
me is this:
I defend my body's destructive
might.
God defends my soul's illumining
light.

The difference between Heaven
and me is this:
I bark at Heaven.
Heaven smiles at me.

The difference between earth and
me is this:
I see earth as a hopeless case.
Earth sees me as a God-manifested
face.

823. MY TWO REALISATIONS

You speak, and yet you say
nothing
When I see the human in you.
This is my earth-realisation.

You speak not, and yet you say
everything
When I see the Divine in you.
This is my Heaven-realisation.

824. GOD-TOUCH

Earth-touch makes me patient;
Therefore
I am grateful to earth.

Heaven-touch makes me
compassionate;
Therefore
I am grateful to Heaven.

God-touch makes me complete,
perfect
and absolute;
Therefore
I am grateful to God.

825. EARTH-PLEASURES, EARTH-JOYS

O man, don't be a fool!
Your earth-pleasures are
perishing like
anything.
You can't hoard them.

O man, don't be a fool!
Your earth-joys will never leave
you.
Just deserve them and use them.

826. VERY OLD FRIENDS

God and I are two very old
acquaintances.
You may call us even friends,
Two very old friends.
But we two friends can never fulfil
each other
Although we consider ourselves as
friends.

God gives me His
Conviction-power
And I give Him my
contradiction-power.
Indeed, this way we sing the song
Of perpetual mutual
wisdom-sacrifice.

827. COMMAND AND OBEY

God has commanded me;
Therefore
I love God.
Indeed, His Command
Is my perfection-seed.

I have obeyed God;
Therefore
God is pleased with me.
He knows my obedience
Is His Satisfaction-tree.

828. EARTH-FEAST AND HEAVEN-FEAST

He descended to earth
To feast his eyes.
He has fulfilled his task.
Earth-beauty his eyes have
enjoyed.

He shall ascend to Heaven
To feed his heart-hunger.
He knows Heaven is generous;
He knows Heaven is
compassionate;
He knows Heaven is all-giving.

829. I LOVE YOU

Although I quarrel with you
I love you.
Although I fight with you
I love you.
Although I speak ill of you
I love you.
Although at times I hate you
I love you.
Why do I love you?
I love you because
I cannot live without you.

830. ANOTHER INSTRUMENT

The moment you displease me
I think of another instrument:
A good instrument,
A divine instrument,
A perfect instrument.
But God tells me that another
instrument,
A good instrument,
A divine instrument,
A perfect instrument
Is only a dream.
Not only my dream
But
The dream of God's Patience-Sky.

831. MY VITAL AND MY HEART

My vital tells me:
Love me or I will go away
Never to return.

My heart tells me:
Whether you love me or not
I shall stay in you, for you.
I shall never return
To the Heaven-Delight
Without you.

832. I SEE HIM

Months passed by;
Years too.
Alas, where is my Lord, my
  Beloved Supreme?
Ah, I see Him in His Beauty's Face!
He is in my crying minute
And in my surrendering second –
In my heart's crying minute
And in my life's surrendering
  second.

833. MY COMPANIONS

Hope, my hope,
You are my conscious companion;
Therefore
I always like you.

Patience, my patience,
You are my conscious and
  constant companion;
Therefore
I always love you.

Surrender, my surrender,
You are my conscious, constant
  and
illumining companion;
Therefore
I always need you.

834. WHEN I CRY

When I cry,
I am my futility-strife.

When I try,
I am Heaven's liberty-soul.

When I surrender,
I am God's Satisfaction-sun.

835. PLEASE ACCEPT ME

Father, please accept me
As Your surrendering son.

Son, please accept Me
As your surrendered Father
Who was once upon a time
A rejected and discarded Father.

Father, let us enjoy
The beauty of mutual acceptance.

Son, indeed,
That is an extraordinary
  suggestion.
Today you deserve My
  Gratitude-sea.

836. THE STORY OF MY POOR TIME

When I spend my time
Underestimating myself
I am, indeed, a great fool.
God, I do not want my body-man
To remain a great fool.

When I spend my time
Overestimating myself
I am, indeed, a greater fool.
God, I do not want my vital-man
To remain a greater fool.

When I spend my time
Hating myself
I am, indeed, the greatest fool.
God, I do not want my mind-man
To remain the greatest fool.

837. HOW DO I FORGET?

How do I forget
My mental pains?
I forget my mental pains
By treasuring my psychic gains.

How do I forget
My earth-failures?
I forget my earth-failures
By remembering my
Heaven-dreams
And
My Heaven-promises.

838. FATE AND FAITH

Fate
Is the slave-surrender
Of the beggar in me.

Faith
Is the God-Light-acceptance
Of the Prince in me.

839. GOD WILL BLESS YOU

You wanted name.
God has given it to you.

You wanted fame.
God has given it to you.

God wanted you
To give Him a smile.
Still you have not played your role.
God will bless you
Since I cannot.

God wanted you
To serve Him in humanity.
Still you have not played your role.
God will love you
Since I cannot.

840. PAST, PRESENT, FUTURE

My mind
Is busy with my unpardonable
past.

My heart
Is busy with my deplorable
present.

My soul
Is busy with my profitable future.

841. NOT WISE ENOUGH

I am wise enough
To tell the world
That God is my might.

I am not wise enough
To feel that what I do
Is nothing but a constant
manifestation
Of God-Light
In me,
For me.

842. MY SECRET SORROW

Lord, finally today
I am giving You
My secret sorrow.

Son, secret sorrow is sacred.

Ah, since You are my only Lord,
I must confess to You
Or
Confide in You.
Why am I not another God?

843. DO NOT WORRY

Heart, do not worry;
Mind will love you.
Give it another chance.

God, do not worry;
I do need You.
Give me another chance.

844. THE HOUR OF NEED

I helped God
In His Hour of need;
Therefore
God is now able to sing and dance.

God helped me
In my hour of need;
Therefore
In Heaven I am complete
And
On earth I am perfect.

845. OUR PROMISES

I have just remembered
My promise to God:
I shall work for
God-Manifestation
On earth.

God has just remembered
His Promise to me:
He will give me
His infinity's Strength
And His Eternity's Patience.

846. LOVE

The human in me says
Love is blind.

The divine in me says
Love is wisdom.

The Supreme in me says
Love is His Eternity's Height,
Infinity's Might
And
Immortality's Light.

847. AN EXTRA SOUL

It is an extra eye
That sees God's Beauty,
And
That eye is my heart.

It is an extra heart
That feels God's Satisfaction,
And
That heart is my soul.

It is an extra soul
That becomes God's Perfection,
And
That soul is God.

848. ETERNITY IS AT MY DISPOSAL

God, I must leave You
Since
You are not pleasing me.

Son, please, please
Give Me another chance.
From now on
I shall be more loving;
I shall be more compassionate.
From now on
I shall try to please you
In your own way.
I have to prove
That Eternity
Is at My disposal.

849. MY DOUBT-CHILD AND MY FAITH-CHILD

My doubt-child will not live with me
For a long time.
He has a very short life;
Therefore
I am treasuring him and cherishing him.

My faith-child will not only have
A long life,
But an eternal life;
Therefore
I am not so fond of him right now.

Once my doubt-child dies,
The joy that I now give to my doubt-child
Will all be given to my faith-child
In addition to what I now give to my
faith-child.
When I am left with only my faith-child,
My faith-child will have everything
That I have and that I am.
What I have is sacrifice
And
What I am is smile.

850. A TEMPORARY EXPERIENCE

"Doubt, my life is bound up in you;
Therefore
I am imperfect."

"Man, your life is bound up in me?
No, your life is bound up
In the pleasure-life;
And that pleasure-life is your ego-life.
And that ego-life is your ignorance-life.
And that ignorance-life is something
That God wants you to have
For the time being."

851. YOURS IS THE HEART

Lord, Yours is the Heart
That loves me
And mine is the heart
That needs You.

Lord, Yours is the Heart
That awakens the soul-life in me
And mine is the heart
That fulfils the Goal-embrace in You.

852. WHEN I SAID TO GOD

When I said to God,
"God, I shall leave You,"
A look of pain crossed His
beautiful Face.

When I said to God,
"God, I shall stay with You
No matter what You do to me,"
God jumped up out of His
Throne,
Gave me His Throne,
Gave me His Crown,
Gave me His Heart,
Gave me His All
And said
I was not only a son of His
And
A vision-fulfilling reality of His
But
His Eternity's All.

853. THE ORDER OF THINGS TO COME

Who can alter the order of things
to come?
Not the devouring tiger in me.

Who can alter the order of things
to come?
Not the roaring lion in me.

Who can alter the order of things
to come?
Only the running deer in me.

854. HIS MIND REFUSES THE TRUTH

His mind refuses to accept the
Truth
Because
Truth is too powerful.

His mind refuses to face the Truth
Because
Truth is too beautiful.

His mind refuses to love the Truth
Because
Truth is too fruitful;
Truth is too soulful.

855. TOO MUCH FOR HIM

God-Beauty was too much for
him;
Therefore
He wanted to stay in
ignorance-ugliness.

God-Smile was too much for him;
Therefore
He wanted to stay with
ignorance-frown.

God-Perfection was too much for
him;
Therefore
He wanted to stay with
imperfection-prince.

856. HE WAS LOST

He was lost in his father;
Therefore
His father's glory was pleased
with him.

He was lost in his mother;
Therefore
His mother's beauty was pleased
with him.

He was lost in his daughter;
Therefore
His daughter's faith was pleased
with him.

He was lost in his son;
Therefore
His son's courage was pleased
with him.

857. MY DIVINE CAPACITIES

You were right, my Lord.
I had divine capacities in
boundless measure.

You are right, my Lord.
I shall be able to reveal these
capacities on earth.

You shall be right, my Lord.
My divine capacities will be only
for
Your satisfaction,
Only for earth's recognition
Of Your Height,
Your Compassion
And
Your Goal-Perfection.

858. MY HEART'S DESIRE AND MY HEART'S LONGING

Who has the audacity to refuse my heart's
desire?
No, not even the child-titan
Who lives on earth.

Who has the capacity to refuse my heart's
longing?
No, not even the omnipotent Lord
Who lives in Heaven.

My desire is my dauntless power
Which
Earth always sees.

My longing is my adamantine power
Which
Heaven always sees.

859. FOR YOUR GOOD

When I say that I have realised God,
Why do I see a look of disbelief in your eyes?

Do you think I am fooling you?
Do you think I have nothing else to do
on earth
Than to tell you who I am
And
To try to convince you why I am here?

No. No. No.
I tell you I have realised God
Just because God wants me to tell you.

I am more than pleased with my God-realisation.
I do not have to proclaim my divinity.
I do not have to share my divinity.
I am complete in myself.
I am perfect in myself.
It is for your good,
For your realisation,
For your perfection
That I tell you I am a realised soul.

860. TELL ME SOMETHING NICE

Father, tell me something nice.
"Daughter, your happiness means
everything
to Me."

Father, tell me something more.
"Daughter, when I don't satisfy
you
I feel simply miserable."

Father, tell me something more.
"Daughter, I live on earth only to
see you
Become divine, perfect and
complete."

861. ONLY TO PLEASE MY BELOVED SUPREME

My heart is living on earth
Only to please my Beloved
Supreme.

My vital is dying on earth
Only to please my Beloved
Supreme.

I am grateful to my heart
For its oneness inseparable
With my Beloved Supreme.

I am grateful to my vital
For its sacrifice-might
For my Beloved Supreme.

862. HIS EARTH-FATE AND HIS HEAVEN-GATE

He realised that his earth-fate
Was too powerful;
Therefore
He gave up fighting
In the battlefield of life.

He has realised that his
Heaven-gate
Is wide open;
Therefore
He has started running fast,
faster, fastest
To his destined goal.

863. MEN LIKE YOU

There will be men like you,
I tell you,
Who are great,
really great,
divinely great,
supremely great.

There will be men like him,
I tell him,
Who are good,
divinely good,
supremely good,
eternally good.

There will be none like me,
I tell myself,
Because I know I am God's failure
  on earth
And
God's hope in Heaven
And
God's Promise to humanity.

864. YOU ARE GREAT

Here on earth you are great
Because
You are impervious to all hearts.

There in Heaven you are great
Because
You are generous, really generous
To earth-cries;
Therefore
You consciously and
  unconditionally
descended
to
earth.

865. HIS SELF-IMPOSED LAWS

He will not find imperfection
In any human being.
He has set this law unto himself.

He will give everything to earth,
Whether earth wants to receive it
  or not.
He has set this law unto himself.

866. THEY CHOOSE FOR ME

My fate chose God
For its Lord
In the past.

Now, the other person
Chooses God for my Lord:
My hope.

867. YOU DO NOT KNOW MY STRENGTH

You do not know the strength of
my mind.
It can
Batter and shatter the whole
world.

You do not know the strength of
my heart.
It can
Purify and unify the whole world.

You do not know the strength of
my soul.
It has
The power to prove to the world
That God is a necessity,
The only necessity,
Here on earth and there in
Heaven.

868. FOR YOUR SAKE

Father, it is for Your sake
And not for my sake
That I need Perfection-Light.

"Son, it is true, it is true.
And it is for your sake
And not for My sake
That I need Satisfaction-Height."

869. EARTH-DUTY AND HEAVEN-DUTY

Earth-duty
was enough
to weaken my austerity.

Heaven-duty
was enough
to strengthen my insecurity.

870. I WOULD HAVE CHAMPIONED YOUR CAUSE

Lord, I would have championed
Your cause:
Love-manifestation,
If I had had the time, the
necessary time.

"Son, I would have championed
your cause:
Ignorance-feast,
If I had found that you really
needed it,
Or that it would do you any good."

871. DENIAL AND ACCEPTANCE

You denied yourself even the bare necessities;
Therefore
You think you are great.
You may be right.
Who knows?

He denies nothing that comes his way.
I tell you
That he is right.
God is well-pleased with him.

I deny the things that God wants me to deny.
I accept the things that God wants me to accept.
Why?
Because my acceptance-light
And my denial-might
Contribute to my God's constant self-transcendence
in me.

872. MY EXPECTATIONS

I do not expect any criticism
From you who love me.

I do not expect any scolding
From you who love me.

I expect only appreciation
From you who really love me.

I expect only admiration
From you who really love me.

You know that if you do
What I expect from you,
I will give you
My heart of love,
My heart of sacrifice
And my soul of constant vigilance,
Eternal vigilance.

873. I HAVE COME TO YOU

Lord, I have come to You as a son.
"Then sit at My Feet."

Lord, I have come to You as a friend.
"Then let us shake hands."

Lord, I have come to You as another Lord.
"Then embrace Me. Let Me embrace you."

874. NOTHING TO EQUAL

There is nothing
to equal
My promise in Heaven.

There is nothing
to equal
My frustration on earth.

There is nothing
to equal
My dream in God.

There is nothing
to equal
My failure in myself.

875. WHAT CAN I DO FOR YOU?

"Son, what can I do for you?"
Why, Father, You can do
everything for me.

"Son, what do you want?"
I want all the wealth that You have
in You.

"Granted, son."

Father, what can I do for You?
I will do everything for You,
Father.

"Son, if you are ready to do
everything for Me,
Then give me only one thing at
least.
That is:
Your dissatisfied earth-heart."

876. LIFE'S COMPENSATIONS

Your life will have its
Compensations for you.
Give your life
What you have.

Do you know what you have?
Do you want to know?
You have only a moment of
Dedicated love in your life.

877. GOD'S ETERNAL CHOICE

Earth-grief
burnt his
body's frame.

Earth-jealousy
burnt his
life-fame.

Earth-ignorance
burnt his
God-Vision.

Yet his soul
loves earth,
treasures earth,
For earth is
God's eternal Choice,
His ultimate Voice.

878. DISAPPOINTMENTS, SATISFACTIONS, GOD-APPOINTMENTS

Disappointments followed one
another
When I tried to perfect
The earth-consciousness.

But
Satisfactions followed one
another
When I tried to perfect
My self, my life, my journey.
God-appointments followed one
another
When I surrendered
My earth-cry to God
And
My Heaven-smile to God.

879. THE CREATION OF GOD, THE GOD OF CREATION

The creation of God
Is the gradual perfection
Of art.

The God of creation
Is the uncertain smile
Of beauty.

880. TWO APOSTLES

Two apostles of atheism:
Doubt and insecurity.

Stupid doubt feels
That God-light can be challenged.

Stupid insecurity feels
That God-power need not be
compassionate.

881. DIVINE INCREASE

Every day the animal in me
Is growing better.

Every day the human in me
Is becoming sweeter.

Every day the divine in me
Is shining brighter;
Therefore
My heart is now big
With rich and divine increase.

882. MELANCHOLY DAYS HAVE GONE

Melancholy days have gone.
There is a lustre divine
In his heart-sky.
No more his mind
Is crowded with doubt-forests.
He builds a bridge
Between
Earth's nothingness
And
Heaven's endlessness.

883. I TELL YOU

Sincerely I tell you:
Poverty wants much.
Unmistakably I tell you:
Prosperity wants more.
Unconditionally I tell you:
God-necessity receives most.

884. DO NOT GRASP

Do not grasp.
If you want to grasp,
You will never reach.
If you do not grasp,
I assure you
Your achievement-reach
Will far exceed your feeble
desire-grasp.

885. REMAIN YOUNG

Do you want to trust
The world?
Then remain young.

Do you want to love
The world?
Then remain young.

How do you remain young?
You remain young
By discovering the true truth
That you are of God's inspiration
And
God is of your aspiration.

886. A SMILE AND A CRY

What is the difference
Between
A smile and a cry?

A cry is the beginning of endless aspiration.
A smile is the undying revelation of aspiration.

887. ACTION! ACTION!

Action! Action!
I must act in the body,
With the body.
Why?
Because I need
Body-transformation and life-perfection.

Action! Action!
I must act in the soul,
With the soul.
Why?
Because I need
God-revelation and God-manifestation.

888. TRUMPETS

You are really good and divine;
Therefore
You blow God's trumpet only.

He is really bad and undivine;
Therefore
He blows his own trumpet only.

I am neither good nor bad,
Neither divine nor undivine;
Therefore
I have no trumpet of my own.

889. YOUR BEAUTY

Temptation-cry:
What is it?
That is your personal beauty.

Illusion-sleep:
What is it?
That is your impersonal beauty.

Aspiration-might:
What is it?
That is your divine beauty.

Realisation-light:
What is it?
That is your supreme beauty.

890. YOU ARE BOUND TO SUCCEED

When other servers fail,
Try your faith-day.
You are bound to succeed.

When other helpers fail,
Try your surrender-light.
You are bound to succeed.

891. AMERICA SINGING, AMERICA DANCING

I hear America singing.
I must say,
America's voice is loud;
America's voice is good,
And soul-stirring, too.

I see America dancing.
I must say,
Although America's dance
Wants to illumine the world,
It ends by frightening the world
Not only beyond the
  world-imagination,
But
Beyond her own loftiest
  imagination, too.

892. WHAT IS IT?

Use it or lose it.
What is it?
Love.

Build it or break it.
What is it?
Hope.

Love it or hate it.
What is it?
Surrender.

893. GOD'S HEAVEN, MY EARTH

God shares with me
His Realisation.
He tells me:
"My Heaven is star-rich."

I share with God
My realisation.
I tell Him:
"My earth is ant-poor,
ant-weak,
ant-helpless."

894. SILENCE

My body
Is the sleeping silence in me.
My vital
Is the dreaming silence in me.
My mind
Is the ignoring silence in me.
My heart
Is the awakening silence in me.
My soul
Is the perfecting,
illumining
and
fulfilling silence in me,
And the ignorance-transforming
silence
In God.

895. WHAT DO WE NEED?

I need.
What do I need?
I need
My God-root in the heart of
humanity.

God needs.
What does God need?
God needs
My man-flower in the life of
Divinity.

896. THE VISION-LIGHT

When
I live with the Vision-Light
I am definitely great.

When
I live in the Vision-Light
I am unreservedly good.

When
I live for the Vision-Light
I am unconditionally God's.

897. THE SPOILS OF BATTLE

His vital wants
The pride of battle-fury.

His mind wants
The garland of victory.

His heart wants
The beauty of glory.

898. JUST THE BEGINNING

To God
I have offered
A flood of tears.
I assure God
That there is nothing left.

To me
God has given
A sea of Joy.
He assures me
That this is just
The very beginning.

899. FOUR MEN

We blame
The living man
Because
He is impure.

We forgive
The dying man
Because
He tried to remain pure.

We admire
The dead man
Because
His is the life that will not worry.

We need
The immortal man
Because
His is the life
That can and will fulfil us.

900. YOU ARE VANQUISHED

You are vanquished;
Don't argue any more
With the inevitable.
Your cheerful surrender
Is the satisfaction
Of God's supreme Heart-Glory
Of Perfection-Light.

901. HOPE ENTERED

Hope entered.
He smiled and danced.
He became God's Vision-Race.

Hope departed.
He cried and slept.
He became Eternity's
ignorance-face.

902. GOD'S GRACE

God's unconditional Grace:
My soul's illumining face.

God's unconditional
Perfection-shower:
My heart's climbing tower.

903. MY SILENCE

My silence
Is the morning light
Of God's God-Vision.

In God-Vision I have become
The angel-eye
Of Infinity's Soul-Smile.

904. GOD THANKED ME

I prayed to God.
He thanked me compassionately.
I meditated on God.
He thanked me smilingly.
I surrendered my gratitude-life to
God.
He thanked me lovingly.
I declared my sovereign equality
to God.
He embraced me unreservedly.

905. MY DARK SECRET, MY BRIGHT SECRET

I love myself only:
This is my dark secret.
I love God only:
This is my bright secret.

God blesses and perfects
My dark secret.
God fondles and treasures
My bright secret.

906. MY ETERNAL SUNRISE

My doubt's desire-life
Is my slow, gradual death.
I know it.

My faith's aspiration-life
Is my eternal sunrise.
I know it.
I love it.
I need it.

907. MY BEAUTY

Yesterday
I was despair-beauty.
Today
I am hope-beauty.
Tomorrow
I shall become surrender-beauty.
The day after tomorrow
I shall become God-Beauty.

908. WHO ARE YOU?

Jealousy, do you know
Who you are?
In case you do not know
I shall tell you who you are.
You are the shameless weakness
Of humanity.

Doubt, do you know
Who you are?
In case you do not know
I shall tell you who you are.
You are the useless sickness
Of humanity.

909. THREE WORLDS

A moment's pleasure
Your vital-world wants.
Eternity's joy
Your heart-world needs.
Immortality's satisfaction
Your soul-world is.

910. MY IDENTITY

Who was I?
Earth's idle dreamer.
Who am I?
Earth's slowest walker.
What shall I be?
My life's frustration
And failure collector.

911. IN SILENCE

In silence you suffered
Because
You were too great.

In silence you suffer
Because
You are too good.

In silence you will smile, sing and dance
Because
The Hour of God before long will strike.

912. WHEN I PRAY AND MEDITATE

When I pray
I enjoy the depth
Of God-Compassion
In my heart-world.

When I meditate
I enjoy the embrace
Of God-Concentration
In my soul-world.

913. THE LIFE OF LIGHT

The life of night
Has only one destructive thing:
The poison of despair.

The life of light
Has not one,
Not two,
But three constructive things:
The love of light,
The path of progress,
The victory of aspiration.

914. ONLY ONE ARMOUR

There is only one armour
Against fate:
God's transcendental
Silence-Grace.

There is only one armour
Against God-satisfaction:
Man's ephemeral
Ingratitude-face.

915. THE ROLE OF TIME

The role of Time:
Duty, constant duty.

The soul of Time:
Beauty, illumining beauty.

The goal of Time:
Love-reality
And
God-necessity.

916. HE IS AFRAID OF THREE THINGS

He is afraid of three things:
Silence, sound and perfection.
When he is afraid of silence
Earth loves him.
When he is afraid of sound
Heaven loves him.
When he is afraid of perfection
The animal in him loves him
Plus
The human in him loves him;
But
The divine in him pities him
And
The Supreme in him forgives him.

917. FATHER AND SONS

Prayer says to God:
"Father, I have come to You.
What will You give me?"
"Son, I shall give you joy.
Look, I am massaging your feet."

Meditation says to God:
"Father, You have come to me.
What can I offer You?
What will give You joy?"
"Son, you can massage My Head."

918. TWO BLESSINGS

Earth-ignorance
Blesses me
By forgetting me.
I am grateful.

Heaven-Justice
Blesses me
By forgiving me.
I am grateful.

919. THE FLAME OF COURAGE

The flame of courage
Illumines me, my earth's life.
I am grateful.

The flame of love
Fulfils me, my soul's role.
I am grateful.

920. ONLY ONE FOOD

His is the body
That cries for only one food:
Night, brooding night.

His is the vital
That cries for only one food:
Might, controlling might.

His is the mind
That cries for only one food:
Light, glowing light.

His is the heart
That cries for only one food:
Delight, flowing delight.

921. THE LADDER OF LIFE

The ladder of humility
Leads us to God-Heights of
Man-emancipation
And
Man-perfection.

The ladder of pride
Is uncertainty's song,
Imperfection's dance
And
Futility's hush.

922. TWO SECRETS

A heart-shattering secret:
My God-realisation
Will not take place
In this lifetime.

A life-illumining
And
Life-immortalising secret:
God's Eternity
Loves me supremely
And
Needs me constantly.

923. A NEVER-ENDING NOW AND AN EVER-ENDING NOW

He lives
In a never-ending Now
And
In an ever-ending now.

A never-ending Now
Is God's choice for him.

An ever-ending now
Is the voice of his treasured
Ignorance-night.

924. IN SPITE OF WHAT I AM

A daily miracle:
The human in me prays to God
In spite of what I am.

A constant miracle:
God-Compassion dreams in me,
God-Joy loves me
And
God-Reality needs me
In spite of what I am.

925. LEAVE ME NOT ALONE

O earth, leave me not alone.
I need you.
I need your heart's
Aspiration-cry
To see the Face of God.

O Heaven, leave me not alone.
I need you.
I need your soul's
Divinity-smile
To discover the Beauty of God.

926. BE NOT PROUD

Death, be not proud;
Life is aspiring.

Life, be not proud;
Death is approaching.

Death and life,
Be not proud;
The Lord Supreme is watching.

927. I LOVE MY HEART

My heart of love
Is divinely beautiful.
I love my beautiful heart.

My heart of devotion
Is eternally soulful.
I love my soulful heart.

My heart of surrender
Is supremely fruitful.
I love my fruitful heart.

928. THEY NEED HER

She embodies
The Eye of Heaven;
Therefore
Earth constantly needs her.

She embodies
The heart of earth;
Therefore
Heaven unreservedly needs her.

She heralds
God-perfection on earth;
Therefore
God supremely needs her.

929. DOUBT-CURE

If you are a doubter,
Then your faith in yourself
Will one day
Come to the fore
And cure you.
But
If you are doubt itself,
Then God alone
Can cure you
And that, too,
He will do at His choice Hour
And not at your hopeful hour.

930. LOVE ME NOT, LEAVE ME NOT

My Lord,
Love me not
If You do not
Want to.

My Beloved,
Leave me not
Even if You
Want to.

931. YESTERDAY, TODAY, TOMORROW

Yesterday
My life was a thorn-crown.
I endured it.

Today
My life is a clown-frown.
I endure it.

Tomorrow
My life shall be a God-town.
The whole world will treasure it.

932. GOD AND WE

God has no Hands
Of His own.
We are His hands.

We have no eye
Of our own.
God is our Eye.

God and we
Have one thing
In common:
Oneness-Heart.

933. YET GOD LOVES US

You are an artist
Who cannot draw;
Yet
God loves you.
Why?
Because you are pure.

He is a singer
Who cannot sing;
Yet
God loves him.
Why?
Because he is humble.

I am a seeker
Who cannot seek;
Yet
God loves me.
Why?
Because I am sincere.

934. MY BODY AND MY HEART

My body says to my heart:
"Beloved, I have only you."

My heart says to my body:
"My sweet little chariot,
For you alone
God's transcendental Crown
And
God's universal Throne."

935. MINE

Mine is the hope-sky
That keeps me alive.

Mine is the faith-moon
That guides me safely.

Mine is the promise-sun
That fulfils me unreservedly.

936. A BROKEN LIFE

Yesterday
I embodied a heap
Of broken hopes.

Today
I reveal the thoughts
Of an arid brain.

Tomorrow
I shall sit down
Quietly
And
I shall weep
Helplessly.

937. WHEN HE DIED

When
His body-vital-mind died,
There was silence in Heaven.

When
His heart died,
There was sound in Heaven.

When
He himself died,
Earth gave him earth's heart-cry
And
Heaven gave him Heaven's
soul-smile.

938. GOD'S HOSPITALITY AND MAN'S HOSPITALITY

God's Hospitality
Tells me:
I need not shout my faith.

Man's hospitality
Tells me:
I must show
Not only
My heart of gratitude
But also
My soul of admiration.

939. WHEN I AM ALONE

Believe it or not,
My eyes do not see
When I look alone.

Believe it or not,
My heart does not breathe
When I live alone.

Believe it or not,
My God does not need me
When I meditate alone.

940. MY PRIDE

My yesterday was proud
Of its wild disbelief.

My today is proud
Of its blind unbelief.

My tomorrow shall be proud
Of its spontaneous belief.

941. O SILENCE

O Eye of Silence,
Your Eye is beautiful.
I need your transcendental Eye.

O Heart of Silence,
Your Heart is beautiful.
I need your universal Heart.

O Life of Silence,
Your Life is beautiful.
I need your immortal Life.

942. YOUR TEACHERS

Let the sky
Become
Your teacher.
You will learn
How to serve.

Let the moon
Become
Your teacher.
You will learn
How to love.

Let the sun
Become
Your teacher.
You will learn
How to become.

943. THE VOICE

Yesterday
I was the trembling voice
Of earth's cry.

Today
I am the illumining voice
Of Heaven's smile.

Tomorrow
I shall become the fulfilling voice
Of God's Promise.

944. LIKE YESTERDAY

God cares for me;
Therefore,
Like yesterday,
Today for me
Is another aspiration-experience.

I care for God;
Therefore,
Like yesterday,
Today for God
Is another satisfaction-dawn.

945. HIDDEN FAILURE AND HIDDEN SUCCESS

My hidden failure:
My dark ingratitude.
My hidden success:
My climbing love for God.

946. REALITY OF LOVE

Intensity of love
My heart of gratitude
Embodies.

Immensity of love
My life of fortitude
Reveals.

Divinity of love
My soul of plenitude
Manifests.

Reality of love
My God of infinitude
Eternally is.

947. THREE GODS

You are, at your best,
A different God.
He is, at his best,
An indifferent God.
And
I am, at my worst,
A transparent God.

948. HEAVEN-SILENCE AND WORLD-SOUND

My life's world-sound
Is my success-plant
Threatened and frightened
By earth-storms.

My heart's Heaven-silence
Is my progress-tree
That shelters and feeds
Earth's excruciating pangs.

949. THEY ARE DEAD

You have deserted your honesty.
Lo, God's Duty-Tree
Which has been pleasing you
Is dead.

You have completely deserted
your humility.
Lo, God's Beauty-Flower
Which has been enlightening you
Is unmistakably dead.

You have deserted your purity.
Lo, God's Spontaneity-Fruit
Which has been nourishing you
Is helplessly dead.

950. VICTORY

Human victory
Is always precarious.

Divine victory
Is always prosperous.

God's Victory
Is always
Precious,
Gracious
And
Advantageous.

951. WHAT DO I DO?

What do I do?
I meditate.
On whom?
On God.
For whom?
For God.

And what do I do
In my spare time?
I write love-letters to God.
I compose love-songs for God.

952. I CAN WAIT FOR HIM

I know that
My Lord Supreme
Will come at His choice Hour.
I know that everything in me
Will reach Perfection's height.
Devotedly I can wait for Him.
I certainly can.

953. THINKING, PLANNING, DOING

Father Supreme,
You know what I am thinking,
You know what I am planning,
You know what I shall be doing.

In case You do not know,
Let me tell You:
I am thinking of loving You more.
I am planning to serve You more.
I shall be doing everything for You
Unconditionally.
Beloved Supreme, I sincerely
mean it.

954. I AM HAPPY

My sweet Lord,
I am happy
Because
I am always in Your world.
I am happier
Because
You are always in charge of my
 life.
I am happiest
Because
I need You only.

955. THE BEAUTY OF EASTERN LIGHT

Why did he leave his church?
He left his church
Not because it was unaspiring.

Why did he leave his priest?
He left his priest
Not because he was uninspiring.

He left his church,
He left his priest,
Because he needs his life's
Total and immediate
 transformation.
And for that what he needs
Is the beauty of Eastern light.

956. ONENESS-HEART

Doubt, I am sorry,
I have already told you
That I shall go with somebody
 else.
I may, however, do you a last
 favour.
You want to know who he is?
He is my very old, forgotten friend
And your eternal enemy:
Oneness-heart.

957. EARTH AND HEAVEN, WHAT IS HAPPENING?

Earth, what is happening?
Why are you so sad?
You mean you do not know
That God needs you?
I tell you, He definitely needs you.
For God's sake, do not treasure
False thought-world.

Heaven, what is happening?
Why are you dancing?
You mean God always needs you?
Don't be a fool.
God can perfectly live without
 you.
I warn you,
He certainly can.

958. SUPREME RELIANCE

Yesterday
I was super-confident
Of my success-life.

Today
I am confident
Of my progress-life.

Tomorrow
I shall rely only on God's
Unconditional Compassion-Life.

959. YOU ARE MORE THAN BEAUTIFUL

O my surrender-light,
All the divine qualities
Are beautiful,
But you are more than beautiful;
You are fruitful.

Love I need
To see the Face of God.
Devotion I need
To feel within my heart
The Presence of God.
But
You I need
To please God constantly,
To fulfil God unconditionally.

960. IN COMMON

Earth, I need you,
Although
We do not have anything
In common.

Heaven, I love you,
Although
We do not have anything
In common.

God, I need you,
I love You
Since
You and I have many things
In common.

Alas, where are You?
And where am I?

961. GOD IS CHARMED BY ME

Alas, why did I fall
In love with ignorance-night?
I should have known long before
What it was really like.

Now God is unmistakably
Charmed by me.
Alas, will I be able to give Him
All my attention
And
Pay Him His absolute due?

I hope it is not too late –
Alas, alas!

962. EARTH-PROMISE AND HEAVEN-INDULGENCE

When
You are on earth,
Be pure in your heart,
Be sure of your life.

When
You are in Heaven,
Be sincere to your earth-promise,
Be careful of your
Heaven-indulgence.

963. MY PRESENCE AND YOUR PRESENCE

Lord Supreme, the difference
Between
My presence in You
And
Your Presence in me
Is this:
My presence helps You
To relax and rest.
Your Presence makes me
Feel safe and secure.

964. WHAT IS WORTH BECOMING?

Lord Supreme, what is worth
loving?
"Son, oneness-beauty."

Lord Supreme, what is worth
doing?
"Son, satisfaction-duty."

Lord Supreme, what is worth
becoming?
"Son, perfection-reality."

965. ALAS, WHY DO I OVERESTIMATE?

Alas, why do I overestimate
The power of my ignorance-life?
No matter how long I swim
In the sea of ignorance-night
My Beloved Supreme shall love
me
And give me another chance
For His tomorrow's Life
In me to blossom.

966. GOD DENIED ME

I was inattentive;
Therefore
God denied me His Message.

I was selfish;
Therefore
God denied me His Smile.

I was impure;
Therefore
God denied me His Dream.

967. DO GIVE ME ANOTHER CHANCE

My Lord, there are things
I would like to do infinitely better.
Do give me another chance.

My Lord, there are human beings
I would try to love infinitely more.
Do give me another chance.

My Lord, there are many promises of mine
Remaining unfulfilled.
Do give me another chance.
Although I do not deserve it,
Do give me another chance, my Lord Supreme.

968. HOW CAN I BE JEALOUS?

Your experiences have enriched me, my heart.
How can I be jealous of you?

His realisation has enriched me, my soul.
How can I be jealous of him?

Earth's sacrifice has enriched me, my aspiration-cry.
How can I be jealous of earth?

Heaven's concern has enriched me, my confidence-life.
How can I be jealous of Heaven?

969. I AM GRATEFUL

My Lord, I am grateful to Your Perfection-Eye,
For it knew me
Long before I knew myself.

My Lord, I am grateful to Your Compassion-Feet,
For they will continue to know me
Long after I have totally forgotten myself.

970. GOD LIKES ME

God likes me
Because
I do not find excuses
In my ignorance.

God loves me
Because
I never put
My own concerns first.

God embraces me
Because
I never defy
My conscience-sparks.

971. I AM GRATEFUL TO GOD

In the physical world
I am grateful to God
Because
He has forgiven me
And
My over-indulgence.

In the vital world
I am grateful to God
Because
He has forgiven me
And
My over-confidence.

In the mental world
I am grateful to God
Because
He has forgiven me
And
My self-absorption.

972. I NEVER WANT TO FORGET

I never want to forget
How ruthlessly I have ignored
God.

I never want to forget
How compassionately God has
forgiven me,
My darkness-pride
And
My ignorance-night.

973. TIME GOES SO FAST

Time goes so fast!
I simply can't believe my eyes.
Just yesterday I had breakfast with
God
In Heaven.
Today I am having luncheon with
the prince
of gloom
On earth.
Tomorrow I shall have dinner
with death
In death's private chamber.

974. A SMALL FAVOUR

Lord, You have not chosen me
To play in Your Dream.
Now can You do me a small
favour?
Can You not make of me a good
sportsman?
Can You not give me the strength
To face the disappointment-night
Like a hero-warrior?
Lord, I am sure You can
And You will.

975. I LIKE BEING WHAT I AM

Earth, I like being what I am:
Heaven's descending smile.

Heaven, I like being what I am:
Earth's ascending cry.

God, I like being what I am:
Your Eternity's Dream-Boat
And
Your Immortality's Reality-Shore.

976. MY SINCERITY SPEAKS

I have enjoyed every minute
Of my stay on earth,
But I do not want
To come back to earth.
You may wonder why.
My sincerity speaks:
Earth-life is too risky.
It is only for the brave.

I have enjoyed every minute
Of my stay in Heaven,
But I do not want
To come back to Heaven.
You may wonder why.
My sincerity speaks:
Heaven-life is quite colourless.
It is only for the dull.

977. NOBODY CARES

Earth, you do not care
If I ruin my life
By serving you.

Heaven, you do not care
If I ruin my life
By dreaming of you.

Who cares for me?
Nobody.
And what do I do?
I just don't care.

978. SOMETHING SPECIAL

I am sure
Earth sees something special in
me.
What is it?
Perhaps my soul's God-promise.

I am sure
Heaven feels something special in
me.
What is it?
Perhaps my heart's
surrender-satisfaction.

979. I DO NOT HIDE FROM YOU

Lord, I do not hide my weakness
from You
Because
Your Compassion-Sea
Is my only strength.

Lord, I do not hide my thoughts
from You
Because
Your Illumination-Sun
Is my only salvation.

980. YOUR OFFERING TO THE WORLD

Your mind offers its unreserved
respect
To the world-mind;
Therefore
Your mind is unmistakably great.

Your heart offers its unalloyed
concern
To the world-heart;
Therefore
Your heart is divinely good.

Your life offers its unconditional
love
To the world-life;
Therefore
Your life is supremely perfect.

981. TWO SERIOUS PROBLEMS

I have two serious problems –
One on earth
And
One in Heaven.

On earth I love myself
Infinitely more than I love God.

In Heaven
I do not value God
Supremely and constantly.

982. GOD WANTS ME TO BE PERFECT

Earth wants me to grow up.
Heaven wants me to glow
Within, without.
God wants me to be perfect
In the heart of silence
And
In the body of sound.

983. CHRISTIAN LIFE

Christian life, as he knew it then,
Was pure but not sure.

Christian life, as he knows it now,
Is sure but not pure.

984. GIVE THEM SOMETHING

Sister-earth is at your door.
Give her something;
Give her at least your love.

Brother-Heaven is at your door.
Give him something;
Give him at least your concern.

Father-God is at your door.
Give Him something;
Give Him at least your gratitude.

985. YOU ARE KNOCKING AT A WRONG DOOR

I don't allow you
To impose your mind's futility
Upon my devoted head;
Therefore,
In your eyes, I am bad.

I don't allow him
To impose his heart's insecurity
Upon my aspiring heart;
Therefore,
In his eyes, I am bad.

I am sorry.
You both are knocking
At a wrong door.

986. I HAVE FOUND ONE THING

Heaven, do you really want to
 know
What I have found on earth?
I have found only one thing:
Necessity's cry.

Earth, do you really want to know
What I have found in Heaven?
I have found only one thing:
Promise-light.

987. HE IS WATCHING ME

He is watching me.
If only I could feel
What is inside his heart.
Perhaps his compassion-sea.

He is watching me.
If only I could read
What is inside his eyes.
Perhaps my liberation-sky.

988. USE YOUR WEAPONS

Use your humour-weapon.
Earth will be afraid of you.
You will be able to stay on earth
At least ten more years.

Use your perfection-weapon.
Heaven will adore you.
Heaven will immediately
Welcome you.

989. A LITTLE HOPE

You are deliberately vain.
Who needs you?

He is insanely vain.
Who needs him?

I am unconsciously vain,
Therefore
I have a little hope,
But not much.

990. AFTER ALL, YOU ARE NOT ANOTHER GOD

Don't be so unthinkably
 impatient.
After all, you are not the wind.

Don't pretend to be supremely
 calm.
After all, you are not another God.

991. NOBODY NEEDS ME

True, you are Heaven's
representative
On earth.
But alas, I am not sure
Of your compassion-light.

True, he is earth's representative
In Heaven.
But alas, I am not sure
Of his sacrifice-height.

Poor me,
Heaven does not want me, my
ignorance.
Earth does not need me, my
indolence.

992. WHAT AM I TODAY?

I don't have to go very far
To see the mouth of hell.
Yesterday I was nothing but that.

I don't have to go very far
To feel the heart of Heaven.
Tomorrow I shall be nothing but
that.

And what am I today?
Frustration-killer
And
Hope-builder.

993. LOVE IS PERFECTION-LIFE

Fear is separation-life.
Doubt is destruction-life.
Faith is satisfaction-life.
Love is perfection-life.

994. ONENESS IS ALWAYS GOOD

Toleration by earth-necessity
Is never good.

Surrender by Heaven-pressure
Is never good.

Oneness for God-satisfaction
Is always good,
Supremely good.

995. LET ME FACE WORLD-PROBLEMS

Let me face
All world-problems.
After all, they are all
Temporary.

Let me not be over-eager
To receive Heaven-Delight.
After all, it will eventually come
And
Once I receive it
I will drink it
Eternally.

996. AT LONG LAST

My sweet Lord, at long last
Today I am thinking less of myself
And more of You.

My sweet Lord, at long last
Today I am loving myself less
And loving You more.

My sweet Lord, at long last
Today I have realised
That I am not only of Your
Realisation-Seed
But also for Your
Manifestation-Tree.

997. A REAL FOOL

I was a real fool
To come to earth.
Neither earth nor I need each
other.

I am a real fool
To go back to Heaven.
Heaven will plead with me
To return to earth.
What for?
To sow the seeds of
Earth-perfection
And
God-satisfaction.

998. A SINCERE "YES"

I should not have stayed
Those extra ten years on earth.
Now I have to pay a heavy duty
In Heaven
For my prolonged, unnecessary
stay
On earth.

God, do tell me:
Have You ever created
A greater fool
Than this blind creation of Yours?

God, why are You so silent?
Let me then take Your silence
As a supremely sincere
"Yes".

999. GOD-REALISATION

In your case
God-realisation is a mere desire.

In his case
God-realisation is a mere dream.

In my case
God-realisation is more than a
living reality;
It only is.

1000. YOU ALONE

Yours is the God
Of perpetual illumination.

Yours is the soul
Of perpetual meditation.

Yours is the heart
Of perpetual aspiration.

Yours is the life
Of perpetual dedication.

Therefore
You alone I love;
You alone I need.

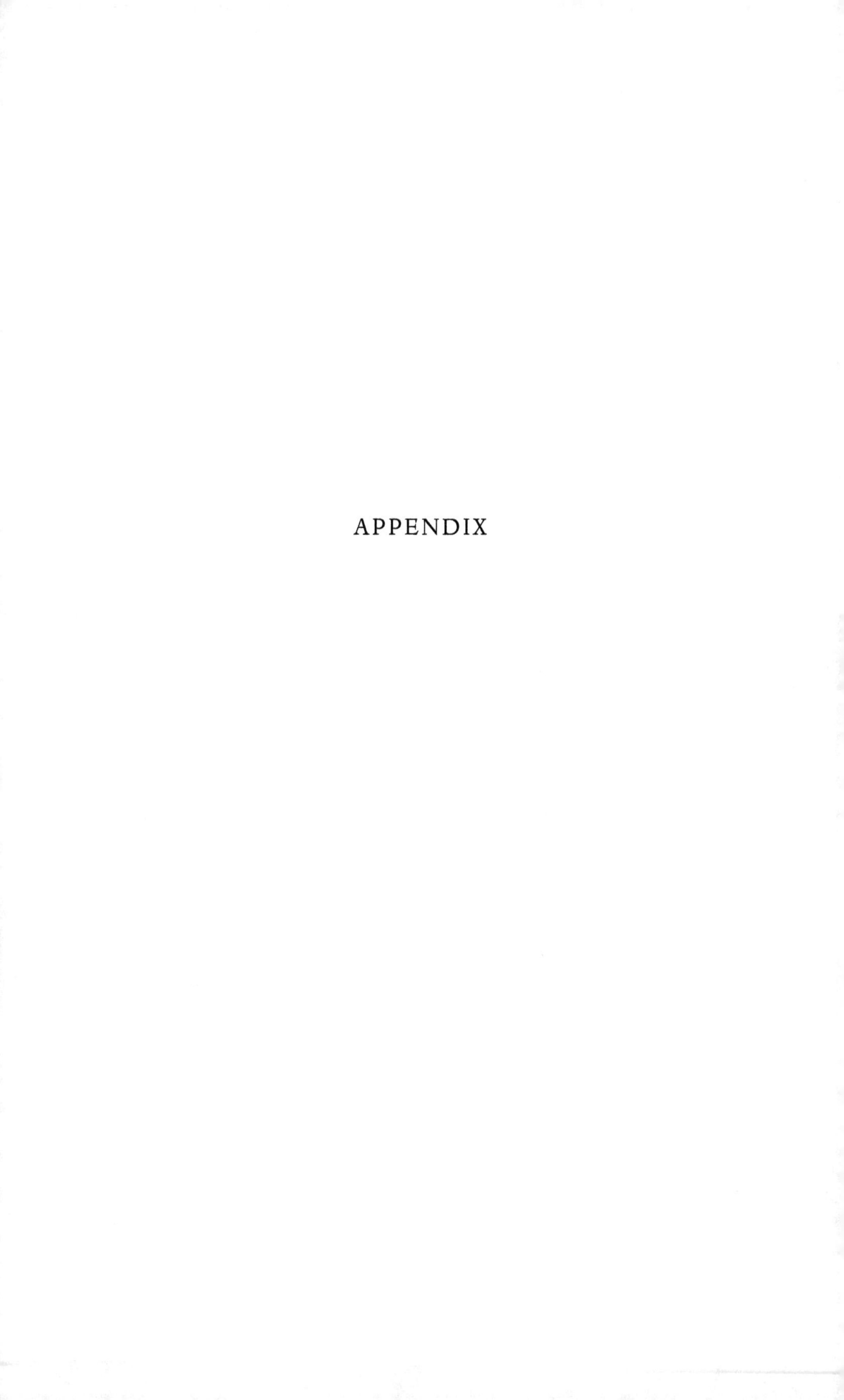

APPENDIX

APPRECIATION-FLOWERS

INTRODUCTION TO "THE GOLDEN BOAT, PART I"

Appreciation-flowers

Today the poet in me has written these 50 poems.

Today I offer my most sincere gratitude to the perfect typist and the untiring server in Nivedan.

Today the great and divine artist in Pratyay deserves my most special gratitude.

Today the exemplary services rendered by Kalyan, Ashpriha, Mangal, Joe, Dhanu, Sevananda, Bansidhar, Jose Luis, Kanti, Indu, Jolie, Daisy, Drona, Madhavi, Ananta, Eulogio, Nadeshwar, Eshana, Aidita, Lester, Ricky, Anna and many more have found their home in my grateful heart for masking, printing, collating and completing this book to my great satisfaction.

(signed by)
Sri Chinmoy
29 January 1974

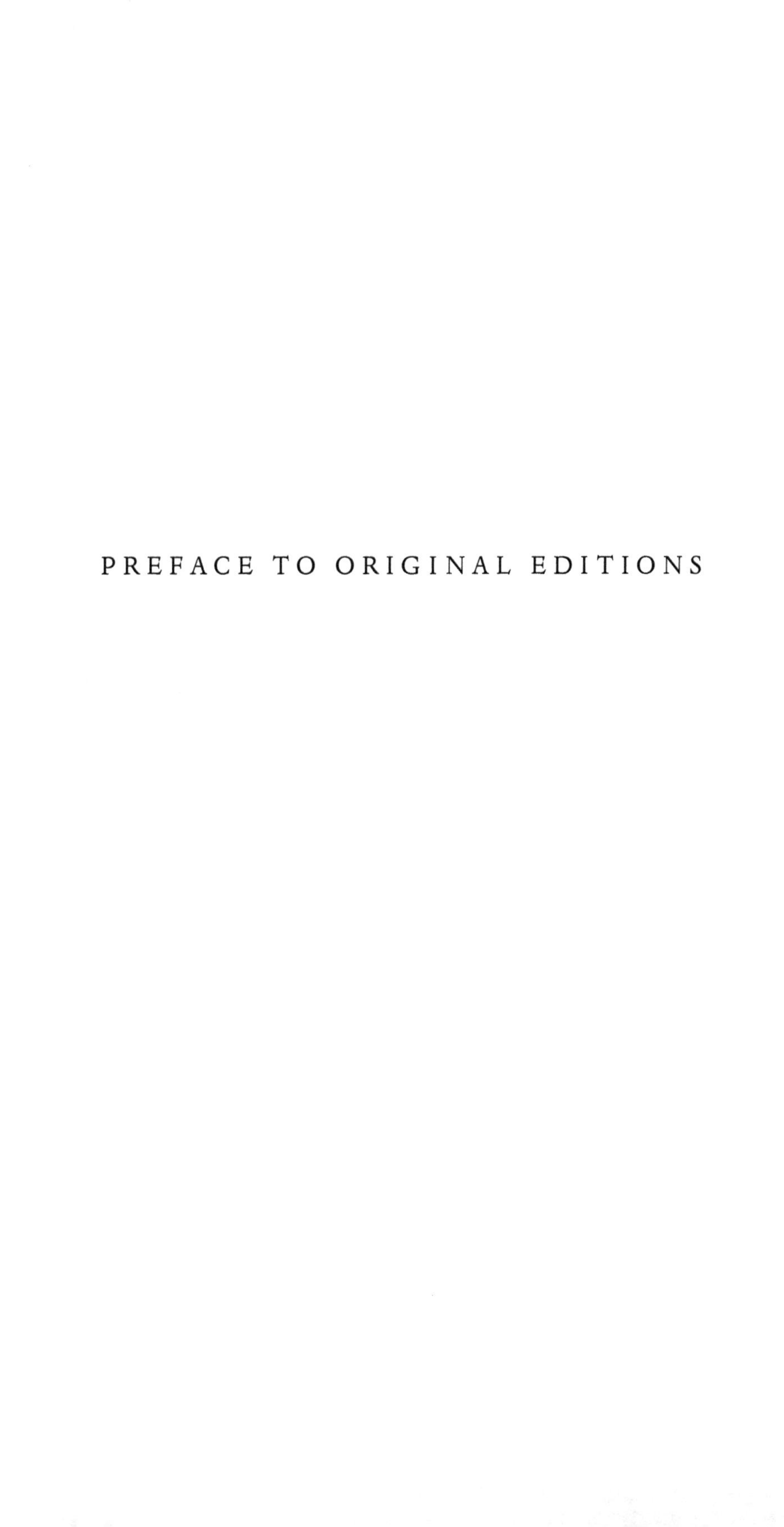

PREFACE TO ORIGINAL EDITIONS

Editor's preface to The Dance of Life, part 7

The 50 poems in this collection were written by Sri Chinmoy on 15 May 1973.

Editor's preface to The Golden Boat, part 2 to 5

This book of 50 poems is part of a four-part series written by Sri Chinmoy in the 22-hour period between 12:01 a.m. and 10:01 p.m. on 2 February 1974. It was also printed on the same day by the group pictured in the photograph above the preface.

Editor's preface to The Golden Boat, part 6

The first eight poems in this book are the last in a series of 208 poems that Sri Chinmoy wrote on 2 February 1974. The first 200, written in the 22-hour period between 12:01 a.m. and 10:01 p.m., were printed as Parts 2 through 5.

Editor's preface to The Golden Boat, part 12

The poems in this volume were written on 4 June 1974.

BIBLIOGRAPHY

THE DANCE OF LIFE (20 VOLUMES)

SRI CHINMOY:

–*The Dance of Life, part 1,* New York, Agni Press, 1973.
–*The Dance of Life, part 2,* New York, Agni Press, 1973.
–*The Dance of Life, part 3,* New York, Agni Press, 1973.
–*The Dance of Life, part 4,* New York, Agni Press, 1973.
–*The Dance of Life, part 5,* New York, Agni Press, 1973.
–*The Dance of Life, part 6,* New York, Agni Press, 1973.
–*The Dance of Life, part 7,* New York, Agni Press, 1973.
–*The Dance of Life, part 8,* New York, Agni Press, 1973.
–*The Dance of Life, part 9,* New York, Agni Press, 1973.
–*The Dance of Life, part 10,* New York, Agni Press, 1973.
–*The Dance of Life, part 11,* New York, Agni Press, 1973.
–*The Dance of Life, part 12,* New York, Agni Press, 1973.
–*The Dance of Life, part 13,* New York, Agni Press, 1973.
–*The Dance of Life, part 14,* New York, Agni Press, 1973.
–*The Dance of Life, part 15,* New York, Agni Press, 1973.
–*The Dance of Life, part 16,* New York, Agni Press, 1973.
–*The Dance of Life, part 17,* New York, Agni Press, 1973.
–*The Dance of Life, part 18,* New York, Agni Press, 1973.
–*The Dance of Life, part 19,* New York, Agni Press, 1973.
–*The Dance of Life, part 20,* New York, Agni Press, 1973.

Suggested citation key: DL.

THE WINGS OF LIGHT (20 VOLUMES)

SRI CHINMOY:

–*The Wings of Light, part 1,* New York, Agni Press, 1974.
–*The Wings of Light, part 2,* New York, Agni Press, 1974.
–*The Wings of Light, part 3,* New York, Agni Press, 1974.
–*The Wings of Light, part 4,* New York, Agni Press, 1974.
–*The Wings of Light, part 5,* New York, Agni Press, 1974.
–*The Wings of Light, part 6,* New York, Agni Press, 1974.
–*The Wings of Light, part 7,* New York, Agni Press, 1974.
–*The Wings of Light, part 8,* New York, Agni Press, 1974.
–*The Wings of Light, part 9,* New York, Agni Press, 1974.
–*The Wings of Light, part 10,* New York, Agni Press, 1974.
–*The Wings of Light, part 11,* New York, Agni Press, 1974.
–*The Wings of Light, part 12,* New York, Agni Press, 1974.
–*The Wings of Light, part 13,* New York, Agni Press, 1974.
–*The Wings of Light, part 14,* New York, Agni Press, 1974.
–*The Wings of Light, part 15,* New York, Agni Press, 1974.
–*The Wings of Light, part 16,* New York, Agni Press, 1974.
–*The Wings of Light, part 17,* New York, Agni Press, 1974.
–*The Wings of Light, part 18,* New York, Agni Press, 1974.
–*The Wings of Light, part 19,* New York, Agni Press, 1974.
–*The Wings of Light, part 20,* New York, Agni Press, 1974.

Suggested citation key: WL.

THE GOLDEN BOAT (20 VOLUMES)

SRI CHINMOY:

– *The Golden Boat, part 1,* New York, Agni Press, 1974.
– *The Golden Boat, part 2,* New York, Agni Press, 1974.
– *The Golden Boat, part 3,* New York, Agni Press, 1974.
– *The Golden Boat, part 4,* New York, Agni Press, 1974.
– *The Golden Boat, part 5,* New York, Agni Press, 1974.
– *The Golden Boat, part 6,* New York, Agni Press, 1974.
– *The Golden Boat, part 7,* New York, Agni Press, 1974.
– *The Golden Boat, part 8,* New York, Agni Press, 1974.
– *The Golden Boat, part 9,* New York, Agni Press, 1974.
– *The Golden Boat, part 10,* New York, Agni Press, 1974.
– *The Golden Boat, part 11,* New York, Agni Press, 1974.
– *The Golden Boat, part 12,* New York, Agni Press, 1974.
– *The Golden Boat, part 13,* New York, Agni Press, 1974.
– *The Golden Boat, part 14,* New York, Agni Press, 1974.
– *The Golden Boat, part 15,* New York, Agni Press, 1974.
– *The Golden Boat, part 16,* New York, Agni Press, 1974.
– *The Golden Boat, part 17,* New York, Agni Press, 1974.
– *The Golden Boat, part 18,* New York, Agni Press, 1974.
– *The Golden Boat, part 19,* New York, Agni Press, 1974.
– *The Golden Boat, part 20,* New York, Agni Press, 1974.

Suggested citation key: GB.

POSTFACE

Publishing principles

This edition of *The works of Sri Chinmoy* aims to obey the Author's wish: scrupulous fidelity to his original words, use of typographical style by him selected, specific spelling choices, end placement of any editorial content (i.e. not written by Sri Chinmoy himself), particular treatment of some personal nouns in special cases, etc.

Textual accuracy

The text of this edition has been checked to ensure faithful accuracy to the originals. Although much effort has been put in proofreading and comparing different versions of the text, this print may still present a few lingering errors.

The Publisher would be grateful to be apprised of any mistypes via postal mail or facsimile, possibly with scan of the original page where the text is different. Please use original books only, specifying the year of publication. Online versions may be not as accurate and should not be considered authoritative.

Acknowledgements

The Publisher is very grateful to the late Professor Lambert and his équipe for his invaluable advice. For many decades Prof. Lambert conducted a small publishing house specialising in hand-made prints of philological edition of the classics. The standard of this edition would not have been the same without his scholarly advice.

The Publisher is also grateful to the international team of collaborators that spent countless hours proofreading and checking the current text against the originals.

Our deepest gratitude to Sri Chinmoy. His living presence can be felt breathing throughout his writings. It is such a privilege to be involved with his works, in any form.

Citation keys

Citation keys are used throughout *The works of Sri Chinmoy* to allow accurate cross-reference of texts across titles and editions. Examples: EA 13, ST 50000, UPA 7.

Sri Chinmoy Canon

We could not use better words than Professor Lambert's, who kindly offered the name *Sri Chinmoy Canon*:

> «By defining Sri Chinmoy's first editions as *editio princeps* we chose to follow classical scholarship criteria, not because we consider Sri Chinmoy's work antique, but because we believe it is among the few post ‹classical antiquity› works to rightly deserve to be considered a *classicus*, designating by that term *superiority, authority* and *perfection*.
>
> «The monumental work Sri Chinmoy is offering to mankind is awe-inspiring and supremely pre-eminent in proportions and quality. It is manifest that Sri Chinmoy's work — which we feel right to call *The Sri Chinmoy Canon* — will be of profound help and source of enlightenment to anyone seeking a higher wisdom, truth and reality supreme.»

[Translated from French by M. G.S.]

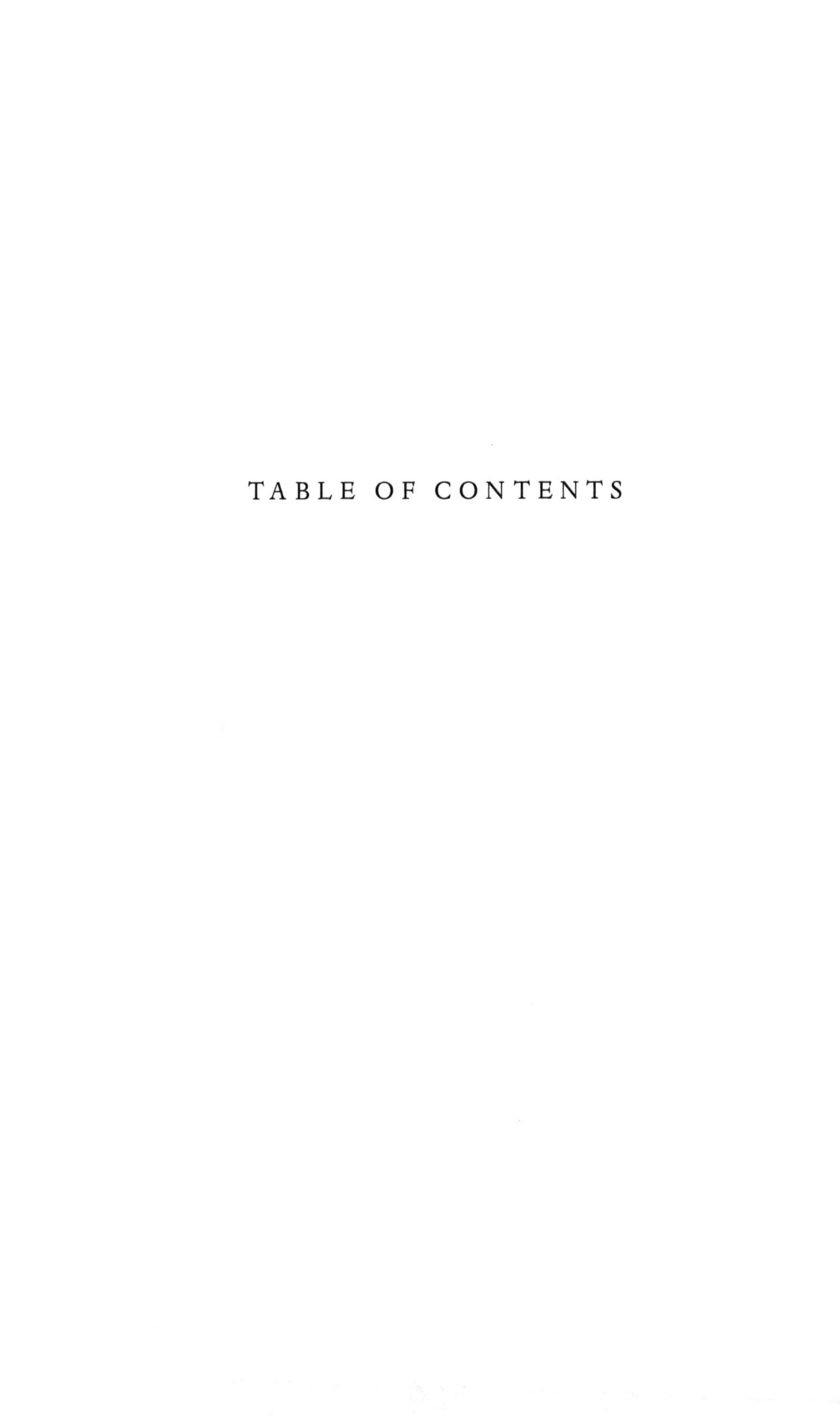

TABLE OF CONTENTS

Composition typographique par imprimerie Ab Academia Aoidon, Paris & Lyon.

Un grand merci à Prof Knuth pour l'utilisation avancée de TEX.

A LYON, LE 13 FÉVRIER LXXXVI Æ.G.

www.ingramcontent.com/pod-product-compliance
Lightning Source LLC
Chambersburg PA
CBHW020814300326
41914CB00075B/1769/J

9780993308062